विष्णुधर्मोत्तरपुराणीयं
चित्रसूत्रम्

THE CITRASŪTRA
OF
THE VISṆUDHARMOTTARA PURĀṆA

कलामूलशास्त्र-ग्रन्थमाला

KALĀMŪLAŚĀSTRA SERIES

इ.गा.रा.क.के.*क.मू.शा* - ३२

I.G.N.C.A. *K.M.S.* - 32

विष्णुधर्मोत्तरपुराणीयं

चित्रसूत्रम्

THE CITRASŪTRA

OF

THE VISṆUDHARMOTTARA PURĀṆA

CRITICALLY EDITED AND TRANSLATED
BY
PARUL DAVE MUKHERJI

INDIRA GANDHI NATIONAL CENTRE FOR THE ARTS
NEW DELHI
AND
MOTILAL BANARSIDASS PUBLISHERS PVT. LTD.
DELHI

First Published 2001

Published by
INDIRA GANDHI NATIONAL CENTRE FOR THE ARTS
Central Vista Mess, Janpath, New Delhi - 110001
in association with
MOTILAL BANARSIDASS PUBLISHERS PVT. LTD.
Bungalow Road, Jawahar Nagar, Delhi - 110007

ISBN : 81-208-1805-9

Typeset by Typographia
C-111, Karampura, New Delhi
Printed in India
at Sri Jainendra Press
A-45, Naraina Industrial Area, Phase-I
New Delhi–110028

CONTENTS

* * *

FOREWORD

The Citrasūtra of the *Viṣṇudharmottara-purāna,* Khanda III Chapters 35-43 is the thirty-second volume in the Kalāmūlaśāstra Series of the Kalākośa Division in the Indira Gandhi National Centre For the Arts (IGNCA). The earlier volumes have included the seminal texts, relevant to the Indian arts: *Mātrālakṣaṇam,* volume 1; *Kāṇvaśatapathabrāhmaṇa,* volumes 12 and 22; *Lāṭyāyana-śrauta-sūtra,* volumes 27, 28 and 29. These lay the foundations for an incipient theoretical framework before a clearly articulated theory of art emerges. Also these texts provide the basic structure and building blocks for the evolution of a language of 'form'. The *Karmakāṇḍa* (popularly called ritual practices) and its systems of a multilayered spatial and temporal design employ a multi-media vocabulary of sound, music, word, movement and gesture. This design-style permeates into the fabric of the specific arts. The texts on music *Dattilam* volume 2, *Bṛhaddeśī,* volumes 8 and 10 and *Saṅgītopaniṣatsāroddhāra,* volume 23, move concurrently on the three planes of concept, form and technique. So also the texts of architecture *(vāstu)*, the *Mayamatam,* volume 14 and 15; and *Śilparatnakośa,* volume 16. Underlying all is a shared world view, a distinctive approach to phenomena and all that we understand by the word 'nature'. Besides there is the affirmation of the principle of inter-connectedness and interdependence. This is the glacial level of thought as articulated in the *Vedas* specially *Ṛg Veda* and the *Upaniṣad.* The texts as also the artistic practice, subscribe to the world-view, accept it as given. It is therefore not considered necessary to explicitly state it in the texts of the specific arts. Understandably they have been considered as treatises, manuals of technique.

Although texts such as the *Śatapaṭha and Śrautasūtra* go back many centuries before the era. The texts on the specific arts roughly open a period from the second century to the eighteenth century. Throughout there is adherence to the fundamental concepts. This is the time of continuity; alongside there is an equal pre-occupation with change and specificity. Now categories and typology of forms constantly evolve.

The contents of the few volumes published by the IGNCA bear testimony to the dynamics of continuity and change, the perennial and the temporal as concurrent movements. Basic to the textual tradition in all the arts is the

Nāṭyaśastra which will be published later. This monumental text lays the foundation of a theory of the Indian arts, which continues to be valid in practice over a millennium and more. The textual tradition flows along one direction, the actual practice *(prayoga)* in turn gives concrete shape in defined space and time. The *Śāstra* (general theory) and *prayoga* (practice) interpenetrate and re- inforce each other.

The Puranas, *Agni, Viṣṇu, Matsya,* and *Mārkanḍeya* provide a necessary bridge between the ritual texts such as the *Śatapatha* and *Lāṭyāyana* and the texts of the particular arts. Now the abstract concept, the philosophic discussions as also structures are couched in a language of myth and a narrative mode. The Puranas are neither a sub-stream of popular discourse as considered by some or narratives of complex mythologies and legends manifesting flights of poetic imagination or shrouding social histories only. Indeed they are another mode of communicating the same ontological and epitomological concerns as the Vedas and the Upanisads and the systemisation of method of the Brahman as they provide another method of relating the abstract and the concrete, the universal and the specific, the philosophic and the artistic. Their mythical world with a staggering variety serves as transition from a system of thought, a knowledge and scheme of ritual to the vocabulary of form in the specific arts. Now myth which was seminal but capsuled earlier, a methodology of ritual which was highly structured is given a fluidity through the expansiveness of the myth. There is plurality of a figurative language. Consequently they provide the basis of the figurative language of iconography where myth collapses into an icon with attributes. The chapters relating to the *Mūrtivinirdeśaḥ* in the *Kālikāpuraṇe Mūrtivinirdeśaḥ*, volume 9 and the chapters on the arts in the *Agni Purāṇa,* not yet published by the IGNCA bear this out. Only on the surface are the Puranas compendiums of disparate concerns. Thus the chapters on the Arts in the Puranas have to be comprehended against the larger concerns. There is the endeavour to contain multi-dimensions of concepts and meanings through narrative myth and its transformation into a vocabulary of formal elements in the arts, singly and together.

While this is not the occasion to delve more fully into the contribution of the Puranas as also the *Upapurāṇas* in facilitating the flow of a tradition through an alternate mode of expression, it is well to remember that no Purana is a single isolated entity, unrelated to the other Puranas or to other texts on the arts. There is a continuing dialogue within their own category and each component also has interaction with the discourse in the specific disciplines. A vertical transmission and a horizontal movement can be discerned.

The *Viṣṇudharmottara-purāṇa* occupies a predominant position amongst the *Upapuranas* and is also related to the discourse within the Puranas. Moreover, it is central to the discourse on the arts, both preceding and succeeding it. The voluminous text can be viewed only within the framework of the Puranas or it can be placed through Khanda III in the mainstream of the discourse on the arts from the *Nāṭyaśāstra* to the medieval texts mentioned above. Its contents can be profitably compared with those of both its predecessors as also successors such as *Mayamatam, Mānasollāsa, Śilparatnakośa, Śilpaprakāśa and Aparājitapṛcchā.*

The *Citrasūtra* (Khaṇḍa III Chapter 35 - 43) constitute an important cluster in the larger concerns of the *Viṣṇudharmottarapurāṇa* on both the nature of art, artistic expression and communication as also its insistence on establishing a meaningful interdependence and inter-relationship between and amongst the arts. As has been pointed out, the Puranic methodology is in the narrative mode. An oft quoted story about a dialogue between Vajra and Mārkaṇḍeya embodies the essence of the theoretical position of the composer of the *Viṣṇudharmottara-Purāṇa.* Since the IGNCA and I as General Editor of the Series are deeply committed to this view point, it would be relevant to quote it in full as a constant reminder:

"King Vajra requests the sage to accept him as his disciple and teach him the art of icon-making, so that he may worship the deities in their proper forms. The sage replies that one cannot understand the principles of image-making without a knowledge of painting. The King wishes for instruction in this art and is told that, unless he is accomplished as a dancer, he cannot grasp even the rudiments of painting. The King requests that he be taught dancing, whereupon the sage replies that, without a keen sense of rhythm or a knowledge of instrumental music, proficiency in dance is impossible. Once again the king requests that he be taught these subjects; to which the sage replies that a mastery of vocal music is necessary before one can be proficient in instrumental music; and so finally the sage takes the king through all these stages before he is taught the art of iconography." [1]

1 Visnudharmottara - purana, III. 2.1-

Equally important is the other statement:

yathā nṛtte tathā chitre trailokyānukritissmṛtā (As in dance so in painting, there is to be a close observation and reproduction of the world around us in as charming a style as possible.) [2]

In the first, quote the method is narrative, in the second, aphoristic and deductive. The chapters relating to the arts have therefore to be seen together. Each is integral to the other. Notions of interdepedence and interpenetration are the norm not the exception at the level of content, form and even technique. A framework of both sharing as also autonomy is developed through the discussion on the diverse arts. The chapters relating to the art specially the visual arts have received considerable attention from scholars since the publication of the first edition. Subsequent editions and translations have appeared. Nevertheless it was time to attempt another edition based on new material.

The Indira Gandhi National Centre for the Arts (IGNCA) is indebted to Dr. (Smt.) Parul Dave Mukherji for having undertaken the arduous task of locating more manuscripts. She has gone beyond her predecessors in carefully pursuing manuscripts which did not receive the attention of her predecessors. The manuscript from Nepal (Ms N) and from Dhaka (Ms D) have obviously been of great help in arriving at new readings. She has drawn up a convincing stemma. This is an invaluable contribution. She has painstakingly taken into account the work of Stella Kramrisch, Priyabala Shah and C. Sivaramamurti. Her introduction gives a lucid account of the contents of each chapter. More importantly, she addresses some basic issues of textual work and textual criticism. Our editor represents like Allyn Miner in the case of *Sangītopaniṣasāroddhāra*, a younger generation of scholars, who understandably are concerned, as much with trying to find a near authentic text as with contextualising the text in its historio-cultural ambience. Besides the preceding discussion on this and other texts is taken into account. Allyn Miner had ably placed her text in the historio-social context. Parul Dave goes further by carefully and critically analysing the histriography of critical discourse on her text in the twentieth century. Her yardstick of evaluation is the socio-historical contexts of colonial and post-colonial India. Logically she offers explanation for particular interpretation of her peers and predecessors situating herself as being distinctively different. All this is welcome.

2 Visnudharmottara - purana, III. 35.5

From her meticulously argued position, it is clear that she considers the question of arriving at particular readings practically inseparable from the 'ideological' position of the editors. Further she attributes these positions to the historio-social situation. She cites a few instances of this from the editorial work and translation of these chapters by her distinguished predecessors. Invaluable is her summary of the chronology of the interest in the Khaṇḍa III of the *Viṣṇudharmottara* during the last seven decades. I have no doubt that the text, translation and the introduction will be widely read and re-invigorate the discussion on this text. It will again convince readers that both historically and artistically the *Viṣṇudharmottara-purāṇa* is watershed and a milestone for comprehending the Indian artistic traditions in general and those of sculpture and painting in particular.

A close reading of the text, its translation and/or interpretation by Stella Kramrisch, A.K. Coomaraswamy, Priyabala Shah and C. Sivaramamurti, has to be juxtaposed with Dr. (Smt.) Parul Dave Mukherji's comment and critical evaluation Two sets of issues emerge on two interconnected planes. The first set relate to the conceptual plane, this is implicit. Each editor translator tacitly or explicitly subscribes to certain notions in regard to the world view in which a text is embedded. The second set of issues relate to not merely correcting scribal errors or those of orthography but others which impel and compel an editior/translator to take options in respect of particular words specially key words of the discourse. It is at the conceptual plane that the subscription or otherwise to a world-view and approach becomes crucial for a contemporary editor. Unless cognizance is taken of the glacial level of thought and the methodologies of systematisation in concrete form, the key terms can be de-contextualised and critically evaluated by other parameters of other times and other thought and perception systems. The second course is undoubtedly valid if it is conceded that the key terms of a discourse can be and do walk out of a particular text to assume other meanings. Nevertheless, at the primary level of textual criticism they have necessarily to be investigated within the context of the text and the tacit assumption underlying the text. Dr. (Smt.) Parul Dave Mukherji has identified the key words of *sādṛiśya, satya, anukṛti* in the *Viṣṇudharmottara* for investigating the interpretation of these terms by her predecessors. Her own interest emerges from investigating the presence or absence of 'naturalism' in Indian art. According to her the cluster of terms which approximate the notion are the Sanskrit terms, *sādṛśya, satya, anukriti* used in the *Viṣṇudharmottara* and of course other texts.

Before commenting on our editor's analysis it is necessary to point out a self evident fact that the frequent use of these terms in the *Viṣṇudharmottara* has a long history of discourse within the textual tradition. The *Nāṭyaśāstra* revolves around the notion of *anukaraṇa* (not imitation) and *anukriti.* The prefix *sa* in *sahṛdaya* for receiver, spectator is as telling as in *Sādṛśya.* Elaboration on this is not necessary at this stage on the history of this discourse in the vertical flow of the textual tradition. Let us return to our editor's comments on and explanations for A.K. Coomaraswamy. Stella Kramrisch's position in regard to *sādṛśya* on the one hand and naturalism on the other. For a fuller examination it would be necessary to re-open the question of what constitutes as Nature in the Indian mind-scape, more precisely, the *mahābhūtas* and *prakṛti.* This comprehension has to be clearly distinguished from the emergence of 'naturalism' as an art movement in Europe in the 18th and 19th centuries. As is well known, the art movement was a corollary to the development of the discipline of natural history. More it pivotally revolves on the distinction between Man and Nature, Matter and spirit. 'Naturalism' then was the doctrine that nature should be represented as objectivity without interpretation. The representation of the 'natural' tantamounted to accepting the notion that 'Nature' exists apart from man. Naturalism in art approximated camera vision via formal naturalism. Thus it parallels nominalism and representation of the particular rather than the universal. When A.K. Coomaraswamy spoke of the self conscious eschewing of 'naturalism' in Indian art, he was undoubtedly aware of and sensitive to the then recent notion of nature as object and naturalism as the style of faithful representation of the visible. What constitutes 'nature' in the Indian tradition and the artists' full and deep pre-occupation with it is articulated in the body of his work particularly the "Yakṣas: Essays in the Water Cosmology" and "The Transformation of Nature in Art". [See Forewords and Introduction in volumes of Kalasamalocana Series Publication of the Indira Gandhi National Centre for the Arts, New Delhi.] The notion of *sādṛśya* in art could hardly be dissociated from the world view and the notions of phenomena what constituted Nature: its manifestation and consequent experience and artistic expression. If organic growth, and transmutability of matter was fundamental to the world view, the artist's concern could not be confined to faithful exact representation of the outer visible. The unmanifest and manifest levels had to be taken into account. Both A.K. Coomaraswamy and Stella Kramrisch bring this home in the body of their writing. Now to attribute these interpretations only to the historico-social situation of a colonised and post-colonial situation and to understand the recognition of the transcendental as nationalist agenda is perhaps to essentialise a more complex situation to a single dimension of the politico-socio. Of course there is no denying that in the case of A.K. Coomaraswamy, he did take a defiant and defensive positions against the colonial onslaughts. Also *Swadeshi* was a nationalist agenda in some of his writing but it would be injustice to the totality of his work to stretch the argument to an interpretation of key words in the textual tradition. This appears to overlook the history of the discourse of these terms within the tradition and the interpretation by scholars mentioned above. A.K. Coomaraswamy strove hard some times giving excruciating details of etymologies, origins of words and concepts. He went further to find parallels in other languages, Greek, Latin, Persian, and other thought systems particularly Christian medieval. Hermeneutics was not ruled out but this was no escape route to justify a deliberate ideological stance. One instance from "The Transformation of Nature in Art" will suffice:

"Now as to *sādṛśya* : literal meanings are sym-visibility, con-similarity; secondary meanings, co-ordination, analogy. That aesthetic *sādṛśya* does not imply naturalism, veri-similitude, illustration, or illustration in any superficial sense is sufficiently shown by the fact that in Indian lists of factors essential to painting it is almost always mentioned with *pramāṇa* "creation of truth", here "ideal proportion"; in the Indian theories of knowledge empirical observation *(pratyakṣa)* as supplying only a test, and not the material of theory, is regarded as the least valid amongst the various *pramāṇas*." and again,

"In Rhetoric, *sādṛśya* is illustrated by the example "The young man is a lion" (Bhartrmitra, Abhidha-vrtti-matrika, p. 17, and commonly quoted elsewhere); and this analogy very well demonstrates what is really meant by aesthetic "imitation". Vasubandhu, Abhidharmakośa, IX, Poussin, pp. 280, 281, explains the relation of knowledge *(vijñāna)* to its object, neither knower nor known existing apart from the act of knowledge."

and finally,

"*Sādṛśya* is then "similitude", but rather such as is implied by "simile" than by "simulacrum". It is in fact obvious that the likeness between anything and any representation of it cannot be a likeness of nature, but must be analogical or exemplary, or both of these. What the representation imitates is the idea or species of the thing, by which it is known intellectually, rather than the substance of the thing as it is perceived by the senses." [3]

Stella Kramrisch may have been handicapped by the lack of access to primary material and her reliance initially on Indian scholars and the first printed edition. Nevertheless throughout the body of her work, she is as concerned with essence as with 'form'. Her interpretations of the *Viṣṇudharmottara* despite the obvious inaccuracies and some mistakes has to be studied along with her work on Indian sculpture and other writings. Although she does not explicitly apply the tenets of *Viṣṇudharmottara* it is clear that she is more than aware of the Indian artist's distinctive response to nature or more precisely nature of embodiment in Indian art. Both the little book Indian Sculpture and writing elsewhere is clear proof that she penetrates into the instrinsic character of the notion of nature in Indian art and assesses the art again from within the tradition rather than application of the term 'naturalism' as evolved in the post 18th context of European Art. If this is an 'ideological' position it is one from within the context of the tradition.

Two quotations from her work will suffice to demonstrate her penetrating insights. To recognise the latent possibilities of artistic expression or form to acquire symbolic significance is not to deny the skill of the artist to capture visible phenomenon.

"Nature, as visible parallel and accompaniment of man, had already begun to gradually disappear. Nature as a whole is taken into and expressed by a transfigured body. A garland of supra-personal figures, in cadences not outspoken and therefore the more suggestive, is gathered according to the subdued rhythm of the ever-recurrent though no longer visible lotus creeper. Not the motif but its rhythm is present, and has become further differentiated." and again

"To measure the degree of maturity of Indian art by western standards—not to speak of influences — is nowhere as futile as it would be in case of the Sanchi reliefs. Daring in diagonal arrangements, furtively broken by light and darkness, modelled with a delicacy and experience that would do credit

3 Coomaraswamy, A.K. Transformation of Nature in Art, pages 8-9 Edited by Kapila Vatsyayan, IGNCA & Sterling Publishers, New Delhi, 1995

to the western Baroque, the genius which produces this seeming similarity assigns it to quite a different level." [4]

Commenting on the *Viṣṇudharmottara - purāṇa* :

"The Viṣṇudharmottara clearly distinguishes between *dṛṣṭa* and *adṛṣṭa,* the latter comprising things invisible or rarely to be seen. The *dṛṣṭa,* things that are seen easily by ordinary mortals, excel in what we call landscape painting. The hours of day and night and the seasons are described (chapter 42). There we find a close connection of mood and time, which reached its height in the Rāgamālā pictures, where season, hour, emotion, and music became fused as paintings. At the same time details are observed with the same sincerity as we find in the pictures of Dutch masters, for instance, in the description of the drinking place. The light effects sought to be producd show a very sensitive reaction to optic effects, as the faded light of the candle in the morning dawn. Yet we are told that moonshine should be shown by a Kumuda flower in full bloom, and sunshine by drawing creatures suffering from heat. In one instance, atmospheric effects are observed, while in the other, the behaviour of one object or the other, reacting to the atmospheric change, is represented suggestively. This interest in the living individuality of the single forms of nature gives to Indian landscape, the charm of storytelling." [5]

C. Sivaramamurti was another mind and another person. He was part and parcel of the tradition and fully immersed in it. It would be correct to state that he was perhaps not self conscious of the usage of the term 'naturalism' in the European art-historical context. Thus when he affirms the presence of 'naturalism' in Indian art, it must be remembered that he was not speaking of 'naturalism' as understood in European art - historical terms. He could not be less concerned with colonial or post - colonial discourse or an anxiety to validate Indian art on terms other than what he was an inheritor of. This too, alas, cannot be considered as a post - colonial ideological stance. In fact C. Sivaramamurti was, through another manner of speaking, affirming again the Indian artists' pre-occupation with 'nature' but not nature as object and nature merely observed and faithfully represented as the other.

4 Kramrisch, Stella, Indian Sculpture, pages 31, 65, Oxfprd University Press, London YMCA Publishing House, Calcutta, 1933

5 Kramrisch, Stella, Exploring India's Sacred Art, page 267, Edited by Barbara Stoler Miller, University of Penssylvania Press, Philadelphia, 1983

Engaging and fascinating as the argument is, one has to most respectfully disagree with the view that textual criticism is or has been governed only by the historico-socio context of the colonial, post - colonial period and the nationalist agenda.

Despite these honest differences in comprehension and perception, I am most grateful to Dr. Parul Dave Mukherji to have sincerely articulated her critical evaluation. This will no doubt stimulate further discussion on scholarship in a continuous journey of dialogue with fresh insights. Further, her observations further convince one to persevere to find an appropriate language to translate an entire system of perception and thought embodied in a single key word or cluster of culturally loaded key-terms. What is the method and tool of communicating one system of thought knowledge and perception into another? *Sādṛśya* (not to speak of *satya*) is an excellent example of the inadequacies of translation or transcreation. A converse situation has occurred in writing in Indian languages on a key word an concept like *katharsis* in Greek. Each contains a whole body of ideas and layers of meaning.

The term *anukṛti* which occurs in the *Viṣṇudharmottara Purāṇa* several times is yet another fundamental term which requires volumes of explanations and qualifications before it can be translated into an equally simple but complex and loaded term *imitation*. From the *Nāṭyaśāstra* to the *Abhinavabhāratī* and numerous other commentators and interpreters, the terms *anukaraṇa* and *anukṛti* have a fascinating history. The theory of aesthetics rests squarely on it. In recent scholarship 're-narration', 're-creation', 're-shaping' are the close approximations offered. The English word *imitation* in turn comes with all its antecedents of an equally vibrant but totally different discourse ranging from Plato to Aristotle to the romantics to modern times. The employment of words which denote terms, concepts, world view and philosophies is a difficult, challenging job, fascinating and complex.

Undoubtedly the editors/translators are affected by the socio-historical milieu of this particular time and the best is undoubtedly perceived from the present, but that is only one dimension. The deeper concerns are of understanding the 'other' (tradition or self, spatially or temporally) on its own terms. The textual scholar must necessarily place his text within the discourse of the specific tradition before adopting a universalist position or undertaking comparative work from the position of immediate present. It is here that the IGNCA's work in the *Kalatattvakosa* becomes relevant and important for both those doing textual work and those others who are interested in understanding the multilayered system of concept word and meaning. A perusal of the volumes already published is ample proof of the pervasiveness as also complexity and change of meaning, and connotation and denotation of the same term. A future volume of this series (volume V) will be devoted to *ākṛti* and the terms *anukṛti* and *anukaraṇa* will be included there. This may also help the readers of the text of the *Viṣṇudharmottara.*

Finally a word about *Citra.* The single and problematic term needs elucidation of another order. The *Viṣṇudharmottara* provides some clues not all. However discussion on this term would demand an independent essay and will have to wait. Once again, I would like to thank Dr. Parul Dave Mukherji for her painstaking effort for undertaking this difficult task and for her refreshing and stimulating introduction. I should also like to thank Pandit Satkari Mukhopadhyaya for guiding and assisting Dr. Parul Dave Mukherji at various stages of her work. Also he has, with usual competence, seen the volume through the press. In this task he was assisted by Dr. (Smt.) Sanghamitra Basu.

October 1998 KAPILA VATSYAYAN

ACKNOWLEDGEMENTS

So many people have contributed to this critical edition; most of all, Prof. Alexis Sanderson, my Ph.D. guide at the Faculty of Oriental Studies, Oxford University. He patiently introduced me to the rigours of textual criticism and let me work within the interdisciplinary space between Indology and Art History.

The late Prof. B. K. Matilal and Dr. Sanjukta Gupta encouraged me at the most critical points of my research. Prof. Richard Gombrich was the first to suggest this text for my doctoral dissertation. Unfailing support from my College, St. Hilda's, especially from Dr. D. Innes, saw me through the most exacting phase of my work. I also wish to sincerely thank Mr. Ebrahim Alkazi and Mr. Re Cavaliero of the Charles Wallace India Trust and Shri Vasudev Dave for their moral support and generous financial assistance.

I am indebted to the staff of the manuscript departments of several libraries and institutions, especially the assistance of the National Archives, Kathmandu, Nepal; the Dhaka University Library, Dhaka, Bangladesh; the National Museum, New Delhi; the Royal Asiatic Society Library, Mumbai and the Bhandarkar Oriental Research Institute, Poona. I particularly extend my special thanks to the staff at the Indian Institute Library, Oxford – Dr Jonathan Katz, Dr Simon Lawson and Mrs. Elizabeth Krishnan.

The list of friends who have directly or indirectly contributed to my thesis is enormous. My Oxford experience, still memorable, will be forever associated with Amrita Cheema, Eugenia Bolognesi, Susanna Boylston, Tapati Guha Thakurta, Sujata Krishna, Gunthard Mueller, Charlotte Purkis, Vidya Rajan, Srilata Raman, Claudia Rapp and Kate Teltscher.

Conversion from thesis to a book entailed a radical rethinking of the conceptual framework informing my interpretation of the text. This was mainly possible after heated discussions with Bhanu Narayan, Deeptha Achar and Santosh Dash. For systematic and meticulous proof-reading across two languages, I thank V. Subbha Rao.

The motivation to see this work to its final outcome, I owe most to Joy and my family. I am grateful to Mayanka who has grown up so graciously in the middle of my hectic schedule divided between teaching at the University and the revision of this thesis.

I thank Dr. Kapila Vatsyayan for the serious attention she has given to the theoretical questions raised and for letting me retain my differences with her. Finally, my sincere thanks to Prof. Satkari Mukhopahdyaya for his scholarly interventions and sound advice and Dr. Sanghamitra Basu for her informed editing of the work.

ABBREVIATIONS

TEXTS

Agni Purāṇa	AgniPu.
Aparājitapṛacchā	ApaPṛ.
Bṛhatsaṃhita	BṛSaṃ.
Citralakṣaṇa	CitLak.
Hayaśirṣapañcarātra	HaŚiPaRā.
Mānasollāsa	MānUll.
Matsya Purāṇa	MatPu.
Samarāṅgaṇasūtradhāra	SamaSūtDhar.
Śatapatha Brāhmaṇa	ŚatBr.
Viṣṇudharmottara Pūraṇa	ViDhPu.
The Monier Williams Dictionary	MW

AUTHORS

Ananda Kentish Coomaraswamy	AKC
Stella Kramrisch	SK
Priyabala Shah	PS
C. Sivaramamurti	SM
Gunasinghe	GS

SYBOLES

{{.}}	an akṣara to be inserted.
{.}	an akṣara to be deleted.
<.>	a missing akṣara.
<<.>>	an insertion/interpolation.
+.+	a corruption, of which no conjec ture or emendation possible so far.
<.?>	uncertain deciphering/faded akṣara
Italics	in the citation are used for emphasis and for pointing out serious mistranslation by the scholars.

INTRODUCTION

To a contemporary editor or a textual critic, an ancient text is a source of knowledge about a *past.* But if that treatise is seen as a *text,* one confronts a different set of problems. The difference is not so much a shift in the nature of the *object* of one's inquiry but a different way of viewing it: either one subscribes to the view that it is possible to approach a *work* directly as transparent, unnegotiated, complete in itself, ready to yield valuable information about that past, or one hazards a reading of it, as a *text,* embedded in the circumstances and time of its production, interpretative, partisan.

Textuality as a modern notion tends to open up this object of inquiry into a *process,* engaging in its historiographical, semiotic and rhetorical aspects. These problems become manifold if the text in question is an already "worked text," edited and translated and interpreted by pioneering scholars and art historians.

A part of Puranic genre, the *Citrasūtra,* has attracted tremendous scholarly attention since its first English translation by Stella Kramrisch in 1924.[1] Subsequently it has come to acquire a hegemonic status on account of its centrality to arguments about Indian art in the works of A.K. Coomaraswamy[2] and C. Sivaramamurti.[3] Its position as the most privileged *Śilpa śāstra* was established by a variety of factors. Foremost is the antiquity of the text whose dating is still a matter of controversy but is generally fixed between 500 A.D. to 900 A.D., corresponding roughly to what is considered to be the classical period in Indian art.

In comparison to other *Śilpa* texts such as the *Citralakṣaṇa* of Nagnajit, the *Samarāṅgaṇasūtradhāra,* or the *Aparājitapṛchha,* the *Citrasūtra* offers a more comprehensive coverage on art. Comprising of the *adhyāyas* from 35

[1]S.K. Kramrisch, "A Treatise on Indian Painting," *Journal of the Department of the Letters,* 2, pp. 1-56, Calcutta, 1924.

[2]A.K. Coomaraswany, "Viṣṇudharmottara Chapter XLI," *Journal of American Oriental Society,* 52, pp. 13-21, 1932.

[3]C. Sivaramamurti, *The Citrasūtra of the Vishnudharmottara*, (New Delhi, Kanak Publications, 1978).

to 43 of the III *khaṇḍa* of the *Viṣṇudharmottarapurāṇa*, the *Citrasūtra* encompasses a wide spectrum to topics related with art practice. The 35th *adhyāya* opens with a creation myth which attributes the origin of painting to the birth of *Urvaśī*. The 36th *adhyāya* is concerned with the five male stereotypes exemplifying the canons of iconometry. The next is *adhyāya* 37 which classifies five types of eyes. The following *adhyāya* 38 deals exclusively with norms of idol-making accompanied by dire warnings in case of any transgression of the prescribed measurements.

The *adhyaya* 39 marks a shift from the strictly religious/ritualistic context to the rules of foreshortening *(kṣayavṛddhi)*, which pertains to the problem of representing three-dimensional figures on a two-dimensional surface, from changing points of view as in a painting or a sculpture in relief.

Devoted mainly to the technical aspects of painting, the 40th *adhyāya* pays attention to the methods of ground preparation and mixing of colours. *Adhyāya* 41 is central to the *Citrasūtra*. It is here that the paintings are classified into four types: the *Satya, Deśika, Nāgara* and the last one *Miśra* being a combination of the first three. Most elaborate and important for iconography is the penultimate *adhyāya* which concerns the typology of various figures such as the kings, the ministers, the wrestlers and so forth, according to their relative placing in the social hierarchy. It also incorporates a section on the conventions for delineating not only different times of the day and night but also the four seasons. As it concludes, the *Citrasūtra* brings within its focus the *citra rasas* or the sentiments to be portrayed in art.

The Citrasūtra: A Founding Moment in Indian Art History

The *Citrasūtra* was "discovered" in colonised India. It coincided with the time when the question of arriving at an essentially Indian indentity of traditional art loomed large for art historians in the first quarter of the twentieth century. The dominant paradigm had already been set when Coomaraswamy launched a powerful defence of Indian art against the prevailing colonial view which had even denied the existence of fine arts in India. Central to Coomaraswamy's strategy was the transcendentalist claim[4]

[4]This appeal to transcendentalism is grounded on a set of binary oppositions setting apart Indian and western art (Greco-Roman and Renaissance traditions). If western art is characterised by naturalism, sensual materialism, Indian art is independant of the visible world and the source of its images is located in the mind.

for Indian art which was considered exclusively Indian in essence, compared to the degenerate materialism of western art. Elevating Indian art to such a refined exclusivity by grounding it on a polarised opposition to western art, Coomaraswamy effectively constructed a counter-discourse to the Eurocentric marginalisation of Indian art/craft. It was inevitable that the interpretation of the *Citrasūtra* would get caught up in the nationalist agenda of rewriting history from the perspective of the colonised.

My work is an exercise in reconstituting the text by approximating the archetype (assumed to be imaginary) on the basis of more MSS available to me than my predecessors. Given the discursive nature of the text itself and the foundational role it has played in the theorisation of early Indian art and aesthetics, any textual study of the *Citrasūtra* is necessarily mediated by the varying interpretations proposed by these scholars.

The genealogy of the scholarly interest in this text calls for a comment, as it offers a trajectory by which the text entered the centrestage of heated polemics, and debates about what constituted the essence of Indian art. The history of scholarly interest, i.e., the constitution of the modern discourse on the *Citrasūtra* can be traced back to 1912, when its first publication was brought out by the Venkatesvara Press.[5] However, this edition did not engender an immediate interest among the art historians. It was only when an English translation by Stella Kramrisch was published in 1924 that it had an impact on art historians and critics. This translation by Kramrisch had totally relied upon the Venkatesvara edition, which in turn had been uncritically prepared from two cognate and corrupt MSS (V1 & V2). Subsequently, Kramrisch returned to this text in 1928 and published a revised translation,[6] signalling the growing importance attached to the *Citrasūtra*.

It was this revised translation that had attracted the attention of Coomaraswamy. Out of all the 9 *adhyāyas*, it was *adhyāya* 41, dealing with the classification of paintings, which was to be the main focus of his article of 1932, as mentioned above.

By now, the two pioneering art historians of Indian art were involved in the interpretation of the *Citrasūtra*. This in turn raised the status of the text

[5] *Viṣṇudharmottarapurāṇa*, (Third Khanda), ed. Pandit Madhusudana and Madhavaprasad Sarma, (Venkatesvara press, Bombay, 1912).

[6] Stella. Kramrisch, "A Treatise on Indian Painting," *The Calcutta Review*, 1928.

and transformed it into a special site for wide ranging extrapolations about Indian art and aesthetics.

After Coomaraswamy's translation of *adhyāya* 41 and the series of articles by him referring back to it in general, and the *Citrasūtra* in particular, attention to this text returned when the first critical edition of the entire III *khaṇḍa* of the *Viṣṇudharmottara* was prepared by a Sanskritist, Priyabala Shah, in 1958.[7] It was followed by an annotated translation of this *khaṇḍa* in 1961.[8] Being a vast improvement on the Venkatesvara edition, Shah's edition broke fresh grounds in the area of textual criticism. More critical than the first, it incorporated the evidence of six new manuscripts (ABCDS1S2), of which five (ABCS1S2) contained the *Citrasūtra.* A seventh MS (F) was identified when the preparation of the edition was complete and its variant readings were inserted in the appendix. Despite the detailed account of the text in the introduction to the edition, her attempts at theorisation were limited to her comments on *adhyāya* 41. There she rejects Kramrisch's and Coomaraswamy's understanding of the text's classification of the types of painting and offers an interesting alternative to their interpretation of "shading" *(vartanā).*

C. Sivaramamurti's *The Citrasūtra of the Vishnudharmottara*[9] followed Shah's edition in 1978 but it relied upon Shah's critical apparatus completely and did not bring in any new MSS.

On the Manuscripts of the Text

Priyabala Shah and the earlier editors of the *Citrasūtra* had access to several MSS for textual construction. These have been listed below:

[7]Priyabala Shah, *Viṣṇudharmottarapurāṇa,* III *Khaṇḍa,* vol. II, (Text, Critical Notes, etc.) Oriental Institute, Baroda, Gaekwad Oriental Series, no CXXX, 1958.

[8]Priyabala Shah, *Viṣṇudharmottarapurāṇa,* vol. II, (Introduction, Appendixes, Indexes, etc.) Oriental, Institue, Baroda, GOS. 137, 1961.

[9]C. Sivaramamurti, *The Chitrasūtra of the Vishnudharmottara,* (New Delhi, Kanak Publications, 1978).

1. MS C.

Place of deposit: Bhandarkar Oriental Research Institute, Poona.

Catalogue no. : 93 of 1875-76

Folios: 488-755"

Size: 10.25" X 9,75"

Lines per page: 17

Substance: "Birch Bark"

Script: *Śāradā*

Date:-

Further comments: It was purchased by Bühler from Kashmir[10].

2. MS F.

Place of deposit: National Museum

Catalogue no.: Acc. no. 57. 106/1

Folios: 89

Size: 14" X 9.45"

Lines per page : 23

Substance: Paper

Script: *Śāradā*

Date: *saṃvat* 34 *(saptarṣi)* 8th, April, 1758 A.D. [11]

Further comments: The colophon mentions the scribe's name as *Makh-* and that it was completed on a Saturday *pratipadā* in the month of *Caitra.*

[10]See G. Bühler, *A Detailed Report of a Tour in search of Sanskrit MSS made in Kashmir, Rajputana and Central India,* 1877, pp. vi, Bombay.

[11]L.D. Swamikannu Pillai, *An Indian Ephemeris* (Madras, 1922).

3. MS A.

Place of deposit: Bhandarkar Oriental Research Institute, Poona.

Catalogue no.: 91 of 1875-76

Folios: 120

Size: 14" X 6"

Lines per page: 12

Substance: Paper

Script: *Devanāgarī*

Date:-

Further comments: This was also purchased by Bühler from Kashmir.

4. MS B.

Places of deposit: Royal Asiatic Library, Bombay.

Catalogue no.: 1758, Bhau Daji's coll. 249-250

Folios: 114

Size: 15" X 7"

Lines per page: 12

Substance: Paper

Script: *Devanāgarī*

Date: 1925 *Vikrama* era, 1868 A.D.

Further comments: The colophon mentions the scribe's name, *Bhūsara,* that it was completed in the month of *Aśvinī,* in the *kṛṣṇā pakṣa,* on a Saturday, the 10th of October, and that it was copied from a very old birch bark MSS.

MSS S1 and S2 are in the Saraswati Bhavan, Varanasi and are the only MSS whose readings I have not been able to check. I therefore had to rely on the editions of Shah and Ashoke Chatterjea Sastri for their readings.

While preparing this edition, I gained access to two MSS during my field trips to Nepal in August 1988 and to Bangladesh in January 1990. Shah was apparently aware of the existence of these MSS but was unable to refer or incorporate their readings in her edition. The MSS I located are as follows:

MS N.

Place of deposit: National Archives, Kathmandu, Nepal.

MS no.: 2-313

Catalogue no.: 8 no. 606

Folios: 249

Size: 30 cms X 11 cms.

Lines per page: 7

Substance: Paper

Script: *Newārī*

Date:

Further comments: MS D.

Place of deposit: Dhaka University Library.

Catalogue no.: 4669

Folios: 9-261

Size: 7 cms X 60 cms

Lines per page: 6

Substance: Paper

Script: *Bengalī*

Date

Further comments: Mohammad Shahjahan Mia, a local expert in Bengali paleography in Dhaka, proposed on the basis of the quality of handmade paper of the MS that it is at least 300 years old. It may be noted that the fact that the script of this MSS corresponds in most of the details, especially with the 12th century paleography, may point to its antiquity. (See *The Paleography of India,* Plate 34, Gaurishanker Ojha, Ajmer, 1975).

In dearth of sufficient external evidence given in the MSS, determining the inter-relationship and the relative chronology of these MSS is a problem. Only MS B, and to some extent F, give us some information in their colophons.

However, that C is the oldest of our MSS is attested by the fact that it has been written on a birch bark, which makes it at least 300-350 years old.

According to Bühler,[12] the use of birch bark came to an end from the time of Akbar (middle of the 16th century), in whose reign paper was introduced in Kashmir for the first time. Certain paleographical details, for example, the use of the double loop *(upadhmānīya)* in place of *visarga* on top of the following (labial) *akṣara* in the *Śāradā* script support its antiquity. The most important form of evidence comes in the form of good readings that it has consistently preserved. Of course, this is assuming that the older the MSS is, the closer it is to the archetype and the better readings it retains. Now let us examine the genealogical relationship between C and other MSS that have so far been used by Shah.

F is another *Śārada* MS but is written on paper, suggesting that it could not have been older than 300-350 years. Its colophon has the date - *samvat* 34. Assuming that it was *saptarṣi* 34, it must have been written in the latter half of the 18th century (1758). It is on the basis of its internal evidence that I conclude that F descended from C, namely that F not only incorporates the errors of C but also many peculiar errors. Still, I do not rule out a certain degree of contamination in F reflected in the corrections of the errors of C.

MSS A and B are on paper and written in *Devanāgarī*. Shah's claim that B is a copy of C on the basis of B's colophon lacks sufficient evidence. What is clear is that both A and B are copies of one MS, for they share substantial number of errors not found in C, and both A and B lack *adhyāya* on *Nṛsiṃharūpanirmāṇam,* which given in C makes it unlikely that this omission was accidental. That A and B are not copies of each other is clear by the fact that when they differ, readings of either of them agree with CFV. Moreover, the observation that where CF lack a verse (eg. 43.28) which A and B do not, inclines me to postulate a lost or an undiscovered MS (c) as their source. This lost MS (c) must have descended from C and also had an access to MSS of another tradition of transmission.

As for V, which was allegedly a copy of 2 MSS (V1, V2), its close affinity with B suggests that one of V's sources was B. The editions of V, or the scribes of V1 and V2, seem to have an access to F. This would account for several corrections made in V on the basis of F. The stemma of the MSS discussed so far can be made as follows:

[12]G. Bühler, 1877, pp. 29.

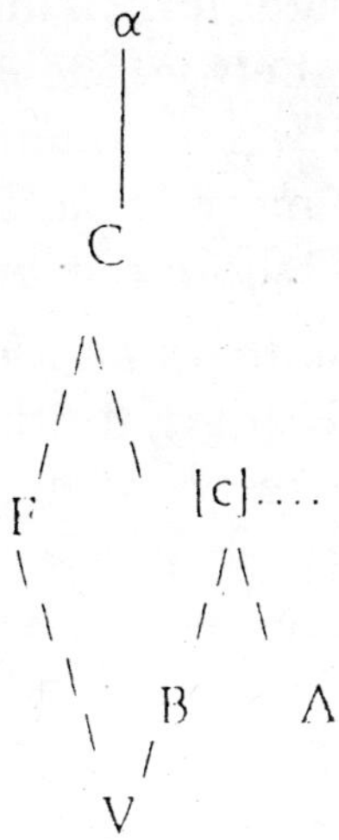

Note that the dotted line next to [c] signifies its access to another MSS tradition.

The MSS from Nepal and Bangladesh

Again we are left in doubt regarding the chronology of the MSS from Nepal and Bangladesh, as none has been dated. Therefore, for fixing the inter-relationship between themselves and with the MSS of the earlier group, we have to rely solely on the internal evidence. It was easily apparent from a study of their readings that they formed a distinct group (II) from the MSS used by Shah. Their readings suggest that they represented a separate branch of transmission and relate to the archetype independant of MSS CFABV. This explains certain sound readings, needs additional word or correction, even in verses retained in N and D but not to be found in any of the MSS of group I. As for example, verse 16 of *adhyāya* 42 is only preserved in D and N. Thus, these two MSS of group I, and diagnosing the peculiar errors in C.

In view of their being independent witnesses to the archetype, at first it seemed possible to place them at the primary split level, chronologically on par with C. However, a closer study of their inter-relationship revealed that they too, like MSS AB of the group I, are copies of a lost MS [d], of which D is more complete copy than N. Where N has left out verses, D's readings become the only guide to [d].

What makes D and N so significant is that they have descended from [d], which in turn relate to the archetype independently, and the latter therefore can be placed at the first split. Again, where N and D differ, the reading that agrees with C is considered more reliable. The fact that both or either of them shared readings with C shows that one was not the copy of the other.

However, it must be admitted that it is not possible to assume a strict distinction between group I and II, for there is some evidence suggesting that a cross-contamination between them occured. It seems that it was through [c] that readings from group II found their way into ABV. A concrete instance of this phenomenon is the presence of verse 29 of *adhy.* 43, तरङ्गग्निशिखाधूमं ..... विज्ञेय: स चित्रवित्, in ABV and its absense in CF. Similarly, while verse 28 of *adh.* 43, सुप्तं च चेतनायुक्तं ..... य: करोति स चित्रवित्, can be found in CFV, it is lacking in AB.

This strengthens the inter-relationship chalked out. The omission of this verse in AB was due to its absence in [c], it being [c]'s peculiar error. On the other hand, V through its access to F rectified this omission. It must be noted that MSS N and D of group II retain both of the above mentioned verses. Significantly, the verse order in V suggests it supplied this missing verse from F rather than D and N. The stemma representing the inter-relationship of all the MSS is as follows:

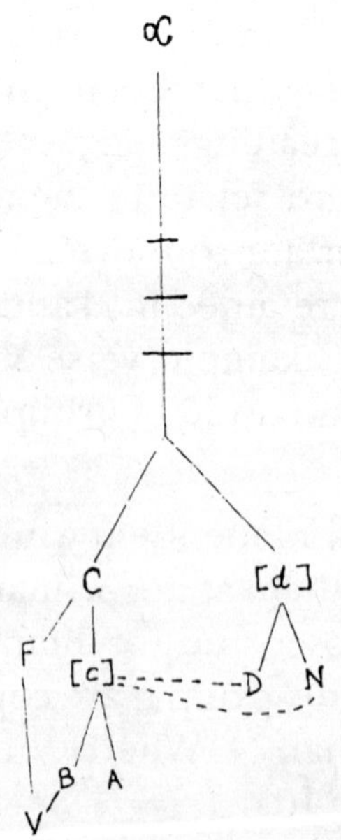

Now arises the question of evaluating the MSS on the basis of their readings. As indicated by the stemma above, it has not been possible to treat any one MS as the "best". Chronologically C preceded all the MSS, yet the readings of D and N have been regarded with equal respect. Where C shows a peculiar error, i.e. against ND, the reading of the latter two is more likely to lead us to the archetype. Again, it is difficult to uphold D as superior to N on grounds of its relative antiquity, simply because there are cases when N agrees with C against D, thus helping us to detect D's peculiar error.

Hence, in my edition, I have regarded MSS CDN as having equal value. Apart from following the basic principles of textual criticism, such as applying the inter-relationships amongst the MSS, the rules of grammar and the metre to the study of the text, I have also been guided by sense and context. In cases where even if all the MSS agree but yield improbable readings, I have proceeded to consider them suspect and wherever possible emend them (eg. *ashy.* 36, II.2 the emendation of *catvāriṃśaddanta-* to *Dvātriṃśaddanta-*). It is quite likely that errors of such kind could have taken place in the transmission before the primary split.

The Dating of the Text

The oldest extant MS of the work C can be approximately dated around the middle or the end of the sixteenth century. However, the original composition of the work of the archetype must have preceded C by centuries. The date of the *ViDhUp.* is widely contested as that of any other puranic sources[13]. The following is a table of dates ascribed to the *ViDhUp.* by various scholars[14].

1. Bühler	(pp. 408, 1890)	500 AD - 1000 AD.
2. Kramrisch	(pp. 5, 1928)	7th century
3. Shah	(pp. xxxvi, 1958)	450 AD - 650 AD.
4. Hazra[15]	(pp. 212, 1958)	400 AD - 500 AD.
5. Kane	(pp. 910, 1962)	600 AD - 1000AD.
6. Pingree	(pp. 472, 1967-68)	5th - 6th centry.

[13]See L. Rocher for the problems involved in dating the Purāṇas, pp. 100ff. 1986.

[14]It must be that there was a tendency amongst the scholars to derive the dates for the *ViDhUp.* as a whole, not considering that their evidence or arguments may not apply to all the *khaṇḍas.*

[15]See Hazra, *Studies in Upapurāṇa* pp. 205-212, for a detailed discussion on the dating of the *ViDhUp.* 1958.

There is an agreement about the ante quem of the text being 1000 AD, based on al-Bīrūnī's citations from the *ViDhUp.*, which have been identified with the *khaṇḍa* I of the text by Bühler.[16] So far it is Hemādrī's *Caturvargacintāmaṇi* that draws directly from and cites from all the three *khaṇḍas* of the *ViDhUp.*, pushing the upper limit of the third *khaṇḍa* to 1260-1309 AD. David Pingree, on the basis of his study of *adhy.*166-174 of *khaṇḍa* II not only dates it to the 5th-6th century AD but also concludes Kashmir as its provenance.[17] His evidence for such dating is that the *khaṇḍa* 2 of the *ViDhUp.* was the source for Brahmagupta's *Brahmasphuṭasiddhānta,* which was written in Bhinmal, Rajasthan, in 628 AD. However, this dating applies only to *khaṇḍa* II of the *ViDhUp.* The *Citrasūtra (adhy.* 35-43) is a part of *khaṇḍa* III and must have followed *khaṇḍa* II. However, it is difficult to ascertain the gap between the last two *khaṇḍas.*

Further evidence for dating the *khaṇḍa* II comes from the close correspondence between the Kashmir sculptures of the 6th-8th century AD and the description of these images in the *ViDhUp.*, as pointed out by Pratapaditya Pal.[18] Pal draws attention to a Kashmiri Viṣṇu trimūrti belonging to the 6th century AD (now in Berlin), which has the lion's head on the right and the boar's on the left. This arrangement of the heads is reversed in the Mathura prototypes. What is of interest to us is that this detail of the Kashmiri Viṣṇu exactly corresponds with the description of Viṣṇu in the *ViDhUp., khaṇḍa* III, *adhy.* 44. This is also an argument for Kashmir as the provenance of the text.[19]

At this point, it needs mentioning that close affinity exists amongst the *adhy.* 34-38 of the *Citrasūtra,* the *adhy.* 8, 58, 68, 69 of the *BṛSaṃ* (550 AD), and the *Adhy.* 4 and 37 of the *Sārāvalī* (800 AD). The fact that none of them cites from one another makes it difficult to form genealogical relationships amongst them. However, to some extent, it is possible to postulate that the *BṛSaṃ* and *Sārāvalī* may have been the source books for the *Citrasūtra.*

[16]Bühler, *Indian Antiquary* xix, pp. 380- 410.

[17]Pingree, pp. 472-473-1967-68 *Adayar Library Bulletin.*

[18]Pratapaditya Pal, *A Brahmanical Triad from Kashmir and Some Related Icons in Archives of Asian Art,* xxvii, pp. 38, 1973-74.

[19]See Hazra, for further evidence for establishing Kashmir as the provenance of the *ViDhUp.* pp. 214-216, 1958.

It is clearly evident that the five male stereotypes in the *Citrasūtra* were closely modelled on the personification of the five planets. The latter has a more natural place in the *BṛSam* and the *Sārāvalī* than the *Citrasūtra*, given that they are primarily texts on astronomy.[20]

It must be added that internal evidence in the *BṛSaṃ* shows that the *CitLak* of Nagnajit preceded it. Varāhamihira refers to this text, mentioning the author on the length of the face of an idol (58.4.). All that this enables us to conclude is that the *Citlak* antedated the *BṛSaṃ.* Nevertheless, the comparison of the iconometrical sections in the *Citlak* and the *Citrasūtra* clearly reveals the relative antiquity of the former.[21]

From the close affinity among the *Citrasūtra*, the *BṛSaṃ*. and the *Sāravalī*, Pingree's dating of the *khaṇḍa* II and the close correspondence between the image of Viṣṇu with the prescription in the *ViDhUp khaṇḍa* III, it seems possible to date the original composition of the text between 500 to 900 AD.

Nevertheless, a wide gap of 800 or perhaps 1000 years divides the Sanskrit archetype and the oldest extant MS. With this limitation, is it possible at all to restore the text to its original form ? The common source from which C, (d) D and N have descended may well have been open to numerous attempts at reconstruction along the long chain of transmission.

An access to primary sources, such as the Sanskrit MSS in various scripts, does not guarantee an access to the original meaning. Rather, it is only from the present that the past is reconstituted. There is no pristine "past" which lies out there to be (un)covered through textual fragments. Every translator relates to an imaginary past from one's location in the present, and the distance between that past and the present is already/always mediated by "other" translations which is synonymous with interpretations.[22]

On the one hand, my textual interest in the *Citrasūtra* has led me to approach the text vertically in my attempt to reconstitute the text on the

[20]I have followed David Pingree for the dating of the BṛSaṃ and the *Sāravalī* Jyótiḥśāstra. *History of Indian Literature,* vol 6 (2). 1981.

[21]If the above argument is valid it contradicts Hazra's statement that the Viṣṇudharmottara does not utilize Varāhamihira's Bṛhatsaṃhitā,..... or any other work written later than 500 AD, pp. 201, 1958.

[22]Steven Mailloux, "Interpretation", pp. 121-134, *Critical Terms For Literary Studies,* ed. Frank Lentricchia & Thomas McLaughlin, (University of Chicago Press, 1990).

basis of readings from the "unworked" MSS (N & D). On the other, weaving pervasively through the first mode of approach is the horizontal relation to the text which makes it impossible to regard any "fresh" reading without considering how my predecessors would have read it.

No textual critic can transcend the dominant views about Indian art and historiography, and I locate my edition and the interpretation of the text within the larger tradition of the modern interpretation of the *Citrasūtra,* and regard it as its latest addition/supplement. Perhaps what marks this edition as different from the earlier ones is that it inscribes a position that every scholar or translator operates within a philosophy or a theory of translation. Rather than repressing it on the grounds of objectivity, it becomes incumbent on the editor to state his/her ideological position.

Central to my interest in the *Citrasūtra* have been my expectations from the text about its stance on the question of naturalism which is a highly problematic terrain.

The Question of Naturalism: Nationalist Reworkings of the Citrasūtra

No term is more complex and ideologically loaded than naturalism. This term has had a long linguistic history in English.[23] Although it finds no direct one-to-one equivalent term in Sanskrit, this does not rule out its relevance in the context of Indian art and aesthetics. It was also a factor contributing to the sustained interest in the *Citrasūtra* shown by its modern commentators. Rather than appearing as a singular term, it seems to be scattered in related terms such as *sādṛśya* (resemblance), *satya* (world-resembling/naturalistic) and *anukṛti* (imitation). Taken as semantically grouped, constituting a family of ideas, they converged towards a view that "imitation" of the visible world was the most vital agenda for an art activity. As my interpretation of "naturalism" goes, it can never be accepted as a neutral, disinterestedrelationship between the observing *subject* and the observed *objects.*

[23]Williams traces concisely the history on "naturalism" from the early 17th century as used in religious and philosophical contexts to its contemporary usages. In its relation to art and literature, it has been contrasted with rhetorical use of language in the mid-18th century. In the 19th century, the term developed a close affinity with the sense of natural history, implying careful observation. "In painting especially, naturalism and the new MC 19 naturalistic were used to describe not only close observation but detailed 'reproduction of natural objects." From these derive the contemporary sense—a style of accurate external representation. Williams, Raymond: *Keywords'* Fontana Press, Great Britain, 1988.

Rather than being a universalconcept, "naturalism" appears to be a very local, culture specific one, in which the visual image and the language in which it is articulated interpenetrate; so much so that it becomes difficult to draw a line between literary and visual metaphors.

However, "naturalism" has posed a dilemma to my predecessors, and their interpretation remains to be historicised against its complicity with the nationalist struggle for identity. Only then, I hope, could one explain the anxiety surrounding its interpretation and the doubt regarding its validity as an aesthetic category in Indian art. "Naturalism", as a criterion in Indian art, was rendered problematic, and even a textual reference to it became suspect precisely when it became imperative to defend Indian art against colonial representations.

By the first quarter of the twentieth century, both Kramrisch and Coomaraswamy emerged as the two most powerful ideologues of Indian art. Their credibility largely rested upon their successful defence of Indian art against the prevailing colonial opinion, which was largely derogatory in that it considered "naturalism" as alien to Indian sensibility.[24] Kramrisch[25] warded off this charge by privileging suggestive symbolism as a constitutive element of Indian art, and thereby created an exclusive space for it which did not lend itself to any easy and favourable comparison with western art.

Kramrisch's view that Indian symbolism was mainly premised upon a metonymical relationship, in which a part could stand for the whole, informed her reading of the *Citrasūtra* (for eg. *adhy*. 42. verse 72). This verse concerns the depiction of moonlight by the means of blooming blue lotuses; the latter is taken in its singular sense against textual evidence, and thereby the significance of metonymy is underlined.[26] Besides, Kramrisch reinvokes

[24]See Partha Mitter's *Much Maligned Monsters,* chapters IV & V, for a fuller discussion of the European interpretation of Indian art from the mid-18th century till the beginning of the 20th century. (Oxford Clearendon Press, 1977).

[25]For Kramrisch's notion of "naturalism", see *A Biographical Essay* by Barbara Stoller Miller. Miller sketches an intellectual background of Kramrisch and mentions the influence of her teachers in Vienna. Max Dvorak, a Viennese art historian, had taught Kramrisch, whose important essay on 'Idealismus und Naturalismus in der gotischen Sculptur und Malerei' must have influenced Kramrisch. *Exploring India's, Sacred Art,* ed. Barbara Stoler Miller, (Univ of Pennsylvania Press, Philadelphia, 1983).

[26]This same view was echoed in Kramrisch's article, "The Representation of nature in Buddist Sculpture," *Rupam,* (Oct. 1921), pp. 9.

One tree, one flower is sufficient to express and to contain the whole nature. One house or citadel represents similarly a town . . . . .

"naturalism" as a term within quotes that had a different status and valency vis-a-vis its western counterpart.[27]

Coomaraswamy, more than Kramrisch, was vociferous in challenging the western evaluation of Indian art by certain norms derived from the Greco-Roman art which privileged "naturalism". As it is to be expected, a vehement denial of this criterion formed the ground on which the essential "Indian" aesthetics needed to be constituted.

This negation of "naturalism" had a strategic value, in the sense that it effectively undercut colonialist critics' denigration of Indian art. In fact, by thus distancing Indian art from the western criteria of judgement, Coomaraswamy made any comparison of the two art traditions suspect, if not impossible. Herein lay the strength of his discourses, which aimed at bringing about a radical reassessment of Indian art, in line with the nationalist agenda.

However, Coomaraswamy's defence of Indian art preceded his encounter with the *Citrasūtra.* This text presented a tremendous challenge to his views on Indian art, with its open endorsement of "naturalism" thereby exposing a gap between his modern expectations and the text. It interpellated him in such a way that there remained two alternatives open to him—a) It demanded a radical paradigmatic shift, which entailed on one hand, the abandonment of the transcendentalist claim for Indian art, and on the other, the recognition that interest in nature was as important in Indian art as in western art. b) The text could not be accepted at its face value and a "deeper" and more significant level had to be "discovered". Thus, the semantic discrepancy had to be negotiated through hermeneutics, i.e., by the act of interpretation as a radical strategy for conserving the text, which was thought to be too precious to be repudiated. Although it appears that Coomaraswamy maintains the sanctity of the text, in effect he radically alters it via the process of interpretation through a well-defined ideological framework.

Coomaraswamy's involvement with the *Citrasūtra* was selective and ideologically grounded. This has been historicised and placed within the given

[27]"The early exprience, that everything is recognised by its limits, is uttered by the means of the line, which circumscribe the objects and pronounce the names. In so far is early Indian art "naturalistic". Outlines have their origin in an intellectual, not sensual, perception of nature", *The Representation of Nature in Buddist Sculpture" Rupam,* 8, pp. 9, (Oct. 1921).

colonial context of the nationalist struggle for identity.[28] Unlike Kramrisch, he was not drawn to the textual problems of diagnosing suspect readings and offering emendations but his project was differently grounded. What situation could prompt this curious project of transforming a text ? The task of interprettaion is virtually one of translation in which Coomaraswamy seems to suggest that X is really Y, or really means Y, or that Y is really B. Interpretation thus presupposes a discrepancy between the clear meaning of the text and the demands of the (later) reader. It seeks to resolve that discrepancy.

> If we understood *sādṛśya* then to mean "illusion" or "realism", "verisimilitude" of any crude or native sort, we should be contradicting all that we know of the oriental conceptions of art.[29]

Here, Coomaraswamy explicates the meaning of *sādṛśya* via an allusion to the "the oriental conception of art." What this implies is a certain circularity where, on the one hand, he holds the text supreme, and on the other, he justifies his particular interpretion by invoking a set of presuppositions about the transcendentalist status of Indian art. Rather than spelling out these notions and examining their bearing on the reading of the text, he forecloses the argument by regarding them as given. In effect, Coomaraswamy's own position would be that of a mirror reflecting the pure text, both avoiding native and crude western conceptions of Indian art and eliding his own orientalist agenda.

For again, he says:

> What follows is derived from all these sources without the addition of any thought or phrase of my own. Verbal authority could be cited for any statement.[30]

[28]A.K. Coomaraswamy, *Essays in Natonal Idealism* Ceylon, 1909 Coomaraswamy, A.K. *Art and Swadeshi*, Madras, 1911.

Tapati, Guhathakurta, *Marking Independance: The Ritual of a National Exhibition, The Journal of Arts and Ideas,* pp. 98, no. 30-31, Dec, 1997

[29]A.K. Coomaraswamy, *Journal of American Oriental Society,* vol. 52 pp. 21, 1933.

[30]"The Painter's Art in Ancient India, Ajanta", *Journal of the Indian Society of Oriental Art* vol. I, Calcutta, pp. 26, 1933.

Again, *"Satya"* type of painting in *adhyāya* 41 comes to acquire the meaning "Pure and Sacred", which following V. Raghavan's criticism,[31] was revised to "intellectual" and "ideal"[32]. Such a project of transforming a text can only happen when there is a perceived gap between the ancient text and the scholar's expectations. Unless Coomaraswamy's modern expectations i.e., what the text ought to say, are contextualised against the historical reality of colonial India and his location in it, his reading of the *Citrasūtra* would simply appear to be a deliberate imposition of his earlier views upon the text. It would be far more accurate to argue that Coomaraswamy's work was underwritten by the nationalist imperatives of his time.

No translator, however, can stand outside the ideology that marks him/her as a product of history. Rather than an act of false consciouness, Coomaraswamy's translation foregrounds certain rules or codes of interprettaion/translation, which no doubt were a part of our nationalist agenda during the colonial period, and therefore, are now in urgent need of intervention in the post-colonial present.

The Citrasūtra in the Post-Colonial Art Historiography : Priyabala Shah and C. Sivaramamurti

Priyabala Shah's critical edition of the *Citrasūtra,* along with the annotated commentary, marks a breakthrough in the area of textual criticism. More of a Sanskritist than an art-historian, Shah makes no attempt at placing the text in a wider art historical context. However, she cannot distance herself from the urgencies of art history. There are instances where she tends to follow Kramrisch's view, even where those stem from corrupt readings of the Venkatesvara edition. Again, *adhyāya* 41 offers a case in point in which the interpretation of *patravartanā,* one of the three types of shading, is involved.

Having access only to the Venkatesvara edition, Kramrisch and Coomaraswamy had the following text before them in *Adhyāya* 41, verse 6 and translated them as follows:

[31]V. Raghavan, "Some Sanskrit Texts on painting", *Journal of Indian Historical Quarterly,* 9, pp. 904-905, 1933.

[32]A.K. Coomaraswamy, "The Painter's Art in Ancient India", *Journal of the Indian Society of Oriental Art,* Calcutta, vol. I, pp. 26, 1933

patrākṛti rekhābhi patravartanā

SK : Crossing lines (lit. lines in form of leaves, *patrajā*)....

AKC : The leaf shading *(Patravartanā)* is done with lines *(rekhā)* like those on a leaf.

In the absence of more reliable readings, the corruption in *patrākṛti* was not obvious to them. Curiously, Shah, who had the advantage of better readings available from *Sāradā* MSS (CF) in the form of *kṛtākṛtibhi* preferred the reading from the Venkatesvara text, and remained under the spell of the leaf metaphor invoked by her predecessors! Shah's translation reads as follows: "When the paint is applied in wavy lines . . . ."

According to her, when *patra* is used alone, it stands for the leaf of the *Tamāla* tree. Although she was aware of the ambiguity inherent in the leaf metaphor, i.e., "whether the lines of a paint are to be taken leafy in shape or whether they are like lines on the leaf" (pp. 127), she did not scrutinise adequately the alternate variants.

I have rejected V's reading as a corruption resulting from banalisation of the more technical sense yielded by the variants of MSS CF, (emended to) *kṛtākṛtābhi.* This new reading gives the following sense:

Patravartanā is a type of shading in which the lines are partly drawn and partly undrawn as in discontinuous line.

Shah's difficulty in not being able to resist the pull of the Venkatesvara edition appears to stem from her identification of certain readings as critical to art history, of which she could not claim enough authority and had to invoke that of her predecessors.

As a Sanskritist, Shah tended to attend mainly to the textual problems, i.e., of collation and the construction of the critical apparatus. Perhaps, this prompted C. Sivaramamurti to redress her bias towards the technical aspects of textual criticism and supplement the insights of a literary critic and an art historian in the study of the *Citrasūtra.*

Sivaramamurti's *"The Citrasūtra of the Vishnudharmottara"*, which appeared in 1978, relied entirely on Shah's collation and critical apparatus. Where there were occasional emendations offered, they were made on grounds of sense alone.

Sivaramamurti justified his translation and commentary as follows:

> . . . a technical text like this is bound to be an enigma in several respects. The text is yet not completely free from errors; and it can never be either. But there were some that yet could be clarified and

> corrected. The translations and interpretation also required looking into.[33]

Underlying this work in the thesis that naturalism was highly respected in Indian art. Extending the evidence given in his much earlier work, "The Artist in Ancient India", he supports his view with copious quotations from Sanskrit literatre. He places the *Citrasūtra* in a wider context of the classical Sanskrit literature and retrieves the *Citrasūtra* terms *sādṛśyā* (resemblance), *pramāna* (proportion) and *anukṛti* (imitation) from the problematic of transcendentalism.

His interest in this text began early in his carrer. "The Artist in Ancient India", which he wrote when still a research student, already quotes extensively from the *Citrasūtra* and makes several comments on the problem of imitation. He claims that both Western and Indian art were commited to the naturalistic techniques which some might associate exclusively with the western artistic tradition.

> Questions of perspective and foreshortening do not appear to have baffled the old artists of our land, as is evident from their talks on such technical details as *Ksayavṛddhi* and the actual conformance of the pictures to those rules so elaborately discussed in books on theory.[34]

He looked for evidence not only to the *Citrasūtra* but also to the descriptions of painting that occur in classical Sanskrit literature. Thus refering to a passage of the *Mṛcchakaṭika* (IX. 34), he says:

> The tendency of imitation in an artist given in the *Mṛcchakaṭika* is healthy sign of progress at a particular stage provided it is directed in the right direction.[35]

Sivaramamurti reinstated naturalism in post-Independent India as an index of progress, as proof that India could measure up and more to the categories and standard set-up in and by the west. Indeed, he writes naturalism back into art historiographical demands of post-Independent India, mapping the

[33]C. Sivaramamurti, *The Chitrasūtra of the Vishnudharamottara,* (New Delhi: Kanak Publications, 1978), pp. xv.

[34]C. Sivaramamurti, "The Artist of Ancient India", *Journal of Oriental Research,* 8, (1934): pp. 189.

[35]Ibid.

term as powerfully on nation-building as Kramrisch and Coomaraswamy had done.

What sets him apart from the earlier interpreters of this text is his stance of pro-naturalism, and therefore his ready acceptance of the *Citrasūtra's* naturalist terminology. This he took to be the text's full endorsement of naturalism as a valid aesthetic criterion. Historically, this position itself seems symptomatic of the fact that in the post-colonial era, the pressure to subscribe to the transcedentalist discourse of Kramrisch and Coomaraswamy did not exist in the same degree for Sivaramamurti.

On Situating the Citrasūtra

Central to the problem of interpretation of the *Citrasūtra* has been the delinking of the textual and the hermeneutic readings. As in the case of Coomaraswamy, where the gap between the syntax and semantics, or that between the signifier and the signified opened the widest, his interpretation acquires optimum resonance and rhetorical force. As the history of modern discourses on the *Citrasūtra* indicates, theorisation and speculation about its contents preceded the first critical edition. When the very order of its construction is inverted, misreadings occuring at the primary level tend to persist even in the most "improved" edition. There is no doubt of the fact that Shah was able to remove a large number of corrupt readings which Kramrisch and Coomaraswamy accepted due to the paucity of available MSS. Nevertheless, there are instances when the manifestly corrupt variants are preferred by Shah simply because they are supported by the deeply entrenched notions about early Indian art and aesthetics.

It seems to be a contradiction to accept the view that every translation/interpretation is ideology-specific, and yet it is possible to distinguish betwen a corrupt and non-corrupt reading since my premise of creating the distinctions would also be bound by my ideology. Let me define the notion of corruption that I use. Within the MSS, it is possible to identify corruption on grounds of acoustics-scribal errors based on similarity of sound (*da/dha; ta/ta; stra/tra* etc.), of paleography—those based on the similarity of written letters (different in different scripts) and of metrical inconsistency—a word or words which does/do not conform to the *anuṣṭubh* meter is/are found suspect. More difficult is to diagnose the ideological readings preferred by my predecessors.

For example, when Kramrisch accepted *vivarṇa* (adhy. 42, verse 58) in the context of how sky the ought to be represented, the alternate reading *svavarṇa* was still not available to her, and hence her attempt at accommodating it within the view of Indian art as being symbolic, in which the sky is to be represented colorless *(vivarṇa),* and indirectly suggested by the means of flying birds. Shah overlooks a reading from a fresh MS and retains *vivarṇa.* This preference of Shah's for a reading preferred by Kramrisch may also be deliberately justified on the grounds of her acceptance of Kramrisch's larger view of Indian art.

For me, this was a "wrong" variant and my acceptance of the other variant *svavarṇa* as better *also* stems from the ideology within which I operate, and also includes the project of critiquing the doxa or the accepted views of my predecessors on early Indian art.

At the outset, my interest in a *śilpaśāstra* like the *Citrasūtra* was that it would aid an entry into concerns that surround and inform art practice in early Indian art. Its stature as the hegemonic *śilpaśāstra* also held fasci-nation for me. This was further egged on by my suspicion on the question of interpretation that surrounded Orientalist discoures of the colonial/post colonial era. Central to this project was the complexity of addressing the question of naturalism and its possible complicity with the nationalist rhetoric.

Not being a sanskritist in Indian Art History can be a severe drawback which I have attempted to redress by entering into textual criticism. While this brought along certain advantages—it equipped me to address certain hermeneutical questions and make them bear upon the practice of textual criticism—it did not ground me firmly in Sanskrit studies in which I still regard myself as an outsider.

Each act of translation also gestures towards historiography, i.e., by a desire to rewrite history. Hence the present edition does not represent a return to a more "authentic" or "true" *Citrasūtra.* Every access to the text is marked by a discourse which is grounded in an ideology of the interpreter. In the case of the *Citrasūtra,* there have been several. In relation to them, I view this edition less a corrective project than an attempt to rework the text in the face of post-colonial concerns. The task of criticism is "not to discover forms of 'truth', but forms of validity".[36] What is valid as an assertion on the

[36]Roland Barthes, *Criticism as Language, in 20th Century Literary Criticism,* pp. 649, ed. David Lodge, Hongkong: Longman, 1988.

Citrasūtra in the colonial context linguistically, historiographically or ideologically may not be so in the post-colonial 90s. Underpinning this is the question of semiotics, constitutive of any interpretation. A translator inevitably deals with words and their meanings. A project of arriving at the most "authentic" meaning of the text presupposes a view that the relationship between words and meanings or between the signifiers and the signifieds is or can be stable.[37]

Finally the question of the rhetoric of translation needs to be addressed. The language of a text is never value-neutral, has is the language into which it is translated.[38] Just as the Sanskrit terms such as *sādṛśya, anukṛti* and *satya,* which have assumed controversial stature, are potentially polyvalent, likewise their English counterparts. The terms used by Coomaraswamy for translating them into English, such as "Pure", or "Sacred", "Ideal" are equally polyvalent, and today the present notions of them may not semantically coincide with the translator's intended meaning.[39] Again, every translator may have very different lists of words which are considered untranslatable.

This would be rhetoric in its limited and technical usage. The larger question of rhetoric[40] opens up the issue of the truth claim implicitly or explicitly put forward by every translator we have considered so far, including those made by me. Each of these translators differed from each other not only in terms of making assertions grounded in their ideologies but also in their style of translation. These assertions, couched as they are in certain rhetoric are made for the purpose of persuading some audience. Their

[37].. translation practices the difference between signified and signifier. But if this difference is never pure, translation is even less so, and a notion of transformation must be substituted for the notion of translation.

Gayatri Chakravarty Spivak, "Translator's Preface pf Grammatology by Jacques, Dervida (Baltimore: John Hopkins University 1975): 9-10.

[38]Walter Benjamin, *The Task of the Translator, Illuminations* pp.74, London: fontana, 1992.

[39]Roland Barthes, (Longman: 1988)

The language that a critic chooses to speak is not a gift from heaven; it is one of the range of languages offered by his situation in time and, objectively, it is the latest stage of a certain historical development of knowledge, ideas and intellectual passions.

[40]Stanley Fish, "Rhetoric", *Critical Terms For Literary Studies;* ed. Frank Lentricchia & Thomas McLaughin, (Univ. of Chicago Press, 1990).

interest in the text was not neutral, professing to uncover some hidden truth even if a claim to this effect be made but loaded where each had a stake in it. Each occupies a certain stage situation, hazarding an interpretation of utterances produced by actors in other stage situations.[41]

Subscribing to the view that every translation is ideological and inscribed with the translator's perspective, it is that very perspective which is enabling. In other words, it becomes possible to create the distinction between the "correct" and the "incorrect" readings amongst the variants available in the MSS and rescue the translator from relativism. What is most problematic to determine is the criteria for "truth" or "accuracy", however provisional or ideology-specific the translator admits it to be. Sometimes, it is on the grounds of grammar or meter, or sometimes that of the context applied not only by the larger text that a chapter is a part of but by other *Śilpa* or related texts such as these concerning astrology, architecture, poetics.

Given the question of naturalism assuming central importance in the interpretation of the *Citrasūtra,* my position towards it needs to be stated. Though it is a highly complex issue defying any simplification, if for the sake of underlining my position, naturalism is assumed to imply an interest in nature or in the visible world, and the desire to imitate it, it has been as much a part of the Indian art tradition as the western one. Each of the terms in this "definition—nature", "interest", "visible", "desire", and "imitate", are culturally loaded.

There is no universal naturalism which transcends cultural diversities but it can only be formulated as a cultural construct. Rather than simply accepting or rejecting it as a valid aesthetic category in Indian art, the specificites of the construct that naturalism is, need to be interrogated and analysed. Although this term defies a word-to-word translation in Sanskrit, this untranslatibility does not rule out its relevance in Indian art practice and theory. Instead of a single term in Sanskrit, as a semantic equivalent of "naturalism", there appear to be a cluster of terms—*sādṛśya, anukṛti,* and *satya,* which constitute a family of ideas converging towards its sense in English. "Naturalism", as is construed in the *Citrasūtra,* lent predominance

[41]Ibid, p. 214.

to metaphors which were as much rooted in linguistics as the tradition of visual imagery (*cf. adhyāya* 37).[42]

Much as a translator desires to bridge the gap between the words and meanings, as to rewrite history through the translator's perspective, and arrive at the most "transparent" interpretation, there is no guarantee that this gap may not be reopened by the deconstructive lever of a future translator.

> ... criticism is neither a "tribute" to the truth of the past, nor to the truth of "the other"; it is the ordering of that which is intelligible in our time.[43]

[42]The adhyāya 37 deals with the five types eyes classified according to their resemblance with a bow, cowrie shell, blue lotus leaf, white lotus leaf and the belly of a fish.

[43]Roland Barthes, pp. 649, (Longman: 1988).

CITRASŪTRA
(Text, Translation and Notes)

ADHYĀYA 35

पञ्चत्रिंशोऽध्यायः

मार्कण्डेय उवाच

अतः परं प्रवक्ष्यामि चित्रसूत्रं तवानघ ।
उर्वशी सृजिता पूर्वं +चित्ररूपा+ नृपात्मज ॥१॥

नारायणेन मुनिना लोकानां हितकाम्यया ।
प्राप्तानां वञ्चनार्थाय देवस्त्रीणां+महामुनि+: ॥२ ॥

सहकाररसं गृह्य उर्व्यां चक्रे वरस्त्रियम् ।
चित्रेण सा ततो जाता रूपयुक्ता वराप्सराः ॥३॥

यां दृष्ट्वा व्रीडिताः सर्वा जग्मुस्ता देवयोषितः ।
एवं महामुनिः कृत्वा चित्रं लक्षणसंयुतम् ॥४॥

ग्राहयामास स तदा विश्वकर्माणमच्युतम् ।
यथा नृत्ते तथा चित्रे त्रैलोक्यानुकृतिः स्मृता ॥५॥

दृष्टयस्तु तथा भावा अङ्गोपाङ्गानि सर्वशः ।
कराश्च ये मता नृत्ते पूर्वोक्ता नृपसत्तम ॥६॥

N lacks adh. 35

1b. D तवानथ 1c ADV उर्वशी AVS1V सृजतः CF सृजता D सृता ABV पूर्वे
1d. चित्ररूपा conj. ABCDFNV चित्रसूत्रं
2c. S1 वाञ्चनार्थाय F वञ्चिनार्थाय
3b. C वरस्त्रियाम् 3c F जातौ
4a. A बीडिताः CF व्रूडिस्तस्सर्वा 4b C जग्मुस्तां 4c CF महामुनिर्कृत्वा
5c. S2 नृत्ये 5DF –नुकृति
6a. ABV दृष्टयश्च तथा D तथा भाषा F भवा 6c CFV महानृत्ते

ADHYĀYA 35

Mārkaṇḍeya spoke:

1-3b. O Sinless One, I shall henceforth teach you the treatise on painting. O Prince, sage *Nārāyaṇa* [who was engaged in penance] for the welfare of the worlds, created *Urvaśī* in form of a painting. The great sage after taking the juice of the mango tree, painted on the ground [a picture of] a beautiful woman to deceive the wives of the gods who had approached him.

3cd. Then she, the best of the *Apsaras*, endowed with beauty came into being as a painting.

4-5b. On seeing her, all the wives of the gods were put to shame and they fled. Then the great sage having painted [this] picture with [all] the marks of excellence made the imperishable *Viśvakarman* learn it.

5cd. As in dance, so in painting, the imitation of the three worlds is prescribed.

6-7. Those eye [and eyebrow] expressions, moods, primary and secondary limbs and hand (gestures) mentioned earlier in the (section

त एव चित्रे विज्ञेया चित्रं नृत्तसमं मतम् ।
नृत्ते प्रमाणं यन्नोक्तं तत्प्रवक्ष्याम्यतः शृणु ॥७॥

हंसो भद्रोऽथ मालव्यो रुचकः शशकस्तथा ।
विज्ञेयाः पुरुषाः पञ्च तेषां वक्ष्यामि लक्षणम् ॥८॥

उच्छ्रायायामतुल्यास्ते सर्वे ज्ञेयाः प्रमाणतः ।
स्वेनैवाङ्गुलमानेन शतमष्टाधिकं भवेत् ॥ ९॥

प्रमाणं नृप हंसस्य भद्रस्य तु षडुत्तरम् ।
चतुर्भिरधिकं ज्ञेयं मालव्यस्य तथा नृप ॥१० ॥

शतं च रुचकस्योक्तमष्टोनं शशकस्य च ।
द्वादशाङ्गुलविस्तारस्ताल इत्यभिधीयते ॥११॥

आ गुल्फतश्चतुर्भागः पादोच्छ्रायः प्रकीर्तितः ।
द्वौ च तालौ तथा जङ्घे पादतुल्ये च जानुनी ॥१२॥

जङ्घातुल्यौ तथा चोरू नाभिस्तालं तु मेढ्रतः ।
तावच्च नाभेर्हृदयं हृदयात्कण्ठ एव च ॥१३॥

7a. A तपव D विक्रेया 7b ABCVF नृत्तं चित्रं परं D चित्रं समं A मत्तम्
7c. D यत्रोक्तं V येन्नोक्तं 7d A शृण्व
8a. CF भद्रोऽय 8b C रुचकस्मकस्तथा F रुचकस्वकस्तथा 8c AB विज्ञेयः ˘B पुरुषः
9b. ABD ज्ञेया 9c B स्वनेवाङ्गुलमानेन DV स्वेनेवाङ्गुल-
10b. D भद्रस्यस्तु यडुत्तरम 10d D मानव्यस्य
11a. F चा 11cd D विस्तार विस्ताले त्यभिधीयते
12a. S1 omits अगुल्फ.....तथा चोरु V अङ्गुल्फन्तच्चतु- ABCF अगुल्फंतश्चतु-V -भागं
13a. B जंघातुल्यो ABS2 तथा द्वौ तु 13cd D नाभिहृदय- ABCFV नाभिहृदयं
13d. AS1S2 हृदयात्कण्ठमेव च B हृदया कण्ठमेव च

on) dance, O Best of kings, are the very ones to be known in painting (for) painting is considered to be parallel to dance.

Now listen [to me for] I shall teach you [the rules of] proportion, which were not mentioned in [my treatment of] dance.

8. Know that there are five [types of] men to be known : *Haṃsa, Bhadra, Mālavya, Rucaka* and *Śaśaka.* I shall tell you the distinguishing features of [each of] them.

9-10. Know that they all are equal in height and width (individually) according to the (given) proportion. O king, the proportion (i.e. height) of the *Haṃsa* should be 108 *aṅgulas* according to its 108th part determined by itself. A Bhadra is 106 *aṅgulas* in height and Mālavya should be 104 *aṅgulas.*

11. The height of a *Rucaka* man is 100 *aṅgulas,* and of a *Śaśaka* man 92. A *tāla* ought to equal 12 *aṅgulas* in extension.

12-13b. The height of the foot up to the ankle is said to be four *aṅgulas (bhāga);* the shank (from the ankle to the knee) measures 2 *tālas* ; the knees measure a *pāda* (i.e.a quarter of a *tāla*); The thighs measure the same as the shanks; the distance between penis and navel is 1 *tāla.*

13cd. The distance between the navel and the heart, and that between the heart and neck is the same. (i.e. 1 *tāla*).

कण्ठस्तालत्रिभागः स्यात्तालं च वदनं भवेत् ।
तालषड्भागमप्युक्तं ललाटोपरि मस्तकम् ॥१४॥

मध्ये मेढ्रं तु विज्ञेयमिति दैर्घ्यं प्रकीर्तितम् ।
तालः प्रोक्तः करो राजन्बाहू सप्तदशाङ्गुलौ ॥१५॥

प्रबाहू तावदेवोक्तौ वक्षसोऽर्धमथाष्टकम् ।
एतदायामतः प्रोक्तं मानं हंसस्य पार्थिव ॥१६॥

अनेनैवानुसारेण शेषाणामपि कल्पयेत् ।
आयामपरिणाहाभ्यां समाः सर्वे नराधिपाः ॥१७॥

सामान्यतस्ते नृपवर्य मानं
प्रोक्तं मया हंसनराधिपस्य ।

प्रत्यङ्गमानं तु मयोच्यमानं
समासतस्तं शृणु राजसिंह ॥१८॥

इति श्रीविष्णुधर्मोत्तरे तृतीयखण्डे मार्कण्डेयवज्रसंवादे चित्रसूत्रे
आयामोच्छ्रायमानवर्णनो नाम पंचत्रिंशत्तमोऽध्यायः ॥

14a. A कण्ठताल- F कठास्तालं त्रिभागस्स्यात् C कण्ठस्तालं त्रिभागस्स्यात्

14b. D वचनं भवेः 14c D तानषड्- C तालसद्भाग-

15a. Cf मेढ्र 15c CF प्रोक्त करे

15cd. D -रोजन्वावाहुक्ष 15d F -दशाङ्गुली

16a. F देवोक्ता 16c A पदताया-

17b. CF शेषामपि 17c D आयास- CD -हाभ्यं 17d ABV नराधिप

18a. CF समान्य-D नृपचर्म ? 18b D महाहंस 18c ABV च D यायाच्यमानं

18d. A भृण्उ D भृण्व

14. The neck measures 1/3 of a *tāla* and the face 1 *tāla*. The head above the forehead (i.e. the crown) is said to be 1/6 of a *tāla.*

15. The penis is understood to be in the centre (of the length of the body). What is taught is the elevation (of the *Haṃsa*).

O King, it is taught that the palm is a *tāla,* the hands (from wrist to the elbow), 17 *aṅgulas.*

16. The forearms are said to be of the same measurement (17 *aṅgulas*). One half of the chest measures 8 [*aṅgulas*]. O King, this proportion is prescribed for the *Haṃsa* male in terms of the width.

17. One may calculate the proportion of the remaining [types], based upon this very model. [For] all the lords of men are equal in height (*āyāma*) and breadth (*pariṇāha*).

18. O Best of Kings, I have taught in general terms proportion of the *Haṃsa* variety of king. Listen now, O Lion amongst Kings, as I teach you in outline the proportions of the minor limbs.

NOTES TO ADHYĀYA 35

35. 1c. *sṛjitā*. Note that this emendation is required to get a complete sense. *Sṛjatā* yields no sense here. The version in *khaṇḍa* I (see below) suggests a past participle of √*sṛj*. I propose, to read *sṛjitā*. This is not a Pāṇinian Sanskrit . However, it is not perhaps beyond the bounds of possibility in a text of this kind.

35. 1d. *citrarūpā*. *Citrasūtram* (<MSS) yields no good sense in the context and is probably a repetition of *citrasūtram* in the same metrical position in the preceding line. *Citrarūpa* restores sense in accordance with the fuller version of the myth (*khaṇḍa I, adhyāya* 129, 1-15) which is summarised here.

1-5ab. Compare this section on the origin of *Urvaśī* with a parallel account found in *khaṇḍa* I, *adhyāya* 129, verses 1-15, *ViDhUp* .

वज्र उवाच उर्वशी च कथं जाता बुधजं पाथिर्व कथम् ।
पतिं कृतवती देवी मानुषं तत्प्रकीर्तय ॥ १ ॥

मार्कण्डेय उवाच साध्यौ धर्मसुतौ प्रोक्तौ नरनारायणावृषी ।
यौ तौ पूर्वं महीपालौ तावुभौ यदुनन्दन ॥ २ ॥

विष्णोरंशौ महावीर्यौ तपस्याभिरतौ सदा ।
तयोस्तदाश्रमं रम्यं सुगन्धिविटपद्रुमम् ॥ ३ ॥

बदर्याश्रममित्युक्तं मृदुस्पर्शहिमं शुभम् ।
उष्णतोयवहा गङ्गा शीततोयवहा परा ॥ ४ ॥

सुवर्णसिकता रम्या काञ्चनोत्पलमालिनी ।
तत्र सा बदरी रम्या नित्यपुष्पफलोपगा ॥ ५ ॥

तत्र तौ मुनिशार्दूलौ घोरं तप उपाश्रितौ ।
भवाय सर्वलोकस्य सर्वलोकेश्वरावुभौ ॥ ६ ॥

तयोस्तपस्यतोरेवं मौनेयाप्सरसो दश ।
तयोस्तु तपसो विघ्नं संभूय कृतनिश्चयाः ॥ ७ ॥

तं प्रदेशमनुप्राप्ता नानाभरणभूषणाः ।
पितामहान्न सौम्योऽस्ति कश्चिद्राजञ्जगत्त्रये ॥ ८ ॥

तासां दर्शनमासाद्य नरः कामवशो भवेत् ।
कुसुमानि विचिन्वत्यो ललन्त्यश्च यथासुखम् ॥ ९ ॥

दृष्टा नारायणेनाथ सर्वा बालमृगेक्षणाः ।
तासामन्तर्गतं भावं ज्ञात्वा वेदविदां वरः ॥ १० ॥

जितक्रोधो महातेजा जितकामोऽर्थधर्मवित् ।
आदाय सहकारस्य रसं मदनदीपनम् ॥ ११ ॥

ऊर्वोश्चित्रेण चार्वङ्गीं निर्ममेऽप्सरसं शुभाम् ।
ऊर्वोः कृता चित्रेण चित्राक (भ ?) रणशालिनी ॥ १२ ॥

तस्मिन्नेव क्षणे नारी बभूवायतलोचना ।
न देवी न च गन्धर्वी नासुरी न च पन्नगी ॥ १३ ॥

तादृग्विधा त्रिलोकेऽस्मिन्यादृशी सा वराङ्गना ।
तां दृष्ट्वा व्रीडितास्सर्वा मौनेयाप्सरसो दश ॥ १४ ॥

जग्मुर्यथागतं राजंस्तच्छुश्राव पुरन्दरः ।
द्रष्टुं कौतुहलात्तां च बदर्याश्रममागतः ॥ १५ ॥

Mārkaṇḍeya narrates to Vajra how Urvaśī came into being. The sage, Nara and Nārāyaṇa were engaged in penance in a beautiful hermitage called Badari for the welfare of the whole world (*bhavāya sarva lokasya*). Then, with the intention of disturbing their penance, ten celestial nymphs entered Badari. Upon seeing them frolicking about and picking up flowers, Nara was overcome with desire. (But) the other sage Nārāyaṇa who had control over anger and desire, sensed their intention. Then he obtained (some) mango juice which induces passion, and painted a beautiful nymph on (his) thighs. (This beauty) endowed with wonderful ornaments (*citraka(bha ?) raṇaśālinī)* was made on his thighs in a form of a painting. At that very moment, a long-eyed woman of incomparable beauty came into being (from that very painting). On seeing her, all the celestial nymphs were put to shame and they departed.

This version (A) is certainly the more coherent and complete of the two. In comparison, the version (B) in adhyāya 35, *khaṇḍa* III appears not only condensed but incomplete. From the former, we gather that the sages were engrossed in deep meditation for the sake of the welfare of the people or the worlds (see verse 6 adh. 129 kh.I.) *lokānām hitakāmyayā* in *adhy*.35 seems correspond closely with *bhavāya sarvalokasya* in *adhy*.129. Given this reason for the sages' meditation, it makes little sense to assume that either Urvaśī or the CitSūt. was created for the benefit of the worlds which follows from the version B.

35. 3b. *urvyām* . SM emends to *ūrvām* and translates " on his thigh" (p 167) on the basis of the version A. But *ūru* is masculine and its locative singular is *ūrau.* However, the emendation is unnecessary since the MSS' *urvyām* gives an entirely satisfactory sense. SM supports his emendation as follows:

> F.N.1 : Here is a clear case of correction of reading. It is well known that उर्वशी is from the ऊरू or thigh of Narayana. Hence the emendation. If it were from उर्वी the derivation would be different. The illustration from Bharhut is also a pointer to the right reading. (pp. 137)

Neither argument is persuasive. The evidence of one etymology does not exclude any other, even in the understanding of a single author. As for the evidence of the Bharhut sculpture, it no more supports SM's emendation than what is given in the text.

35. 3cd, SK translates *citreṇa sā tato jātā rūpayuktā varāpsarāḥ* as "By means of (the science of citra) she was endowed with beautiful form and became the best Apsara". I take *citreṇa* to mean "as a picture", i.e. as a condensed expression for *citrarūpeṇa;* see Speiyer * 67. Rem. 2.

35. 5c. *nṛtte.* SM prefers S2'5 *nṛtye. Nṛtte,* the reading of all MSS, is, however, acceptable, since the distinction between *nṛtta* as formal dance and *nṛtya* as a mimetic dance is a later development; see ***Classical Indian Dancing A Glossary,*** M. Bose, p.9 ff Calcutta, 1970. SM's emendation of *nṛtte* to *nṛtye* is, therefore, quite unnecessary.

> F.N. 2 : The reading नृत्य is better then नृत्ते as it is only the former by its abhinaya that can achieve interpretation of the world around, trailokyānukṛti. (pp. 137).

35. 6a. *dṛṣṭayastu.* SK translates *dṛṣṭayah* as "eyes" (p. 29), SM as "glances" (p. 167) and PS as "eyesights" (p. 105). However, adhy. 25 (*Nṛttasūtra*) gives it a more precise and technical sense namely "transformation in facial expression brought about by the movement of the eyes and the eyebrows".

Aṅgopāṅgāni again stands specifically for the major limbs or members of the body such as trunk, head, arms, and legs and the minor limbs are the forehead, nose, chin, fingers, ears etc.

35. 7b. *nṛttasamam.* D provides a sound reading *samam* as opposed to *param* given in all other manuscripts. It has to be treated as one word to make it grammatically tenable. It would have made more sense if the order were reverse i.e. *citram nṛttasamam matam.* Note how *param* affects the following translations:

SK: Dancing and chitra are considered as (*equally*) *excellent.* (p. 29)

SM: .. *as dance is art supreme.* (p.167)

PS leaves it out in the translation.

35. 7cd. PS's criticism of SK's translation of this line is valid.

SK: Hence I am going to speak about *that by which measurement* in dancing was said (to be *regulated*). (p. 29)

PS: This is obviously wrong. The question of bodily proportion has no place in dancing . (p. 105)

What the text implies is that as far as bodily gestures and facial expression are concerned, dance and painting are alike. The *pramāṇa* or proportion of the body is what differentiates painting from dance.

35. 9ab. *ucchrāyām atulyāste sarve jñeyāḥ pramāṇataḥ.* It, in this case means, by implication the various measurements of the height given in the succeeding verses. As for instance, a *Haṃsa* type is 108 *aṅgulas* in height and width i.e. the width across the outstretched hands from the tip of a finger of one hand to that of another. Similarly, a *Bhadra* man is 106 in height and so on.

SK's translation is rather obscure:

Equal in height and breadth, they are all to be known from (*other respective*) measurements. (p. 29)

SM links up 9a with 9b and translates it as :

These all have *equally proportionate* height and width in *terms of their own aṅgula, finger.* (p. 168)

Svenaivāṅgula- cannot be translated as "their own finger". See below.

35. 9c. *svenaivāṅgulamānena*. This term has a more specific and technical meaning; see BṛSaṃ 57.4 with Bhaṭṭotpala's commentary:

स्वैरङ्गुलप्रमाणैर्द्वादश वीस्तीर्णमायतं च मुखम् ।
नग्नजिता तु चतुर्दश दैर्ध्येण द्राविडं कथितम् ॥ ४ ।। ५७ बृ. स.

However, it may be noted that his exposition suffers from a transposition of numerals underlined below. See AgniPu., HaŚiPaRat. (18.8), ApaPṛ. (210.1) for support for my observation.

Bhaṭṭotapala:

यस्मात्काष्ठात् पाषाणादिकाद्वा प्रतिमा क्रियते तद्दैर्घ्यः पीठप्रमाणविवर्जितः
द्वादशभागविभक्तं कृत्वा तत्रैको भागो नवधा कार्यः सोऽङ्गुलसंज्ञा भवति ।
यस्मादष्टाधिकमङ्गुलशतं प्रतिमाप्रमाणं वक्ष्यति - स्वैरङ्गुलप्रमाणैरिति ।

"The measurements of their own units" means the follows: Divide the entire length of that wood or stone etc. out of which an idol is to be made, into 9 (12) parts, each of which subdivided into 12 (9) equal parts, that one part (i.e. the lowest unit) is called an *aṅgula.* Becausethe proportion of an idol is said to be 108 *aṅgula.*

This means that this term *aṅgula* does not stand for a finger-breadth but the lowest unit of measure of any whole divided into 108 parts which makes any 108th part an *aṅgula.* In CitSūt., it is the *Haṃsa* type which is alloted with this division and hence it is this type which becomes the standard for all the other types. See Diagram III

This artist divides his material into 108 units, lets it remain as it is in case of the *Haṃsa* or subtracts 2, 4, 8, or 16 for *Bhadra, Mālavya, Rucaka* and *Śaśaka* respectively. If the interval between the units is a constant factor, and height a variant, then the four types would get progressively stouter. Note that this is at variance with PS's following deductions:

> The measurements of these five types is given in terms of aṅgula. The phrase *Svenaivaṅgulamānena* would mean the measurements according to one's own *aṅgula*. If this interpretation is true, then the measurements of each one of these types would be relative to their respective *aṅgulas*. This means that no standard measure of *aṅgula* irrespective of the measure of individual *aṅgulas* was fixed. (p. 105-106)

The theory that *Haṃsa* type forms the standard for other types gains support from verse 16b, 17 and 18a. Perhaps the reason why *Haṃsa* becomes a model is because its height coincides with the *aṅgula* system. It is evident in this and the following chapter that the *Haṃsa* type is central. The section on proportion in adhy. 36 ends : इति हंसप्रमाणं भवति । cf. 35. 18a:

सामान्यतस्ते नृपवर्य मानं प्रोक्तं मया हंसनराधिपस्य ।

35.10-11ab. Different texts record different measurements for the five male types. In BṛSaṃ., the chapter *"Pañcamānuṣyavibhāga"* gives two irreconcilable sets of proportion, a fact acknowledged by the commmentator, Bhaṭṭotpala on 7.68.

एतदुत्तरत्र वक्ष्यमाणग्रन्थेन विरुध्यते ७.६८

This contradicts what is going to be mentioned later.

35. 11b. *maṣṭonam* . This is an emendation of *daśonam* against all MSS evidence. In the *Śāradā* script, it is easier to explain the confusion between the *da* of *daśonam* and *ma* of *maṣṭonam* than between the so of the former and the *ṣṭo* of the latter. The main consideration prompting the emendation is a mathematical program into which 92 *aṅgulas* for *Śaśaka* fits in better than 90

aṅgulas. It is obvious that the *Haṃsa* type comprising of 108 *aṅgulas* is assumed to be the model - the remaining types for *Bhadra, Mālavya, Rucaka* and *Śaśaka* as 106, 104, 100 and 92 (under question) are derived by subtracting from 108 multiples of 2: (108-2=106; 108-4=104; 108-8=100 & 108-16=92) Cf. BṛSaṃ. which also gives 92 *aṅgulas* for *Śaśaka.* See Diagrams III-VII in which attempt is made to reconstruct the four male stereotypes derived from the Haṃsa Model.

The table recording the variation in proportion is as follows:

	BṛSaṃ	BṛSaṃ	CitSūt	CitLak		SamSūtDhar
Haṃsa	96	96	108	Cakravartin	108	88
Bhadra	105	84	106	Sadhu	106	94
Mālavya	108	108	104	Mālavas	104	96
Rucaka	102	100	100	Vyañjanas	100	92
Śaśaka	92	99	92	Giridhara	98	90

35.12a. *ā gulphataś ca caturbhāgaḥ* . SM emends to *āgulphāntaṃ caturbhāgam* on the basis of *agulphantaśca* from AC and F which is corrupt. I have adopted D's reading.

35. 13c. *nābherhṛdayam.* All MSS give *nabhihṛdayam.* I have emended in accordance with the obviously intended sense. The resulant *pāda* is a 3rd *vipulā* of the *anuṣṭubh.* This agrees with PS's conjecture and SM's emendation.

35. 15a. *madhye meḍhram.* What the text intends to convey is that the penis is located in the centre of the length of the body.

35. 15b. Note that 15ab with *-iti dairghyam prakīrtitam* concludes the section on "elevation" and is followed by that on the lateral dimension or *āyāma.*

35. 16b. *etadāyāmataḥ.* SM translates it as "in terms of length" (p. 168) Note *āyāma* in this case precisely means "breadth" or "width". This distinction between the height of human body measuring

from feet upwards till the head and the horizontal measurements starting from palm laterally indicates that the model was conceived of as standing with outstretched arms.

35. 17c. *āyāmapariṇāhābhyām.* In this context, *pariṇāhā* means "width". This verse only reiterates what was mentioned earlier (supra 9a). SK takes it as "the proportion between the breadth and circumference".

We know that as far as height or elevation is concerned, all the five types differ, but that they are similar individually with regard to the ratio between the height and breadth.

PS reads in "circumference" which the text does not mention.

PS: All the types are equal in their length, breadth and *circumference.* (p. 106)

35. 17d. *narādhipāḥ.* The five male stereotypes are referred to here as "lords of men", as in verse 17b in the case of the *Haṃsa* type. Considering that C, D and F show *narādhipāḥ,* I regard the reading of AB and V *(narādhipa)* as a corruption. Note how it affects the translations:

SK: In all cases, the proportion between breadth and circumference is constant, *O lord of Men,* (p. 30)

PS leaves it out in the translation.

SM (p. 138) emends to *narādhipa:*

F.N. 1) it should be नराधिप addressing the king, not in plural.

BṛSaṃ throws light on the interpretation of the five male stereotypes being referred to as "Lords of men". Bhaṭṭotapala cites an interesting verse allegedly from a work on proportions by Parāśara.

उच्छ्रायः परिणाहस्तु यस्य तुल्यं शरीरिणः ।
स नरः पार्थिवो ज्ञेयो न्यग्रोधपरिमण्डलः ॥ ७.६८ बृ. स.

Know that embodied man to be a king whose height and breadth are equal (and) who is a fathom in a circumference.

MatPu. (p. 118) mentions this in the same context:

महाधनुर्धराश्चैव त्रैतायां चक्रवर्तिनः ।
सर्वलक्षणसंपन्ना न्यग्रोधपरिमण्डलाः ॥

न्यग्रोधो तु स्मृतौ बाहू व्यामो न्यग्रोध उच्यते ।
व्यामेन उच्छ्रायो यस्य अघ ऊर्ध्वं च देहिनः ॥

समोच्छ्रायपरिणाहो न्यग्रोधपरिमण्डलः

In CitLak of Nagnajit (ch. III v 556-573), the same rule is mentioned in the same context. Its translation reads as follows:

> With regard to the expression "extent", it stands for the length; width stands for (the shorter) direction measured straight. Now shall be fully expounded the measurements and human beings. Hear now what concerns the surface extent of a cakravartin as it is explained. He is well-proportioned, as the Nyagrodha tree. Concerning the length of the cakravartin, it should amount to 108 digits according to the measurements of his own finger;

(***An Early Document of Indian Art***: The Citralakṣaṇa of Nagnajit, p. 80-81, Dahman Dallapicolla, B.N. Goswamy, 1976)

ADHYĀYA 36

षट्त्रिंशोऽध्यायः

मार्कण्डेय उवाच

I

१ अथ प्रत्यङ्गविभागो भवति । तत्र द्वात्रिंशाङ्गुलपरिणाहो मूर्धा ।

२ चतुरङ्गुलोच्छ्रायमष्टाङ्गुलं ललाटम् । शङ्खौ चतुरङ्गुलौ द्व्याङ्गुलोच्छ्रायौ ।

३ पञ्चाङ्गुलौ गण्डौ। चतुरङ्गुलौ हनु द्व्यङ्गुलोच्छ्रायौ । द्व्यङ्गुलौ कर्णौ चतुरङ्गुलोच्छ्रायौ ।

४ कर्णमध्योऽङ्गुलम् तद्रन्धं तदर्धकम् पालिरनियमेन । नासा चतुरङ्गुला

५ अग्रे द्व्यङ्गुलोच्छ्राया तदायामा च । नासापुटावर्धाङ्गुलविस्तारौ

६ द्विगुणद्विगुणायामौ ।

1. ABVS2 द्वादशाङ्गुल-
2. N संखं चतुलाङ्गुलौ D < .. > ङ्खचतुर- N द्व्यङ्गुलोच्छ्रयौ
3. V चतुरङ्गुलो हनुः F हन्य N हस्त D द्व्यङ्गुलोच्छ्रायौ N कर्णौः A चरंगुलोच्छ्रायौ ABCFN lack द्व्यङ्गुलोच्छ्रायौ
4. VN कर्णमध्याङ्गुलं CF कर्णममध्यङ्गुलम् D कर्णमध्योऽङ्गुलौ

   ABV तद्रन्ध्रमुदकम् N तद्रन्धतर्ध D-तदर्धम् C तद्रन्ध्रतमुदकम् F तद्रन्ध्रत्वुदकम् N पाशि-ABS2 << कर्णस्य लुटिका पालिः >> N चतुरङ्गुलौ
5. N द्व्यङ्गुलौच्छ्रायेतिदायिमाच CF -तिदायामा च A तिचायामा B तिचयामा V -त्रिकायामा S1 lacks तदायामा ABCFV -पुटावङ्गुलि- N पुटावङ्गुली D -पुटावलिविस्त- N -गुलौ विस्तारौ B द्विगुणायामौ F द्विगुणुयामौ
6. N द्विगुणाद्विगुणाङ्गुलौद्यात्रौ

ADHYĀYA 36

Mārkaṇḍeya spoke :

I.1. Now begins the section on the secondary members of the body. The head measures 32 *aṅgulas* in circumference.

I.2. The forehead is 4 *aṅgulas* in height and 8 in width; the temples measure 4 *aṅgulas* [in breadth] and 2 in height.

I.3. The cheeks measure 5 *aṅgula*. The jaws are 4 *aṅgulas* (in width) and 2 *aṅgulas* in height. The ears are 2 *aṅgulas* [in breadth] and 4 in height.

I.4. The centre of the ear measures 1 *aṅgula* and its hole, half an *aṅgula*. Regarding the earlobe, there is no rule. The nose is 4 *aṅgulas* [in length].

I.5-6. At the tip it is 2 *aṅgulas* in height and breadth. The wings of the nostrils are half an *aṅgula* [in thickness] and four times as much (i.e. 2 *aṅgulas*) in length.

II

१ नासौष्टमध्यमर्धाङ्गुलम् । ओष्ठश्चाङ्गुलम् । चतुरङ्गुलायाममास्यम् । अधरोऽङ्गुलम् ।

२ द्व्यङ्गुलं चिबुकम् । द्वात्रिंशद्दन्तास्तेष्वष्टौ दंष्ट्राः । अर्धाङ्गुलोच्छ्रिता दन्ताः ।

३ साङ्गुलद्वादशभागिका दंष्ट्राः । अङ्गुलविस्तृते त्र्यङ्गुलायामे नेत्रे । नेत्रत्रिभागं

४ कृष्णमण्डलम् । तत्पञ्चभागास्तारा । अर्धाङ्गुलविस्तृते चतुरङ्गुलायामे भ्रुवौ ।

५ तयोर्द्व्यङ्गुलमन्तरम् । चतुरङ्गुलं नेत्रान्तकर्णविवरम् ।

1. F नसौष्ट- B नासाष्टमध्यमर्धांगुलम N -ध्यमध्यमार्धाङ्गुलं N ओष्ठाश्चाङ्गुलः
ABCFV -चाङ्गुलः N चतरंगुलाद्यासौम्यं F -याममास्यात्

2. C द्व्याङ्गुलो N द्व्यङ्गुलचिबुकम् N चत्वारिंशदन्ताः ABCFV चत्वारिंशद्दन्तास्तेष्व D चत्वारिंशङ्गेलतास्तेषु N ओष्टो दंष्ट्राः CF दन्तास्तेष्वष्टौ दंष्ट्रा D दन्ता B दन्ताः

3. ABCDFNV अङ्गुलद्वादशभागिका N भागिका दन्ताः CDF दंष्ट्रा N दन्ताः ABCF अङ्गुलि -N विस्तृतं V विस्तृता F विस्तृतै F -लायामनेत्री N त्र्यंगुलयामे नव

4. N कृष्णमण्डल N तत्पंचभागस्ताराः V पञ्चभागास्तारा ABCDF पञ्चभागस्तारा C अर्धाङ्गुली C चतुरङ्गुलयामे A त्र्यंगुलायामे V- लिविस्तृते व्यङ्गुलायामे C चतुरङ्गुलयामे F चतुरङ्गुलुयामे D भ्रुलौ

5. V तयोद्व्यंगुलमन्तरम् N तयाद्व्यङ्गुलमन्तरम् F द्व्यङ्गुलमन्तरम् AB तयोर्द्व्यगुलमांतंगुलमांतरम N चतुरङ्गुलनेत्र- A करर्ण-

II.1. The distance between the nose and the upper lip is half an *aṅgula.* The upper lip measures an *aṅgula* [in thickness]. The mouth is 4 *aṅgulas* in width. The lower lip [too] measures an *aṅgula.*

II.2. The chin measures 2 *aṅgulas* . There are 32 teeth of which 8 are canines. The teeth are half an *aṅgula* in height.

II.3. The canines are $1\frac{1}{2}$ of an *aṅgula* [in height].The eyes are an *aṅgula* in width and 3 *aṅgulas* in length.

II.4. The black orb of the eye is 1/3 of the eyes. The pupil is 1/5 of the orb. The eyebrows are 1/2 an *aṅgula* in breadth and 4 *aṅgulas* in length.

II.5. The space between the two [i.e. eyebrows] is two *aṅgulas.* The intermediate distance between the end of the eyes and the ears is 4 *aṅgulas.*

III

१ दशाङ्गुलविस्तृता ग्रीवा एकविंशत्यङ्गुलपरिणाहा । षोडशाङ्गुलं स्तनान्तरम् ।

२ षडङ्गुलं स्तनजत्र्वन्तरम् । षोडशबाहुमूलपरिणाहः द्वादशाग्रे । सप्ताङ्गुलं

३ करतलं पञ्चाङ्गुलविस्तृतम् । पञ्चाङ्गुलप्रमाणा मध्यमिका । तत्पर्वदलहीना

४ प्रदेशिनी । तत्तुल्या चानामिका । तत्पर्वदलहीना कनिष्ठिका । सर्वाः

५ समत्रिभागपर्वाः । पर्वार्धा नखाः । त्र्यङ्गुलमङ्गुष्टं द्विपर्वम् । जठरपरिणाहो

६ द्वाचत्वारिंशदङ्गुलः । वेधप्रमाणाम्यामङ्गुलं नाभिः । कटिरष्टादशाङ्गुलविपुला ।

७ तत्परिधिः चतुश्चत्वारिशंत् । चतुरङ्गुलविस्तृतौ वृषणौ । षडङ्गुलं तावत्परिणाहं

८ मेद्रम् । [तन्] मध्ये ऊरू चतुर्दशाङ्गुलौ तद्द्विगुणपरिणाहौ ।

1. N विस्तृतग्रीवा:N ङ्गुलीपरिणाहो D षडङ्गुलं स्तनान्हं
2. AB स्तनजत्रन्तरम् C स्तनजत्ववरम् F स्तनुजत्ववरम् CF मूलपरिणाहा: N lacks षोडशाङ्गुलं ......बाहुमूलपरिणाह: N द्वादशाग्रं
3. N- ङ्गुलकर- AFV पंचाङ्गुलं N मध्यमिम्क A तत्पर्वदल- B तत्सर्वदलहीना
4. N तत्तुल्यानासिका D तत्पूर्वदलहीना कनिष्टा AV तत्परीहीना FC lack तत्पर्वदलहीना ....कनिष्ठिका
5. B समित्रिभागसर्वाः A समित्तिभाग- F समुत्रिभागपर्वाः D पर्वार्द्धनखा: N पर्वार्द्धन्नखा: AB पर्वाधं CF पूर्वाधं F -नख: S1 द्वयलमङ्गुष्टं ABCFV द्विपर्वः D द्विपर्व N स्विप
6. N -रिशांङ्गुल: CV -रिशांगुल: ABD वेद V वैद्य N -मङ्गुन्नभि: N कटिरष्टाङ्गुलत्रिपूणा D -दशाङ्गुलि- C -ङ्गुलाविपुला
7. N -चत्वारिंश D -वृषणो: N षतंगुलं D -परिणाह- N -परीणाहं CF -परेणाह
8. N तन्मध्ये CDFV तन्मध्यत ऊरूचतुरङ्गुलौ AB तन्मध्यउक्ष ABCFNV -परिणाहा--

III.1. The width of the neck [along the curvature] is 10 *aṅgulas* and its circumference is 21 *aṅgulas.* The distance between the nipples is 16 *aṅgulas.*

III.2. The distance between the nipple and the clavicle is 6 *aṅgulas* and the circumference of the base of the arm [lit.root, where it leaves out of the shoulder] is 16 *aṅgulas.* At the forearm the circumference is 12 *aṅgulas.*

III.3. The length of the palm is of 7 *aṇgulas* and the breadth, 5 *aṅgulas*. The middle finger measures 5 *aṅgulas* [in length].

III.4. The middle finger is longer than the index by 1/2 a phalange. The ring finger is equal to it. The little finger is less by half a phalange of the ring finger.

III.5. All [the fingers] are equally divided into 3 phalanges. The nails are half of a phalange. The thumb is 3 *aṅgulas* [in length] and has 2 phalanges.

III.6. The belly around the navel measures 42 *aṅgulas* in circumference. The navel is an *aṅgula* in depth and breadth. The hips are 18 *aṅgulas* in width.

III.7-8. Their circumference is 44 [*aṅgulas*]. The testicles are 4 *aṅgulas* in width. As much in circumference, the penis is 6 *aṅgulas* in length.In the middle, the thighs measure 14 *aṅgulas* in width. Their circumference is twice as much [i.e. 14 X 2 = 28 *aṅgulas*].

IV

१ अष्टाङ्गुलविपुले जानुनी तत्त्रिगुणापरिणाहे । जङ्घाग्रं पञ्चाङ्गुलं

२ चर्तुदशपरिणाहम् । द्वादशदीर्घौ षडङ्गुलविस्तृतौ पादौ ।

३ त्रिकायतावङ्गुष्ठौ । अङ्गुष्ठतुल्या प्रदेशिनी । तदष्टांशोना: सेषा: ।

४ अङ्गुलचतुर्भागहीनोऽङ्गुष्ठनख: । तदर्धप्रमाण: प्रदेशिन्या: । तदष्टभागोना:

५ शेषाणाम् । सपादमङ्गुलमङ्गुष्ठोत्सेध: । त्र्यङ्गुले पार्ष्णी

६ चतुरङ्गुलोच्छ्रायाविति हंसप्रमाणम् भवति । भवन्ति चात्र [[श्लोका:]]

1. CV तद्द्विगुण F तद्द्विगुणौ- D तद्द्विगुणपरिणाहा जंघाग्रं ABCFNV -परिणाङ्गुल- F विपुलं N -विपुलो जानूनी S2 विपुले च जानुनी ABN तत्द्विगुण- N उंतत्त्रिगुणपरिणाहो- VBS1S2 गुणपरिणाहं N गुणपरिणाहौ C माङ्घाग्रं N पंचांगुलीम्

2. C -परीणाहं D द्वादशदी < . > NF दीर्घा D डषङ्गुलविस्तृतौ BDV पदौ

3. BC त्रिकारयतांगुष्टौ N भूपाताङ्गुष्ठौ CFV त्रिकायताङ्गुष्टौ D त्रिकायताङ्गुष्ठं A त्रिकारयतांगुलौ D -तुल्य- N तदष्टानां A तदष्टांशेना: D -शेषा

4. N अङ्गुलं F अङ्गुलाचर्तु N -हीनाङ्गुष्टनख: ABF तदर्धं प्रमाणं CDNV तदर्धप्रमाणं CFN प्रदेशिन्या D प्रदेशिन्यास्तद- ABCDFNV तदष्टभाग: शेषाणाम्

5. N repeats from चतुर्भागहीना to शेषाणां ABCFVS1S2 सर्वपादमङ्गुलमष्टाङ्गोत्सेध: N सर्वपादमङ्गुलमष्टाङ्गुोत्सेधा D सर्वपादमङ्गुलमष्टाङ्गुलोत्सर: AS1S2F त्र्यंगुली

6. N चतुरंगुलौच्छ्रायै CD -लोच्छ्रायो इति N हंसप्रमाणो D -प्रणामम्भवति CNDF भवति चात्र

IV.1. The knees are 8 *aṅgulas* in breadth (along the curvature) and their circumference is thrice as much (i.e. 8 X 3 = 24 *aṅgulas*). At the end of the shank, the width is 5 *aṅgulas* and the circumference, 14 *aṅgulas*.

IV.2. The feet are 12 *aṅgulas* in length and 6 *aṅgulas* in width.

IV.3. The big toes are 3 *aṅgulas* long. The index toe is the same in length as the big toe. The rest [of the toes] are less by 1/8 [of the big toe progressively].

IV.4. The toe-nail is less than the size of the toe by a quarter. The nail of the index toe is half of that of the big toe. The remaining [toes] are less by the 1/8 of the index toe-nail [progressively].

IV.5-6. The height of the big-toe consists of $1\frac{1}{4}$ of an *aṅgula.* The heels are three *aṅgulas* in breadth and 4 *aṅgulas* in height. Such is the measurement of a *Haṃsa* man. There are also [the following verses] on this subject:

शेषाणां पार्थिवेन्द्राणां मानं युक्त्या प्रकल्पयेत् ।
अनेनैवानुसारेण स्वमानस्यानुसारतः ॥ १ ॥

मध्वक्षश्चन्द्रगौरस्तु नागराजभुजो बली ।
+ हंसगामी + सुमध्यश्च हंसश्च सुमुखो भवेत् ॥ २॥

रोमरुद्धकपोलस्तु गजगामी महामतिः ।
वृत्तोपचितबाहुस्तु भद्रः पद्मनिभो भवेत् ।।३।।

+ मुङ्गश्यामस्तु + मालव्यः कृशमध्यस्तनुच्छविः ।
आजानुबाहुः पीनांसो दंतिघोणो महाहनुः ।।४।।

शरगौरस्तु रुचकः कम्बुग्रीवो महामतिः ।
सत्त्ववान् श्रमिकश्चैव बलवांश्च प्रकीर्तित ।।५ ।।

+ रक्तश्यामस्तु + शशकः किञ्चिद्दन्तुरकस्तथा ।
पूर्णगण्डश्च चतुरो + महावर्त्मा + च कीतिर्तः ।।६ ।।

इति श्रीविष्णुधर्मोत्तरे तृतीयखण्डे मार्कण्डेयवज्रसंवादे चित्रसूत्रे प्रमाणाध्यायो नाम षट्त्रिंशत्तमोऽध्यायः

1b. N मानो D सानं

1bc. CDF अनेनेवानुसारेण A अनेनैवान्वसारेण N अंगेनैवानुसारेण 1d D सुमानस्य-

2a. CF मध्यक्ष- V1B मधक्ष- AS1S2 मधुक्ष- V2 मध्यकृच्चन्द्र D मक्षश्चन्द्र F मम्यक्ष-

2b. A बलीः 2c D हंसणामी Nहंससमी Aसुमधश्च

3b. D सहामतिः 3c. N वृत्तौपरितबाहुस्तु 3d N पद्मनिभा

4a. N मुङ्गम्याम्- C मालव्य D मलव्यः 4b CFNV1 कृशमध्यतनु- V2 कुशभमध्य- AB कृष्टमध्य-

4c. C आजानुबाहु N अजानुबाहुः N पीनांसा

5a. N सरगौरस्तु ABCFV शरङ्गौरस्तु 5b D कल्यग्रीवो 5c D सत्वर < ? > F सन्यत्समिक- C सन्यत्स < .. > मिक- AB सन्यस्तुं V सत्यस्तु सिकतश्चैव N इत्येतत् N समकश्चैव

5d. A बलावांश्च

6a. F शशक 6b N किञ्चिःदन्तुरकस्तथा D किञ्चिःदन्दुरकस्तथा C किञ्चिद्दान्तुरकस्तथा AB किंचिद्दन्तरकस्तथा V2 किं चिद्दमुरकस्तथा V1 किंञ्चिःरन्तुकस्तथा V किःचित्कर्बुरकस्तथा

6d. ABNV मध्वक्षश्च CF मध्याक्षश्च D मर्वमश्च CDFN प्रकीर्तितः

1. The remaining of the great men should be made by employing the proportion conforming to this very (type) and according to their respective height.

2. A *Haṃsa* man has honey coloured eyes, is as fair as the moon, has arms which resemble the king of snakes, a swan-like gait, a slender waist, is strong and handsome.

3. A *Bhadra* man has cheeks covered with hair, a gait like that of an elephant, is highly intelligent, has rounded and well-developed arms and who resemble[s] a lotus (in complexion).

4. A *Mālavya* man is dark as a green bean (?), slender waisted, has a symmetrical body, with arms reaching down to his knees[and] has broad shoulders. [His] nose resembles that of an elephant ['s nostrils] and has large jaws.

5. A *Rucaka* man has reddish brown complexion, conch like throat, is highly intelligent, courageous, laborious and strong.

6. A *Śaśaka* man is said to have a reddish brown (a dark blue or black ?) complexion, slightly protruding teeth, full cheeks, is clever and has large eyelids.

NOTES TO ADHYĀYA 36

36.I.1 *pratyaṅga.* This term technically means "the members of the body such as the forehead, nose, chin, fingers etc" as opposed to the 6 *aṅgas* or the chief members which refer to the torso, head-neck, 2 arms and 2 legs. Note that all the earlier translations lack this technical sense.

SK (p. 30) takes it as "division of limbs *one by one*", PS (p. 106) as " the measurement of *each limb*" and SM (p. 169) "the limbs are treated *separately.*

Carakasaṃhitā gives the division of the body into *aṅgas* and the *pratyaṅgas.*

तत्रायं शरीरस्याङ्गविभागः । तद्यथा द्वौ बाहू द्वे सक्थिनी शिरोग्रीवम् अन्तराधिर् इति षडङ्गमङ्गम् । ७.५

It lists the following parts of the body as the *pratyaṅgas:*

षट्पञ्चाशत् प्रत्यङ्गानि षट्स्वङ्गेषूपनिबद्धानि ...... तद्यथा - द्वे जङ्घपिण्डिके द्वे ऊरूपिण्डके द्वौ स्फिचौ द्वौ वृषणौ एकं शेफः द्वे उखे द्वौ वङ्क्षनौ द्वौ कुकुन्दरौ एकं वस्तिशीर्षम् एकमुदरम् द्वौ स्तनौ द्वौ श्लेष्मभुवौ द्वे बाहू पिण्डिके चिबुकमेकम् द्वौ ओष्ठौ द्वे सृक्कण्यौ द्वौ दन्तवेष्टकौ एकं तालु एका गलशुण्डिका द्वे उपजिह्वके एका गोजिह्वका द्वौ गण्डौ द्वे कर्णशुष्कुलिके द्वौ कर्णपुत्रकौ द्वे अक्षिकूटे चत्वारि अक्षिवर्त्मनि द्वे अक्षिकनीनिके द्वे भ्रूवौ एकावटुश्च चत्वारि पाणिपादहृदयाणि ।

1. Two calves 2. Two thighs 3. Two buttocks 4. Two Testicles 5. A penis 6. Two upper legs (Axillae) 7. Two groins 8. Two cavities of the loins 9. A neck of the bladder 10. A belly 11. Two nipples 12. Two glands (of phlegm) 13. Two biceps 14. A chin 15. Two lips (upper and lower) 16. Two outlines of the lips 17. Two [rows of] gums 18. A palate 19. An Uvula 20. Two tonsils 21. A tongue 22. Two cheeks 23. Two ear flaps 24. Two conches of ear 25. Two ear cavities 26. Four eye lids 27. Two pupils 28. Two eyebrows 29. A nape of the neck 30. Two palms and two soles.

In this *adhyāya,* the parts of the body discussed under *pratyaṅga* correspond closely with what are listed in Carakasaṃhitā; the latter being a medical text is more detailed.

In adhy. 37.1 *aṅgapratyaṅgamānena* or "following the measurements of the major and minor limbs" confirms this division.

36.1.1. *dvātriṃśadaṅgulapariṇāho.* MānUll 1.3.244 gives a slightly larger circumference for the head:

> षड्त्रिशंदङ्गुलो ज्ञेयः परिणाहो विचक्षणैः । २४४.३.१
>
> The experts know (the circumference of the head) to be 36 *aṅgulas.*

See MānUll. 1.3.235-237 and ŚilpRat. 8.5-7a for elaborate details concerning the shape of the head. Both the texts are remarkably similar in their treatment of the matter.

36.1.2. All the Śilpa texts agree that the width of the forehead is 4 *aṅgulas* except MānUll 1.3.244 which makes it 3.

> भ्रूपृष्ठात्केशपर्यन्तं ललाटं त्र्यङ्गुलं भवेत् ।। २४४.३.१
>
> The forehead from the eyebrows to the hairline measures 3 *aṅgulas.*

36.I.2. The table prepared by SK (p. 20) wrongly gives the height of the temple according to BṛSaṃ. 57.6. as 3 *aṅgulas.* In fact, like CitSūt. it gives it as 4:

> चतुरङ्गुलौ तु शङ्खौ ६.५७

36.I.3. Note CitSūt. is the only *Śilpa* text which mentions the measurements of the cheeks.

caturaṅgulau hanū. Hanū being dual clearly refers to the jaws and not the chin as previous translators have taken it. SK, (p. 30), PS (p. 106) and SM (p. 169) take *hanu* to refer to the "chin". As for the measurement of the chin, II.2. has already stated that the chin measurment is 2 *aṅgulas - dvyaṇgulam cibukam.*

In BṛSaṃ., the measurement of jaws is given as 2 *aṅgulas.*

> द्वे अङ्गुले च हनुनी ५.५७
>
> The jaws are that which join the face with the neck.

Whereas MānUll. and ŚilpRat. agree with CitSūt. and are more detailed on this:

> क्रमशो हीयते तत्तु यावत् स्याद्धनुमण्डलम ।
> सार्द्धाङ्गुलं भवेदूर्ध्वं तिर्यक् स्याच्चतुरङ्गुलम् ।। २८०.३.१
>
> It should be reduced progressively so that there is a (jaw-curve) jaw-line. Heightwise, it is 1 and 1/2 *aṅgula* and diagonally, it should be 4 *aṅgulas*.

ŚilpRat., 69.8 merely parrots this.

The discrepancy between the two measurements i.e. 2 and 4 *aṅgulas* for *hanu* can be explained from the context. The 2 *aṅgulas* prescribed in the BṛSaṃ. refers to the height of the jaws i.e. from the base of the ear downwards where the jaws join the face. The 4 *aṅgulas* found in the CitSūt., MānUll. and ŚilpRat. refer to the length of the jawline.

36.I.4. *tadrandhram tadardhakam.* This emendation is based on N's *tadrandham tadardha,* D's *tadardham* and that CF's *tadrandhram tamudakam.* SK omits *tadrandhramtadardhakam pāliraniyamena* from her translation.

PS translates *karṇamadhyo 'ṅgulam* as "The *cavity of the ear* is one *aṅgula* (p. 106). Yet in the footnote she expresses misgivings.

> F.N. 1) Something is said about the hole in the reading.

SM takes *karṇasya lu?bu?puṭikā pālih.* as a part of the text but it is clearly an interpolation. It is put in parentheses in PS's text and is to be found only in ABS2. It is probably an incorporated gloss on *pāliḥ.* SM emends *tadrandhramudakam* to *tadrandhramūlat* and connects it with this "gloss", SM explains his emendation as follows:

> F.N.2) The correct reading here should be this, as रन्ध्रमुदकम् makes no sense and it is clearly a clerical error मु for मू, द an extra, क in the place of ल, and म् in the place of त् (pp. 139)

SM's emendation of *lu?bu?puṭikā* to *puṭikā*is explained as follows:

> F.N.3) It is clearly पुटिका same as पुटि that is well known as कर्णपुट same as कर्णपाली, लुटिका is scribe's error. (pp. 139)

SM's translation is thereby affected.

The lobe from the root of the ear cavity in undefined in length. (p. 169)

Note that it is depression in the centre of the ear which is referred to and not the earhole. Besides, an *aṅgula* is too large a measurement for the latter.

36.I.5. *agre dvyaṅgulocchrāyā tadāyāmā ca. Trikāyāmā ca* ("there [*aṅgulas*] in length") accepted by SK (p. 30), PS (p. 106) and SM (p. 169) appears to be an emendation of CF's *tidāyāmā ca.*

It results in following misleading translations in which the breadth of the nose is taken as 3 *aṅgulas:*

SK: The nose (measures) 4 *aṅgulas,* the elevation of its top (being) 2 aṅgulas, *the breadth* 3 *aṅgulas.* (p. 30)

PS: At the tip, it is 2 *aṅgulas* in height and it is 3 *aṅgulas in breadth.* (p. 106)

SM: The nose is four *aṅgulas,* two *aṅgulas* in depth and 3 *aṅgulas in width.* (p. 169)

When, in fact, according to D the breadth of the nose is same as the height from the base of the nostrils and tip of the nose i.e. 2 *aṅgulas.*

ŚilpRat. (50.9) confirms this:

अङ्गुलद्वयविस्तारं नासायामिति कीतिर्तम् ।।

The width of the nose is prescribed as 2 *aṅgulas.*

36.I.5. *nāsāpuṭāvardhāmgulavistārau.* All MSS read *nāsāpuṭāvaṅguli-* or a corruption thereof. I have emended following sense - a measurment 1 *aṅgula* is preposterously large and the ŚilpRat. 9.50 reads :

घोणाग्रमङ्गुलं तच्च तदर्धेन पुटो भवेत ।

The tip of the nose measures one *aṅgula.* The nosewing is half of that.

PS and SM translate *nāsāpuṭa* as "nostrils".

PS: The extent of *nostril* is an aṅgula and the width double. (p.106)

SM: The *nostrils* are an aṅgula wide and twice that in length. (p.169)

ŚilpRat. states the measurement of nostrils as:

घोणबिलं समुद्दिष्टं कनिष्ठाङ्गुलिमात्रकम् । ५१.९

The nostril is said to be merely of the size of a little finger.

36.I.6. *dviguṇadviguṇāyāmau.* PS and SM follow B in reading *dviguṇāyāmau.* I have preferred CDN's *dviguṇadviguṇāyāmau,* seeing B as a case of haplography. Since this gives a more satisfactory sense if we accept the emendation *nāsāputāva rdhāṅgula.* If the nosewing measures 1 *aṅgula,* then the right reading would have to be B's.

36.II.1. All the texts are in agreement about the width of the mouth CitSūt. gives 1 *aṅgula* as the width of the upper lip. But BṛSam. (57.8) differs making it 1/2 *aṅgula.*

अधरोऽङ्गुलप्रमाणस्तस्यार्धेनोत्तरोष्ठश्च । । ८.५७

The lower lip is an aṅgula in thickness and the upper one, its half.

36.II,2. *cibuka* confirms my reading of *hanū* in 1.3 as "jaws". Note in SK's chart, the height of the chin is given as 4 *aṅgulas. Cibuka* is ambiguous in meaning for it can mean two different things as pointed out by Bhaṭṭotpala. It can either mean from the root of the nose downwards to the chin when 4 *aṅgulas* are stated:

चिबुकग्रहणेन नासायाश्चतुरङ्गुलो भाग उच्यते.

Or it can refer to the width of the chin proper when 2 *aṅgulas* are mentioned :

चिबुकं च द्व्यङ्गुलं विततं विस्तीर्णं कार्यम् । चिबुकशब्देनात्र मुखस्याधोभाग उच्यते ।। ५७.५

36.II.2 *dvātriṃśaddanta.* It is clear that the MSS' *catvāriṃsad* - is a corruption of *dvātriṃśad-*. This scribal error can also be explained as resulting from the careless addition of 8 canines to the total number of teeth. Since the iconometry in this text is based on human scale and proportion, 40 teeth seem most unlikely. If there were any other superhuman features stated, then perhaps one might entertain the reading. Only SK (p.30) accepts it- ((there should be) 40 *teeth,...*) PS emends to *caturviṁśad.* But this is impossible in the light of what follows, namely the statement that 8 of their (*teṣu*) are canines. SM accepts PS's emendation but seeing the problem emends *teṣv* ("of these") to *tathā* ("and") bringing the total to the normal 32.

36. II.2. The CitSūt., MānUll. and ŚilpRat. differ on the size of the teeth. In the CitSūt. a distinction is made between the teeth and the canines. In the MānUll. and ŚilpRat. give in addition the measurements of the visible portion of the teeth.

> ऊर्ध्वा पञ्चयवा दृश्यास्तलस्थास्त्रियवास्तथा । MānUll 275.3.1.
>
> Five *yavas* of the teeth in the upper row are seen. Of the lower row, three *yavas* are visible.

36.II.3 *sāṅguladvādaśabhāgikā.* The MSS read *aṅguladvādaśā.* This emendation is required by sense. It is unlikely that a canine should measure only 1/12 of an *aṅgula.* The acceptance of this reading leads to a contradictory sense in the translation by SK (p. 30) and SM (p. 106):

SK: .... of which eight should be large tooth, 1/12th of an *aṅgula* in elevation; a large tooth is one *aṅgula* broad.

PS. The tusk is 1/12*th of an aṅgula.*

SM. understanding this problem, emended to *aṅguladvādaśa-bhāgādhikā* and took it to mean that the teeth are $1\frac{1}{2}$ *aṅgula* in height. This gives the required sense but at the expense of the normal order of words in a compound. One would have expected *dvādaśabhāgikāṅgulā.*

36.II.5. *tayor dvyaṅgulam antaram.* This reading of N,D and V is corroborated by other *Śilpa* texts; see, e.g. BṛSam. 57. 12b.: भ्रूमध्यं द्व्यङ्गुलकं, "The space between the eyebrows is 2 *aṅgulas*" SK acceps it but PS and SM follow the corrupt reading of A, though PS translates as though she had accepted V's reading, SM emends A's reading to *tayorangulamantaram,* "...... an *aṅgula* space between them" (p. 169); but such a measurement is uncorroborated.

36.II.5. *netrāntakarṇavivaram.* SK (p. 31), PS (p. 106) and SM (p. 169) translate *netrantakarṇavivaram* to mean the space between the end of the eye and the earhole. Since they take *karṇavivaram* to mean the latter, they presume that "the space between" is implied though necessarily not expressed. This is improbable Sanskrit. But it also yields an impossible sense, since the distance between these two points must be more than 4 *aṅgulas.* In fact *vivaram* is not the "hole" of the ear but "the space between" the end of the eye and the ear [where it joins with the face]. cf. BṛSaṃ.57.8ab: चतुरङ्गुलं वसिष्ठः कथयति नेत्रान्तरकर्णयोर् विवरम्, "The space between the end of the eye and the ear is 4 *aṅgulas,* says *Vasiṣṭha*".

36.III.1 *daśāṅgulavistṛtā grīvā.* PS (p. 106) and SM (p. 169) take this to mean that the neck is 10 *aṅgulas* in height. CitSūt. 35.14 has already given the height as 4*aṅgulas,* a measurement confirmed by BṛSaṃ 57.5: नासाललाटचिबुकग्रीवाश्चतुराङ्गुलास्तथा कर्णौ, "The nose, forehead, chin, neck and ears measure 4 *aṇgulas*"

Regarding the width of the neck, cf BṛSaṃ. 57,15 : ग्रीवा दश विस्तीर्णा परिणाहाद्विंशतिः सैका,"The width of the neck (along the curvature) is 10 *aṅgulas* and the circumference is 20 *aṅgulas* plus one *aṇgula.*" Note that this width does not equal diameter but the width along the natural curve of the neck which approximately is an *aṇgula* less than half of the circumference.

36. III.2. *stanajattvantaram.* D retains the correct reading. SK and PS emend correctly to *stanajatvantaram* but they translate it incorrectly, taking it to mean 'the distance between the clavicles'.

SK: The distance between the nipples is 16 aṅgulas and *that between the clavicles* 6 *aṅgulas.* (p. 31)

PS: ..... six aṅgulas *between the clavicles.* (p. 107)

6 *aṅgulas* is far too large a measurement for the distance.

36.III.2 *dvādaśāgre.* The measurements of the arm and the forearm agree with BṛSaṃ. 57.26, though the latter is more specific, *dvādaśāgrahaste,* 'twelve at the [lower] end of the [fore[arm.' It is difficult to see by what reasoning SK (p. 31) arrived at "the whole length of the hand being twelve aṅgulas", correct though that measurement happens to be. SM's translation is ambiguous:

The girth of the arm near the armpit is sixteen *aṅgulas* and *further up, twelve.* (p. 169)

36.III2-3. *saptāṅgulam-vistṛtam.* Here there is a slight discrepancy between the CitSūt. and the BṛSaṃ., 57.26 and Kāśyapa quoted ad loc. by Bhaṭṭotpala. The latter prescribe 6 *aṅgulas* for the width of the palm, विस्तारेण करतलं षडङ्गुलं सप्त दैर्घ्येण (BṛSaṃ.), षडङ्गुलं हस्ततलं सप्त दैर्घ्येण च स्मृतम् (Bhaṭṭotpala).

36.III.3. *tatparvadalahīnā* NA's *tatparvadalahīna* confirms PS's conjectural emendation of the reading *tatpūrvā* (MSS DV etc.). However, all have wrongly taken *dala* here to refer to a phalange. It is *parva* that means a phalange, *dala* meaning "half" as is clear from Bhaṭṭotpala's gloss on BṛSaṃ. 57,27. The latter has : अङ्गुष्ठादनन्तरं या अङ्गुली सा मध्यमायाः पर्वदलेन पर्वणोऽर्धेन हीना कार्या, " The forefinger is that which is close to the thumb, it is to be made less by half a phalange."

36.III.5. *jaṭharapariṇāho.* SK (p. 31) and SM (p. 169) take *jaṭhara* to mean "belly" or "abdomen". It is clear however, from BṛSaṃ. (57.24), that it refers to the waist, i.e. circumference at the level of the navel चत्वारिशंद्द्वियुता नाभिमध्येन मध्यपरिणाहः "The circumference around the navel is 40 *aṅgulas* plus 2.

36.III.6. *vedhapramāṇābhyām.* N, F and C preserve the correct reading, the latter two being ignored by the editors. The corrupt reading *vedyapramāṇā* misled the following translations:

SK (pp. 31) accepts V's *vedyapramāṇābhyām* and translates "from (all) known sources" inspite of the dual ending and the fact that vedya- is not used in this sense.

SK: The navel is one aṅgula according to the information to be gathered from *(all) known sources.*

PS ans SM accept AB's *vaidyapramāṇābhyām.* The former connects it with the measurement of the abdomen:

> The abdomen measure one aṅgula *according to the physicians* and measurements (p. 107)

SM: *According to physicians* and in terms of proportion the navel is an aṅgula. (p. 169-170)

The dual ending is no less acceptable. It is surprising that they preferred solecism to the good sense and grammar of *vedhapramā-nābhyām* which they had in F and C. That this is the correct reading is confirmed by BṛSaṃ. 57,23: अङ्गुलमेकं नाभी वेधेन तथा प्रमाणेन, "The navel is one aṅgula in depth and breadth."

Bhaṭṭotpala glosses *vedha-* here as depth *(gāmbhīrya)* and *pramāṇa* as breadth *(vaipulya)* : नाभी वेधेन गाम्भीर्येण तथा प्रमाणेन वैपुल्येन चाङ्गुलमेकं भवति

36. III.8. *madhye ūrū caturdaśāṅgulam.* Following *tanmadhye ūrū catu-raṅgulam,* the reading of all the MSS, SK (p. 31) PS (p. 107) and SM (p. 170) take the text to mean that the distance between from "the middle of that" (i.e. the penis) to the thighs is 4 *aṅgulas.*

SK: from the middle of that (i.e. the penis) the thighs are 4 aṅgulas.

PS: the thighs are 4 aṅgulas from its middle.

SM: From its centre (i.e. penis) to the thigh is four aṅgulas.

The Sanskrit, even allowing for Puranic licence, cannot possibly accommodate this sense. In any case, one wonders at the relevance of such a measurement. It is certainly not found in any other source on the subject. My emendation to *madhye ūrū caturdaśāṅgulam* follows the indication of BṛSaṃ.

> विपुलौ चर्तुदशोरू मध्ये द्विगुणाश्च तत्परिधिः ।। २२.५७
>
> In the middle, the thighs are 14 (*aṅgulas*) in width and twice as much in cicumference (i.e. 28 *aṅgulas*).

The corruption in the CitSūt. can be eliminated by consulting its counterpart in BṛSaṃ. To do so, we need to examine the corrupt reading and point out where exactly the problem begins.

(i) तन्मध्यत ऊरूरचतुरङ्गुलौ (ii) तद्द्विगुणपरिणाहाङ्गुलविपुले जानुनी तत्तिगुणपरिणाहे Note the corruption spreads to the entire line. In all the preceding lines, *vipula* or "circular width" precedes the *pariṇāha* or "circumference." Let us suppose "X" is what (i) refers to. What follows it is तद्द्विगुणपरिणाहा. This measure of circumference belongs to "X" and not to the knees. Note that all the scholars connect it with जानुनी and translate it as "the length of the knees". *Pariṇāha* is a strictly technical term for the circumference and cannot be translated as "length". The length of the knees is already mentioned as measuring 4 *aṅgulas* in *adhyāya* 35.

द्वौ च तालौ तथा च जङ्घे पादतुल्ये च जानुनी ।। १२.३५ चि. सू.

This makes it clear that तद्द्विगुणपरिणाहा refers to "X". This corresponds directly with द्विगुणश्च तत्परिधिः mentioned in the BṛSaṃ. for the thighs. Therefore "X" stands for the width of the thighs and "मध्ये" for the middle of the thighs. What is missing is दश after चतुर which needs to be supplied from the BṛSaṃ. With the above mentioned emendation, what follows it falls back into place. The following line on the knees is अङ्गुलविपुलजानुनी makes no sense. The circular breadth of the knees cannot be 1 *aṅgula*. So we have to posit that this line is corrupt as well and something is missing.

Let us turn to BṛSaṃ. which is clear about this:

> अष्टौ तु जानुमध्ये वैपुल्यं त्र्यष्टकं तु परिणाहः ।
>
> विपुलौ चतुर्दशोरू मध्ये द्विगुणश्च तत्परिधिः ।।२२।।५७

The missing part in the CitSūt. can be supplied from the above. Hence the emendation of अङ्गुलविपुले to अष्टाङ्गुलविपुले. Note that तत्रिगुणपरिणाहे supports this emendation. This means that the circular breadth of the knees comprises of 8 *aṅgulas* and the circumference is 24*aṅgulas*. It seems logical that the measurement of the thighs be mentioned after that of genitals and before that of the knees conforming with a downward progression. The parallel reference in the BṛSaṃ. shows that द्विगुणपरिणाह or "twice as much" and त्रिगुणपरिणाह or "thrice as much" are associated with the circumferences of the thighs and the knees respectively. In the CitSūt., same rule can be gleaned.

SK's (p. 31) translation is thoroughly misleading :

> As much in circumference the penis (is) 6 aṅgulas long-from the middle of that the thighs (are) four aṅgulas. The breadth of the knees (is) twice as much aṅgulas in expanse. The breadth of the forepart of the leg beneath

> the knee (is) thrice of that (the length being) 5 aṅgulas and the circumference is 14 aṅgulas.

Note that the breadth of the forepart of the leg would be 24 *aṅgulas* ! (4 x 2 = 8, 8 x 3 = 24). Note PS's criticism of SK's translation is valid.[3]

F. N. 3) Dr. Stella Kramrisch seems to take tattriguṇapariṇāhe with jaṅghāgram but pariṇāhe is in dual and therefore should be taken with jānunī. (pp. 107)

PS emends it to *taddviguṇāṅgula vipule jānunī tattriguṇapariṇāhe* and thinks that there is an "Intrusion of *parināha* between *dviguṇa* and *aṅgula*". (see. fn. 2. p. 107) Her translation is as follows:

> The *width* of the knees is its double, *i.e.* 8 aṅgulas. Its circumference is triple *i.e.* 12 *aṅgulas.*

Note that 12 *aṅgulas* is too small a measure for the circumference of the knees. *Pariṇāha* is taken to mean "width" which is inaccurate. Note interestingly, SM's translation is correct despite the corruption and the mistake of taking *pariṇāho* as "breadth".

SM: The knees is twice four (i.e. eight) in width and three times that in girth. (p. 170)

36. IV. 2. *dvādaśadīrghau.* Both PS and SM emend to *dvādaśāṅguladīrghau.* This is unnecessary since it merely makes explicit what is already implicit. cf. BṛSaṃ. 57.18: द्वादशदीर्घौ षट् पृथुतया बृ. स. १८. ५७

36. IV. 3. *trikāyātāvaṅguṣṭhau.* This measurement applies only to the big toes and certainly not to all the toes. Both PS (p. 107) and SM (p.170) translate *aṅguṣṭhau* as "toes"!

36. IV. 3. *tadaṣṭāṃśonāḥ śeṣāḥ.* That this means that the remaining three toes should be progressively shorter by 1/8 of the length of the big toe is evident from the parallel passage in BṛSaṃ. 57.19 : अष्टांशाष्टांशोना: शोषाङ्गुल्य: क्रमेण कर्तव्या:, "Each of the remaining toes should be made less by a 1/8th progressively.

Note how misleading the following translations are :

SK: .....and *the rest* (are) *less* (in length) *by an eighth part.* (p. 31)

PS: .....and *the others are small by one eighth* (p.107)

SM: The rest are shorter by an eighth part. (p. 170)

The translators have not understood the implied progressive diminution, taking all three remaining toes to be of the same length.

36. IV. 4. *tadaṣṭabhāgonāḥ*. I have emended the MSS' *tadaṣṭabhāgaḥ* to *tadaṣṭabhāgonaḥ* in accordance with sense and the parallel at BṛSaṃ. 57.20. अङ्गुष्ठनखः कथितश्चतुर्थभागोनमङ्गुलं तज्ञैः । शेषनखानामर्धाङ्गुलं क्रमात् किञ्चिदूनं वा ।। The nails of the three toes too decrease in size progressively.

36.IV. 5. *sapādam aṅgulam aṅguṣṭhotsedhaḥ*. SK, PS and SM do not challenge the reading of the MSS *(sarvapādam aṅgulam aṣṭāṅgulotsedhaḥ)*. Yet the translation of the first appears to understand some emendation since it can hardly have been thought to be justified by the reading, as it stands, while those of the other two give impossible sense even if they do not execute violence to the rules of grammar. Thus SK (p. 31-32) translates *sarvapādam aṅgulam* as "the toes of all the feet":

> (*the sum total of ?*) all the toes of the feet is 8 aṅgulas in height.

PS (p. 107) takes the following sense:

> *The whole foot* measures an *aṅgula in thickness* (?) and *its* height 8 aṅgulas.

SM (p. 170) takes it in yet another way:

> The foot is all along an aṅgula but eight *aṅgulas* at its *highest point.*

No foot let alone that of an ideal type, is that thin. He takes *aṣṭāṅgulotsedhaḥ* as "*eight* aṅgulas at its highest point", as though he had a *bahuvrīhi aṣṭāṅgulotsedham* agreeing with *sarvapādam.*

The parallel passage in BṛSaṃ. throws light on this problem clarifying that *pāda* here means "quarter" as opposed to "foot":

सचतुर्थभागमङ्गुलमुत्सेधोऽङ्गुष्ठकस्योक्तः १९. ५७

अङ्गुष्ठस्योत्सेध उच्छ्रायः सचतुर्भागमङ्गुलमुक्तः कथितः ।

36.IV. 5-6. *tryaṅgule pārṣṇī.* This measurement applies to the breadth of the heel. PS wonders whether it refers to its thickness (p. 107). SK and SM do not tell us how they take it.

36. 1a. *pārthivendrāṇām.* See BṛSaṃ. and 18.35 17d (supra) for the use of the term "king" for these ideal types. SK's (p. 32) "best inhabitants of the earth" misses the fact that *pārthivaḥ* means "king" rather than earthling. The BṛSaṃ. provides the correct background which facilitates our understanding for this equation between kings and the standards of human proportion.

36. 2. Cf. BṛSaṃ. 68.24:

रक्तं पीनकपोलमुन्नतनसं वक्तं सुवर्णोपमं
वृत्तं चास्य शिरोऽक्षिणी मधुनिभे च रक्ता नखा : ।
स्रग्दामाङ्कुशशङ्खमत्स्ययुगलक्रत्वङ्गकुम्भाम्बुजै-
श्चिहैर हंसकलस्वनः सुचरणो हंसः प्रसन्नेन्द्रियः ।। २४ ।। ६८

Note that this verse makes the face red whereas CitSūt. states that the *Haṃsa* type is "fair as the moon". Where the MSS of CitSūt. have *Haṃsagāmī* "with the gait of goose" BṛSaṃ. has *haṃsakalasvanaḥ* "with voice melodious as a goose's ". Perhaps we should look for a synonymous expression in CitSūt. *Haṃsanādi* is a possibility.

36. 3. Compare it with BṛSaṃ. :

उपचितसमवृत्तलम्बबाहु-
र्भुजयुगलप्रमितः समुच्छ्रायोऽस्य ।
मृदुतनुघनरोमनद्धगण्डो
भवति नरः खलु लक्षणेन भद्रः ।। १३ ।।
त्वक्शुक्रसारः पृथुपीनवक्षाः
सत्त्वाधिको व्याघ्रमुखः स्थिरश्च ।
क्षमान्वितो धर्मपरः कृतज्ञो
गजेन्द्रगामी बहुशास्त्रवेत्ता ।।१४ ।।
प्राज्ञो वपुष्मान् सुललाटशङ्खः
कलास्वभिज्ञो धृतिमान् सुकुक्षिः ।
सरोजगर्भद्युतिपाणिपादो
योगी सुनासः समसंहतभ्रु ।।१५ ।। ६८

These verses give some additional attributes not found in the CitSūt. SK incorrectly translates *kapola* as "forehead" (p. 32) as opposed to cheeks.

36. 4. Cf. BṛSaṃ. 68. 10: For *mudgaśyāmastu,* see p 344.

मालव्यो नागनासः समभुजयुगलो जानुसम्प्राप्तहस्तो
मांसैः पूर्णाङ्गसंधिः समरूचिरतनुर्मध्यभागे कृशश्च ।
पञ्चाष्टौ चोर्ध्वमास्यं श्रुतिविवरमपि त्र्यङ्गुलोनं च तिर्यग्-
दीप्ताक्षं सत्कपोलं समसितदशनं नातिमांसाधरोष्ठम् ।।१०।।६८

BṛSaṃ. is silent about the complexion. However, Bhaṭṭotpala's commentary throws light on CitSūt.'s *tanucchaviḥ,* glosses its counterpart in BṛSaṃ. *samaruciratanur* as follows:

समरुचिरतनुः समाः तुल्या रुचिरा श्रेष्ठा तनुः शरीरं यस्य ।

Samaruciratanuḥ [means] one whose body (*śarīram* [< *tanuḥ*]) is even (*tulya*[<*samăḥ*]) [and] excellent (śreṣṭha[< *rucirā*]).

If we follow Bhaṭṭotpala, *tanuchaviḥ*. "having an excellent physique".

36. 5a. *śaragaurastu.* SK etc. accept AFCV's *śaradgauras tu,* taking it to mean that the complexion is as fair as the autumn (*śarad*). But is the autumn fair ? I have followed ND's reading *śaragauraḥ* meaning "reddish brown". For the sense see, e.g. **Mahābhārata**, where it is used for monkeys *(śaragauraiś ca vānaraiḥ).*

तरुणादित्यसदृशैः शरगौरैश्च वानरैः ।।२७।।
प्राकारं ददृशुस्ते तु समन्तात्कपिलीकृतम् । २८. २६८ .३

Cf. BṛSaṃ 68.27:

सुभ्रकेशो रक्तश्यामः कम्बुग्रीवो व्यादीर्घास्यः ।
शूरः कूरः श्रेष्टो मन्त्री चौरस्वामी व्यायामी च ।।

raktaśyāmaḥ is the counterpart of *śáragauraḥ* and lends support to the reading accepted from N and D.

36. 5c. *sattvavān.*SK (p. 32), PS (p. 107) and SM (p. 170) accept V's reading *satyastu* and translate it as "truthful". The reading *sattvavān* is D's. It makes better sense and is consistent with other given attribute like *balavān. Sattvavān* means "resolute",

"energetic", "courageous" and so forth. On the other hand, *satyastu* finds no support in the parallel verse of BṛSaṃ while *sattvavān* is paralleled by *śuraḥ*.

Cf. ***Mantreśvara*** (68. 32) cited by Bhaṭṭotpala :

दीर्घास्यो बहुसाहसाप्तविभवः शूरोऽरिहन्ता बली ।
गर्विष्ठो रुचको प्रतीतगुणवान् सेनापतिर्जित्वरः ।।

36. 5c. *śramikaścaiva.* None of the MS readings (*samika, samaka, saṇaka*) is acceptable. My emendation *śramika* meaning "laborious" is backed by BṛSaṃ. 68.27, which describes the *Rucaka* as *vyāyāmī.* Bhaṭṭotpala glosses *vyāyāmī* as *śramaparaḥ* "given to exertion" ("hardworking"). He also cites from Sārāvalī : श्रमककरणरतो, "one who is fond of exertion".

SK find *sikataḥ* unobjectionable and translates it as "high souled" (p. 32). PS's emendation *rasikah,* "of good taste" (p. 107) is based on V's *sikataḥ* . It is also acceptable to SM (p. 170). Perhaps, they were largely guided by the term *Rucaka* itself.

36. 6. Cf. BṛSaṃ. 68,20:

ईषद्दन्तुरकस्तनुद्विजनखः कोशेक्षणः शीघ्रगो
विद्याधातुवणिक्क्रियासु निरतः सम्पूर्णगण्डः शठः ।
सेनानीः प्रियमैथुनः परजनस्त्रीसक्तचित्तश्चलः
शूरो मातृहितो वनाचलनदीदुर्गेषु सक्तः शशः ।। २० ।। ६८

36. 6a. *raktaśyāmas tu.* All MSS read *raktaśyāmas tu.* But this is term used in BṛSaṃ. to describe the previous type, the Rucaka, and CitSūt.'s *śaragauraḥ* is synonymous with it. The complexion of the Śaśaka is not given in BṛSaṃ. and there is of course, no necessity which would prevent the *Śaśaka* of the CitSūt. being said to have the same complexion as the *Rucaka.* However, the planet associated with the *Śaśaka* is Saturn and the colour associated with that planet is black or deep blue. This suggests that CitSūt. may have read *nīlaśyāma, atiśyāma* or *ghanaśyāma.*

The BṛSaṃ. states the following on Saturn and colours:

वैदूर्यकान्तिविमलः शुभकृत्प्रजानां ।
बाणातसीकुसुमवर्णनिभश्च शस्तः ।। २१.१०

Note the colour of *atasi* is jet black.

Bhaṭṭotpala cites Parāśara:

स्निग्धोऽमलः श्यामो विस्तृतार्चिः शनैश्चरः ।
मार्गस्थश्च प्रसव्यश्च नक्षत्रद्धित इष्यते ।।

36. 6b. *kiṃciddanturakas tathā.* SK, PS and SM read *kimcitkarburaka* following V. The *kimcit* ("somewhat") which modifies *karburaka* ("multicoloured") makes the description no less improbable.

SK: A Śaśaka is .....of a *slightly variegated colour* .. (p.32)

PS: A Śaśaka is *somewhat spotted,* (p. 108)

SM: a Śaśaka is .. a *little grey and mottled...* (p. 170)

F preserves the correct reading. It is backed by BṛSaṃ which has the exact synonymn *īṣaddanturakaḥ*. Cf. Bhaṭṭotpala'comments:

दन्तुरकः । दन्ता उन्नता यस्य ।

danturaka [means] he whose teeth are projecting."

36. 6d. *mahāvartmā.* AV's *madhvakṣa* followed by SK, PS and SM is suspect. This attribute has already occured shortly before in the description of the *Haṃsa* and is not backed by BṛSaṃ. The latter does refer to the *Śaśaka's* eyes but in form of the term *kośekṣanaḥ,* which Bhaṭṭotpala glosses *vipulapuṭekṣaṇaḥ,* "having eyes with large lids". I conjecture *mahāvartmā* on the ground that it has the same sense. The corresponding verse in the BṛSaṃ. has no parallel attribute to support it. The attribute in the latter with a reference to the eyes is *kośekṣaṇaḥ* meaning "one who has large eyelids". There is possibility that it could be a corruption of a similar attribute, as for instance *mahāvartmā* or "large lided". Note that N shows *madhvadmaśca.*

सप्तत्रिंशोऽध्यायः

मार्कण्डेय उवाच

अङ्गप्रत्यङ्गमानेन यथा पञ्च नराः स्मृताः ।
स्त्रियः पञ्च तथा ज्ञेयास्तथैव मनुजोत्तम ।। १ ।।

पुरुषस्य समीपस्था कर्तव्या +योषिदीश्वरा+ ।
नरस्कन्धप्रमाणेन कार्यैका सा यथामति ।। २ ।।

अङ्गुलौ द्वौ नरात्क्षामं स्त्रियो मध्यं विधीयते ।
अधिका च कटिः कार्या तथैव चतुरङ्गुलम् ।। ३ ।।

उरः प्रमाणतः कार्यौ स्तनौ नृप मनोहरौ ।
नृपाश्च सर्वे कर्तव्या महापुरुषलक्षणाः ।। ४ ।।

जालपादकराः कार्यास्तथा वै चक्रवर्तिनः ।
+और्णेयः+ च भ्रुवोर्मध्ये तेषां कार्यं तथा शुभम् ।। ५ ।।

1b. AF नरा

1cd. CF ज्ञेयात एव A ज्ञेयास्ता एव N ज्ञेयो NV ता एव

2a. A समीपस्थाः 2b ACFV योषिदीश्वर N योषिदेश्वर D योषिदीश्वरः B योषिदीद्वर

2c. A नरस्कन्द- 2d A यथामतिः V यथामिति N कार्य्या कामा

3a. D अङ्गुल्यौ N नराक्षामं 3b D मान्त्रयौ यः

3c. F कटि 3d N चतुरंगुला B चतुरङ्गुलीम्

4c. N सर्व 4d C मलापुरुष- F -पुरुषलक्षणः

5a. F जालं- 5c ACFV ऊणेर्य D ऊणेर्पः N भ्रुवोर्म्मध्ये 5d D कर्त्तव्यं शुभाशुभम्

ADHYĀYA 37

Markaṇḍeya spoke :

1. O Best of Men, know that just as men are understood to be of 5 types according to the measurement of the major and minor limbs, so are women.

2. When standing next to the men, a woman should be made, O Lord, as tall as the man's shoulder. When she is by hereself, she may be made as one sees fit.

3. A woman's waist is to be made 2 *aṅgulas* less than that of a man [i.e. 40 *aṅgulas*]. Likewise, the hips exceed that [of a man] by 4 *aṅgulas* [48 *aṅgulas*].

4. O king, the breasts should be made beautiful, in proportion to the chest.
   All kings should be made with [all] the characteristics of Great Men.

5. Kings should be made with feet and hands webbed; and in the middle of their eyebrows there should be a tuft of hair (*ūrṇā*) which is auspicious.

रेखाश्च करयोः कार्यास्तिस्रो राज्ञां मनोहराः ।
शशक्षतजसंकाशास्तथा वै क्षामकोटयः ।। ६ ।।

तरङ्गभङ्गिनः सूक्ष्मा निजस्नेहाभ्यलङ्कृताः ।
घनेन्द्रनीलसदृशाः केशाः कार्यास्तथा शुभाः ।। ७ ।।

कुन्तला दक्षिणावर्तास्तरङ्गाः सिहंकेशराः ।
बर्बरा जूटकसटा इत्येताः केशजातयः ।। ८ ।।

चापाकारं भवेन्नेत्रं मत्स्योदरमथापि च ।
नेत्रमुत्पलपत्राभं पद्मपत्रनिभं तथा ।। ९ ।।

वटाकृति महाराज पञ्चकं परिकीर्तितम् ।
चापाकारं भवेन्नेत्रं प्रमाणेन यवास्त्रयः ।। १० ।।

6b. F मनोहरा N मनोत्तरा

6c. C शशक्षत्रज- N संकाशास्तथा ACF शस्ता BV शस्त्रा D शास्त्राता

6d. D तथैव ABV क्षामकोटका:

7a. ABV तदङ्गभङ्गिनः F सूक्षा 7b CF निजघ्रेदाम्यलंकृतमः N लङ्कृता

7c. A चनेन्द्रनील- 7cd A केशाकार्या- 7d N केशकार्य्या N शुभा

8a. D दक्षिणावस्तास्तरङ्ग V -तरङ्गा 8b AV सिहंकेसराः N सिहंकेशरा

8c. ABCFNV वर्धरा ABCDFV जूटटसरा D जूटटमरा N कूटजमरो

9b. ABFV वा

A repeats from9b to 10c.

10a. D शराकृतिर् S1F शाराकृतिर् N शरोकृति ABV शानाकृतिर् S2 शाणाकृतिर् C माराकृतिर् 10b N पंचकं ABCV पञ्चमं 10d NV यथास्त्रियः

6. Three beautiful lines, red as hare's blood and finely tapered (*kṣāmakoṭayaḥ*), should be made on the palms of kings.

7. Hair should be made beautiful-wavy, (*taraṅgabhaṅginaḥ*) , fine *(sūkṣmā)*, beautified with its natural oil, *(nijasnehābhyalaṅkṛtāḥ)* resembling a dark sapphire *(ghanendranīlasadṛśāḥ)*.

8. The following are the [various] types of hair : (i) locks, (*kuntalāḥ*), (ii) curls common in the south (*dakṣiṇāvartāḥ*), (iii) wavy, *(taraṅgāḥ)* ,(iv) like lion's mane, *(siṃhakeśarāḥ)*, (v) curly, *(barbarāḥ)*, (vi) twisted, *(jūṭakāḥ)* (vii) matted *(saṭāḥ)*.

9. An eye may be in the shape of a bow or the belly of a fish. It may resemble the petal of a blue or red lotus.

10. O Lord, the fifth type is said to be cowrie shell-shaped. The bow-shaped eye should measure 3 *yavas* in width. [1]

1. The width refers to the height of the eye from top to bottom.

मत्स्योदराख्यं कथितं तथा यवचतुष्टयम् ।
नेत्रमुत्पलपत्राख्यं प्रमाणात्षड्यवं स्मृतम् ।। ११ ।।

पद्मपत्रनिभं नेत्रं प्रमाणेन यवा नव ।
वटाकृति च विज्ञेयं तथैव च यवा दश ।। १२ ।।

स्वमानाङ्गुलमानस्य यवमानं प्रकल्पयेत् ।
चापाकारं भवेन्नेत्रं योगभूमिनिरीक्षणात् ।। १३ ।।

मत्स्योदराकृति कार्यं नारीणां कामिनां तथा ।
नेत्रमुत्पलपत्राभं निर्विकारस्य शस्यते ।। १४ ।।

त्रस्तस्य रुदतश्चैव पद्मपत्रनिभं भवेत् ।
क्रुद्धस्य वेदनार्तस्य नेत्रं वटाकृति स्मृतम् ।। १५ ।।

11d. D प्रमाणा मे < रं ? > स्मृतम् N -षट्यव A -षड्यवं

12b. A प्रमानैन N यवान्नच

12c. NF शराकृतिं D शवाकृति C मराकृतिं ABS1S2B शशाकृतिं A शशकृतिं

12d. N यथादश:

13c. A चापकारं 13d N योगं

14a. N -राकृति: A मत्स्योदराकृत्यं <..> 14d N सस्यते
D repeats from 9d to 14 after 14c.

15a F ददतश्चैव 15c A वेदनात्रस्य V वेदनान्तस्य 15d D शवाकतिर्भवेत् AV शाराकृतिर् N सारकृति BCVF चाराकृतिर् 15d ACDF भवेत्

11. The fish- belly type is said to be 4 *yavas*; 6 *yavas* are prescribed for the width of the eye called the blue lotus petal type.

12. The eye which resembles the petal of a red lotus is 9 *yavas* in breadth and that which resembles a cowrie shell is known to measure 10 *yavas*.

13. The measurement in terms of *yavas* should be formulated from the peculiar[2] measurement of the *aṇgula (svamānāṅgulamānasya)*.

The eye will be bow-shaped when the subject ['s mind] is focussed [in trance] on a level of *Yoga*.

14. For women and male lovers, the eye should be made in the shape of a fish-belly.

The eye of a subject, who is not under the sway of passion, should resemble a petal of blue lotus.

15. An eye, with the shape of a lotus petal, is for a frightened and weeping subject. For someone who is angry and afflicted with pain, the eye resembling a cowrie shell is recommended.

2 The measurement of the *yava* is relative to the size of an aṅgula. Likewise, an *aṅgula* is relative to the Tāla system.

ऋषयः पितरश्चैव देवताश्च नराधिप
सुप्रभाभरणाः कार्या द्युतिमन्तस्तथैव च ।

मुष्णन्तस्तेजसां तेजः परेषां नृपसत्तम ।। १६ ।।
सम्यग्विचार्य नृपते स्वधिया यथोक्तं

ह्येतत्प्रमाणमनुरूपमनिन्दितं च ।
स्थानैरनेककरणैः स्थिरभूमिलम्भैः

कार्यं तदेव सुकुमारमजिह्मरेखम् ।। १७ ।।

इति श्रीविष्णुधर्मोत्तरे तृतीयखण्डे मार्कण्डेयवज्रसंवादे चित्रसूत्रे सामान्यमानं नाम सप्तत्रिंशत्तमोऽध्यायः ।। ३७ ।।

16b. AFNV स्वप्रभा- 16cF -स्तेजसातेजः ADF -तेजसा A तेनः
N ends after v. 16

17a. CF नृपतिस्स्च- AV नृपतिः FC यथोक्तमेतत्प्र- D यथोक्तप्रमाण-

17c. ACFV -किरणैः D भूमिवन्तैः (रन्तैः?) A -लम्वौः

17d. V सकुमार- CDF -जिह्मलेखम्

16-17. O King, sages, forefathers and gods *(devatāśca)* should be made, adorned with splendid ornaments halos, so bright that they outshine those of others with their lustre. O king, after deliberating carefully with all your intelligence, following the proportion just stated, make the [drawing], free of faults, based on postures and various *karaṇas* ascertained by the help of stable plumblines and delicate and fluid lines.

37. 1a. *aṅgapratyaṅgamānena.* For the meaning of this expression see Notes 36.1.1.

37. 2a. *samīpastha.* This qualifies the subject *yoṣit* ("a women, [when] in the company of a man .....") not as SK. etc. take it as a part of a predicate (i.e. "A woman should be portrayed in the company of a man"). The latter interpretation contradicts what follows, namely "(When alone (*ekā*) she may be portrayed as one sees fit)" SK avoids this contradiction by forcing *ekā* to mean "everyone": *Everyone* (of them) should be made to reach the shoulder ...." (p. 32). PS's paraphrase pays no heed to *ekā;* " A woman should be placed near her man ...." (p. 108); as does SM's translation: "The female is to be located close to the male,....." (p. 171)

Note to get the sense correct, "when" must be supplied. When a female figure is to be portrayed in the company of a male figure, then alone her height is up to man's shoulder but when she is by herself, the man's shoulder ceases to determine her height.

37. 2b. *īśvara.* Note that in the ViDhUp., *Īśvara* as a masculine vocative is very unusual. I suspect that it is a corruption of *īśvarā*, forming a compound with *yoṣit* and meaning "a queen amongst women". This could possibly be a feminine counterpart of *narādhipa* by which the five male stereotypes are referred in the earlier chapters.

37.3. These measurements here refer to the circumference of waist and hips.

37. 6ab. Cf. BṛSaṃ. 68.44:

तिस्रो रेखा मणिबन्धनोत्थिताः करतलोपगा नृपतेः । ४४.६८

A King has three lines rising from the wrist and going towards the palm.

This verse of BṛSaṃ. is only the first of a long series on the subject of palmistry listing a great variety of palm-marks / lines and what they suggest and foretell.

Bhaṭṭotpala cites a verse from Prahlāda along similar lines:

मणिबन्धने त्रिरेखासु मणिभूषणभाग्भवेत् ।
राज्ञां तिस्त्रस्तु नारीषु कामिन्यां द्वितयं स्मृतम् ।। ibid

37. 6d. *kṣāmakoṭayaḥ.* This reading comes from CNDF. SK and PS take this to mean "slenderly curving / curved?" *koṭi* meaning "the end or top of anything ? it denotes something curved where it refers to a bow or the wings of the moon; but the curvature is incidental. My interpretation ("finely tapered") is supported by CitLak. (verses 845-866), see p.92 for translation:

> Both the palms should resemble the red lotus: the lines in these are deep. At both the ends they are just a little deep and fine; resembling the colour of the blood of a hare...

37.7a. *sūkṣmā.* Note that it should be translated as "fine" and not as "thin" (see PS p. 108). SM takes it as "thin and fine" (p. 171).

37.8a. *dakṣiṇāvartāḥ.* According to BṛSaṃ., this is one of the features associated with kings:

मांसलमृदुभिः पार्श्वः प्रदक्षिणावर्तरोमभिर्भूपाः । २६. ६८

37.8c. *barbarā.* Only MS N preserves this reading *(varvarā).* PS, SK and SM accept the reading *vardharā* found in all other MSS. SK translates it as "parted" (p. 33), PS as "broom or brush like". (p. 108) and SM leaves it untranslated. SK's translation is evidently based on the fact that the root √ *vardh* means to cut, divide etc. How she justifies proceeding from this to vardhara "parted", she does not say. PS's translation is inspired by the lexical entry *vardhanī* "broom, brush". Perhaps she meant to emend to *vardhanāḥ.* Of course, this would not yield the meaning "broom, brush like". N's reading restores a familiar word in an appropriate sense. Cf. Citlak. 957-968:

> The hair is fine, resembling a spiral figure, shimmering with its natural rich shine, like the sapphire in its beauty similar to the colour of the bee, like antimony, like the neck of the peacock, like the breast of the cuckoo,like an unchanging colour in its shine,

falling down to the shoulder blades wound in locks and spiralling to the right. The spiral resemble the mane of the lion, the bun on the head (cikhanbadha) spirals leftwards. Such is the appearance of the hair of the head.

37. 8b. *jūṭakasaṭā.* The reading *juṭaṭasara* (ABCDFV), which yields no meaning, seems to have involved a transposition of the *akṣaras*-sa- and -ta- (ṭā) under the influence of the -ṭa- of *juṭa-*. Note that it is to be taken as a compound with *barbarā. Jūṭaka* or "twisted hair" and *saṭā* or matted / clotted hair form two more varieties of hair.

SK and PS's "matted" rests entirely on the *juṭa* element and ignores the rest. SM takes both *vardharā* and *jūṭaṭasarā* as 'frizzled". (p. 172)

37.9cd. *netram utpalapatrābham padmapatranibham.* SM interprets them differently: "*....dark and charming like the blue lotus (utpalapatrābha)"; "pinkish like the petal of the red lotus (padmapatranibha).* (p. 172). These similes are based on the shape of the lotuses and not their colour or beauty. This is obvious from the fact that the various types of eyes so described are distinguished from each other in terms of *yavas.*

37. 10a. *vaṭākṛti.* None of that MSS reading is acceptable. The order in which the five types of eyes are mentioned is significant. Every succeeding eye is larger than the preceding, where size (*pramāṇa*) means the perpendicular width of the eye and not its length. Within this order, the simile of a bow works very well for the first type, since this does have the least width. *Matsyodara* or the fish-belly type is wider by one *yavas.* A blue lotus petal is narrower than that of a red lotus and therefore is mentioned before the red lotus type. The type in question *(vaṭākṛti)* is said to be 10 *yavas* in width and hence the largest.

Let us note the various interpretation of the fifth type of eyes:

SK accepts *śāṇākṛti* and translates it as:

> a fifth (oh) great king, is said to be of the form of a *grindstone.*[2]

2. There words are used in three places (1) sānā, (2) śaśa, (3) sāra,i.e., grindstone, hare, deer, śaśa and Sāra do not yield any sense, sāna may be read in all three cases. (pp. 33)

Besides, "a grindstone" can hardly be an appropriate standard of comparison for the eyes.

PS accepts *śarākṛti* from A and interprets it to refer to an eye "in shape of an arrow" (p. 108). This does not yield good sense given the fact that according to the CitSūt., this type is the widest. SM's emendation *śaṃkhākṛti* derives from Goswamy's and Dallapiccola's translation of the Laufer's German translation of the Tibetan translation of the CitLak. A parallel passage in that text has "like a cowrie shell" in the corresponding position in the list. Note that CitLak. is very clear about this type of eye. Given the fact that all the other four types mentioned in CitLak. run closely parallel to what is stated in CitSūt., one is cempelled to take the Tibetan reading-mgron-bu seriously.

> mig ni ḥod mahi gshu ḥdrahi shen / nas gsum gyi ni tshad du bya
> eye bamboo bow like wide / yava three size make
>
> utpala ḥdab ḥdrahi mig la ni / nas drug gis ni tshad du bśad
> blue lotus petal like eye / yava six size declared
>
> ña lto ḥdra bahi mig gaṅ yin / nas brgyad kyi ni tshad du bśad
> fish stomach eye which is / yava eight size declared
>
> padmaḥi ḥdab ma ḥdra bahi mig / nas dgu yi ni tshad yin no
> red lotus petal like eye yava nine size is
>
> mgron bu ḥdra bahi mig gan yin / de ni nas dag bcu yin no
> cowrie shell like eye which is / that yava ten is (verses 619-628)

Note: not only do the measurements coincide but also the facial or mental states associated with them. Mgron bu or the conch shell type is mentioned again:

> Khros daṅ sdug bsṇal gzir baḥi mig / mgron bu ḥdra bar bri bar bya angry and distress aflicted -of eye mgron bu like draw
> (verses 639-640)

SM arrives at *śaṃkhākṛti* perhaps because of metrical consideration. Note that all the synonymns for "cowrie shell" are polysyllabic and would not fit in with the *anuṣṭubh* metre. *Vaṭa* is the only synonymn which fits in metrically if not paleographically with the MSS readings and hence it is preferred:

काकिनी कपर्दकः (वटः) वराटकः हिरण्यं

In the ***Vyutpatti***, mgron-bu is given as the Tibetan for the following Sanskrit words:

	Sanskrit equivalent	Tibetan	
5994	*Kapardika*	Mgron	bu
9374	*kapardaka*		‹
9375	*kākinī*		‹
9377	*māṣaka*		‹
9377	*kārṣāpaṇaḥ*		‹

As for the readings of the MSS, in the *Śāradā* script, *-va/ṣa-* and *-ma-*, similary *-ta-* and *-ra-* are easily confused. This would explain how *vaṭā* became *śarā-* (MSS ADN), *śārā-* (MS F) or *mārā-* (MS C) and so on.

37.12b. Note SM translates *saṃkhākṛti* differently:

The *globular* eye is understood as ten *yavas* in its proportion. (p. 172)

37.13ab. *svamāna .... prakalpayet.* Note the odd use of genitive in *svaṃānāṅgulamānasya.* One would expect an instrumental *svāṅgulamānena.* For its techincal sense missed by SK, PS and SM, see Notes 35.9b. If an *aṅgula* is defined as a 108th part of a given whole as it is by BṛSaṃ., the same rule should be applied to *yava* which is 1/8 of an *aṅgula.* Or the size of a *yava* is dependant upon that of an *aṅgula.*

37. 13d. *yogabhūmi-* SK (p. 34) and PS (p. 108) translate it as "looking at the ground in meditation"; and SM (p. 172) as [eyes] set down in "Yoga". I take *yogabhūmi-* in the technical sense "stage or level of Yoga", for which See, e.g. Yogasūtra 3.6 with Bhojarāja's commentary on Mṛgendratantra, *Yogapāda* 8 (KSTS edn. p. 9). Note that in meditation, the eye are to be focussed on the tip of the nose or inwards.

37. 14a. *matsyodarākṛtir.* I have preferred to N (>ABCDF) here at the expense of grammar, rather than to restore grammar at the expense of metre by emending to *matsyodarākṛti kāryam.* SM, aware of the dilemma has rendered the words of the *pāda* to preserve both grammar and metre.

नारीणां कामिनां कार्यं तथा मत्स्योदराकृति । १४. ३७

But this is, perhaps, to assume too high a standard of conformity to rules.

37. 15b. *vedanārtasya.* This reading, preserved in N and D, confirms PS's conjecture and SM's emendation. CF's *vedanāntasya* results from the similarity of -nta- and -rta- in the *Śāradā* script.

37. 15b. *smṛtam.* N's *smṛtam* is preferred to ABCDF's *bhavet,* since the latter is likely to be the result of dittography from the end of the preceding line, and makes the *pāda* unmetrical. SM came close with his conjecture *śaṅkhākṛti smṛtam.*

37.17a. *nṛpate.* This reading is preserved by D confirms PS's conjecture and SM's emendation.

37. 17c. *sthānair anekakaraṇaiḥ.* D against AVFV (*-kiraṇaiḥ*), confirming SM's emendation. SK and PS try to make sense of the corruption. SK takes it to refer to "positions with various rays of light upon them". PS takes *kiraṇa* to mean "beam-like line". SM emends well but mistranslates *karaṇa* as "flexion". It is, in fact, a term of the dance literature, where it refers to coordination of the movement of the hands and of the feet; See NS 30,4.

हस्तपादस्तमायोगो नृत्तस्य करणं भवेत् ।। ३०.४

अष्टात्रिंशोऽध्यायः

मार्कण्डेय उवाच

नेत्रमुत्पलपत्राभं रक्तान्तं कृष्णतारकम् ।
प्रसन्नं दीर्घपक्ष्मान्तं मनोज्ञं मृदुवर्त्म च ।।१।।

देवतानां कृतं राजन्प्रजाहितकरं भवेत् ।
समे गोक्षीरवर्णाभे स्निग्धे जिह्माग्रपक्ष्मले ।।२।।

प्रसन्ने पक्षपत्राभे मनोज्ञे प्रियदर्शने ।
कृष्णतारे विशाले च नयने श्रीसुखप्रदे ।।३।।

चतुरस्रं सुसंपूर्णं प्रसन्नं शुभलक्षणम् ।
अत्रिकोणमवक्रं च अविकारि मुखं भवेत् ।।४।।

दीर्घमण्डलवक्राणि त्रिकोणादीनि यानि च ।
वर्ज्यानि तानि देवानां प्रजासु शिवमिच्छता ।।५।।

1a. N रक्ताभं F रक्तान्त

1c. N प्रसन्न N दीर्घपक्ष्मात्रं 1d ND मृदुवर्त्तिर्नम् D मृदुवर्तिनम् V मृदु सत्तम ABCF मृदुसत्तमम्

2a. V करं 2c N सतं D -नोक्षीर- 2cd N -वर्णाभं स्निग्धं 2dBCF जिह्माश्रिपक्ष्मले

3a. N पद्मनेत्रान्त ACDFV पद्मनेत्रान्ते

3c. CF कृष्णताले 3d N नयन D नषने B श्रीमुखप्रदे N श्रीमुखप्रदी

4c. ABCFV -कोणमवक्रं DN अतिकोणसचक्रं

4d. D अविकारं FCV अधिकारमुखं AB अधिकारसुखं

5a. ADN दीर्घमण्डलचक्राणि 5c F तात्रि 5d N प्रजास्वसितमिच्छता

ADHYĀYA 38

Mārkaṇḍeya spoke:

1-2b. O King, it is beneficial to the people if the eyes of the gods are made similar to a blue lotus petal, with reddish corners, black pupils, benevolent, possessing long eyelashes, pleasing to the mind and having delicate eyelids.

2cd. [The eyes should be] level [looking straight ahead], with their whites of the colour of cow's milk and with long-ended eyelashes.

3. [The eyes that are] benevolent, with reddish corners, pleasing to the mind, beautiful to look at, with black pupils, and large, grant wealth and happiness.

4. The standard face *(avikāri mukham)* should be symmetrical *(caturasram)*, fully complete *(susampūrṇam)*, benevolent, possessing auspicious characteristics, neither triangular *(atrikoṇam)* nor crooked *(avakram)*.

5. In the case of gods, face which are long, circular, crooked, triangular etc. should be avoided by one who desires the well-being of the people.

कार्या हंसप्रमाणेन देवा यदुकुलोद्वह ।
तेषां च लोम कर्तव्यमक्षिपक्ष्मसु च भ्रुवोः ।। ६ ।।

अतः शेषेषु गात्रेषु देवाः स्युर्लोमवर्जिताः ।
द्विरष्टवर्षाकाराश्च तथा कार्या दिवौकसः ।। ७ ।।

प्रसन्नवदना नित्यं तथा च स्मितदृष्टयः ।
मुकुटैः कुण्डलैर्हारैः केयूरैरङ्गदैस्तथा ।। ८ ।।

भूषितास्तेऽथ कर्तव्याः शुभस्रग्दामधारिणः ।
श्रोणीसूत्रेण महता पादाभरणधारिणः ।। ९ ।।

यज्ञोपवीतवन्तश्च सावंतसास्तथैव च ।
जान्वधोलम्बिना कार्याः शोभिना कटिवाससा ।। १० ।।

6a. CF कार्यहंस- N हसप्रमाणेन N देवी
6cd. AB कर्तव्यमक्षपक्ष्मसु N कर्तव्यमक्षिपद्मसु D कर्त्तव्यं सक्षियक्ष्मसु 6d N च प्रेमी
7b. N देवा B स्युलोमवर्जितः ND म्युलोमदर्जिताः
7c. N द्विरष्टावर्षाकाराश्च
8d. N केयरैरंगदैस्तथा
9ab. N विभूषितास्ते कर्तव्या शुभम्रग्दामदारिणः 9a D –कर्तव्या D शुभस्वग्दामचारिणः
9b. F –दामकारिणः
9d. V पादाभरणचारिणा CF –चारिणः
10a. D –पवीतवर्णश्च 10b N सावतं-
10c. A जान्वु- C कार्या

6. O Perpetuator of the *Yadu* race, the gods should be made according to the *Haṃsa* measurements. Their [only] hair should be on the eyelashes and eyebrows.

7. Therefore, the gods are hairless on all other parts of their bodies. They should be portrayed as [though they were] 16-year olds.

8a. [They should] always be portrayed with benevolent faces and with a smile in the eyes.

8b-9a. They should be decorated with crowns, ear rings, necklaces, armlets and bracelets. They should be portrayed wearing beautiful garlands and an elaborate girdle, foot ornaments, sacred thread and ear ornaments.

10b. They should be represented with loin cloths *(kaṭivāsa)* extending down to left knee.

वामे मनुजशार्दूल दक्षिणं जानु दर्शयेत् ।
अंशुकं च तथा कार्यं देवतानां मनोहरम् ।। ११ ।।

प्रभा च तेषां कर्तव्या मूर्ध्नि मूर्धप्रमाणतः ।
मण्डलाभा महाराज देवताभानुकारिणी ।। १२ ।।

ऊर्ध्वा दृष्टिरधोदृष्टिस्तिर्यक् तेषां विवर्जयेत् ।
हीनाधिका वा दीना वा क्रुद्धा रूक्षा तथैव च ।। १३ ।।

ऊर्ध्वा तु मरणायोक्ता शोकायाधः प्रकीर्तिता ।
तिर्यग् धनविनाशाय हीना भवति मृत्यवे ।। १४ ।।

अधिका शोकजननी दीना च नृपसत्तम ।
रूक्षा भयावहा प्रोक्ता क्रुद्धा भयविवर्धिनी ।। १५ ।।

11a. F वाम 11b A जान्वु
11c. CF अस्तुम् ND कार्य्य
12a. D प्रभाव
12b. F मूध्न- V मूर्ध्नः AB मूर्ध्व- D मूर्धि मूर्ध्व C मूर्ध्नप्रमाणतः N मूतिर्मूर्ध्व
12d. ABCNVD देवतातोऽनुकारिणी F-ऽत्रकारिणी
13a. N उर्ध्वो 13b. CF विसर्चयेत्
14a. D ऊर्ध्वास्तु मरणाप्रोक्ता 14b CF शोकया-
14c. D तिर्यग्धनविनाशाय F तिर्यग्धवि- V तिर्गग्धन-
15c. N क्षयावहा ABCDFV धनक्षयाय स्यात् 15d. N क्रुद्धो F क्रुद्धमय- FD विवर्धनी

11. O Tiger amongst men, the right knee should be exposed. Gods should also have a beautiful upper garment.

12. The gods should be given halos around their heads in accordance with the latter's size. O Lord, the colour of the halos should be the same as that of the gods themselves.

13. [In the case idols to be worshipped], an upward, downward gaze, or oblique gaze should be avoided. [They should] neither be too small or too big, neither sad, wrathful nor harsh [to look at] *(rūkṣā)*.

14. [Regarding these idols], an upward gaze is said to bring death, a downward one grief, a diagonal look the destruction of wealth. [An idol which] is less [than the given proportion] causes death.

15. O Best of Kings, too large an idol causes sorrow and as does one which is sad. An idol with a harsh appearance brings fear and one with an angry expression predicts danger.

शातोदरी न कर्तव्या न कार्या चाधिकोदरी ।
सक्षता च न कर्तव्या तथा यदुकुलोद्वह ।। १६ ।।

हीनाधिकप्रमाणा च रूक्षवर्णा तथैव च ।
∓विवृतेन च वक्रेण∓ नता च यदुनन्दन ।। १७ ।।

प्रमाणहीनैरङ्गैश्च त्वधिकैरपि पार्थिव ।
शातोदरी क्षुद्भयदा मरणायाधिकोदरी ।। १८ ।।

सक्षता मरणायोक्ता हीना धनविनाशिनी ।
अधिका शोकजननी रूक्षवर्णा भयप्रदा ।। १९ ।।

विवृतेन च वक्रेण कुलनाशकरी भवेत् ।
प्राङ्नता धननाशाय दक्षिणेन च मृत्यवे ।। २० ।।

16b. ABDFCN छातोदरी N राधितोदरीम्

16c. ABCDV सुक्षता 16d N यदुकुलोद्वहा

17a. N -प्रमाना 17b. N रूक्षकर्णा

17c. A विवृत्तेन N निवृतेन वक्रेण 17d CD कुलनाशकरी भवेत्

18a. D < ? > 18bc NF अधिकैरपि

18c. ABCFN छातोदरी D हातोदरी

19a. N साक्षतो D -मरणप्रोक्ता 19b CDFN धनविनाशनी

20a. A विवृत्तेन N निवृतेन

20c. ND प्राङता CF प्रात्राता ABV प्राच्याभा

16. An idol should be made neither thin-waisted nor large-waisted. O Scion of the *Yadu* race, it should be undamaged.

17. It should neither be too thin nor too large in proportion; nor harsh coloured. O Son of the *Yadus,* the face of the deity should not be made either turning away or bent down.

18. O King, nor should it possess limbs which are too small or too large. An idol with too thin a waist gives rise to hunger and fear and one with too large a waist brings death.

19. An idol which is damaged causes death and one that is undersized destroys wealth. An oversized idol causes sorrow and one that is harsh- coloured brings fear.

20. An idol with the face turned away will lead to the destruction of one's family.

An idol which stoops towards the east *(prāṅnatā)* brings about the destruction of riches; and if it bends towards the south, it brings death.

पश्चिमेन सुतघ्नी स्यादुदग् भयविवृद्धये ।
प्रमाणहीना नाशाय अधिका देहनाशिनी ।। २१ ।।

अश्लक्ष्णा मरणायोक्ता क्रुद्धा रूपविनाशिनी ।
प्रमाणहीनां प्रतिमां तथा लक्षणवर्जिताम् ।। २२ ।।

आवाहितापि विप्रेन्द्रैर् नाविशन्ति दिवौकसः ।
आविशन्ति तु तां नित्यं पिशाचा दैत्यदानवाः ।। २३ ।।

तस्मात् सर्वप्रयत्नेन मानहीनां विवर्जयेत् ।
चित्रलक्षणसंयुक्तं प्रशस्तं सर्वमुच्यते ।। २४ ।।

आयुष्यं च यशस्यं च धनधान्यविवर्धनम् ।
तदेव लक्षणापेतं धनधान्यविनाशनम् ।। २५ ।।

21ab. AV सुतघ्नी च चोदग्मय- 21b D भवविवर्द्धनी
21c. C -हीनापाशाय 21d ABD देशनाशिनी CDNS1S2 देशनाशनी F चेशनाशनी
22a. A अश्लक्ष्णा N अश्लल? D मरणाप्रोक्ता
22b. DFN क्रुद्ध DN रूपविनाशनी C रूपाविनाशनी
23a. V आवाहिताश्च 23ab F विप्रेन्द्रैन्नाविशन्ति 23b N हि देवता
23cd. CF तु ता नित्यं पिशाचै- N lacks तु तां नित्यं but has सुतत्रेव and ends.
24a. D प्रयत्ने 24b CDF मानहीना
24c. CDFS1S2 चित्रं
25c BCDF लक्षणोपेतं A तदेवालक्षणोपेतं

21. If the idol leans towards the west, it annihilates sons, and if towards the east, it increases fear. If too small, it brings destruction; if too large, it destroys [one's] body *(dehanāśinī)*.

22ab. An idol which is not polished is said to cause death. If it looks wrathful, it destroys beauty.

22c - 23. Gods, even though invoked by the best of *brāhmins*, do not enter an idol which lacks proportion and is bereft of the [auspicious] characteristics.

Instead, such an idol is always haunted by *piśācās*, *daityas* and *dānavas*.

24. Therefore every attempt should be made to avoid an idol which lacks [the prescribed] proportion. Any [idol] which has [all] the characteristics prescribed for a painting is said to be praiseworthy.

25. It brings about longevity, increases fame, wealth and material prosperity. Any [idol] which has inauspicious characteristics destroys wealth and prosperity.

देवा नरेन्द्र कर्तव्याः शोभावन्तः सदैव तु ।
मृगेन्द्रवृषनागानां हंसानां गतिभिः समाः ।। २६ ।।

सलक्षणं चित्रमुषन्ति धन्यं
देशस्य कर्तुर्वसुधाधिपस्य ।

तस्मात्प्रयत्नेन सलक्षणं त-
त्कार्यं नरैर्यत्नपरैर्यथावत् ।। २७ ।।

इति श्रीविष्णुधर्मोत्तरे तृतीयखण्डे मार्कण्डेयवज्रसंवादे चित्रसूत्रे प्रतिमालक्षणाध्यायो नाम
अष्टत्रिंशत्तमोऽध्यायः ।। ३८ ।।

26a. CFDV देवा D नरेन्द्राः
26b. V मृगेद्र- F मृगेक्र-
27a. AB चित्रमुष्यंति CDF चित्रमुषन्ति 27c D मात्प्रसवेन
27d. A नरैयत्न-

26. O King, the gods should always be made magnificent and resemble lion, bull, serpent and swan in gait.

27. A painting endowed with auspicious characteristics increases the glory of the country, the patron [*yajamāna*] and the king. Therefore the [image] should be made carefully, with all the auspicious marks, by diligent men according to the rules.

NOTES TO ADHYĀYA 38

38. 1a. *netram utpalapatrābham.* This type of eyes was discussed in adhy. 37, 11b and 14b and prescribed for *nirvikārasya,* "one who is unaffected by emotions". It is clear from the present context (v. 2a) that this indicates the gods. Cf. CitLak. :

> Eye resembling an utpala petal are red at the corners, the pupils are black and shiny, the lashes have long points and are pleasing with the lustre of their colour appearing in soft tones. When one has painted the eyes of the Gods, the well - being of the kings and of all beings shall increase. (The eyes of the Gods) are lustruos and rich (snigdha) like the colour of cow's milk, having lashes devoid of coarseness, resplendant like a petal of a padma lotus and constantly changing in their play of colours because of the blueness of the conjunctive, with pupils black and large; the painting of eyes such as these bring riches and fortune. (p. 84)

38. 1d. *mṛduvartma ca.* SK and PS accept *mṛdusattama* from V and take it as a vocative. In CitSūt. this form of vocative is uncorroborated. SM emends *mṛdusattama* from the vocative case to *mṛdusattamam* or the accusative case and connects it with the eyes. His translation (p. 172) of it as "exceedingly soft" is accounted in the foonote:[4]

> F.N. 4 मृदुसत्तमम् would qualify the eye as it should and is no epithet of the king addressed.

Whereas N and D show *mṛduvartinam* which yields a vague sense - "moving gently" or "behaving gently". On the basis of CitLak. where "the luster of their colour appearing in soft tones" seems to be a parallel, I conjecture *mṛduvarṇitam.* The other possibility is *mṛduvartma ca.* N and D have preserved - va - in *vartinam* and AFC retain - ma - in *-sattamam.* Note - ca - has to be postulated for the sake of the metre. This may not be farfetched given how closely - ma- and -ca- resemble in the *Śāradā* script. The meaning that it yields is relevant to the context - "having delicate eyelids".

38. 2a. *kṛtam.* SK accepted V's *karam* : "The hands of the gods ..." (p. 34).

38. 2c. *same.* See verse 13 (infra) for the context. *Same* refers to the gaze of the idol and not to the size of the eye as was thought by all the translators. It means "straight" or "level", i.e. that which is neither upwards nor downwards, neither sideways nor diagonal.

Cf. ŚilpRat.:

अधोदृष्टिश्चोर्ध्वदृष्टिः सततं दुःखदा नृणाम् ।
पार्श्वदृष्टिश्च तत्तुल्या समदृष्टिः शुभावहा ।। २६.४०

Cf. ***Kriyāsamuccaya*** **:** समे दृष्टी प्रसन्नास्ये सौम्यस्निग्धावलोकने । p. 449.

Cf. a passage cited by Bhaṭṭotpala, 68.64:

समे गोक्षीरवर्णाभे रक्तान्ते कृष्णतारके ।
प्रसन्ने च विशाले च स्निग्धे चैवायते शुभे ।।
अतसीपुष्पसङ्काशे भवतां यस्य लोचने ।
भूपतिः स तु विज्ञेयः समुद्रवचनं यथा ।।

38. 3a. *padmapatrābhe.* The *padmanetrānte* of all the MSS is suspect. It is evident from the context that the verse introduces the next type of eye, which, in the order of the original listing at *adhy.* 37, verse 9, is that which has the shape of the petal of a red lotus. Hence my emendation. Cf. BṛSam. 68.64: पद्मदलाभैर्धनिनो रक्तान्तविलोचनाः श्रियो भाजः "Those who have eyes resembling lotus petal and with red corners will be prosperous."

SK (p. 34) fails to see connection between this and earlier type pointed out by PS (p. 109) and merely translates it as ".... with ends like those of a blue lotus petal". This is surprising, since the reading SK follows refers to the *padma*-which means the red rather than the blue lotus *(utpala)* SM follows SK.

38.4a. *caturasram.* Both PS (p. 109) and SM (p. 173) interpret this mean "squarish". Although there are several references to specific shape in this passage it is clear that *caturasram* means "regular" in the sense of symmetrical rather than "square" as interpreted by PS and SM given that both CitSūt. and BṛSam. regard squareness of face as a negative attribute. According to BṛSam. 68.56, The possession of a square face portends fraudulence.

स्त्रीमुखमनपत्यानां शाठ्यवतां मण्डलं परिज्ञेयम् ।
दीर्घं निर्द्रव्याणां भीरुमुखाः पापकर्माणः ।।५५ ।।

चतुरस्त्रं धूर्तानां निम्नं वक्रं च तनयरहितानाम् ।
कृपणानामतिह्रस्वं सम्पूर्णं भोगिनां कान्तम् ।।५६ ।।६८ पुरुषलक्षणम्

Know the childless by [their] effeminate (face), rogues by their round (faces), the poor by long [and] the sinners, timid faces.

Wicked people have a square face, and those without any issue have sunken and crooked face; misers, a very small face, and those who enjoy the pleasures (of life) possess a fleshy and attractive face.

Bhaṭṭotpala cites the following from an unknown text:

स्त्रीमुखं निरपत्यानां मण्डलं शाठ्यसेविनाम् ।
दीर्घं मुखं च निःस्वानां भीरुवक्त्रा दुराशयाः ।।
चतुरस्त्रं तु धूर्तानां निम्नं सुतविवर्जितम् ।
कृपणानां तथा ह्रस्वं चिपिटं परजीविनाम् ।।
यन्मुखं मांसलं स्निग्धं सप्रभं प्रियदर्शनम् ।
वर्णाढ्यां सन्धिविश्लिष्टमजस्त्रं सुखभागिनाम् ।।

Given the fact that there seems to be a close parallel between the CiSūt. and BṛSam. in regarding triangular, circular, long and crooked faces as inauspicious, *caturasram* cannot be taken to mean square.

38.4a. *susampurṇam.* Its technical meaning related with foreshortening needs to be recognised. A figure when viewed strictly from the front is not given to any foreshortening and hence is fully complete in all its details.

38. 4d. *avikāri mukham.* The reading *avikāramukham* comes from N and D. SK etc. follow ABCFV's *adhikāramukham.* It is difficult to see how SK proceeds from that reading to the following translation:

SK The face beautiful all over should be *fully developed*; (p. 34)

PS (p. 109) takes it to mean "The *principal face*". SM realises the problem and suggests the emendation *mugdhākāram mukham* (... but charming in shape should be the face. p. 173) on the following grounds:[3]

F.N. 3) This reading is corrupt. If च and अ coalesce as they should there is a slip in the metre. And what is अधिकार ? अधिकारमुख Can it be मुग्धकारं मुखं भवेत्? p.142

Such a drastic emendation is unnecessary. The corruption of *avikāra* to *adhikāra* is probably the result of the close similarity of -v- and -dh- in the *Śāradā* script. I have emended *avikāra* - to *avikāri* for reasons of sense. The verse is evidently a description of the faces [of the gods], a particular kind of face, as it would have to be if we accepted *avikāramukham. avikāri,* a small change given the Kashmirian propensity to confuse - a and -i- in pronuciation, given as appropriate attribute of such faces, namely that they should be "free of deformities".

38.5a. *-vakrāṇi.* I take *vakra* - to mean "crooked", this being one of the inauspicious facial characteristics listed at BṛSam. (supra). 68.56. SK, PS and SM sacrifice any connection with the preceding verse by taking it to refer to one of a number of prohibited abstract shapes. SK interprets the verse along the same lines but omits to translate *vakra-* "One who wishes good to the people should discard (a too profuse employment of) *large* circles, triangles and other (geometrical shapes) when representing gods." (p. 35) and PS takes it, "Long, circular, *oblique* and triangular shapes should be avoided for the welfare of the people." (p. 109); SM: " In the case of celestials, excess of length, rotundity, *curvature,* angularity and other such traits should be avoided,.... (p. 173).

In my interpretation, v. 5 merely continues the subject matter of v. 4. in reaffirmation of verse 4. This interpretation has the support of CitLak. 693-704:

> The face should be made squarish in form, sharply delineated, beautifully full and endowed with brilliant and pleasing marks. It shall not be made triangular, nor sloping; it shall not be made angry nor round: he who has painted such a face shall always gain earthy rewards. For common persons should be employed a face desirous of composure, whether round, or sloping or triangular etc. The characteristics mentioned before are suitable also for the faces of the Gods and Kings whose measurements have already been laid above. (p. 85-86)

38. 12a. *mūrdhapramāṇataḥ.* I have emended C's *mūrdhnapramāṇataḥ,* since *mūrdha-* is the grammatically correct stem form. This might be thought to be an arbitrary upgrading of the Sanskrit of the text.

However, where the language of the CitSūt is un-Pāninian this licence is motivated by metre.

38.12c. *maṇḍalābhā. ābhā* refers to the colour of the halo and not to its shape as SM (p. 174) takes it.

38.12d. *devatābhānukāriṇī.* This emendation is suggested by the sense required by the context. All MSS read *devatāto'nukāriṇī'* which yield no good sense as is evident in all the translations which accept it. It is not clear from any of these translations how the translators analyse the *devatāḥ* which they presumably see here.

SK: The halo should be drawn around their heads, proportionate to the measurement of the head and *the colour of the halo circle,* (p. 35)

SM: Their halo should fit the head it decorates, sin due proportion to it, should be circular, *following the requirements of each of the celestials.* (p. 174)

They certainly do not appear to be taking it in the sense of an ablative of *devatā* which is the only obvious interpretation. My emendation fits the context well, because it means that the text requires the artist to take the colour of the halo from that of the deity's body. These colours are given at ViDhUp., *adhy.* 42,v.22-23.

Note that from this point onwards what the text discusses pertains only to temple idol which is located in the *garbhagṛha* or the inner sanctum and not to the representations of other images such as the five ideal types. Cf. ***Pratimālakṣana***, *adhy.* 58 of BṛSam. which treats it as a separate topic :

Bhaṭṭotpala introduces it as :

अथार्कमुद्दिश्य सर्वप्रतिमानां शुभाशुभमाह-

Now, he after mentioning about the good and bad omens of (the idol) of Sun he speaks about all the images(i.e. which applies to all images).

Note that the proportions assigned to the temple idols are different from what has been discussed in the CitSūt. so far :

सौम्या तु हस्तमात्रा वसुदा हस्तद्वयोच्छ्रित प्रतिमा ।
क्षेमसुभिक्षाय भवेत् त्रिचतुर्हस्तप्रमाणा या ।। ४९, ५७

An image measuring 1 cubit is benevolent, 2 cubits high, gives prosperity, 3 and 4 cubits high, happiness and abundant food respectively.

38.15ab. *adhikā-*. Note that here it refers to the size of the deity's eye as opposed to its waist. The latter is mentioned in 38. 19c. PS (p. 109) translates *adhikā-* as "wide".

38.15c. *bhayāvahā proktā*. ABCDFV read *dhanavināśāya*. I have emended to *bhayāvahā* in accordance with N and 38.19d. The first reads *ksayāvahā* and the second states that this sort of gaze causes fear / danger *(bhayāpradā)*. N's *kṣayāvahā* yields sense and it might be thought that it is original. But -ks- and -bh- are easily confused in the *Newārī* script of N. The reading of ABCDFV's followed by SK etc., is explicable as dittography of the same pāda in the preceding verse. *(tiryag dhanavināśāya)*.

38.15d. *bhayavivardhinī*. This reading is doubtful since it seems little more than a repetition of the *bhayāvahā* so while qualifies the preceding type of gaze.

38.16a. *śātodarī*. This slight emendation of CDF's *chātodarī* is confirmed by BṛSam. 57.50. This emendation is implicit in the translation though not shown in the editions. SK (p. 35) translates *śāta-* "shrunk". PS (p. 110) translates it as "depressed" and SM (p. 174) as "sunken". I take it to mean "[too] thin", "[too] slender"; See Bhaṭṭotpala on BṛSam 57.50 शातोदर्यां तनूदरायां क्षुद्भ्यं भवति । *Śātodarī* means "thin-waisted".

38. 16c. *sakṣatā*. This means simply "damaged" or "broken". SK (p. 35) and PS (p. 110) take it to mean "wounded".

38.20c. *prāṅnatā*. SK, PS and SM follow AV's *prācyābhā*, taking the verse to be referring therefore to the halo *(ābhā)* of the deity. However, *ābhā* is not recorded in the sense of halo and it is in any case, surprising that the subject should suddenly deviate : the next verse like the preceding contains attributes of the images as a whole. I read *prāṅnatā*. This reading is supported by BṛSam. 57.51.cd. which speaks of the consequence of idols that lean to the left *(vāmāvanatā)* or the right *(dakṣinavinatā)* in exactly the same position within the parallel sequence of verses. The CitSūt. seems to have elaborated the latter by speaking of idols leaning in each of the four cardinal directions.

SK *A halo* in the east causes loss of wealth, in south death, in the west destruction of sons, in the north fear. (*i.e. it should be behind and round the head.*(p. 36).

PS *If the halo* is eastward, it causes loss of wealth and southward death; if westward, destruction of sons and if northward, it increases dangers. (p. 110)

SM ...*the pronouncedly east gazing* depletes wealth, similarly south-gazing brings on death. The *pronouncedly west-gazing* destroys the offsprings, the north-gazing enhances fear. (p. 175)

My emendation is based on DN's *prāntā.* Taking this as a corruption of *prāṅnatā* restores the metre and yields sense. Note that the BṛSam. 57.51, supports this emendation:

वामावनता पत्नी दक्षिणविनता हिनस्त्यायुः ।।

Note that the BṛSam. provides the context to interpret verse 20b and 21a in the CitSūt. The temple idol should not bend or lean towards any of the four cardinal directions.

38. 22ab. *aślakṣṇā.....rūpavināśinī.* SK and PS take this verse to concern the halo discovered in V's reading of 20c when it refers to the deity itself.

SK *A nimbus* short of measurement and one exceeding the appropriate measurement bespeaks ruin to the country (p. 110)

PS *If it is* less than the proportion, it leads to destruction, if it exceeds, it ruins the country. (p. 160)

38. 23a. *āvāhitapī.* I take this to be a case of double sandhi *(āvāhitāḥ api > -tā api- > -tāpi-)* such as is not uncommon in Purāṇic and Tantric texts. SM emends to *āvāhitām:*

आवाहितां नाविशन्ति विप्रैरपि दिवौकसः

This restores Pāṇinean grammar but at the expense of sense: it is not the idol that is summoned but the deities.

38. 25b. *tadeva lakṣaṇāpetam.* For once I have followed V here against the other MSS since this alone yields the appropriate sense. An alternative would be to emend *tadeva lakṣaṇopetam* of the other MSS to

tadevā lakṣaṇopetam. But this seems rather strained in comparison to V's appropriate and idiomatic reading.

एकोनचत्वारिंशोऽध्यायः

मार्कण्डेय उवाच

शुभाकारविकाराणि नानावर्णधराणि च ।
नव स्थानानि रूपाणां श्रृणु तान्यनुपूर्वशः ।।१।।

ऋज्वागतं भवेत्पूर्वमर्धर्जु तदनंतरम् ।
साचीकृतशरीरं च्र भवत्यध्यर्धलोचनम् ।।२।।

ततः पार्श्वगतं नाम परावृत्तमनंतरम् ।
पृष्ठागतमथ कार्यं पुरोवृतं समानतम् ।।३।।

एतान्यनेकभेदानि नवस्थानानि भूपते ।
एकैकस्येह भणतः श्रृणु मे नृप लक्षणम् ।।४।।

तत्राभिमुखमेवादौ स्पष्टमानगुणान्वितम् ।
सुसंपूर्णं सुचार्वङ्गं सुश्लक्ष्णामलवर्तकम् ।।५।।

1a. F शुभां - ABCFNV -कारविहाराणि 1b D लावर्णधराणि

2ab. CDF -पूर्वमवर्जु V -पूवमनृजु AB ऋजुस्तदनंतरम् D -द्धर्जुनमदन्तरम् N भवेत्पूर्वमवक्रान्त 2c. N सारीकृत- D वाचीकृत-

2d. ACDFV -त्यर्धविलोचनम् NV अर्धविलोचनं

3a. N पार्श्वगतं N नाश 3b ABCFV पुरावृत्त-

3c. C पृष्ठगत- N -गतमथः कार्य्यं DV -मधः कार्यं ACF -मधः कायं

3d. V पुरावृतं BDN परावृत्तं A परावृत्तां V2 (ख) शरावृत्तं F सरावृत्तं C मरावृत्तं B परावृत्तांतमानतम् N समानतः D समाततं B -तमानतम्

4a, N एतान्येनेक 4b AB स्थानि विभूषिते FCV भूषिते

4c. ABCFV भवतःN भवति D < .. तः ? > 4d N यन् नृप

5c. A -मुखसेवादौ D -सुखमेवा-

5c. N सुसर्वाङ्ग 5d ABCV सुश्लक्ष्णमल- N -वन्तकं

ADHYĀYA 39

Mārkaṇḍeya spoke:

1. Figures have nine postures whose transformations are beautiful *(śubhākāravikāraṇi)* in shape and possess various colours. Listen to them one after another.

2. The first is *Ṛjvāgata* (Frontal), followed by *Ardharju* (Afrontal), *Sācīkṛta,* (Averted) and *Adhyardhalocana* (One - and- a- half- eyed).

3. *Pārśvāgata* (Profile) comes next, followed by *Parāvṛtta* (Turned away), *Pṛṣthāgata* (Backview), *Purovṛtta* (Turned towards the front or Reverted) and *Samānata* (completely Bent).

4. O King, these nine postures have innumerable variations. Listen to me about each of the characteristics as I speak.

5. Amongst them, *Ṛjvāgata* (Frontal) is the first. It is [drawn with] the measuring thread straight *(spaṣṭamānaguṇānvitam)*. It is fully complete *(susampūrṇam)* [being unforeshortened], with beautiful limbs and is sketched very smoothly and faultlessly.

सुशुद्धं मधुरं स्पष्टरेखासंस्कारभूषितम् ।
यद्भवेत्स्थानमक्षीणगात्रं ऋज्वागतं तु तत् ।। ६ ।।

मुखं स्यादर्धतः क्षीणं वक्षसः उदरं तथा ।
कट्याश्च स्फिप्रदेशाच्च ऊरूतलं क्षयं गतम् ।। ७ ।।

नासापुटाधरोष्ठानां चतुर्थांशं च बुद्धिमान् ।
क्षयं नीतं त्रिभागं च यस्य गात्रेम्य एव च ।। ८ ।।

कान्तं रूपधरं स्थानं स्तनलम्बोपपादितम् ।
एतदधार्जु नामोक्तमनेककरणान्वितम् ।। ९ ।।

यत्तिर्यग्भूमिलम्बेन नेत्रहारि सुवर्तनम् ।
सुकुमारं चतुर्भागं क्षीणं सर्वाङ्गशोभनम् ।। १० ।।

6a. D सुशुद्ध ACF मधुर N स्पष्टं
6cd. N यत्भवेत्स्थान-CFN मक्षीणं गात्र D -मक्षीणगतं ऋज्वाकरन्तुतः 6d. ACFNV पृष्ठगतं
7a. ABV मुखस्यादावतोऽक्षीणं CF मुखस्यादवतोऽक्षीण N सुखस्यादर्द्धतोऽक्षीणं Dसुखस्यादर्द्धतः
7b ACDF वक्षसं N वक्षसं N तदनन्तथा
7cd. ABCDV कट्याच ABCDFNV स्कन्धदेशाच्च ABCNFV ऊरुतश्च D ऊरुकश्च NV गता A गतः D गताः C[ ]यं गताः F[ ]यो गताः
8a. N नाशा- N चतुर्थांस च F चतुर्थांश D चतुर्वासं ABV बुद्धिमत् 8d. N यस्या
9a. CF कान्तारूपधरं N कान्तारूपतरं D कान्तरूपतरं AV कान्तारूपं परं
9b. BCFNV स्थानलम्भो- A स्थानलंबो- D स्थानंलम्भो- CFN -पदादितम् B -पचादितम् A-पचादिर्तम्
9c. D एतदर्द्धजुना BC एतदेव V एतदेवर्जु N एतदेवार्जु A एतद्देवर्जु F एतदेर्जु A नामोक्ताम- N नोनोक्त D प्रोक्तम- 9d N तनेककरणात्मकं A -करुणा-
10a. D यतिर्य्यग्भू- N पक्तिर्य्यष्भ्रमिलम्भेन AV -लम्भेन
10b. N सुवर्तलम् 10c N चतुर्भागक्षीणं

I. *Ṛjvāgata:*

6. [Because] it is drawn with clearly defined lines *(spaṣṭarekhāsaṃskāra)*, [this posture] is very pure *(suśuddha)* and appealing *(madhura)*. [Because] the body [in this posture] is unforeshortened, it [the posture] is called *Ṛjvāgata*.

II. *Ardharju:*

7. [In the *Ardharju* or Afrontal, not only is] half of the face foreshortened but also of the chest, belly, waist down to the buttocks and the thighs.

8. O Intelligent One, 1/4 of the nosewing and the lips are foreshortened; as for the (rest of) body, a third part (of 8 *aṅgulas*) is foreshortened.

9. This posture called *Ardharju* possesses a beautiful form and is drawn employing the perpendiculars passing through the nipples [*pakṣasūtras*] and various coordinations of hand and foot movements (*karaṇa*) are possible [in this posture].

II. *Sācikṛia:*

10. That [half of the body] which meets the perpendicular at an angle *(yattiryagbhūmilambhena)* which is attractive *(netrahāri)* and delicate *(sukumāra)* is foreshortened to its one fourth (i.e.1/4 of 8 = 2) [and] is beautifully rendered with lines. *(suvartanam)*.

अध्यर्धभ्रूललाटं चाप्यध्यर्धः घ्राणपुष्करम् ।
भागद्वयावशेषार्धं कलार्धं क्षीणलोचनम् ।। ११ ।।

कलार्धलुप्तभ्रूलेखं लिखितं स्निग्धलेखया ।
न च छायागताकारं न चार्धर्जुकलोपमम् ।। १२ ।।

वैकारिकत्वाच्च नृप साचीकृतमिहोच्यते ।
अर्धं नेत्रं मुखे यस्य लुप्तमर्धभ्रूवे तथा ।। १३ ।।

भङ्गि ललाटं मात्रार्धं दृश्यनासार्द्धमेव च ।
मात्रार्धं चैकतो गण्डं दृश्येतार्धकृतक्षयम् ।। १४ ।।

मात्रार्धं कण्ठरेखाया यवमाविष्कृतं हनोः ।
उरसेऽर्धं मुखं लुप्तं नाभ्याः स्याच्छिष्टमङ्गुलम् ।। १५ ।।

11a. D प्यर्धभ्रू-F अम्यर्धभ्रू- BV -भ्रूललाटे 11b V चाप्यध्यर्ध- F चाप्यम्यर्धा- N वाप्यध्यर्द्ध CFD घ्राणमुत्करम् VA -घ्राणमुत्कटम्

11c. DV भागक्षयावशे.षार्धं B भागक्षायवशेषार्ध्वं AS1S2 भागक्षयावशेषोर्ध्वं CF भागक्षयावशेषोव्वं N -वशेषाध 11d ABCFV कलापक्षीण- N कलांचंक्षीणलोचेनं D कलाचक्षीणचोलनम्

12a. ABCV कलावलुप्त- ND कलाचलुप्त- F वलावलुप्त

12c. ABCFV च्छायागतं कालं N चे छयागतं D न च हायागतकर 12d N चावैत्रृजु- ABCFV चावत्रृजु- ABCDFV कोपनम् N कोपलम्

13a. N वैकारिकत्वात्तु CF वैकारिवद्वाश्च AB वैकारिकताच्च V खेकारिकत्वाच्च

13c. D अर्धनेत्रं N अर्ध्वनेत्रे N यस्यालुप्तमर्द्धभ्रुवे V यस्य लुप्तवभ्रुवे

14a. ABCFNV भङ्गो- ABCDFV ललाट- CFV ललाटमात्रश्च N ललाट्यमात्रा च AD -मात्राश्च

14b. N दृश्यानासार्द्धमेव CF दृश्यानां सार्धमेव ABS1S2V दृश्यानां सारमेव तु

14c. N मात्रार्द्ध D मात्राद्धं ABCFV मात्रार्धां F चेकतो

14d. AB दृश्येतार्य कृतं N दृश्यतार्य्यकृतो क्षया F दृश्यतार्य कृतं V दृश्यमर्धकृत- C दृश्यकार्यकृतं

15a. N मात्रार्द्ध ABCV कण्डरेखाया 15b. N -विप्लुतं CDF-विष्कृतं N हरौ D भवेत्

15c. N उरसोर्द्धमुखं S1S2 उरसोर्ध्व ABCDF उरसोर्ध्वो ABVD लिप्तं

15d. ABDNV नाभ्यास्याच्छिष्ट- C नाभ्यासाच्छिष्ट-

11. One and a half side of the [elephant-] *trunk-like* nose and the forehead are shown. [i.e. one whole side and half of the other). The remaining half (of the foreshortened part of the body) has 2 parts *(aṅgulas)* and the foreshortened eye measures half a *kalā* (i.e. 1 *aṅgula*).

12-13b. The foreshortened eyebrow measuring half a *kalā* is drawn with a tender line. (This posture) O King because it is deviant *(vaikārikatvācca)*, [i.e.] it is neither like *Chāyāgata* nor like *Ardharju*, it is called *Sācīkṛta* (Averted).

IV *Adhyardhākṣam:*

13c-14. That (figure) whose half an eye and eyebrow are foreshortened, whose forehead [on the foreshortened] is half a *mātrā*(i.e. 1/2 *aṅgula*) and whose only half of the nose is visible [is *Adhyardhākṣa*]. It has one side of one cheek measuring half a *mātrā* (1/2 *aṅgula*) and one [entire] side foreshortened *(ardhakṛtakṣayam).*

15. The region [lit. line] of the throat [on the foreshortened half] measures half a *mātrā* and that of the chin, a *yava* is shown. The front *(mukha)* of the chest is foreshortened by half and one *aṅgula* remains of the (foreshortened side of the) navel.

अध्यर्धशेषा च कटी अन्यच्चादर्शनी कृतम् ।
अध्यर्धाक्षं परिज्ञेयमाकारेणैवमादिना ।। १६ ।।

छायागतमिति प्रोक्तं पर्यायेणैतदेव तु ।
यस्यावलोक्यते पार्श्वं दक्षिणं सव्यमेव वा ।। १७ ।।

कृत्स्नमन्यत्क्षयं यातं तदङ्गसंहतिस्तथा ।
एकाक्षमेकभ्रूलेखमर्धनासाललाटवत् ।। १८ ।।

एकं श्रोत्रं ⁺पदार्धं⁺ स्याच्चिबुकार्धं शिरोरुहम् ।
अहीनमानलावण्यं माधुर्यादिगुणान्वितम् ।। १९ ।।

पार्श्वगतमिति प्रोक्तं तत्स्याद्भित्तिकसंज्ञितम् ।
अपाङ्गे ऽर्धकलाक्षीणे कण्ठदेशे तथैव च ।। २० ।।

16a. D अन्यर्द्ध- C अम्यर्ध- F अम्यर्द्धशेषाश्च N कंटी A कटे
16b. N अन्यच्चादर्श- V अन्यच्चदर्श S1S2 अन्यश्चादर्श-
16c. N अध्यद्धाक्ष- D अन्यर्द्धा Cf अम्यर्धाक्षं AN परिज्ञेयं- N -मकारे- A अकारे- CF-मकारलैवंमादिना D -मादिया
17a. F पर्यायेणेदेव B पर्यायेणेतदेव N पर्य्यायेणतदेव A पर्यायेनेतदेव 17c. N पार्श्व
18a. AB कृत्स्नमन्यत्क्षयातं V कृत्स्नमन्यर्क्षयातं D कृत्स्नमन्यक्षयं यात CF कृत्स्नमन्यत् < . > यात N कृत्स्नमन्यक्षयं यात
18b. CV तदङ्गमङ्ग- AB तमंगमंग- FD तमङ्गमङ्गगति N संगसंग-
18cd. D भ्रूलेखार्द्धनासा- N भ्रूल्लेखा अर्द्धनासा- ABCV भ्रूलेखमरनामा- F भ्रूलेखाभरनासा-
19a. ACND एक N पदर्द्ध ACDFV यदर्द्ध 19b ACDF -श्चिबुकार्ध N स्याश्चिकुकार्द्ध A चिबुकार्ध 19c. V गृहीतमान- 19cd CDFV -लावण्यमाधुर्यादि-
20a. BCDV पार्श्वा- B -गतिमिति 20b D -भित्तक- N -द्भिन्नक-
20c. ACFV अपाकुद्धे N अवाक्कुद्धेऽ D र्धे < कले? > BV कलक्षीणे AFS!S2 कले क्षीणे
20d. B कंठदेश

16. One and a half of the [unforeshortened] waist is visible [lit. is remaining] [whereas] the other half becomes invisible. (This) posture is known as *Adhyardhākṣa* (One and a half eyed) because of its appearance etc.

17ab. It is also known by its synonym, *Chāyāgata.*

V. *Pārśvāgata:*

17c-19. (That posture) whose only one side can be seen, either left side or right side, whose entire other side undergoes foreshortening and along with it disappears the symmetry of its body *(aṅgasaṃhati)*. It has one eye, one eyebrow, half a nose and forehead; one ear, *half the distance between the eyebrows (pada)*, half a chin and hairline; It is one whose loveliness is not devoid of proportion and full of qualities such as sweetness etc;

20ab. (Such a posture) is called *Pārśvāgata* (Profile). It is (also) called *Bhittika.*

बाहुगण्डललाटेषु कलार्धं क्षयमागतम् ।
बाहुवक्षःकटितटे स्फिग्गुल्फद्वयसेष्वपि ।। २१ ।।

द्विकलं द्विकलं 'ज्ञात्वा' यथाभागं कृशीकृतम् ।
अनुरूपप्रमाणेन नातितीक्ष्णाङ्गमेव च ।। २२ ।।

एतद् गण्डपरावृत्तं स्थानं च परिकीर्तितम् ।
पृष्टतो यदपि व्यक्तं देहबंधं मनोहरम् ।। २३ ।।

वलितश्लक्ष्णसर्वाङ्गं संधिबंधनमेव च ।
'ईषच्चदर्शितापाङ्गं' कपोलजठरेऽपुनः ।। २४ ।।

प्रकाशितैकपार्श्वेन सुस्थिरं दृष्टिहारि च ।
अहीनमानलावण्यं माधुर्यादिगुणान्वितम् ।। २५ ।।

21a. N बहुगण्ड-21b CF कलाख्यं ABFS2V कालाख्यं D कलाक्षं A क्षययागतम्
21cd. NV बाहुवक्षः CF बहुवक्षर्कटितटंस्थितिगु < .... > ष्वपि V बाहुवक्षः कटितटस्थिगु <..> A बाहुवक्ष्यः कटितटस्थितिगु < < ह्मतले > > ष्वपि N -स्थितिगुल्फद्वयेष्वपि D-स्फिविगुदेष्वपि
22a. F द्विकालंद्विकलं N द्विलकंद्विलक- 22b D यथा भाग F यथा भाचं V -कृमीकृतं
22c. D -प्रमाणश्च F रूपप्रमाणे च AS1S2 अणुरूपप्रमाणे च
23a. D एतदण्ड N एतत् गंत
23c. CF -व्यक्त A यदप्यव्यक्तं N यदधिष्वक्तं 23d N मनोहलम्
24a. N lacks 24a D < वन्धतिश्च? > ABCFS1S2 वक्रभ्रूश्लक्ष्णसर्वज्ञ- V वक्रभ्रूकुटिसर्वज्ञ- D वल्गतिश्चसर्वाङ्गं 24b. D < . > सन्धिवान्धरः
24c. CF ईषञ्च- A ईशच्च- CFV -दर्शितापाङ्ग AB -दर्शतापांग D -दलितायाङ्ग
24d. N कपालजठरं D -जठरं F पुनः C कपोलचठरे F थुनः
25a. N प्राकाशि- A प्रकाशतै 25b. F दृष्टहारि N दृष्टिहानि S!S2 दृढहारि
25c. ABCFS1S2V स्वहीन- 25d DFV लावण्य- C लावण्या-

VI. *Gaṇḍaparāvṛtta*:

20c-21b. When (one) corner of eye [of the figure] measures half a *kalā* and the throat region measures the same; the chin (arm ?), the cheek and the forehead are foreshortened by half a *kalā* (i.e. 1 *aṅgula*), [it is said to be in *Gaṇḍaparāvṛtta* posture).

21c-22b. [Its] arm, chest waist, buttocks are also right down to the ankle are foreshortened in the appropriate places by 4 *kalās* [lit. after doubling the *kalā*].

22cd. (The foreshortening should be done) in terms of correct proportion [so as not to] make the body look too angular *(nātitīkṣṇāṅgam)*.

23ab. This posture is called *Gaṇḍaparāvṛtta* (Averted by the cheek).

VII. *Pṛṣṭhāgata*:

23c-24. Even though the body is shown from the back, the joints of the body are beautiful of all the parts of the smooth body which are turned *(valitaślakṣṇasarvāṅga)*. (One half of the body is shown thus ?) The corner of the eye is shown slightly [but] the cheeks and the stomach not again *(apunaḥ)*.

25-26b. (This) posture which is very stable, beautiful to look at, whose loveliness is not devoid of proportion, and is full of qualities such as sweetness etc. It is called *Pṛṣṭhāgata* in painting and sculpture.

लेख्येषु पुस्तदेशेषु पृष्ठागतमिति स्मृतम् ।
यस्यार्द्धमङ्गं पादोनभागेन तमवस्थितम् ।। २६ ।।

स्थितेऽप्यभिमुखेऽर्धाङ्ग परिवृत्तिवशाद्भवेत् ।
किञ्चिच्छायागताकार उपरिष्टादतः पुनः ।। २७ ।।

अर्धार्धगतसारूप्यं विरसं ग्राम्यसंस्थितम् ।
मध्येन नेत्ररम्येण यथायोगविलोपना ।। २८ ।।

विज्ञेयमग्रतः कायं परिवृत्तं नरेश्वर ।
समग्रदृष्टस्फिग्देशं दृष्टपादतलं च यत् ।। २९ ।।

ऊर्ध्वतःक्षीणपृष्ठार्धं दृश्यशेषकटिस्थलम् ।
लुप्तपादाङ्गुलितलं दृश्यारत्नितलद्वयम् ।। ३० ।।

26a. ABCV लेखेषु D -देशेषु

26c. N यस्यार्द्धमगपत्येन VS1S2 यस्योर्धमङ्गपत्येन ABCF यस्योर्ध्वमङ्गपत्येन D यस्योर्ध्वमङ्गमध्येन

27a. NF स्थितेप्याभिमुखेवाङ्गे V स्थितेर्ष्याभिमुखेर्धाङ्गे 27b. D चाङ्गो A-वृत्तिवशाद्भवेत्

27cd, DN किञ्चि:छायागताकार ACFV किञ्चिश्छायागतौ BS1S2 किञ्चिम्कार्यागतौ CFS1S2 कार्य उपरिष्टादधः पुरः BS!S2V कार्यावुपरिष्टादधः पुरः- DN -कार उपविष्टादधः पुनः

28a. N lacks 28ab. 28b. ABCF विरस- V चिरसग्रा- D रसवता < or भा? > स्य

28d. ABV विलोपिना N विलेपिना

29ab. AD विज्ञेयं तदधः ACFNV दधतः D कायपरिवृत्तं N काय V कार्यं

29c. CDFV दृष्टिस्फिग्देशं A -स्फिक्देशं 29d AV दृष्टंपाद CF दृष्टिपादतलं V तु यत्

30a. D क्षीणपृष्ठार्द्धं Nक्षीणाष्टष्ठार्द्ध ABCF दृष्टार्धं 30b. CFNDV दृश्या- AB दुष्टाशेष- V शेषं

30c. D लुप्तपादाङ्गुलतलं CFS1S2 लुपातपादाङ्गुललितं

30d. AB दृश्यारंतितलद्वयम् V दृश्याशेषतलद्वयम् C दृश्यपत्नितलद्वयम्

VIII. *Purovṛtta:*

26c-27. (That posture) whose half of the body is foreshortened to three-fourths of a *bhāga* [which is] 3 *aṇgulas (padonabhāga),* [is called *Purovṛtta*]. Even though it has the other half facing the front, having been rotated, it is somewhat like *Chāyāgata* [of *Adhyardhalocana*] in appearance (seen) from behind again.

28-29b. A quarter-based symmetry *(ardhārdhagatasārūpyam)* is lacking in interest *(virasa)* and vulgar *(grāmyasaṁsthitam)* [lit. established in villages]. O king, [that posture] is known as frontally rotated body *(agrataḥ kāyāparivṛtta)* [brought about] by an intermediary *(madhya)* [angle of vision] which is pleasing to the eye and by the appropriate foreshortening.

IX. *Samānata:*

29c-30. (That posture) in which the buttocks and the soles of the feet are fully visible [and] the half of the back is foreshortened vertically [is called *Samānata*]. The waist is visible [from the back] and the toes and the front part of the soles is foreshortened. The elbows *(aratnitala)* are [also] visible on either side.

चतुरस्रं सुसम्पूर्णमभयानकदर्शनम् ।
प्रकाशीकृतबाहूर्धमदृष्टमुखकन्धरम् ।। ३१ ।।

+ विलुप्तस्यैकतं + ज्ञेयं नाम्ना स्थानं समानतम् ।
नवान्येतानि सर्वाणि तथोक्तैः प्रविभागशः ।। ३२ ।।

लक्षणैर्लक्षितव्यानि त्वयानुक्रममेव च ।
एषां प्रज्ञाविशेषेण विकाराणि बहून्यपि ।। ३३ ।।

एकैकशश्चन भूभागे कर्तव्यानि यथाविधि ।
त्रयमानं समासाद्य सम्यग्मानं तदन्तरे ।। ३४ ।।

स्थानानीमानि मानाद्यैर्गुणैर्लेख्यानि यत्नतः ।
नवैवैतानि दृष्टानि सर्वभागेष्वनिन्दितम् ।। ३५ ।।

31b. D -भयाकन- 31cd. D प्रकाशकृतबाहूर्ध्व- S!S2 बाहुवर्धमदृष्ट- CF -बाहुवनमदृष्ट- BV बाहुश्च सुदष्ट- F -मुखन्धरम् N बाहुवनं अदृष्टसुखकम्बलम्

32a. N विलुप्तस्यैकंत- F लुप्तै जङ्कैकतो D लुप्तजंङ्गैकत- ABCV लुप्तंजङ्गैकतो

32b. FN स्थान- N -समानत ABCFV समानतः D समातनम्

32c. N नवात्येतानि CF नवचान्येतानि ABV नीचान्येतानि D स्थानान्येतानि

32d. V तथोक्तै- F तथोक्त- ABCFV -र्भिराजितम् N-भिचारितम् D रभिगामिभिः

33a. CDFV लक्षितैर्

33b. V त्वयानुक्रमशो D त्वयानुक्रमणेने A तयानुक्रमशो CF क्रमको CFV नव AN नवा

33c. ABCFN एषा CFV प्रज्ञावशेषेण

34a. ABCFN एकैकशेन D एकैकन्येन N भागस्तु ABV भूभागैः S!S2 भ्रूभागैः CF भ्रूभागः D भ्रूभागक-

34b. V यथावधि 34c N त्वया मानःसमासाद्य ABCFV सन्तस्समासाद्य ABCDV त्वया D षन्तःसमासाद्य F त्वषा 34d N सम्यक्मानं CF सम्यमानत A सम्यङमनं D सम्यगान- CFN भूतले ADV तु भूतले

35d. AB सर्वभावेषु निन्दितम् D सर्वाभावेषु निन्दित CFV सर्वभावेष्वनिन्दित

31. It is beautiful from all sides, beautifully accomplished, without appearing dangerous (?) with [only] the upper part of the arm made visible and the face and the shoulders, unvisible.

32ab. This posture is called *Samānatam* (Completely Bent).

32c-34. All these new [postures] can be characterised (*lakṣitavyāni*) according to their distinguishing marks already mentioned (*tathoktaiḥ lakṣaṇaiḥ*) by you following the [same] division (*pravibhāgaṣaḥ*) and order (*anukramam*). These can have many more variations (*vikārāṇi*) with specialised skill (*prajñāviśeṣena*[1]). Make three [main] divisions of a single quadrant [of a circle] one after another (*ekaikaśyena*) and then all the [further] divisions (*samyagmānam*) be made in between (*tadantare*) [the main divisions].

35. O Blameless One, these postures (i.e. nine in a quadrant) can be visualised (*dṛṣṭāni*) in all the [remaining] three quadrants (*sarvabhāgeṣu*) [and] should be carefully drawn by multiplying the *mānas* etc. [divisions and subdivisions][2].

1. The other possible interpretation which expresses a more technical sense is "by means of a different design/ arrangement/ scheme of distribution."
2. The primary mānas amount to 3 giving rise to 4 intervals and the secondary ones are 4 making the total number of intervals to 8. Technically, it is these intervals which are referred here which are to be multiplied by 4 (standing for the quadrants) bringing the total number of postures in a circle to 32.

स्थानानि नाधिकमतः परमस्ति हि किञ्चन ।
जीवलोकं परिक्रम्य सततं स्थाणुजङ्गमम् ।। ३६ ।।

उत्तमाधममध्येषु प्रमाणगुणतस्सदा ।
चित्रं विचित्रमद्वैधं प्रमाणत्रयमेव च ।। ३७ ।।

क्षयवृद्धी च कार्त्स्न्येन मया तेऽभिहिते नृप ।
अतः परं प्रवक्ष्यामि क्षयवृद्धिविधिं क्रमात् ।। ३८ ।।

चित्रविद्भिरसंज्ञेयं समासेनेतरेण च ।
त्रयोदशविधैवात्र क्षयवृद्धिरुदाहृता ।। ३९ ।।

स्थानानां बहुसंख्यत्वादङ्गावयवसंभवा ।
स्थानं ऋज्वागतं पूर्वमर्धर्जुगतमेव च ।। ४० ।।

36a. N < . > धिकमतः AC नाधिकतमः B नाधिकततः 36b. AD किं चिन
36c. N जीवलोक 36d. C स्थानुजङ्गैङ्गम् A स्थानं जगमम् N स्थानजंगमम्
37c. ABCDFVN त्रिविधं 37d AV प्रमाणं N प्रमाणत्रयनुवच
38a. V कात्स्येन 38b N ते भिहितानृप V तेऽभिहिते ऽनघ
38d. N क्षयवृद्धिविधिः A क्षयवृद्धिविधो CF क्षयवृद्धिवधो S1S2 क्षयवृद्धीवीधी
39a. A चित्रविद्धार- D चित्रचिभिर-
39c. N-विधिचांत्र 39d N रूदाहताः A -रूचाहृता
40ab. N बहुसंख्यत्वादं CFV बहुसंस्थत्वाद- A बहुसंस्थतादंगावयव- D बहुसंस्थिद्वाद-
40c. AB स्थानपृष्टगतं S1S2 पृष्टगतं D पृष्टगता CF दृष्टगतं
40d. ABV -वर्जुगतमेव CFN अवर्जगतमेव

36. Having circumambulated the entire world of immovable and movable things, I have not found any posture which is superior to and surpassing the [given] postures.

37. The *Uttama* (Best), *Madhyama* (middling) and *Adhama* (Inferior) [types of postures] based on the criterion of manifoldness / variety of postures/ proportions, *(Pramāṇaguṇataḥ)*[3] are [also] classifiable into the variegated *(Citra)*, hyper-variegated *(Vicitra)* and variety-less/ unique *(Advaidha)*.

38. O King, you have been told by me the (rules of) foreshortening in its entirety. Now, I shall speak about the method of foreshortening *(kṣayavṛddhividhi)* in due order.

39-40b. (Regarding the application of foreshortening), there is no harmony of opinion reached by the experts in painting either in its concise or detailed form. Here, foreshortening has been exemplified by (only) a thirteenfold examples for [it is not possible to list them completely] because of the countless variations arising from different parts of the body.

40cd. *Ṛjvāgata* is the first, followed by *Ardharju*.

3. It can be further explained as "the 'multipliability' of the proportions/ postures". That is, the more varieties a posture yields, the higher its status.

अध्यर्धांक्षं पुरोवृत्तं साचीकृतमुखं तथा ।
नतं गण्डपरावृत्तं पृष्ठागतमथापि च ।।४१ ।।

पार्श्वागतं च विज्ञेयमुल्लेपं चलितं तथा ।
उत्तानं वलितं चेति स्थानानि तु त्रयोदश ।।४२ ।।

कार्याण्येतानि सर्वाणि नामसंस्थानतो नृप ।
मण्डलानीह वैशाखप्रत्यालीढक्रियाक्रमैः ।।४३ ।।

समाश्चार्द्धसमाः पादाः सुस्थितानि चलानि च ।
समासमपदस्थं च द्विविधं स्थानकं भवेत् ।।४४ ।।

तद् ऋज्वापदभूयिष्ठं स्थानं समपदं स्मृतम् ।
मण्डलं च द्वितीयं स्यात्स्थानान्यन्यानि यानि च ।।४५ ।।

41a. ABCFVD मध्यार्धाधं तथाधार्धं N मध्याधावं तथाधार्द्धं 41b N साचीमुखकृतं
41c. N ततः 41d. N –थापि वा
42a. N पश्चात्गतं C विज्ञेयुल्लेषं 42b.N उल्लोमं F -मुल्लर्षं A चवितं D वलिनं
42c. N उत्तानं चलितं F वर्णितं D वडिल्लतां
43a. A कार्याणि तानि
43c. CF- lack मण्डलानीह वै D वैशाखं
43d. N –क्रियाक्रमौ D –क्रियाक्रमे A –क्रयाक्रमैः
44a. S1S2 समासार्धसमाः FN समसार्द्धसमः C समसार्धतमः A समसर्धसमा- D समार्द्धसमपादानि B समायार्द्धसमः N पाद AF पादा
44c. C समासपदस्थं N समासपदसंस्थं 44d. D द्विविध S1S2 द्विविधे स्थानके ABCFN स्थानके
45a. V तद्रत्वा D –तत्रर्जयमभूयिष्ठं C –ऋज्वापद- N भवज्वापादं 45b. D समयतं

41-42. (Then) *Adhyardhākṣa* (One and a half eyed), *Purovṛtta* (Frontally Reverted), *Sācīkṛta* (Averted), *Nata* (Bent), *Gaṇḍaparāvṛtta* (Turned away by the cheek), *Pṛṣṭhāgata* (Backview), *Pārśvāgata* (Profile), *Ullepa* (Sporting), *Calita* (Walking), *Uttāna* (reclining) and *Valita* (turning around) - are the thirteen types of postures.

43. O King, all these [i.e. the following] shooting postures ought to be made here according to [their] appearance in a regular succession of the action [made by] *Vaiśākha* and *Pratyālīḍha*. [4]

44. The feet are straight or partially straight [depending on whether] they are stationary or in motion. [Combined] with straight [i.e.stationary stance] and partially straight [i.e. in motion], the stance *(sthānaka)* evolves into two types.

45abc. [The first type i.e.] is called *Samapada* and has straight legs [unbent] as its distinguishing feature *(Ṛjvāpadabhūyiṣṭha)*. The second type is the *Maṇḍala* (shooting posture).

4. *Vaiśākha* and *Pratyālīḍha* are two types of shooting postures. In *Pratyālīḍha*, the left foot is advanced and right is drawn back.

तान्येकसमपादानि विचित्राणि चलानि च ।
तत्र वैशाखमालीढं प्रत्यालीढं च धन्विनाम् ।।४६ ।।
चित्रगोमूत्रकगतं विषमं खड्गचर्मिणाम् ।
चलितं स्खलितायस्तमालीढैकपदक्रमम् ।।४७ ।।

शक्तितोमरपाषाणभिन्दिपालादिधारिणाम् ।
सवल्गितं चक्रशूलगदाकुणपधारिणाम् ।।४८ ।।

एकपादसमस्थानं द्वितायेन तु विह्वलम् ।
शरीरं च सलीलं स्यात्सावष्टम्भैः क्वचिद् वृत्तम् ।।४९ ।।

लीलाविलासविभ्रान्तं विशालजघनस्थलम् ।
स्थिरैकपादविन्यासं स्त्रीरूपं विलिखेद् बुधः ।।५० ।।

प्रमाणहीनस्तु जनोऽस्ति भूयान्
कालस्य भावस्य बलात्पृथिव्याम्
इति प्रचिन्त्यात्मधिया बुधेन
कार्यं प्रमाणं क्षयवृद्धियोगे ।।५१ ।।

इति श्रीविष्णुधर्मोत्तरे तृतीयखण्डे मार्कण्डेयवज्रसंवादे चित्रसूत्रे क्षयवृद्ध्यध्यायो नाम एकोनचत्वारिंशत्तमोऽध्यायः ॥ ३९ ।।

46a. AS1S2 -समुपादानि D समसानि 46b D वलानि N चा
46c. A वैशाखमलीढं D वेशाख- 46d. Aधन्विताम् N धन्वितं
47a. CF -शतं 47b. N खड्गचर्म्मिणं
47cd. ABV खलितायस्तमाली- N कलितं A वलितं D स्तसालीचैक-
N शूलितायस्कमालीढै- 48b AN -भिण्डिपाला- N -दिधारिणम्
48cd. N सवल्भित CF -चक्रस्थल- A गदाकणपधारिणाम् F -करणपधरिणाम् C गदाकरणायधारिणाम् D गदाकरणधारिणां N गदायंनयंधारिणं
49a. NS1S2 एकपादंसमस्थानं S1S2 समं AB एकपादसमं F -सुप्रस्थानं
49b. ABVS1S2 विङ्गलम् D विद्वल 49c. Fसुलीलं N च शरीरं
49d. A-सावष्टम्भै CF स्यात्सावष्टकैः N -साचष्टम्भैः
CN क्वचिदवृतं A कुविद्रुतम् ADFV दुतम्
50a. C -विमासविभ्रान्तं F -विसासविभ्रान्ते N विविनाशविभ्रान्तं
50b. N विनाशजघन- A -जगन- 50b. ACDFN -कपद-
51a. N जनास्ति ABCD भूयात्कालस्य V जनोऽनुभूयात्कालस्य N क्षयात्कालस्य N हलापृथि- (N lacks 51ab). 51d. CF प्रमाणक्षय-

45d-46. And amongst the postures which are different, are those which have one foot kept straight and [the other] in various movements. Amongst them, are the [postures] *Vaiśākha, Alīḍha* and *Pratyālīḍha* for the arches.

47-48b. The bearers of sword and shield have a dynamic and fascinating *"gomutrika"* [zig-zag] stance.

Persons holding a lance, a javelin, a stone and an arrow etc. should be walking, staggering, exerting and shooting respectively.

48cd. Those carrying, a wheel, a spear, a mace and a lance should be leaping.

49-50. The wise [painter] should depict a female form [in the following manner]- One foot should be made straight and the other languid. The body should be made pliant in some part and firm in some.

The enormous hips should be [depicted] swaying in playful abandon. One leg should be stiff [while the other, relaxed].

51. People in this world, as a rule, lack [fixed] proportion because of being conditioned by time. Keeping this in mind, the proportion is determined by the wise [artist] using his own discretion, in conjunction with the [laws] of foreshortening.

NOTES TO ADHYĀYA 39

39.1a. *vikārāṇi*. I have accepted PS's conjecture against the *-vihārāṇi* of the MSS. This emendation (not incorporated in PS's edition) facilitated by the similarity between -k- and -h- in the *Śāradā* script. *Vikārāṇi* in 33d further supports it. PS takes the compound as "having ordinary forms and their modifications" or "having forms and emotions". I take it as "having transformations *(-vikārāṇi)* whose forms are beautiful *(śubhākārā)*".

39.2a. *ardharju tadanantaram.* None of the MSS retains the correct reading. Sense, grammar and usage in parallel art treatises strongly suggest the emendation of *Avarju* (CFD) to *Aṛdharju.* Cf SamSūtDhār. (infra). The similarity between -va- and -dha- in *Śāradā* supports it. SM emends to *syād anantaram* to restore the metre. But this is unnecessary. A final *pada* which begins with a run of five short syllables *(ardharju tada-)* is unusual but not irregular.

39.2d. *bhavatyadhyardhalocanam.* Thus I emend the *bhavaty-ardhavilocanam* of all the MSS and the translation. I do so because the context clearly indicates a reference to a view of the face in which we can see one eye completely and half of the other, i.e. the three quarter profile. *Ardhavilocana* would here mean "[a view of the face] in which one can see only 1/2 of one eye" But this view cannot be intended here since it is mentioned separately under the term *parāvṛtta-* in v.3b. It would seem that *ardhavilocana* arose by the insertion of -vi- to restore the metre after the loss by corruption of the initial adhy- The emendation is further supported by parallel accounts in SamSūtDhār. (81), MānUll. (1.3.372-373) and ŚilpRat. (64). These mention *adhyardhākṣa* and *dvyardhākṣa* in the corresponding position. The first, for eg., lists 1. *Ṛjvāgata* 2. *Ardharjvāgata* 3. *Sācīkṛta* 4. *Adhyardhākṣa* ..... SK (p. 37) translates, ("the position with one eye (lit, with half eyes) *(ardhavilocanam)*". PS (p. 111) and SM (p. 176) list it a *ardhavilocana.*

39.3b. *parāvṛttam.* I have followed N and D since this reading alone yields an appropriate sense meaning "turned away". It is a fitting description of the face turned away from the spectator until only the corner of the eye is visible.

SK (p. 37) only had an access to V's reading- *purāvṛttam* which is amended to *parāvṛttam*:

> Then comes the "Cheek-turned" position *(parāvṛttam)*, it is explained in the foot note thus:
>
> F.N. 1. The text has Purāvṛttam a copyist's slip for parāvṛttam cf verses 20-24.

PS accepts the reading of C,F and V -*purāvṛttam* in the text but emends it in the translation to "*parāvṛttam*". (p. 112)

SM follows the reading of C, F and V -*purāvṛttam.*

It is clear from the order in which the postures are given that the human figure was rotated a full circle stage by stage around its axis. At stage VI i.e. posture 6, it is averted i.e. turned away from the viewer and at stage VIII, posture 8, the body turns towards the stationary viewer. The text seems to signify the former by *parāvṛtti* and the latter by *purovṛtti* or "frontally averted".

39.3d. *purovṛttam.* This reading has been accepted from V which restores the technical sense. It is derived as follows: *puras* + *vṛtta* = *purovṛttam.* It differs from *parāvṛttam* in so far as it is "turned [partially] towards the front". SK emends V's reading *purāvṛttam* to *parivṛttam.*

Note that the emendation of *dadhataḥ* to *agrataḥ* in verse 29a reiterates the sense conveyed by *purovṛttam.* PS (p. 112) emends *parāvṛttam* found in B, N and D to *parivṛttam* on the basis of verse 29.

The reading in our text are *purāvṛttam* (Slo. 3a) and *parāvṛttam* (Slo. 3b). These should be corrected as *parāvṛttam* and *parivṛtta* respectively in the light of verse 23 (*gaṇḍaparāvṛttam*) and 26 (*parivṛttam*).

My emendation above weakens the argument put forward by SK and PS. SM adopts *parāvṛttam.*

39.4b. *bhupate.* This is N and D's reading against all other MSS *(bhūṣite)*, confirming PS's conjecture and SM's emendation. SK (p. 37) follows in the corrupt reading from V and translates:

In painting (bhūṣite),....

39.4c. *bhaṇataḥ*. Neither *bhavataḥ* (ABCDFV) nor *bhavati* (N) yields sense. The emendation gives the meaning -"O King, listen to me as I speak about each of the characteristics".

Note the various translations:

SK now (Oh) King, hear from me, one by one, (what is) the nature of each of them *(and how) it comes into existence.* (p. 37)

PS leaves it untranslated.

SM does not translate *bhaṇataḥ ...me.*

39.5b. *spaṣṭamānaguṇānvitam.* All the scholars miss the technical sense. SK (p. 37) translates this compound as:

> In this way it is *accompanied by the various organs of sense.* [4]
>
> 4. i.e., in this way all the organs of sense (the 2 eyes, mouth, nose,ears) are visible.

Pramāṇaguṇa here means "cord/string employed for measuring the body". And *spaṣṭa* means "straight" as opposed to crooked or oblique. Cf. *yattiryagbhūmilambena* in verse 10a recommended for *sācīkṛta* posture. The compound means "with the measuring thread straight". In all the other postures the measuring thread *(mānaguṇa)* is oblique; See Diag. II. In this posture, which is fully frontal, foreshortening is kept to a minimum. The body is completely parallel to the *brahmasūtra* and the *pakṣasūtras.*

SK takes the compound to mean "accompanied by the organs of sense". PS (p. 112) has "The quality of its measurements (mānaguṇa) is distinct". SM (p. 176) has "clear in its proportion and characteristics". In none of these interpretations does the compound differentiate the *Ṛjvāgata* from the other figures. Also Cf. the definition of *Ṛjvāgata* given in the CitSūt. with that in Mān Ull. :

> सम्मुखं स्यादृजुस्थानं परभागोऽत्र नेष्यते ।। ३७९ . अ१ व.३
> पूर्वभागगतं गात्रं सम्पूर्णं दृश्यते स्फुटम् । ३८०

39.6d. *ṛjvāgatam.* Only D preserves this reading. All other manuscripts show *pṛṣṭāgatam,* an error affecting the C group and its presence in

N can only be through contamination. D's reading confirms PS's conjecture and SM's emendation. SK (p. 38) follows V's corrupt reading- *pṛṣṭāgatam* :

> *the portions on the back* should be without foreshortening (lit. diminished limbs).[1]

39.7a. *mukham syād ardhataḥ kṣīṇam.* CF's *mukhasyādavatokṣīṇa* is obviously corrupt. N's *sukhasyādardhato 'kṣīṇam* and D's *sukhasyādardhataḥ kṣīṇam* are also corrupt but suggest the emendation. The fact that *Śāradā* -ma- and -sa- are so similar is the probable cause of their corruption. D's *ardhataḥ kṣīṇam* is preferred to N's *ardhato' kṣīṇam* because the former expresses the partial foreshortening required by the context. CF's corruption of ***ardhato*** to ***avato*** is evidently due to the similarity of *Śāradā* -rdh- and -v-. What *ardhataḥ* means in this context is that the foreshortening takes place in one half of the body (i.e. from C to B, see Diagrams I and II. By implication, with every decrease in proportion in one side of the body say CB there is the same degree of increase on the side AC.

Both SK and PS follow V's reading *-mukhasyādāvato* which is a step removed from the correct reading:

SK (p. 38) takes it as a part of the defination of the previous posture namely the *ṛjvāgata:*

> *The front view, face,* chest and abdomen should also remain *unforeshortened, (undiminished)...*

PS (p. 112) :

> In the anṛju sthāna *the frontal position has undiminished* chest and abdomen...

This contradicts the context. The body at this stage undergoes a certain degree of rotation (22.5 approximately) and the diminution sets in along one half of the body.

SM (p. 176) is misled by CFV's corrupt reading :

> That is *Aṇṛju* where the *face is full and undiminished,* ....

39.7cd. *kaṭyās ca sphigpradeśāc ca ūrūtalaṃ gatam.* N and F's ablative *kaṭyāśca* makes better sense than the instrumental *kaṭyā* of the other MSS. A greater problem is posed by the *skandhadeśācca ūrutaś ca* which follows. It cannot be sound since it refers to subject to make it intelligible. Since the text is proceeding down the body and has just mentioned the stomach, I emend *ūrutaśca* to *ūrutalaṃ* (thighs), making this the subject; and emend *skandhadeśāc ca,* which is incomprehensible in the context, to *sphikpradeśāc ca.* In *Śāradā* -dh- and -pr- are similar enough to invite confusion, as are -sk-and-sph. The corruption *ūrutaś ca* may be attributed to the influence of the preceding ablatives + ca. SK (p.38) takes 7b as a part of the description of *ṛjvāgatam* :

> (The figures) (Oh) Intelligent one, *grow narrower towards the waist from the thighs* (as well) as *from the shoulders.*

PS: .... and the *portions from waist to shanks and shoulders are diminished.* (p. 112)

SM: .... waist, *shoulder,* thigh are slightly diminished, "(p. 176).

39. 8c. *tribhāgam.* To understand the measurement of the foreshortening given in the CitSūt. in terms of fractions, we need to look at this chapter as whole and also to study similar measurements in other sources. The MānUll. is much more systematic in regarding these measurements. It divides the body vertically into three divisions by means of three perpendiculars. The central, which divides the body into two equal parts, is called the *brahmasūtra* (represented in the diagram as C). The other two on either side of it ("lateral cords") pass through the nipples - (represented in the diagram as A and B). Supposing the body is rotated in the anti-clockwise direction, and that the viewer is fixed to one spot, then the distance between C and B would decrease as that between A and C increases. In other words, if the viewer is stationary as the figure is rotated he will see the distance between A and C increased. In the MānUll. the measurements for the 5 postures are given as follows:

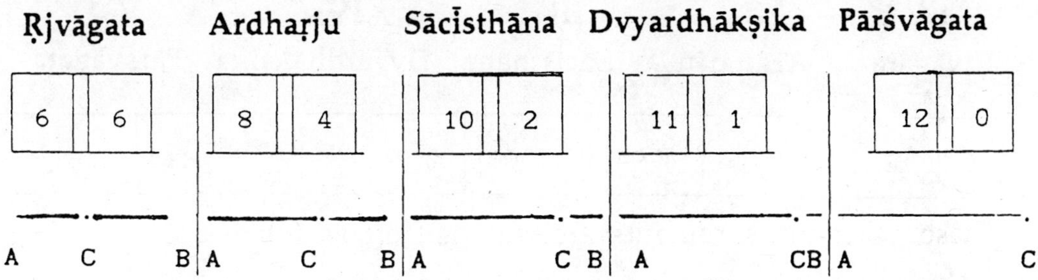

The basis of these measurements in both texts is the distance between the two nipples, points A and B. In MānUll. the distance between them is a *tāla* or 12 *aṅgulas* therefore there are 6 *aṅgulas* on either side.

द्वयोश्चूचुकयोर्मध्ये तालमानमुदाहृतम् । २९० .अ. १. वि. ३

In the frontal posture, the central line C is equidistant from the "lateral lines". With every rotation to the right, the right hand side of the body is seen to contract. The distance between C and B reduces and that between A and B increases, so that the left hand side increases in the manner stated in the CitSūt. in which the distance between the nipples is 16 *aṅgulas.* षोडशाङ्गुलं स्तनान्तरम्। III.1. adh. 35

Despite this discrepancy, the CitSūt. seems to follow the same formula of foreshortening the MānUll. states in greater detail. In both cases, between the frontal posture which is at 0 degree and the one in profile in which the body has rotated 90 degree, there are 3 stages.

So the interval between each of the five stages is a fourth of a right angle, i.e. 90 degrees by divided 4, 22.5 which equals degrees. For the sake of these calculations, we need to suppose either (i) the human figure (ii) the viewing point is fixed. Refer to the diagrams I and II following the two possibilities and the results in both are the same. There is another constant necessary to such deductions namely that distance between the figure and the vantage be fixed. The results from the measurements given in the CitSūt. are as follows, calculated according to the trignometric formula 8±8 sin (X x 22.5):

Note that the results for the 5 postures from this formula are :

I		II		III		IV		V	
Ṛjvāgata		Ardharju		Sācīsthāna		Dvyardhākṣika		Pārśvāgata	
8	8	11.06	4.94	13.66	2.34	15.39	0.61	16	0

These exact measurements are rounded off as follows:

I		II		III		IV		V	
8	8	11	5	14	2	15	1	16	0

As for the *tribhāga* of posture II, understand it as 1/3 rd of the foreshortened half of the body i.e. 8 (i.e. 2.66 rounded of to 8 - 3 = 5). This agrees with the table above or it could be taken as 1/3 of AB (16*aṅgulas*), i.e. 5.33.

SK takes *gātra-* as "limbs" rather than "body" and verse 8 as the definition of posture I:

> and their *limbs* are foreshortened by a third part (*of their breadth*) [2]
>
> 2. The second position 'anriju' is not described; it is the reverse of the first one. (p. 38)

PS: The *three-fourth* of the *limbs* is diminished. (p.112)

SM: ... only *three fourths* of the*from is visible,* (p. 176)

39.9a. *kāntaṁrūpadharam.* I have emended " *kantā* " of all the MSS on grounds of meaning. *Kāntārūpaparam* of MSS AV I take to be a secondary corruption. SK overlooks verse 9cd in the translation, which explains the footnote cited above to the effect that the text lacks a reference to posture II.

PS (p. 112) and SM (p. 176) follow MSS AV translating as follows: PS: This is an *excellent* beautiful sthāna .....

SM: ... and that beautiful *to behold,*....

39.9b. *stanalambopapāditam.* All the manuscripts have *sthānā*-which I take to be corruption of *stana-*, of the error echoing *sthāna-* in the preceding compound. The perpendiculars *(lamba)* passing through the nipples on either side of the *brahmasūtra* were used to measure the increase and decrease in proportion on either side. To extract an appropriate sense from *sthānalamba-* by translating "the perpendiculars (for measuring the) postures" would not explain what point there is in mentioning *sthāna* at all.

PS: This is an excellent beautiful sthāna accomplished by sthānalamba *i.e. by proper perpendicular position.* (p. 112)

SM: .... *with its pose as a fitting background* for several lovely *karaṇa* stances. (p. 176)

39. 10a. *yat tiryagbhūmilambena.* It seems from the measurements given in all the cases of foreshortening, that the two dimensional projection of the foreshortened side was determined by deducting the distance between the lateral-line B3 say in posture II and the base line A1B1. The remaining distance stands for the projection of the foreshortened half. (see Diagram II). So what the compound means is "that which is oblique with or to the perpendicular". This, as the text continues, is to be reduced to its (i.e. one half consisting of 8 *aṅgulas*) quarter which is equal to 2 *aṅgulas.* Note that in diagram II, the perpendicular joining B3 and the base line measures is 5.6 cm. When this is subtracted from 8, it gives 2.4, which has been rounded down to 2. Note all the translations overlook this sense:

SK: What (looks) charming due to the attainment of a curved posture(triyak), (p.38). In the sācīkṛtaśarīra the bhūmilamba - perpendicular *reaching the ground level is sideways.* (p. 112)

SM: That is *Sāchīkṛta* which has a *horizontal background,* (p. 176)

39. 10cd. *caturbhāgakṣīṇam.* This reading from N refers to the foreshortened half reduced to 1/4 i.e. 2 *aṅgulas.* So the ratio between the increase on side AC and the decrease on CB is 14 : 2. SK takes *kṣīṇam* as "slender"

.... well rounded, tender, *all over (lit. all the four parts being) slender* .....(p. 38)

PS: It is diminished by caturbhāga[2] i.e. one quarter.

F.N. 2. According to Kbhi. Cintā, and Śilparatna a bhāga is equal to 4 aṅgulas. If we accept this measurement caturbhāga means 'diminished by one aṅgula' but Abhi Ci. and Śilparatna show the bhūmilamba 'diminished by 2 aṅgulas'. (p.112)

Note that this problem of discrepancy can be resolved by taking *caturbhāga* as a "quarter" of 8 *aṅgulas.*

SM: ... with a fourth part diminished. (p. 176)

This does not specify what whole is this a fourth part of.

39.11a. *ghrāṇapuṣkaram.* N's reading has been adopted. All the editiors seem to follow V's reading *-ghrāṇamutkaṭam* which must be corrupt. Note *puṣkara* means 'the tip of an elephant's trunk". SK does not translate *-mutkaṭam.*

PS: Similarly the *high bridged* nose. (p. 112)

SM: .... and *raised* nose,.....(p. 176)

39.11c. *bhāgadvayā-.* (>N). It is not clear whether D reads *bhāgadvaya-* or *bhāgatraya-.* All the other manuscripts show *bhāgakṣaya-*which makes no sense in the context. The reading from N which means "2 out of a *bhāga/4 aṅgulas*" is equal to 2 *a.ıgulas* which is the measurement of the foreshortened half. This is consistent with *caturbhāgam* i.e. "1/4 th of 8" which equals 2 *aṅgulas* mentioned earlier in verse 10b. SK connects this compound *bhāgakṣaya-* with *kṣīṇalocanam*:

The eye that represents the half that remains after division (i.e. the one eye that is to be seen in profile) is foreshortened.....(p. 38)

PS: The remaining half is diminished by a *bhāga* i.e. 4 *aṇgulas* (p. 112)

SM : .... the remaining half of the *body visible,....* (p. 176-177)

39.11d *kalārdhākṣīnalocanam.* This emends CF's *kalāpaksīṇam.* The sense is that the size of the diminished eye is 1 *aṅgulas* i.e. 1/2 a *kalā (kalārdha-).* In the *Śāradā* script of CF -p- and -rdh- are easily confused. SK translates *kalāpakṣīṇalocanam-* as:

The eye ..... is foreshortened (lit. suppressed) by artistic means.... (p. 38)

PS: The eye is diminished by *a kalā* i.e. 2 *aṅgulas* (p. 112)

SM: ... the eye diminished *slightly,.....* (p. 177)

39.12cd. *na ca chāyāgatākāram na cāṛdharjukalopamam.* Neither D's *na ca hāyāgatakara* nor ACFV's *-gatam kālam* give sense; but they and the context suggest the emendation. An alternative , *-gatam kāryam,* is closer to the Kashmirian MSS but the meaning is clumsier and takes us further from D. The metre requires that the 6th and 7th syllables be lengthened to *-tākāra. Cāvarjukopanam* in C and F is a corruption of *cārdha* (-v- and -rdh- look alike in the *Śāradā* script) The emendation is made on the basis of context. '*Kala*' in '*cardharjukalopamam*' is understood as a unit of measurement employed in the posture mentioned.

The term *ardharjuka* appears at MānUll.

उत्केऽप्यर्धर्जुके स्थाने .... verse 383b, *viṃ.* 3,*adhy.*1

The meaning that the emendation conveys is this; "This posture i.e. *Sācīkṛta* (III) is neither like *Anṛju* (posture II) nor like *Adhyardhalocanam* (posture IV)." It is the posture intermediate between posture II and posture IV. (see the Diagrams I and II). SK follows V's reading –न च च्छायागतं कालं न चावऋजुकोपनम् :

> The face is neither straight nor irritating, neither black nor shady (p. 39)

PS: The *black part of the eye* should not be *shaded* (chāyāgata),[1] nor should be *straight* (Ṛju), nor should it be *as in anger* (kopanam).

> F.N.1. Dr. Stella Kramrisch the word chāyāgata as "coming out of the shade". Chāyayā āgata, (2) Chāyāṃ gatam -gone to the shadow or shade i.e. not even in silhouette. It should not be shown (?). (p. 113)

SM emends it to :

न च छायागतं वालं च चापि ऋजुकोपनम् [6]

> F.N. 6. It is ऋजुकोपमम् and not ऋजुकोपनम् No anger is meant here. It means it is not like ऋजु either. (p. 146)

One is tempted to agree that the original ended in *-upamam,* considering *-ākāram* in the preceding pāda. Unfortunately, the text restored does not yield the appropriate sense. The present posture is not intermediate between posture I and V as SM takes it but between II and IV. Note how SM also mistranslates *vaikārikatvācca* :

> ... not quite a *silhouette* or a *front view, but just a modification.* (p. 177)

In fact *vaikārikatvācca* here means that the posture under discussion *(sācīkṛta)* is neither like *ardharju* (posture II) nor like *chāyāgata* or *adhyardhalocana* (IV) ***because it is deviant.*** *Chāyāgata* does not mean "silhouette" which is what *pārśvāgata* refers to. It is merely a synonym for *adhyardhalocana* cf. verse16b and 17a:

अध्यर्धाक्षं परिज्ञेयमाकारेणैवमादिना । । १६
छायागतमिति प्रोक्तं पर्यायेणैतदेव तु । १७

39.14a. *bhaṅgi lalāṭam mātrārdham. Bhaṅgi-* is the reading of D. What it means in this compound is ("the foreshortened part of the forehead") measures half a *mātrā* which is 1/2 *aṅgula.* Note that this emendation of *mātrāśca* (ACD) and *mātrā ca* (N) to *mātrārdham* is demanded by the context and is consistent with *mātrārdham* mentioned in 14b and 15a.

Note the various translation:

SK: .... the *cure* of the forehead is *half its usual size* ..... (p. 39)

PS :The *contraction* of the forehead or better the contracted forehead should be of *one mātrā.*[2]

F.N.2. The phrase intended seems to be lalāṭabhaṅgo mātrāśca. It is changed as bhaṅgo lalāṭamātrāśca possibly for the sake of metre; mātrā = l aṅgula. (p. 113)

SM: ..... half a brow invisible, *part of the forehead,......* (p. 177)

39.14b. *dṛśyam nāsārdhameva ca.* This follows N and D except that I emend their *dṛśyā-* to *dṛśyam* - as required by the sense. The *Śāradā* manuscripts C and F suffer from this corruption *-dṛśyānām sārdhameva.* Note this reading has led all the scholars to various speculations. SK follows *dṛśyānām sārameva tu* from V:

(lit. the *only essential part of the rest of face* [that is] to be seen is the curve of the forehead....... (p. 39)

PS: The *conspicuous part* should be shown half or adopting the reading sāra only essential part, what is to be shown, *should be exhibited slightly.* (p. 113)

SM: .... a visible half of the nose, ... (p. 177)

F.N. 8. The reading दृश्यानां सार्धं is obviously wrong. The word cannot be split and the *dīrgha* for य and *bindu* for न have no place being clerical errors. (p. 146)

39.15d. *nābhyāḥ syāc.* The *nābhyāsyāc* of all MSS is evidently a case of haplography for *nābhyās syāc.*

39.17. *chāyāgatāmiti ....savyameva va.*

SK (p.39) is wrong in thinking that it is the *pārśvāgata* (side view) of which *chāyāgata* is said to be the synonymn here.

> That position ocassionally is called Chāyāgatam, (छायागतं) *i.e.*, coming out of the shade, whose side is seen, either the right or the left, ... (p. 39)

The text clearly states that *chāyāgata* is another term for *adhyardhākṣa:* See verse 27b which mentions that posture VIII i.e. *purovṛttam,* is nothing but a diagonal counterpart of this posture, in other words "Reversed *chāyāgatam*".

> स्थितेऽप्यभिमुखेऽर्धाङ्गे परिवृत्तिवशाद् भवेत् ।
> किञ्चिच्छायागताकार उपरिष्टादतः पुनः ।। २७ .३९

SM is mistaken in taking verse 17cd as a definition of *adhyardhākṣa/ chāyāgata. chāyāgata* is not a strict silhouette but 22.5 degrees off a complete profile. (see diagrams I and II). From 17cd onwards, the subsequent posture (V) is defined as a strict profile *pārśvāgata* or *bhittika.*

> SM: This is also known as *Chāyāgata*(Silhouette), a word which is a synonymn. Here can be had a side view whether from the right or from the left. (p. 177)

39.18ab. *anyat kṣayaṃ yāta.* This reading is derived from N and D. The corrupt reading resulting from haplography *(Kṣayam yātam -> kṣayātam)* only affects the C group (i.e. C,F,A,B,V). The sense of the reading accepted is that one entire side is diminished, literally "goes into foreshortening". All editors have followed the corrupt reading: SK's translation is rather bizzare:

> ...whose limbs and movement enter into quite a new (lit. different) constellation, (p.39)

PS connects *anyat* which actually goes with *pārśvam* with the *aṅga* of *aṅgam aṇgagatis tathā* :

> The rest of the limbs vanishes or diminishes. (p. 113)

SM leaves 18a out in the translation.

39.18b. *tadaṅgasaṃhatistathā.* This is an emendation of "*tadaṅgamaṅga-gatistathā*" supported in its 4th syllable by N *(saṅgasaṅga-)*. CV's *aṅgamaṅga* and FD's *tamaṅgamaṅga-* and N's *saṅgasaṇga-* are evidently dittographic errors. The term *aṅgasaṃhati* is found in the appropriate sense of "symmetry" at, e.g. ***Kirātārjunīya*** (13.50). Note that in a strict profile, one whole side which, in the frontal view (posture I) lends symmetry to the body, is not visible as a result of foreshortening. The sense in short is this: Just as the view of one whole side vanishes, the body symmetry which is concommitent with it also disappears.

Let us turn to other translations:

SK: ...... *whose limbs and movements* enter into quite a new (lit. different) constellation, (p. 39)

PS: The rest of the *limbs* vanish or diminishes. Similarly also the *movement of the limb.* (p. 113)

SM overlooks this line i.e. 18a. in the translation.

39.18cd. *-bhrūlekhamardhanāsā-*. This is the reading of N and D. It has been preferred on grounds of sense. The corrupting of *-nāsā* to *nāmā* is easily explained by the similarity between -s- and -m- in the *Śāradā* script. Note SK leaves out "nose" in the translation owing to V's corrupt reading- "एकाक्षमेकभ्रूलेखमरनामा ललाटवत् ":

SK: .... of whom one eye only, one eyebrow, one temple, ... (p.39)

Note how *ekā* and *lalāṭa* are connected.

PS emends ABCV's reading to एकाक्षमेकभ्रूले [खाध] रना [सा] ललाटवत् :-

> *like one lower lip, a nose* and a forehead, an eye and an eyebrow are also shown one, singly. (p. 113)
>
> SM's translation follows PS's emendation:
>
> ...that shows only one eye, one line of the brow, *lip nose* and forehead,.....(p.177)

39.19a. *yadardham.* This reading is found in ABCDFV and does not yield sense. N has *padardha* which if emended to *padārdha* gives out some sense. *Pada* means "the space between the eyebrows". In a strict profile view, even this space would be reduced to its half. In the context, it makes good sense but the evidence for this meaning is inadequate. SM, PS and SM overlook "*yad(pad)ardham*" in the translation.

39.19c. *ahīnamānalāvaṇyaṃ mādhuryādiguṇānvitam.* This follows N. This has been preferred on grounds of style. The other MSS give -*lāvaṇyamādhuryādi*- which yields the same sense but is more clumsy.

39.20c. *apāṅge 'rdhakalā kṣīṇe.* The nearest reading to this emendation is D's *apāṅge 'rdhekale.* The meaning that this emendation yields, namely that there is foreshortening of the outer eye to half a *kalā,* i.e. 1 *aṅgula,* encouraged by ***Pratimāmānalakṣaṇa*** (D.H.I., J.N. Banerjea, p. 591):

> अपाङ्गे द्वे कले ज्ञेये नेत्रमध्यञ्च द्व्यङ्गुलम् । २३
>
> This is the full breadth of the eye then one would expect this measurement of 1 *aṅgula* in this posture.

Note the other translations:

SK takes *kalākṣīṇe* and *apākrudde* as :

...*artistically foreshortened* (lit. made slender)[1] and looks *tender.*

F.N.1. Read instead of Kalakshiṇe, Kalākshīṇe (artistically slender).

PS emends *apākrudde* to *apākṛṣṭe* :

> (Here the reading apākruddhe is amended into apākṛṣṭe (?). The averted face (?) is diminished by one kalā; (p. 113)

SM emends it to "*apākṛte*" justifying in the footnote as follows:

F.N.1. अपाकृते should be the right reading as अपाकुद्धे has no sense (pp. 147)

Note SM's translation in which *kalā* has been taken as "a sixteenth part":

> That is styled Gaṇḍaparāvṛtta where the form partially cut off from view has a *sixteenth measure of the neck,* ... (p.177)

39.21b. *kalārdham.* This reading comes from N and seems to fit into the given cotext. *Kalākhyam* and *kalākṣam* found in C and D respectively are corruptions. They make no sense.

Note the various translations:

> SK: and has attained kṣaya (diminution) *called "dark"* in forehead, cheek and arm...(p. 39)

PS adopts C's reading *kalākhyam*:

> ... so also shoulder, cheek and forehead are diminished by *one kalā.* (p. 113)

> SM: ... where the form partially cut off from view has a *sixteenth measure* of the neck, the cheek, forehead, ... (p. 177)

39.21d. *sphiggulphadvayaseṣvapi.* The corruption has affected all the manuscripts. All the major manuscripts only have *gu* < ... > with 3 syllables missing. It is evident from MS A that it also originally had *gu* < ... > which was later filled in by a different hand and it became *guhyatale.* N alone preserves the original to any extent with its *-sthitigulphadvayeṣv api. -dvayeṣu* is obviously improbable since it is not pairs (*dvaya*) that are affected by foreshortening, but only the parts of one side of the body. For *gulphadvayasa-* whose rarity must have been responsible for the corruption see MW under *gulpha-*. *Sthiti-* too is suspect, since we need reference to some part of the body here. For the same reasons, *gulpha-* has been preferred to *guhya-* (private parts) of A followed by the editors and translators. Since the verse is working down the body from top to bottom, and since the waist precedes, *sphig-* (buttock) is strongly suggested. The sense is certainly appropriate. This posture is between a strict profile and a back view so the buttocks begin to face the spectator.

SK omits its translation.

PS follows A's reading with its interpolation as stated above:

> The arm, chest, waist and *the private parts* may be diminished by 2 kalās each. (p.113)

Note "each" makes no sense.

SM, like PS adopts MS A's reading:

> an eighth (?) or the arm, chest, waist, legs and the private parts, all diminished carefully ... (p. 177)

dvikalam dvīkalam jñātvā (22a) is translated by SM as "taking every part into account" (p. 177). Also note that the text has no reference to the "**eighth**".

39.22d. *nātitīkṣnāṅgam eva ca* follows ACFDVN. PS and SM follow *nātikṣīṇāṅgameva ca.* The former reading is preferred being supported by most reliable MSS. Even though SK follows V's correct but she mistranslates: ... whose limbs are *not very sharply (delineated);* (p. 39)

PS: Its limbs should *not be very much diminished.* (p. 113)

SM: *...no limb diminished overmuch.* (p. 177)

Note what the text intends to convey is that the foreshortening should not lead to the limbs of the body seeming too harsh i.e. the transition of the planes should not be too abrupt.

39.24a. *valitaślakṣṇasarvāṅgam.* ABCFS1S2's and V read *bhrū* or bhṛ as the third syllable. But a reference to the brow is impossible since this posture is the backview. My emendation draws on D's *valgitaścasarvāṅgam* and ABCFS1S2's *-ślakṣṇa-* D's *valgati-* looks like a corruption of *valgita-* ("leaping"), but this is surely itself corrupt since there is no scope for referring to movement here. It probably entered the tradition under the influence of the moving posture *savalgita-* which is mentioned in this *adhyāya* at 48c.

39.25c. *ahīnamānalāvaṇyam cf.* verse 19b.

39.26cd. *yasyārdham aṅgam pādonabhāgena samasvitam.* This emendation attempts to restore the meaning expected from the context, though it is suggested with some hesitation, since *ardhaṃ aṅgam* for "half the body" is bad sanskrit and the staddling of the break between the *pāda* by *pādonobhāgena* somewhat unusual. The next verse refers to this position as *kiñcicchāyāgatākāra-,* i.e. "somewhat like the *Chāyāgata* position", and the foreshortening in the *chāyāgata* is precisely that given here if the emendation is sound. Note the various translations:

SK follows V's reading *-yasyordhamaṅgapatyena:*

> (A figure) whose *upper part of the body* should be turning back and only to be seen on the account of its reversed position ... (p. 40)

PS: Its upper part should fall by (diminish) by one *bhāga, i.e.* four aṅgulas. (p. 114)

SM emends *-aṅgapatyena* to *-aṅgapātena* with the following footnote:

> 3. Can it be अङ्गपात or diminishing or loss from sight of certain limbs?

SM's translation reads:

> That is to be understood as *Parivṛtta* where the top of the head (*abhi-mukha?)* has a diminution of visibility, does not show some limbs (like nose, lips chin etc.,) on account of its being a back view, ... (p. 177)

39.27cd. *kiṃcicchāyāgatākāra upariṣṭātaḥ punaḥ.* Note that *kiṃcichāyāgatākāra* and *punaḥ* are adopted from D and N. All the manuscripts in the 'C' group suffer from corruption in form of a dual case as in *-chāyāgatau kārya.* Surely what the text intends to convey is that this posture, VIII, somewhat resembles posture IV i.e. *Chāyāgatākāra* otherwise called *Adhyardhalocanam* seen from the reverse side. Note *upariṣṭāt* i.e. "from behind" is a counterpart of *purastāt* i.e. "from front". The measurements for the foreshortening here do coinicide with that of posture IV, i.e. in terms of 15 : 1 *aṅgulas.*

SK's translation based on V's corrupt reading hence the translation makes no sense:

> (A figure) whose upper part of the body should be turning back and only half to be seen on account of its reversed position with a face *tainted with envy* (*V's "sthitesyārbhamu- khe-"*), whose upper and lower portion of the body should be somewhat lost in shade towards the front ... (p. 40)

PS is misled by the usage of dual in the corrupt reading found in all the manuscripts in the "C" group:

> On the account of parivṛtti the turning back, the upper part is evenly placed with the diminishing part even

> though the half of the limb is frontally placed. The two halves should be shown up and below as if they were somewhat in chāyāgata *style* (silhouette). (p. 114)

SM follows the reading from V:

> It thus appears *without facial contour as a silhouette in its upper and lower parts* (face and legs).
>
> SM (p. 178) supplies the following in the translation:
>
> *Only the buttocks are seen in this threefourth back view ...*

39.28. *ardhārdhagatasārūpyam ... yathāyogavilopanā.* The sense of the verse has been overlooked by all the translators. *Ardhārdhagata-sārūpyam* or "symmetry based upon the quarter *(ardhārdha-)* view or angle" is to be understood in the larger context of the chapter. It is evident from the definitions and the description the postures that the human figure or model has been rotated on its axis 22.5 degrees at every stage (at least from stage I to V through 90 degrees).

The term *ardhārdhagata* has to be interpreted within this circular format. Ideally, to get all the stages of foreshortening, the figure is to be rotated through a full circle. A quarter of this would be 90 degrees. *Sārūpyam* has to be understood in the following way. Divide a circle into 4 equal parts. (i) at 0 degree, *Ṛjvāgata* (posture I) is located. (ii) At 90 degrees, *Pārśvāgata* 1 (posture V) say its right side is located. (iii) At 180 degrees, *Pṛṣṭhāgata* (posture VIII) is seen. At 270 degrees, *Pārśvāgata* 2 revealing its left side is located. The *sārūpyam* ("similarity") refered to is that of *Pārśvāgata* 1 and 2; see fig. (i), B and D in which these can be seen to be identical except that one shows the right side and the other the left. The text disapproves of these postures, calling them *virasa* ("boring"), prefering the subtle angles intermediate between these cardinal postures. In other words, the usage of these 4 angles was considered monotonous because *Ṛjvāgata* resembles *Pṛṣṭhāgata* in so far as one is a counterpart of the other. Likewise, *Pārśvāgata* 1 and 2 are mirror images.

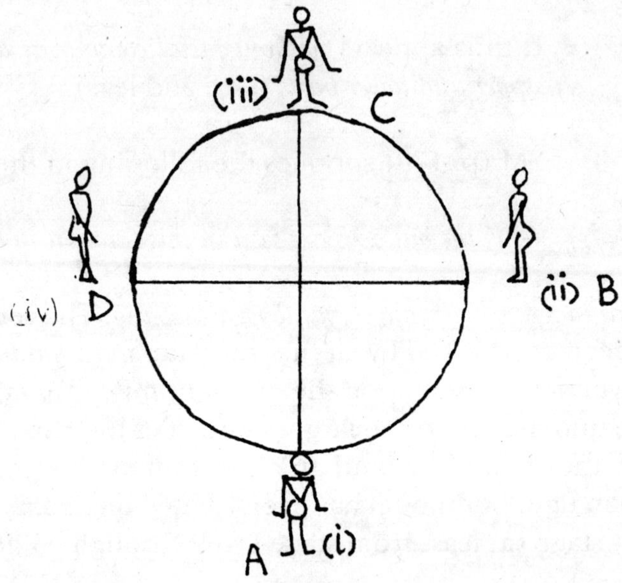

Fig. (i)

Note that it is the postures A, B, C, and D which are *ardhārdha,* occupying the quarters *(ardhārdha)* of the circle. *Sārūpyam* refers to the similarity between the pairs directly opposite i.e. AC and BD. Such a format is indeed simplistic and the four postures tend towards being uninteresting *(virasa)* and rustic or simple *(grāmyasaṃsthitam).* Note that in folk art these postures predominate. An antidote to this postural monotony would be the intermediary angles of vision which the text refers to as *madhya* referred to in fig. (ii) as "M" which bring delight to the eyes (*netraramya*). These provide the necessary variations to the *ardhārdha* or "quarter" based format.

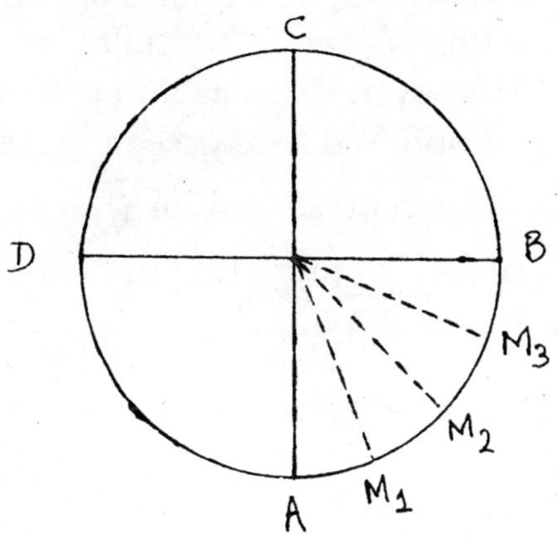

Fig. (ii)

Let us turn to other translations:

SK: .... (while) the (lower) half (of the body) should be like that of a rustic, whose middle (is drawn) properly foreshortened and agreeable to the eye,.....(p.40)

PS: The similarity in the *two halves* is vulgar and without interest and therefore the *middle portion* should be properly diminished as to please the eye,... (p. 114)

Note *ardhārdha* can never be translated as "two halves".

SM: Only the buttocks are seen in this threefourths back view which revealing similarly of form partially is not so pleasing and refined as the same view from the front. (p. 178)

Note that SM's translation is most unrelated with the given text.

39.29a. *vijñeyamagrataḥ*. Note that the emendation of *dadhataḥ* (> MSS ACFNV) to *-magrataḥ* is demanded by the sense. It is supported by the similarity -d- and -ma- in the *Śāradā* script. Likewise, when -g- gets 'compressed' it tends to resemble -dh-. As mentioned earlier, the text distinguishes between 2 kinds of rotation or *parivṛtti* of the body -one type which takes the front part of the body away from the spectator and the other kind brings it back towards the spectator. The former is *Parāvṛtti* and the latter is *Purovṛtti*. By *agrataḥ*, the text conveys precisely this notion of "frontally averted body" or *agrataḥ kāyaparivṛttam.* Moreover, *kāryam* accepted by all the editors is found only in V as opposed to *kāya* seen in A,N,D,C and F.

SK: .... and should be represented for (the purpose of) *upholding*(?), (oh) lord of men. (p. 40)

PS and SM overlook it in the translation.

39.29cd. *dṛṣṭasphigdeśam dṛṣṭapādatalam.* All the MSS have *dṛṣṭisphig-* which does not yield good sense. Metrically, the third *pāda* of this verse falls under one of the permitted variants (c, Appendix 3, Coulson, p. 310). Regarding the latter half, ABV's reading is adopted against CF's *dṛṣṭipāda* and DN's *dṛṣṭampāda-*. SM adopts the reading from C and F.

PS translates *samagradṛṣṭisphigdeśam* as:

> The whole eye is turned towards the region of buttocks. (p. 114)

39.30d. *dṛśyāratnitaladvayam.* Note that the correct reading is preserved in D, F and N as opposed to C's *dṛśyāpatni-*, A's *dṛśyāreti-*, B's *dṛśyāranti-* and V's *dṛśyaśeṣa.* All the editors follow V which yields some sense but not pertinent to the context. The correct reading means that in this posture which is a backview of a bent figure, the lower part of both the elbows *(aratni)* should be shown. Note the other translations:

SK: ... with the two entire soles shown, with *foreshortened lower parts of the toes,...* (p. 40)

PS: The foot and fingers (toes) are dropped while the *two soles are completely seen.* (p. 114)

SM overlooks it in the translation.

39.32a. *viluptasyaikatam.* This reading remains a problem and hence left untranslated. None of the readings is satisfactory.

39.32d. *pravibhāgaśaḥ.* All MSS show *abhirājitam.* The verb *abhirājate* is ill attested and its apparent sense "to shine" is inappropriate here. The context demands this emendation. What it means is that new postures can be characterised *(lakṣitavyāni)* according to the division *(pravibhāgaśaḥ)* of the aforesaid method and distinguishing features *(tathoktair lakṣaṇair).* Note that grammar demands the emendation of *lakṣitair* (33a) to *lakṣaṇair.*

39.33b. *-ānukramameva ca.* It follows N's reading. Note that D retains the *ca.* N retains the *ca.* All the MSS from the C group show *nava* at the end which is redundant given that *navany-* is mentioned in the preceding verse.

On the other hand, these nine postures can be distributed differently within a similar circular format by following another method. It can be demonstrated as follows. Let us refer to it as System II:

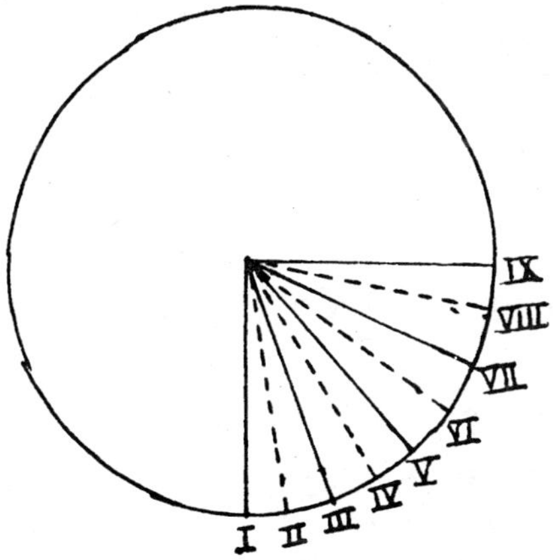

Fig. (iii)

Note that the system II is also given in the SamaSūtDhār (8.4) according to which *Pārśvāgata* or Profile is classifiable as the ninth posture (पार्श्वागतं च नवमं स्थानं भित्तिकविग्रहम्), What the verse tells us is that nine postures defined earlier can be said to have many more variations *(vikārāṇi bahunyapi)* by following a different method of distribution of the angle of vision.

39.34ab. *ekaikaśyena bhūbhāge. Ekaikaśyena* is derived from D's *ekaikānyena* and the emendation is based on the similarity between -ś- and -n- in the Bengali script. The meaning is "seriatim, one by one in a succession, individually, etc." The emendation *bhūbhāge* is based on S1 and S2's *bhūbhāgaiḥ* and D's *bhūbhāga-*.

The verse 34ab refers to another system which yields the same postures distributed more closely so as to accommodate many more variations of the five principal postures- I, II, III, IV and V. Let us compare the system 2 with system 1.

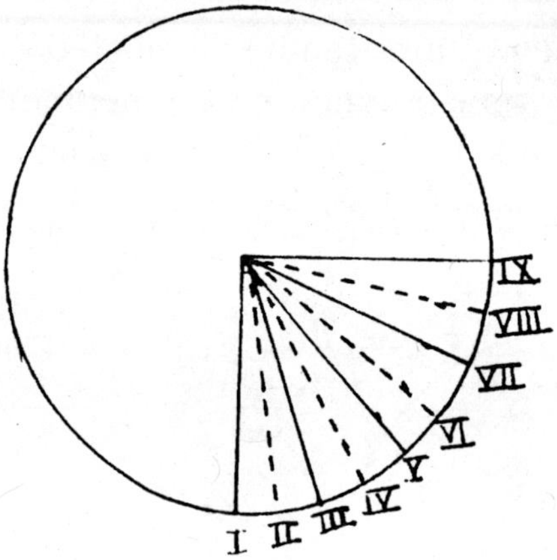

(System 2) fig. (iv)

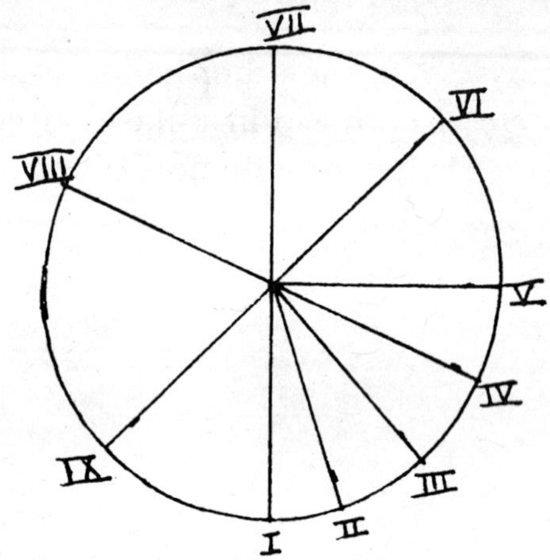

(System1) fig. (v)

In system 1, the nine postures described (5-32) appears to be distributed within a circular format in which only postures I - V maintain an equidistance while the rest are arranged erratically. According to system 2, referred to by verse 35-36, a single quadrant forms the locus of the nine postures, the latter being elaborate modification of postures I - V of the system 1. These *(eṣām)* [i.e. the 9 postures as described already] have more variations by following a different mode of distribution. [They] are to be made *(kartavyāni)* on a "ground" quadrant *(bhūmibhāge)* one by one in a succession *(ekaikaśyena)* as instructed *(yathāvidhi)* [below].

It should be noted that the system 2 of the postural distribution is given in the SamaSūtDhār. (8.4) according to which the *Pārśvāgata* or the side view is classified as the ninth posture. (पार्श्वागतं च नवमं स्थानं भित्तिकविग्रहम् ।) Also see the ApaPṛ.: उभयर्ज्वागतमध्ये प्रत्यङ्गाङ्गकशोभनम् । इति पार्श्वागतं प्रोक्तं स्थानकं नवमं विदुः ।। (211.8)

SK does not translate it.

PS seems to emend to *ekaikaṃśena* and takes *bhūmibhāga* as "background":

> The background should be divided properly and then the different portions. (p.114)
>
> SM closely follows PS:
>
> Of these there can be many more created by the artist's imaginative fecundicity in the case of each one with proper background and in accordance with the major principles governing them. (p. 178)

39.34c. *trayamānam.* Note this is an emendation of *tvayā mānaḥ* from N. All the manuscripts show corrupt readings. Note this is supported by verse 37b which mentions *pramāṇatrayameva.* This means "after ascertaining the threefold measurements" which are arrived at by the threefold divisions of 90 degrees. Note that *māna* here means "division" as opposed to "measurement" given the context. (cf. *śatamāna* meaning hundredfold).

SK does not translate this line.

PS :

> On the background first proper measurement should be achieved and then these 9 sthānās should be drawn in accordance with the qualities of measurement etc. (p. 114)

SM does not translate it.

39.34d. *tadantare.* All MSS have *bhutale* which yeids an unspecific meaning and I suspect *tu bhūtale* to be a corruption of *tadantare.* This conjecture is based on the close similarity between -bhū - and -nta- in the *Śāradā* script and the context. The *bhūbhāge* in 34a may have been the cause for this corruption.

39.35a. *mānādyair guṇair. -adyair* here raises a problem. From the context, it appears to allude to the three *mānas* dividing the quadrant into 4 parts and the four secondary divisions dividing the same into 8 parts.

It is the 8 parts of intervals that the *mānādyair* refers to. Each of the remaining 3 quadrants can have the nine postures by repeating or multiplying *(guṇair)* the 8 parts [by 4]. This brings the total number of posture in the entire circle to 32.

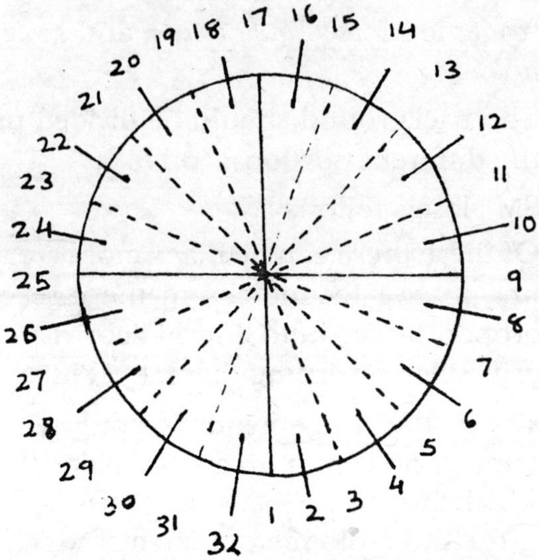

Fig. (vi)

39.35d. *sarvabhāgeṣvanindita. -bhāgeṣv-* is only preserved in N which further supports my interpretation of the preceding *padas.* The verse 34 speaks of the distribution of only one quadrant which is now applied to the remaining 3 quadrants *(bhāga).* All the scholars followed *bhāveṣv-.*

SK (p. 40) translates it as "conditions":

> These positions should be drawn with care (accompanied), by qualities like māna (proportionate measurement), etc. (Oh) blameless (one), these nine positions are seen in all conditions.
>
> PS, (p. 114) :
>
> On the background first proper measurement should be achieved and than these 9 sthānas should be drawn in accordance with the qualities of measurement etc. These 9 postures can depict all the bhāvas.

SM, (pp. 178):

> These nine positions as seen in all attitudes are to be drawn flawless in their proper measurements ....

The vocative in *anindita* based on D's *nindita* makes a good sense. It means the same as *anagha* a common vocative addressing *Vajra.* Note only SK translates it correctly (supra). PS's text shows - *aninditam* but it is not translated. SM translates it as if it were *aninditāni,* qualifying the postures (supra).

39.37c. *advaidham.* All the MSS show *trividham* which gives out a redundant sense given the mention of *pramāṇatrayam* which immediately follows it. *Trividham* is evidently a gloss on *pramāṇatrayam* displacing the third type of category for postures. *Pramāṇaguṇataḥ* in verse 37b gives us a clue to the criterion governing the threefold classification of the postures. The three tiered hierarchy namely the *Uttama, Madhyama and Adhama* are based upon the [lack] of manifoldness [lit. multipliability] of the postures.

SamaSūtDhār. for instance throws a significant light on this problem and actually puts one of these terms (i.e. *Citra, Vicitra* and X) into use for defining the Profile view.

वैचित्र्यं मित्तिके नास्तीत्येव चित्र्यं विदो विदुः । 79.13ab.

The experts understand the Profile view as *Citryam* because it lacks variety.

Let us examine this notion against the wider scheme of organization of the postures. When a human figure is rotated around its axis a full circle with threefold intervals in every quadrant, the diagram that will result is as follows:

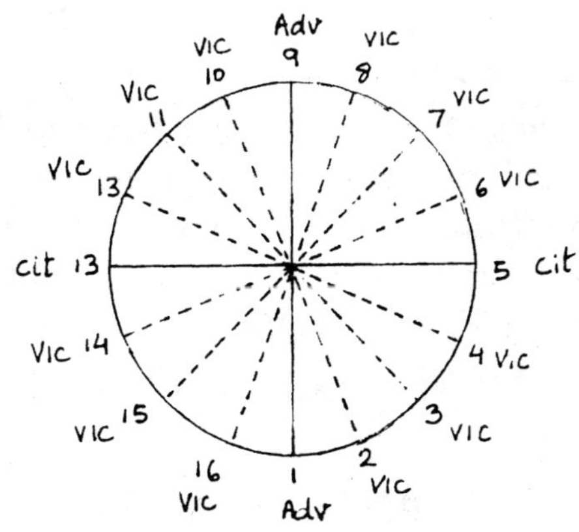

Fig. (vii)

Notice that a profile view is repeated twice at 5 and 13. So it can be said to have two varieties. On the other hand, Anṛju, Sācī, and *Adhyārdha* have their counterparts in each of the quadrants and have the most number of variations. In contrast, the *Ṛju* and *pṛṣṭhāgata* have no counterparts in any of the quadrants. Hence, they are unique and were referred to as *Advaidham* or "that which has no other or variety". Apart from yielding good sense, this emendations draws support from the latter half of its corruption- *trividham.* The number of varieties that each of the postures incorporate are listed as follows:

Postures	**Varieties**	**Type**
Ṛjvāgata :-	1.	*Advaidha*
Pṛṣṭhāgata:-	1.	*Advaidha*
Pārśvāgata :-	2.	*Citra*
Sācī :-	4.	*Vicitra*
Anṛju :-	4.	*Vicitra*
Adhyārdhākṣa :-	4.	*Vicitra*

39.39a. *citravidbhirasaṃjñam.* Note *asaṃjñam* has not been translated by the scholars. What it means is that regarding the method of foreshortening *(kṣayavṛddhividhi)* which determines the distribution and the number of postures, there is a difference of opinion amongst the experts of painting. The CitSūt. itself mentions two methods of foreshortening but there are many more as can be gleaned from various other *Śilpa* texts.

For instance, in the ApaPṛ. 211.1, (अथ वक्ष्ये स्थानविधिं क्रमयोगमुपागतम् । ऋज्वागतादि स्थानानि पञ्च वै पूर्वभागतः ।। ११ ।। कार्याण्यपराङ्मुखानि चतुर्वृत्ताभिधानि च । २१), the nine postures are distributed as follows:

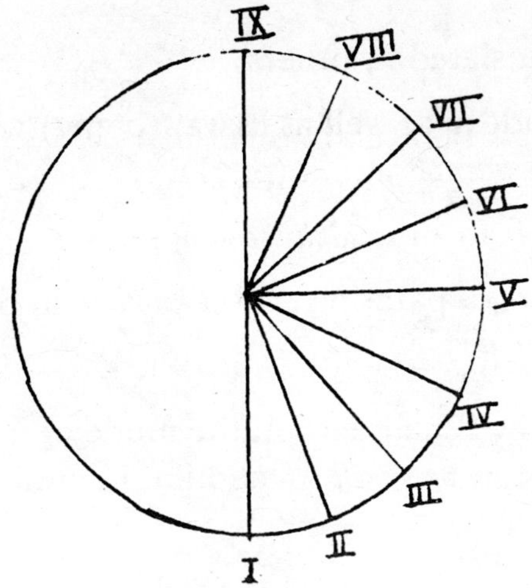

Fig. (viii)

This method is also mentioned in the SamaSūtDhār., 78.3. Apart from this, this text put forward two more methods, the first one being the same as the system 2 of the CitSūt. and the second one, by far the most complex yielding as many as 27 variations along one half of a circular format.

> ऋज्वर्धऋजुनोर्मध्ये चत्वारि व्यन्तराणि च। अर्धर्जुसाचीकृतयोर्मध्ये च व्यन्तरत्रयम्
> ।।५।।
> (द्व्यर्धार्ज्वा ? क्ष)साचीकृतयोर्मध्ये द्वे व्यन्तरे परे। द्व्यर्धाक्षपार्श्वयोर्मध्ये व्यन्तरं
> चैकमन्तरे ।।६।।
> एकोनविंशदेवंच स्थानानिव्यस्तवर्त्मना ।। १३ ।।

It can be illustrated as follows:

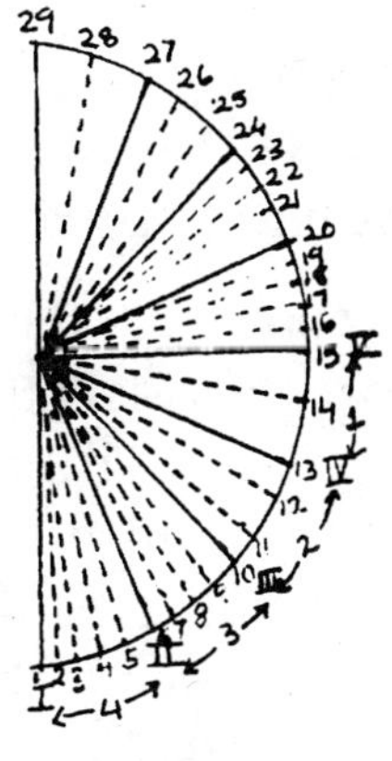

Fig. (ix)

Note how this is translated by others:

SK: This vriddhi as well as kṣaya, (being) without any *(other) name known to the painters,........* (p. 41)

PS emends it to *citravidbhissasaṃjñeyam :*

The knowers of painting *should know it* in brief or at length.

(p. 114)

SM: .... and now I shall tell you the mode of foreshortening, as *artists should know very well* all about it in epitome and in detail.

(p. 178)

39.40ab. *bahusaṃkhyatvād-*. Note this reading has been adopted from N against *bahusamsthatvād-* in CF and its variations in A and D. In the given context, it means "because of (their) being innumerable or many in number". Understand this to imply the impossibility of listing all the possible variations. Hence the author cut them down to only 13 types as discussed *(trayodaśavidhaivatra).*

Note the various translations:

SK: .... is said succinctly to be of thirteen varieties (here) and *(varies) otherwise according to the manifoldness of the positions (lit. of manifestations).* (p. 41)

PS: ... are of thirteen types *on account of the many ways in which the sthānas are composed.* (p. 114)

SM: Foreshortening *(Kshayavriddhi)* is thirteenfold, *as there are several positions* depending on the limbs....... (p. 178)

39.40c. *Ṛjvāgatam.* Only D preserves the reading required by sense. The other MSS have either *dṛṣṭāgatam* (CF) or *Pṛṣṭāgatam* (ABNVS1S2).

39.41a. *adhyādhārkṣam purovṛttam.* This *pāda* calls for a drastic emendation and it is made on the basis of the earlier list of postures given in verse 2-3 of the same *adhyāya.* All the postures mentioned earlier tally with the ones in the second list except *madhyādhārdham* and *tathādhārdham.* This is most irregular and on the grounds of consistency and sense, one expects these two to be corresponding to *adhyārdhalocanam* and *Purovṛttam.* In the *Śāradā* script, -a- and -m- look quite similar and hence the emendation *adhyārdhākṣam.*

Tathārdham appears to be gloss echoing the preceding *madhya-* and in the process one posture namely *Purovṛttam* got eliminated. Paleographically, the emendation relates poorly with the emendation but it yields good sense and is in line with the metre.

39.42c. *calitam tathā uttānam-*. Note that these four stances, *Ullepam* etc. deal more with movement and flexion of human form and less with angles of vision. These four stance actually have more in common with the succeeding postures *maṇḍala* etc. than the *Ṛjvāgata* etc. My view on this irregularity is that originally the first nine postures formed one separate group and it was later that the distinction between postures concerned with the angle of vision and those about movement was blurred. Cf. SamaSūtDhār. 80.1 where a term *ceṣṭāsthāna-* is employed to refer to the second group. (अथान्यान्यभिधीयन्ते चेष्टास्थानान्यनेकशः ।).

39.47c. *skhalitā-* Note this reading is adopted from CF. All the editors seem to prefer V's reading *-khalita. Skhalita-* means "faltering" with reference to the postures of throwing a javelin. Note the other translations:

SK overlooks *khalita* in the translation:

... walk with difficulty and with one leg in ālīḍha position.

PS seems to follow SK :

> ... should be shown in the calita posture showing unsteadiness and one foot in ālīḍha position. (p. 115)

SM: ... one leg is either moving or *shaking*, or fatigued or in ālīḍha while the other is steady. (p. 179)

चत्वारिंशोऽध्यायः

मार्कण्डेय उवाच

त्रिप्रकारेष्टकाचूर्णे त्र्यंशं क्षिप्त्वा मृदस्ततः ।
गुग्गुलुं समधूच्छिष्टं मधुकं कुन्दुरुं गुडम् ।।१।।

कुसुम्भतैलसंयुक्तं कृत्वा दद्यात्समांशकम् ।
त्रिभागमग्निदग्धायास्सुधायास्तत्र चूर्णयेत् ।।२।।

बल्वजं द्व्यंशमिश्रं तत्प्रक्षिप्य सशणांशकम् ।
वालुकांशं ततो दद्यात् 'स्वानुरूपेण' बुद्धिमान् ।।३।।

ततः शर्करतोयेन प्लावयेत्पिच्छिलेन तम् ।
परिक्लिन्नं समग्रं तन्मासमात्रं निधापयेत् ।।४।।

मार्दवं मासमात्रेण गतमुद्धृत्य यत्नतः ।
दद्यात्प्रलेपं निपुणः शुष्ककुड्ये विमृज्य तु ।।५।।

1a. V त्रिप्रकारेष्टिका N त्रिप्रकारेष्टिया ABC चित्रकारेष्टका F चित्रकानेष्टका V चूर्णं A त्रुघ्रं
1b. D त्र्यंशक्षिसा A त्रंत्प्रक्षिप्ता CF मृतस्ततः
1c. ABDFV गुग्गुलं 1d D मधुकुन्दुरक FN मधुकुन्दरुकं C मधुकुन्दूरुकं B मधुकुंडरुकं A मधुकुन्मुरुकं V मुरुकं N गुदं CF गुदुम् B गुरुम्
2a. ABCFV कुसुम्भं D सुकुम्भं 2b N वास्यात्समांशकं
2c. CF त्रिभागमपि- N -दग्ध्या- 2cd D -दग्ध्वप्राः-
3a. N वल्वजं D वल्वजा V बिल्वजं AB बिलुजं 3b D चुत्क्षिप्य N शशणं D शशण- CFV मषणं AB मषकं ACDFNV कषम् B कथम् 3c A बालकांशां D बालुकासं
4a. ABV शकल- N सकल- D सूकल- F तनश्चकर C मकल-
A repeats 4 cd.
4c. B परिक्लन्नं 4d D तन्मासुमास-
5a. A मार्दव D मार्गवं 5c N -प्रलेयं D -प्रलापं N निपूनः 5cd F रिपुणः 5d ABFCV शुष्कं N कुड्य A कुडे ABCDFN विमृष्य V विमृश्य

ADHYĀYA 40

Mārkaṇḍeya spoke :

1-2b. Adding clay to the brickdust of three kinds in the proportion of 1 to 3, he should add bdellium *(guggulu)*, beeswax *(madhucchiṣṭam)*, (an extract of) *Bassia latifolia (madhuka)*, an extract of Deodar of *Avaria longifolia, (kundurū)* and jaggary (*guḍa*) in equal parts, after he has mixed them with safflower oil *(kusumbhataila)*[1].

2cd. Into that [mixture of clay, brickdust, bdellium etc.] he should powder a third part of burnt plaster[2].

3. When he has added that, [having first] mixed [it] with two parts of coarse grass *(balvaja)*, and one part of hemp-fibres *(śaṇa)*, the wise [painter] should add one part *accordingly.*.

4. Afterwards, That [whole mixture] should be thoroughly *(samagram)* soaked in the slimy sugar solution *(śarkaratoyena)* and it should be left (in this state) for only one month.

5. This plaster, which after a month and no more will have become pliant [he should take up*(uddhṛtya)*] and carefully apply as plaster to a dry wall.

[1] oil of Carthamus Tinctorius.
[2] i.e., calcinated [anhydrous] gypsum [calcium sulphate].

श्लक्ष्णं सममवष्टब्धं निम्नोन्नतविनाकृतं ।
न चातिघनतां नीतं न चातितनुतामपि ।। ६ ।।

यदा शुष्कं भवेत्कुड्यं सुधालिप्तं समं कृतम् ।
तया मृदा सर्जरसतैलभागावियुक्तया ।। ७ ।।

श्लक्ष्णीकुर्यात्प्रयत्नेन लेपनं श्लक्ष्णसञ्जनैः ।
मुहुर्मुहुश्च क्षीरेण सिक्त्वा मार्जनं यत्नतः ।। ८ ।।

सद्यः शोषमुपायातः स कुड्यो मनुजेश्वर ।
अपि वर्षशतस्यान्ते न प्रणश्येत्तु कर्हिचित् ।। ९ ।।

अनेनैव प्रकारेण विविधैर्वर्णकैर्युताः ।
कर्तव्याश्चित्रवपुषा विविधमानभूमयः ।। १० ।।

6a. N शुक्लं ABV समं स्ववष्टब्धं CF सम N स्ववष्टध्वं 6b N निम्नोन्नतविवर्जितं
6c. CFD चातिघनता N चातिघनतान्वीतं V चानिघनतां यातं
6d. V चातितनुताङ्गतम् D -तन्वतामपि A चातिवनतां
7a. ABCDFN शुष्को CDFS1S2 कुड्यः N कुद्य AB कुम्पः 7b D सुदालिप्त- N मृदालिप्तम- ABCFS1S2 तदालिप्तम V तत्प्रलिप्तम- D समतृकृतं ABCFNV सत्कृतम्
7c. ACDFNV तया N सर्जरसस्तैल- ACFV सर्जरसा-
7d. C -भागावियुक्तसा F -भागवियुक्तसा N -भागवियुक्तया
8b. N लेपनश् ABCDFN लेपनैः DN सज्जनैः F सज्जनै V श्लक्ष्णमञ्जनैः A -मजनैः C -मज्जनै
8c. N मुहुर्म्मुहु 8d N कृत्वा B मर्जन N मार्ग्शो DN -प्रयत्नतः
9a. V शोषमुपायातं N शेषमुपायातः 9b N कुद्यो V कुड्यं तन्मनु-
9c. F अपि वर्ष- D अपिवर्षगतस्यान्ते 9d ABCD प्रणश्येत N प्रणम्येतु
10b. ABDV द्विविधै- C द्विविधैव- F द्विविदैर्वणकैकृता CN -र्युता
10c. ABCFN कर्त्तव्या D चित्रवपुषो 10d ABCDFNV विविधा N -मभूमयः ABCFV मणिभूमयः

6. [One should apply plaster in such a way that] it is smooth, stands firm (*avaṣṭabdham*), without ups and downs and is laid neither too thick nor too thin.

7-8. When the wall which has been smeared with plaster and levelled becomes dry, then [it] is carefully smoothened by clay mixed with oil of *Vatica robusta (sarjataila)* and rubbed continuously and carefully with milk so as to achieve smoothness on the plaster *(lepanaślakṣṇasañjanaiḥ)*.

9. O Lord of men, that wall having quickly dried will never degenerate even for hundred years.

10. Following this very method, grounds of various dimensions *(mānabhūmayaḥ)* mixed with various colours should be made possessing exquisite beauty.

कुड्ये शुष्के तिथौ शस्ते ऋक्षे च गुणसंयुते ।
चित्रायोगे विशेषेण श्वेतवासा यतात्मवान् ।। ११ ।।

ब्राह्मणान्पूजयित्वा तु स्वस्तिवाच्य प्रणम्य च ।
तद्विदश्च यथान्यायं गुरुंश्च गुरुवत्सलः ।। १२ ।।

प्राङ्मुखो देवताध्यायी चित्रकर्म समारभेत् ।
श्वेतकाद्रवकृष्णाभिर्वतिर्काभिर्यथाक्रमम् ।। १३ ।।

आलेख्ये स्थापयेद्विद्वान् प्रमाणस्थानके तथा ।
ततस्तु रञ्जयेद्रङ्गैर्यथास्थानानुरूपतः ।। १४ ।।

श्यामा गौरी यथा तस्य छविः स्यात्तां प्रदर्शयेत् ।
तस्याश्च लक्षणं प्रोक्तं प्राङ् मया नृत्तविस्तरे ।। १५ ।।

11a. N कुद्य 11bV
11c. CNF चित्रयोगे 11d D श्वेतावासा D यतात्मनाम् N यतान्मवा F यतात्मराम्
12a. N ब्राह्मणां DN च 12b N वाच्यं
N lacks 12cd-14.
12c. AB तद्विधश्च
13b. ABV समाचरेत्
13c. A -कृष्णाभिवर्तिका- 13d F -यथाक्रमम्
14a. ABCDFNV आलिख्य 14ABCFV प्रमाणे स्थानके तथा
14c. CF गञ्जयेद्र- A यजुयेद्र- F -द्राङ्गै-
15b. CD छवि D स्यात् C स्मृतां D प्रदशयेत् 15c A तस्याः च
15d. CF प्रात्माया BV प्राप्ताया ABCDF नृपविस्तरे N भृ (?) तविस्तरे

11-13b. When the wall dries up, on an auspicious lunar day, under positive asterism, especially when the moon is in *Citrā*, when with due procedures he has made offerings to brahmins, those who know this [art], and his teachers and after having wished them well and bowed before them, the self-composed artist should begin to paint *(samārabhet)*. He should be dressed in white garments, should face the east, meditate upon his deity and he may begin to paint.

13c-14b. After sketching first in white, then brown and finally in black paint (or chalk), the well-versed (in painting) should mark out the proportions and in the same way the postures.

14cd. Afterwards, he should paint with colours each according to the right place.

15. The tone of the colour *(chavi)* should be shown depending on whether it is dark [shade] or light [tint]. Its characteristics have been told by me in the detailed exposition of the dance.

मूलरङ्गाः स्मृताः पञ्च श्वेतः पीतो विलोहितः ।
नीलः कृष्णश्च राजेन्द्र शतशोऽन्यतराः स्मृताः ।। १६ ।।

पूर्वरङ्गसमायोगाद् भावकल्पनया तथा ।
स्वबुद्ध्या कारयेद्रङ्गाञ्छतशोऽथ सहस्रशः ।। १७ ।।

नीलपीतव्यतिकृतिः पलाश इति शस्यते ।
स शुद्धश्चैव मिश्रश्च नीलाभ्यधिक एव च ।। १८ ।।

श्वेताधिकश्च भवति छवीनामनुरूपतः ।
श्वेताधिको वा न्यूनो वा समांशस्त्वेति स त्रिधा ।। १९ ।।

स एकस्तम्भनायुक्तो बहुधैवं विकल्पयेत् ।
तेन दुर्वाङ्कुरापीतः कपित्थहरिताः शुभाः ।। २० ।।

16a. F फूलसङ्ग N फूलरङ्गः D फूलसङ्ग N स्मृता
16b. N श्वेताः D श्वेतं N पीताविलोहिताः ABCFV –विलोमतः
16c. N नीलाकृष्णाश्च ABCFV कृष्णो नीलश्च D कृष्णो नीलः 16d ABCDFNV ऽन्तरतः AVDF स्मृतः
17a. ABCDFN पूर्ण– ABCDFNV –रङ्गविभागेन 17b ABCF तया
N lacks 17cd. 17c. AB सुबुद्धया !7cd ABCDF कारयेद्रङ्ग 17d ABCF –शतशो–
18a. V2 नीलपीतकृतिर्वृतिः V नीलेष्वतिव्यतिकृतिः 18b V पालाश
18c. V शुद्धः D सुशुद्धश्च ABCF शुद्धश्वेतमिश्रश्च Nचेतमिश्चश्च DN श्वेतमिश्रश्च
18d. D नीलीम्य–
19a. N एकाधिकश्च D एकाधिश्च CFV एकाधिकं च AB एकादिकं च
19d. V समांशश्चेति N समांस्थो तिवासयेत् CF समांशस्त्वेति <.. >वा AB वा न वा
20a. N स (?) कस्तम्भना– 20b N वहुवैधं F बहुधेवं D बह्वाधेवं ABCD विकल्प्यते VB विकल्पते 20c N दूर्वाङ्कुरो पीतः
20cd. ACF –पीतकपित्थ– 20d. ACF –हरितः ABN हरिता ACF शुभः N शुभा D शुभ

16-17. The five basic colours *(mūlaraṅga)* are said to be white, yellow, red, blue and black. [But] O King, other [colours] are in hundreds. By combining the primary colour *(purvarangavikāreṇa)* using one's imagination *(bhāvakalpanayā)* and discretion one could make hundred, even thousand-fold colours.

18-19. [For example] green is said to be the combination of blue and yellow. It could be [of the] pure [i.e. unmixed] *(śuddha)* and of mixed [types] *(miśra)*. [As for the mixed type], according to the tone *(chavi)* [desired], it is [either a shade] augmented with black *(nīla)*[3] [or a tint] when mixed with white. It [tint][4] is of three types depending on whether white is added to the [secondary] colour in greater, lesser or equal proportion.

20-21b. [Similarly] it [the secondary colour eg. green] can yield many varieties [by increasing or decreasing the proportion of the component colours] by keeping one colour as constant [i.e. fixed] *(stambhanāyuktā)*. It [such a method] results in beautiful [variations of green such as] greenish yellow like that of the *dūrva* grass [and] yellowish green, like that of wood-apple or *Feronia elephantum.*

[3]It must be noted that *nīla* in this context means "black" as opposed to "blue".
[4]When white is added to any colour, it results in a tint (which is same as *Gaurīchavi*, adh. 27) and when black is added, it becomes a shade (*śyāmāchavi*, adh. 27)

मुद्गश्यामप्रभृतयः कर्तव्याश् छवयो नृप ।
नीलः पाण्डुरसंपृक्तो विरागस्सोऽप्यनेकधा ।। २१ ।।

अन्योन्याभ्यधिकं न्यूनं समांशं वा स कल्पयेत् ।
तेन नीलोत्पलनिभा चाषसच्छायसत्प्रभाः ।। २२ ।।

क्रियन्ते छवयो रम्या यथायोगविनिश्चयात् ।
†लाक्षया श्वेतया युक्ता लाक्षारोध्रपिनद्धया†।। २३ ।।

रक्ता रक्तोत्पलश्यामा छविर्भवति शोभना ।
सापि नानाविधानन्यान् वर्णान्विकुरुते बहून् ।। २४ ।।

रङ्गद्रव्याणि कनकं रजतं ताम्रमेव च ।
अभ्रकं राजवर्तं च सिन्दूरं त्रपुरेव च ।। २५ ।।

21a. Dमुङ्गश्याम- ABCFV -प्रकृतयः 21N -चवयो
21c. ABCDFN नील- CFN -रसस्पृक्तो A -संप्रक्तो B- संप्रोक्तो D संयुक्तो
21d. N विरा < .... >सौप्यनेकधाः F विरस्सो CF विर्रस्सो < . > प्यने- V विरङ्ग:सोप्यने- A विरङ्गस्मोप्यने-
22ab. D -भ्यधिकन्यूनसमांस व ABFNV समांशवसकल्पना C समांशवमकल्पना
22d. V माषसच्छायसुप्रभा A माषसच्छायासुप्रभा CF माषमच्छायनप्रभा N मोषसछायाप्तप्रभाः D निभाश्वासच्छायप्रभाम्
23a. CFV क्रियते N छवया D चाया 23b N -विनिश्चया
23c. N श्वेतयान् D लाक्षेपाश्वेर्तया 23d D -रोध्रयि < ? > नद्धया
24a. N रक्तरक्तोत्पलश्यामो
24cd. CF नानाविधानन्यावर्णान् D नानाविधारम्यान्वर्णान्हिकुरुते N -द्यावणान्विकरुणा बहूं
25b. F ताम्र एव च
25c. D रास्तवर्त BCFV राजवन्तं N राजवर्णं 25d ABDF त्रिपुरेव

21c-22b. [On the other hand] tones [of primary and secondary colours] are made starting from [dark] bean green [Phaseolus mungo] etc. (*mudgaśyāmaprabhṛtayaḥ*). A [monochromatic] shade *(virāga)* [results] when black is mixed with white.

A Shade *(śyāmā chavi)* [too is three-fold] according to the amount of black added to the colour in more, less or equal proportion.

22c-23b. By that [earlier method whereby black is added to the primary and secondary colours] *(tena)*, [shades of blue such as] dark blues like that of a blue lotus and blue jay *(cāṣa)* can be made.

23c-24. [Thus] beautiful tones can be made by fixing appropriate combinations. A beautiful [tint] of red comes about when [red] lac and the red powder of the bark of *Symplocos racemosa* combine with white lac.

Red [when mixed with black] becomes a beautiful shade, dark as the red lotus. That [shade] too transforms many colours into different types [depending on the amount of black added.]

25-26b. Gold, silver, copper, mica, lapis lazuli, ultramarine *(rājavarta)*, Red lead, tin, yellow orpiment, lime, lac, vermillion and indigo form the substance of (mineral) colours.

हरितालं सुधा लाक्षा तथा हिङ्गुलकं नृप ।
नीलं च मनुजश्रेष्ठ तथाऽन्ये सन्त्यनेकशः ।। २६ ।।

देशे देशे महाराज कार्यास्ते स्तम्भनायुताः ।
लोहानां पत्रविन्यासं भवेद्वापि रसक्रिया ।। २७ ।।
[चूर्णं तु रंगकेशानां इन्द्रगोपकसंयुताम्]

संकटलोहविन्यस्तमभ्रकं द्रावकं भवेत् ।
एवं भवति लोहानां लेखनीकर्मयोग्यता ।। २८ ।।

अभ्रकं द्रावकं प्रोक्तं सुरसिन्धुजभूमिजे ।
चर्मक्काथोऽथ वकुलनिर्यासस्तम्भनाद्भवेत्
सर्वेषामेव रङ्गाणां सिन्दूरक्षीर इष्यते ।। २९ ।।

†मतङ्गदूर्वारसपट्टबद्धैः†
संस्तम्भितं चित्रं भुदारपुच्छैः ।
धौतं जलेनापि न नाशयेत्
तिष्ठत्यनेकान्यपि वत्सराणि ।। ३० ।।

इति श्रीविष्णुधर्मोत्तरे तृतीयखण्डे मार्कण्डेयवज्रसंवादे चित्रसूत्रे रङ्गव्यतिकरो नाम चत्वारिंशत्तमोऽध्यायः ।। ४० ।।

26a. N भविताल B लक्षा 26b N यथा N हिंगुलकं
26c. D मनुक्तश्रेष्ठ? 26d N तथाऽन्यै CF सन्त्यनेककः
27b. D स्तम्भनायुता 27c B लहानां 27d D नसक्रिया ABCFVS1S2 lack चूणं ......संयुताम्
28a. N lack 28-30 ABCFV संकटं D सटङ्कं लोह-
28ab. F -विन्यस्तंमभ्रकं D विन्यस्तश्चतुस्व ? AB -स्तमभ्रका-
28b. V1 -स्तं शूद्रकं ABCDFV द्रावणं 28d V लेखने
29a CV अभ्रक- AB अभ्रका- ABCV -द्रावणं CFDV द्रावणं AS1S2 सुरसेन्दुज- CDF सरसेन्दुज V सुरसेन्द्र-
29b. V2 चर्म्मक्काथो CF चर्मक्काथं D चर्म्मकचाथो V1 चम्भाकुथो D बहलनिर्यासस्तम्भन ACF -स्तंभना भवेत्
29c. D सङ्गाणां D सिन्दूरे क्षार 30a ABCF मतङ्ग D एमङ्गं F -पुर्वारसपद्धबन्धैः A -पट्टबंधैः C रसपद्धबन्धैः 30b ABCVF चित्रमुदार- D चित्रमुदार < पृ? > ष्टैः
30cd. D नाशयेतिस्तिष्ठ-

26cd. O Best of Men, likewise, there are many more types (of mineral colours).

27. O Lord, in different regions, they are combined with astringent, Of the metals, they are either spread out in foiles or they liquified.

27. [The powder of *Raṅgakeśa* (?) is combined with *Indragopaka* (fire-flies ?).]

28-29. Mica when added to impervious metals acts as a liquifier. Thus the metals become fit for painting. Mica is said to be a liquifier regarding that which is born in the earth (metals?) or that which is born in the Ganges (?). The decoction of leather comes about from stiffening the extract of *Bakula* tree (or by astringent made out of its extract).

30. The milk of *Sindūra* tree is recommended for all the colours. A painting which is astringed by hogs' tail tied together by a cloth [dipped] in the juice of *Mataṅga* and *dūrvā* grass is never destroyed even by water and lasts for many years.

NOTES TO ADHYĀYA 40

40 1a. *triprakāreṣṭakācūrṇe.* Note that this reading found in N, D, and V is the correct one. PS appears to consider *citrākareṣṭacūrṇe* as a possible alternative :

> First crush the bricks into powder. These bricks, according to one reading are of three kinds (triprakāra). We are however, not what these three kinds are! According to another reading (*citrakāreṣṭakā*) they are painter's bricks. What are these painter's bricks? Are we to take them as tabloids or what are called goṭi in Gujarati ? (p. 115-116)

Note *citrakāreṣṭikā* is obviously a corruption and can be accounted for by the preceding *ca* of *mārkaṇḍeya uvāca.* It is easier to understand how *triprakāreṣṭakā-* might be corrupted to *citrakāreṣṭa-* than viceversa. It leaves us with the problem of what these three types of brickpowder are, about which the text is silent.

Note how SM interprets the three types:

SM: Brickpowder of three varieties (i.e. smooth, middling and coarse) (p. 180)

40.1c. *guggulum.* This reading from N and C is better than *guggulam* as accepted by all the scholars. The BṛSaṃ. confirms it in chapter 56 called *Vajralepalakṣaṇam* as follows :

> श्रीवासकरसगुग्गुलु - 56.3.

The commentator Bhaṭṭotpala considers it to be well known:

> गुग्गुलु : प्रसिद्धः

Note that the sense remains the same meaning bdellium or the exudation of *Amyris agallochum,* a fragrant gum resin used as a perfume and mendicant.

40.1d. *madhukam.* This emendation is based on a cross reference to *madhukam* in the chapter 57 of BṛSaṃ. mentioned in the second kind of plaster.

लाक्षाकुन्दुरुगुग्गुलुगृहधूमकपित्थबिल्वमध्यानि ।
नागफलनिम्बतिन्दुकमदनफलमधूकमञ्जिष्ठा:
सर्जरसरसामलकानि चेति कल्कः कृतो द्वितीयोऽयम् । 57.5

Bhaṭṭotpala explains it as *madhukaphalam.* Note this emendation is crucial to set the meter right or else the fifth syllable becomes long in form of -rū- . SK adopting V's *murukam* emends it to *mudgakam:*

> Having mixed saffron with oil (one) should mix (lit. place) (with it) gum resin, bees wax, liquorice, molasses and *mudga* preparation in equal parts. p.42

PS misses it out in the translation. SM accepts *madhu* and translates it as *"honey"*. (p. 180). The use of honey in plaster is uncorroborated.

40. 1d. *kundurūm.* This reading is a slight emendation of *kundurūkam.*

Note its mention in BṛSaṃ. :

> लाक्षाकुन्दुरुगुग्गुलु - 56.5

Bhaṭṭotpala explains it as :

> कुन्दुरुदेवदारुवृक्षनिर्यासः
>
> an extract from the *deodara* (Avaria Longifolia) tree.

40.2a. *kusumbhatailasamyuktam.* The reading from N and D is adopted which takes it as a compound. The oil extracted from the seeds of safflower oil is commonly used for lamps etc. Note the following mistranslation. SK (p. 34) takes it as "Having mixed saffron with oil.", PS (p. 116) as "Kusumbha with oil" and SM (p. 180) as "safflower soaked in oil".

40.3a. *balbajam.* Note that this reading comes from C and F. All the scholars prefer *bilvajam* from V and translate it as "woodapple" identifying it with *bilva. Balbajam* which is a more reliable reading meaning "a species of coarse grass not liked by cattle" *(Eleusine indica)* fits in well with context. It forms one of the binding ingredients along with *śaṇa* meaning "hemp".

SK: Finally the astringent made of the bel-tree *(Feronia elephantum)* destructive (of all injurious agents)...... (p. 43)

PS : Add to this, the pulpa of bilva in two parts .... (p. 116)

SM : To these two parts already composed is added powder of lime three fourths burnt, with bel fruit pulp and lampblack. (pp. 180)

40.3b. *saśaṇamśakam.* This emendation is mainly derived from N's reading *śaśaṇam kaṣam śaṇa* means a kind of hemp (*Cannabis sativa*). Its function must have been to act as a binder by the virtue of being fibrous. Note that this emendation is confirmed by the findings of the composition of the ground employed in the Ajanta murals.

The ground of the paintings is composed of mud-plaster containing about 10 to 12 per cent of combined water and organic matter such as vegetable-fibres, paddy-husk, grass and other fibrous material of organic origin, and rock-grit or sand.

Ajanta Murals, p. 53. ed. A. Ghosh, New Delhi, 1967

This emendation is further confirmed by an interesting reference to the plastering of wall in *Ādiparva*, **Mahābhārata** :

शणसर्ज्जरसादीनि यानि द्रव्याणि कानिचित् । 1.132.9

(see Note 12.40.7 cd. for a fuller citation).

Note how the corrupt reading leads the scholars to a serious error:

SK : follows *maṣakam kaṣam* translates verse 3ab as :

> Finally the astringent made of the Bel-tree (Feronia Elephantum) destructive (of all injurious agents) mixed in the proportion of two to one should be added by the intelligent artist (p. 43)

PS: Add to this, the pulp of bilva in two parts and put in it the black powder of touch stone. (p. 116)

SM : To these two parts already composed is added a powder of lime three fourths burnt, with *bel* fruit pulp and *lampblack.* (p. 180)

40.4a. *śarkaratoyena.* This emendation comes primarily from cross reference in the parallel art treatises. *Śarkara* is taken to mean "sugar" or "jaggary". The reading that MS N offers is *sakala.* In the *Newārī* script, -la- and -ra- often get mixed up caused by the confusion in the regional pronunciation.

Note that F has *cakara.*

ŚilpRat.(adhy. 64) in the same context mentions *gulavāriṇā* :

गुलतोयेन संसिञ्चेत् तच्चूर्ण बालुकान्वितम् ।। १६ ।।
पेषयेद् दृषदि क्षिप्त्वा दृषदा गुलवारिणा ।
नवनीतमिवायाति यावत् तावत् सुपेषयेत् ।। १९ ।।

Note that -da- and -la- in this case are variations in regional pronunciation. In the CitSūt. as well in the ŚilpRat, the function of the sugar of jaggary solution seems to be the same i.e. to soften the plaster. There is mention of *śarkara* in SamaSūtDhāra. (GOS 25):

पूर्वोर्क्त (नियार्सा पुना विधात्तयः ?) कटशर्कराम् ।
तोयेन तां (प्रचांकृत्य ?) पटमालिखयेत् तया
अनेन विधिना बन्धश्चित्रर्मणि शस्यते (p. 587 verse 38/39)

MānUll. likewise mentions "sugar" *(sitā)* in *vimśati* 3, adh, 1, verse 138 :

शङ्खचूर्णसितापिष्टं वज्रलेपसमन्वितम् ।

ŚilpRat. too, mentions *śarkaraśuktyoścūrṇam* in a section called *Sudhā* in chapter 40. (p. 64)

I translate *picchilena* as "slimy", an adjective to *śarkaratoyena.*

Note how ŚilpRat. employs it to mean the same :

पिच्छिलं त्रिफलाम्भश्च त्र्यंशादिकमिदं क्रमात् । (p. 64. part I)

SM emends *śakalatoyena* to *kalaśatoyena* :

> Then it is soaked in water stored in a pot so as to get lubricous... (p. 180)

SK translates (p. 43) V's *śakalatoyena* as "moist split pulse dissolved in water"! PS adopts *śakalatoyena* and connects it with *picchila* taken as a tree.

> Fill this with water of the bark of *Picchila.* (p. 116)

40.5d. *śuṣkakuḍye.* This reading is adopted from D. All MSS show *śuṣkam* which the scholars connect with *pralepam* or coating of plaster. It does not yield good sense.

SK : a skillful (artist) should put (this) *dried (yet still damp)* plaster on the wall. (p. 43)

It should be taken a compound meaning "on the dry wall". This is supported by MānUll which mentions *śuṣkabhittau* in the same context (see above). Note how SK connects *śuṣkam* with *pralepam* and translates it "dried (yet still damp) plaster". This contradiction results because SK realises that dry plaster cannot be smeared.

40.5c. *vimṛjya. Vimṛṣya* found in all MSS is a corruption of *vimṛjya* "after having rubbed".

SM translates it as "after testing":

> a coat applied by the skillful artist on the wall after testing *that it is quite dry.* (p. 180)

40.6a. *samamavaṣṭabdham.* Note without this emendation, the verse fails to conform to the *anuṣṭubh* meter with the 5th syllable being long. In *Newārī* and more so in *Śāradā* script, -ma- and -sa- are easy to mistake. The meaning remains unaffected and the metre rectified.

40.7b. *sudhāliptam samamkṛtam.* D's reading *sudāliptam* has been emended to *sudhāliptam* to derive the appropriate meaning. In the given context, this makes good sense. It is a brief recapitulation of the stages of plastering already stated- "When the wall which has been smeared with plaster and levelled becomes dry ... ".

SK follows V's reading *-tatpraliptamasatkṛtam :*

> Should it look *ill done* after having become (quite) dry (due to shrinkage), then it ought to be carefully smoothed .... (p. 43)

PS emends it to *tapraliptamasatkṛtam* :

> When the wall thus plastered becomes dry and is *unpolished,* (p. 117)

SM emends it to *tatpraliptamasatkṛtam* on the following grounds :

> F.N. 1. Since smoothening is mentioned next, it should be here असंकृत, असत्कृतम् does not convey the sense. (p. 151)

Note SM's translation:

> When the wall is dry after coat and is still *not quite smooth*...(p. 180)

40.7cd. *tayā mrdā tailabhāgāviyuktayā.* Note that *yadā* at the beginning of the verse requires *tadā* and this makes the meaning clearer. "When the wall (which) is smeared with the plaster and smoothened, then the plaster is polished ... ".

Note since both the MSS CFN have *tailabhāgaviyukta-*, its correct interpretation becomes a problem. In the *Ādiparva, **Mahābhārata***, there exists an interesting section on the instructions about the plastering of the wall:

शणसर्ज्जरसादीनि यानि द्रव्याणि कानिचित् ।
आग्नेयान्युत सन्तीह तानि सर्वाणि दापय ।। १.१३२.९
सर्पिषा च सतैलेन लाक्षया चाप्यनल्पया ।
मृत्तिकां मिश्रयित्वा त्वं लेपं कुड्येषु दापयेः ।। १.१३२.१०
शणान्वसं घृतं दारु यन्त्राणि विविधानि च ।
तस्मिन्वेश्मनि सर्बाणि निक्षिपेथाः समन्ततः ।। १.१३२.११

So the correct reading seems to be preserved in N and D - *tailabhāgaviyuktayā* and *tailabhāgavimuktayā* respectively. Both convey the same sense but N's reading is closer to C and F and hence adopted.

SM is right in treating *sarjarasataila-* as a compound but in the translation, he appears to accept the reading given in C :

> it should be smoothened by an application of the clay bereft of sarjarasa and oil. (p. 180)

Note that *sarja rasa* is an extract from the tree *Vatica robusta* (Turner, R.L.).

40.8b. *lepanam.* This is minor emendation derived from N's reading *lepana.* It is the coating of plaster already applied which now requires to be smoothened and refered to by *ślakṣṇīkuryāt.*

40.8b. *ślakṣṇasañjanaiḥ.* This again is derived from D's and N's reading *sarjanaiḥ. Sañjanaiḥ* means "the act of attaching, fastening, sticking or adhering". All other MSS read *mañjanaiḥ* accepted by all scholars.

SK leaves it out in the translation.

PS adopts V's *-mañjanaih.:*

Then one should again polish it with *black collyrium.* (p. 116)

SM too adopts V's reading

> it should be smoothened by an application of the clay bereft of *sarjarasa* and oil *by coats of lamp black*. (p. 180)

Note how the gross error results from a corrupt reading. The use of lamp black or collyrium would only result in a dark background would not be ideal for painting.

40.8c. SK translates *kṣireṇa* as "with water":

> (It is further made) smooth by (repeated) anointing, constant sprinkling **with water** ạnd by careful polish. (p. 43)

Kṣīra here means "milk" or "thickened milk".

40.8d. *kṛtvāsiktvā mārjanaḥ yatnataḥ* Here the readings of CFV are adopted.

40.10b. *vividhair.* This is adopted from N. All the other MSS read *dvividhair* which does not make a very good sense given that in the following line, 10d, *vividhair* is mentioned and there is no reference to the two types.

SK accepts *dvividhair* from V:

> By this means various jewelled floors can be made of variegated texture in *two fold colours*. (p. 43)

PS not only mistranslates the term *varṇaka* as a type of smear but proposes that *dvividhavarṇakair* corresponds to two types of plaster given in verse 1-8. This is a misinterpretation because it is obvious from these verses that only one type of plaster is discussed. In fact, *anena prakāreṇa* in 10a contradicts the above mentioned view of PS *varṇaka* should be taken as "pigment" or "colour".

> PS: The various manibhūmis (lit. surfaces having the crystal like brightness) should be prepared in this way with two varṇakas i.e. two types of smear (described above). If we, however, take the meaning of varṇakas as merely pigments, there should be two kinds of pigments on the wall on which the paintings are to be drawn. (p. 116)

SM suggests a conjecture in the footnote which is confirmed by the reading in N.

> 4. It may be वि instead of द्वि as it fits विविधा better. (p. 151)

Hence, SM gives an alternative interpretation in the translation:

> In this manner a variety of mosaic floors can be made in picturesque fashion by the use of two or different colours, (p.43)

40.10d. *-mānabhūmayaḥ*. Note that this reading comes from D and makes good sense. *Māna* here means "measure/dimension". Regarding *-Bhūmayaḥ* there is a slight ambiguity in its interpretation. It could either mean "ground (of various dimensions)" or "postures (of various dimensions)".

In this context, it means the former.

Note that the corrupt reading *-maṇibhūmayaḥ* was responsible for the following translations:

> SK : By this means various jewelled floors can be made of variegated texture in twofold colours. (p. 43)
>
> PS : The various *maṇibhūmis* (lit. surfaces having the crystal like brightness) should be prepared in this way with two varṇakas i.e two types of smear (described above) (p. 116)
>
> SM : In this same manner a variety of mosaic floors can be made in picturesque fashion by the use of two or different colours. (p.180)

11a.bc. Note that all the translations lack the technical sense of *tithau śaste ṛkṣe ca guṇasaṃyute citrāyoge.*

tithau śaste: Note *tithi* refers to a lunar day which may begin at any time in the nychthemeron. The connection of the lunar day with the date is that the day of the month (i.e. the *sāvana* day) takes it number from that of the lunar day which is current at sun-rise. *śaste* here means "auspicious". Hence, "On an auspicious lunar day". *Ṛkṣe ca guṇasaṃyute* means "and under positive asterism".

citrāyoge:

Note that there are 27 divisions of space measured in degrees along the line of the moon's circuit. They are named after constellations within them. *Citrā* is one of them. *viśeṣeṇa* goes with *citrāyoge* meaning "especially when the moon is in *Citrā*". Note the various translations :

SK : In painting with care on a wall, dry brilliant and smooth, an artist devoted to his master, should begin his work on auspicious day , ...(p. 43)

PS : He has to start his work in the Citrā Nakṣatra. (p. 116)

SM emends *guṇasaṃyute* to *gaṇasaṃyute* :

When the wall is dry, on a good day [*tithau śaste*] with an excellent constellation [*rkṣe*] that is appropriate to the *gaṇa* (*deva* in preference to *manushya* and *rākshasa*) [*gaṇasaṃyute*] specially suited for starting a picture [*citrāyoge viśeṣeṇa*] (like *Punarvasu* for *Rama. Ardra* for *Naṭarāja, Rohini for Kṛishṇa, Mṛigaśira* for *Śiva*, etc.). (p. 181)

The text within the square brackets is inserted by me.

40.12b. *svasti vācya.*

SM : ... having adored Vedic seers and uttered auspicious hymns,... (p. 181)

40.13b. *samārabhet.* This reading comes from C, F and D. Its meaning "should commence" fits in well. All the scholars follow *samācaret* from A and V which is corrupt.

40.13cd. SK translates *śvetakādravakṛṣṇābhir vartikābhir as* "with unoozing black and brushes". This must have come about by her splitting the compound into *śvetaka* and *adrava.* (p. 43)

PS translates *vartikair* as "brushes" (p. 116). From the given context, it is clear that it refers to the colour of pigments with which the initial sketch is done. It is for this reason that the colour employed are neutral such as white, reddish brown and black in increasing darkness.

SM appears to overlook this line in the translation.

40.14b. *pramāṇasthānake.* Note that this reading is adopted from D and is taken as an accusative dual meaning "body measurements and the postures". All the scholars follow the corrupt reading from C,F and V - *pramāṇe sthānake.*

Note the various translations:

SK : ... and fix them on the duly measured ground. (p.43)

PS : Then he should place it on a proportionate position or background or frame. *(sthānaka).*

SM omits verse 14 in his text but the translation includes it and is correct.

40.15a. *yathā.* N's reading is preferred to *tathā* found in other MSS. *yathā* used with *tasya chavih* here means "skin" and not the use of darker of lighter shades, i.e. light and shade.

SM: Darker and lighter shades should be shown as they occur. (pp. 181)

40.15b. *chaviḥ.* N preserves the correct reading and it confirms SM's emendation.

PS takes *chaviḥ* as the colour of the skin or of a surface in case of a painting. From the context in this adhy. it clearly refers to the tonal quality of a colour i.e. the tone. It can be defined as "the prevailing effect of the combination of light and shade,.... " (see ***The Oxford Dictionary, ed. James Murray***). This interpretation of chavi is confirmed by its use in adhy. 27 of the ViDhUp. of the *khaṇḍa* III. There it is subdivided into *Gaurī* (tint) and *śyāmā* (shade).

द्विप्रकारा छविर्यस्मात्सर्वस्येह प्रकीर्तिता ।
गौरी पञ्चविधा तत्र श्यामा द्वादशधा भवेत् । ।

40.15d. *nṛttavistare.* This emendation comes from N's reading *nṛ (bhṛ)tavistare.* I accept this reading because the chapter 27 from the Nṛttasūtra section is what this verse here refers to. SM translates *chaviḥ as* "chiaruscuro" and translates :

> This chiaruscuro has been earlier explained by me at length. (p. 181)

40.16b. *vilohitaḥ*. Note both SK and PS follow *vilomataḥ* whereas SM rightly emends it to *vilohitaḥ* on conjecture which is confirmed by N's reading:

SK: Primary colours are said to be five : white, yellow, of the colour of the emblic *myrobalan,* black and blue. (p. 44)

PS : According to verse 8 of adhyāya 27, the primary colours are Śveta-white, Rakta- red, Pīta-yellow, kṛṣṇa-black and Harita-green. While according to verse 16 of this adhyāya (ad.40) white, yellow, *vilomataḥ* (produced from *viloma ? mi*) i.e. emblic (*myrobalam amalaki)* black and blue are primary colours. (p. 117)

Note that PS's failure to diagnose *vilomataḥ* as corrupt leads her to postulate "a difference in the tradition of primary colours" in the adhy. 27 and 40.

40.17a. *pūrvaraṅgasamāyogād-.* Note that *pūrva-* is found in CFN which here, as SK interprets, refers to the primary colours. The bold emendation of *-vibhāgena* to *samāyogad-* draws support from verse 9 of the adhy. 27 of the ViDhUp :

श्वेतो रक्तस्तथा पीतः कृष्णो हरितमेव च ।
मूलवर्णाः समाख्याताः पञ्च पार्थिवसत्तम ।।
एकद्वित्रिसमायोगाद्भावकल्पनया तथा ।
संख्यैवान्तरवर्णानां लोके कर्तुं न शक्यते ।।

Note that the *ekadvitri-* refers to the three primary colours just as the term *pūrvaraṅga* does in the adhy. 40. On the other hand, -*vibhāgena* yields a poor sense. SM adopts *pūrvam* translating it as "first" in an adverbial sense. (p. 181)

40.17c. *raṅgānśataśo.* Here V's reading is adopted against the *raṅgam śataśo* of all the other MSS as it makes a good sense.

40.18c. *sa śuddhas caiva miśraśca.* The sense demands this emendation of *śvetamiśraśca* to *ścaivamiśraśca.* Note the similarity between -śva- and -śca- in the *Śāradā* script. However, *sa* is ambiguous for it can refer either to any colour or to the green mentioned in the preceding verse.

A colour is either pure or mixed. In the latter, where we are discussing the tone, either white or black is mixed with it. So *nīlābhayādhika* (here *nīla* means black) and *śvetādhika* refers to the types of mixed colours. When black is added to any colour, it results in a shade of that colour and when white it becomes a tint of that colour. Cf. ManUll. *adhy.*1, *vim* 3, v. 164.

एवं शुद्धाश्च मिश्राश्च वर्णभेदाः प्रकीर्तिताः ।

Note that the preceding this verse of the text cited is an account of shades and tints (158-163).

SK: It is either pure, with an admixture of white, or blue-predominating. (p. 44)

PS takes *sa* as referring to "green" of *palāśa:*

> *Palāśa* would either be śuddha-pure, when white predominates or one in which *Nīla* would predominate Nīlābhyadhika. (p. 118)

SM: It may be pale with a greater modicum of white or deeper with blue. (p.181)

40.19d. *samāṃśastveti.* Note this reading is taken from C,F,D, and A. All scholars prefer V's reading *-samāṃśasceti* which would appear to be lectio facilior. The sense remains unaltered. Note SK. translates this verse in which there is no reference to blue:

> Blue (too) is of three kinds : with white predominating, with very little white or with both in equal parts. (p.44)

40.20. *stambhanā* poses some problem in interpretation. It is quite obvious that it has technical meaning which has to be derived from the context. The range of meaning given in the lexicons -"stopping/ arresting/ checking/ restraining/ paralyzing" prove inadequate. What verse 20ab means is "That (i.e. colour in a compound) is thus varied in many ways (when) one (of its components) is constant (or fixed)". The preceding line mentions how there results three types of colour depending upon the proportion of white mixed. Verse 20 is about the manifold transformation which results if one component of the mixed colour remains constant. The example given are variations of green without the addition of white or black. They result from the alteration of the proportion of the primary colours which make up green.

Durvāṅkurāpītaḥ : greenish yellow

Kapitthaharitāḥ : woodapple green

Note the various translations :

SK: Thus it is variously transformed by being connected with anything applied as an astringent. (p.44)

PS : it would be thus variegated by making one of them a binding substance. (p. 118)

SM : With one tone predominant many tints are produced. (p. 181)

40.21a. *mudgaśyāmaprabhṛtayaḥ.* The correct reading is preserved in DN. It refers back to the list of shades given in adhy. 27 verses 13-15. *Prabhṛtayaḥ* then makes sense for it means all the shades starting from *mudgaśyāma, dūrvāṅkuraśyāma, pāṅduśyāma, haritaśyāma* and so on. Note that the verse 22cd in which *nīlotpalanibha* and *cāṣasatchāya-satprabhā* appear, again refers back to this list. Cf. *nīlotpalaśyāma* and *Cāsaśyāma.* Note the various translations in which in place of *-prabhṛtayaḥ, -prakṛtayaḥ* is followed:

SK: Thus beautiful (lit. auspicious) paintings should be made yellowish like the dūrvā sprouts, ... (p. 44)

PS: With it one can have the following colours of skin: Dūrvāṅkurā-pītā,.. (p.181)

40.21cd. *nīlaḥ pāṇḍurasampṛkto.* Note *nīlaḥ* here means "black" again since it is mentioned alongside *pāṇḍura* or "white". *Virāga,* an emendation of *viraṅga,* in my view, refers to a monochromatic "shade"; for eg, a variety of grey can be obtained from mixing white and black.

SK: Blue tinged with yellowish white (becomes) changed in colour ... (p. 44)

PS: Similarly by making *Nīla* astringent with *pāṇḍura* (p. 118)

SM : *Blue* mixed with white is a tertiary colour ... (p.181)

40.22b. *samāṃśam vā sa kalpayet.* Note that D preserves the correct reading. *Sa* refers to "shade" or *virāga* which like the tint or the tone, may be of three types depending upon the quantity of black mixed. Note SM's emendation in form of *samāṃśam vāṃśakalpanā* is unnecessary, given D's reading. SM explains thus:

> F.N. 4) It should be समांश and other smaller proportions, अंशकल्पना, समाशवश कल्पना is not easily construed. (p. 152)

40.22d. *cāṣasacchāyasatprabhā.* All MSS read *māṣa-* which yields poor sense. It is clear that the text reverts to shades and focuses on those of blue. The colour of *Māṣa* (*Phaseolus radiatus*) or the green bean is most inappropriate. N reads *moṣasachāyasaprabhā* from which is derived the emendation of *-suprabhā* to *-satprabhā.* It also draws support from verse 15cd of adhy. 27 :

> ततो नीलोत्पलश्यामा चाषश्यामा च ततः परम् ।
>
> A *cāṣe* or a blue jay (coracias benghenlensis {Linnaeus}) possesses various shades of blue.

The following is a quote of its field characters:

> A striking Oxford and Cambridge blue bird with biggish head, heavy rather crow like bill, ruffous brown coloured breast and pale blue abdomen and vent ... In flight, the dark blue and pale blue portions of the wings flash as brilliant bands.

***Handbook of the Birds of India and Pakistan,* Salim Ali and S. Dillon Ripely, OUP, 1983.**

The translation of the compound would be "light and dark shades (of blue) found in *Cāṣa.* Note that *suprabhā* and *satprabhā* convey a technical sense standing for "dark" and "light". Cf. *satchāyā* in the ViDhUp. in verse 71, adhy. 55.

SK : For that reason the blue-lotus-colour (nīlotpala) appears beautiful when partly shaded dark like the *māṣa*. (p. 44)

PS : Similarly by making Nīla the astringent with pāṇḍura the subsidiary in either equal, smaller or greater proportion, one can have the colour having the blue of Nīlotpala, *Māṣa* (? cāṣa) etc. (p. 118).

SM's translation makes better sense.

40.23cd. *laksaya ...... pinaddhaya.* This line is regarded as suspect though it is possible to guess the sense from the context. What is being discussed is the transformation of red into tint and shade.

40.25c. *rājavartam.* Only MS A preserves this reading. Cf. MānUll. adhy. 1, viṃ 3, verse 161 : राजावर्तः स एव स्यादतसीपुष्पसन्निभः ।

40.27c. Note that the translation of *lohānām* should be metals as opposed to "iron".

SK: A fluid should be made of iron leaves. (p. 45)

This translation is also in accurate because it does not account for the *va*. PS takes it as "irons or metals" (p. 118).

SM : Metal colours are to be laid in delicately thin sheets or by liquefying them by chemical methods. (p.182)

Note the additional half verse found only in D and N- *Raṅgakeṣānām* appears to be a technical name of a metal or a mineral. The mention of *indragopaka* is obscure.

40.28a. *saṃkaṭaloha-. Saṃkaṭa* makes better sense if taken as a compound with *lohavinyasta-* and as a qualifier of *loha* to mean impervious metals.

SK: A mica defile placed in iron should serve as a *distiller.* (p. 45)

PS: The iron and mica can be turned into liquids by putting them in a *narrow vessel.*

Note the emendation PS suggests:

> F.N. 1) I have emended the reading of the text thus I o ham samkaṭa viyastamabhrakam drāvaṇam bhavet. (p. 118)

40.28b. *drāvakam.* Note that *drāvaṇam* means causing to run, putting to flight whereas *drāvaka* has a technical meaning a flux to assist the fusion of metals. This emendation is necessary to get the correct sense.

SK: A mica defile placed in iron should serve as a *distiller.* (p. 45)

PS: see note 41.

SK: Ibid

40.29b. *surasindhujabhūmije.* The interpretation of this term is regarded as a problem.

Note SK. accepts the reading - *Surasendrabhūmije* which lacks one syllable and translates:

> *In the (work called) Surasendrabhumija,* a decoction of hides was said to be a distiller of mica ..... (p. 45)

PS : derives the following meaning :

> The mica can be turned into liquid bitumen and bellium. (p. 118)

Based on reading from S1 and S2 *surasenduja-*, I have derived *surasindhuja-*. *Surasindhu* is one of the synonyms for river Ganges. It could stand for riverborn substance used for painting and *bhūmija* could mean minerals found in earth. However, these meanings are vague and should be dealt as a problem.

40 29c. *carmakvātho.* This reading is adopted from C with a slight correction. Note *carmakvotho* found in other MSS is a corruption.

40.30a. - *paṭṭabaddhaiḥ.* This reading yields a poor sense and is regarded as suspect.

40.30a. *mataṅga-.* It is a kind of wild grass, Eleusine Aegyptica (***see K.M. Nadkarni's Indian Materia Medica, p. 476***)

40.30b. *bhūdārapucchaiḥ*. *Bhūdara-* is a conjecture based on the context and paleography. The text seems to refer to some kind of instrument i.e. brush in this context with which a painting is coated (varnish or astringent) to ensure that it is durable. Perhaps the tail of a hog may have been employed in this process. In the *Śāradā* script, -u- and -bhu- are very similar and interchangeble.

SK accepts the reading *udāra* and translates it as "magnificent" ie. a qualifier to *puccha* translated as a "hairy brush". (p. 45) PS. derives the meaning "a kind of corn with long stalks" for *udāra* (p. 119). SM, like SK, connects *udāra* with *puccha* and translates as "brushes of high quality hair".

ADHYĀYA 41

एकचत्वारिंशोऽध्यायः

मार्कण्डेय उवाट

सत्यं च दैशिकं चैव नागरं मिश्रमेव च ।
चित्रं चतुर्विधं प्रोक्तं तस्य वक्ष्यामि लक्षणम् ।।१।।

यत्किञ्चिल्लोकसादृश्यं चित्रं तत्सत्यमुच्यते ।
दीर्घाङ्गं सुप्रमाणं च सुकुमारं सुभूषणम् ।।२।।

चतुरस्त्रं सुसंपूर्ण न दुर्घटोल्वणाकृतिम् ।
समानस्थानलम्बाढ्यं दैशिकं तन्निगद्यते ।।३।।

दृढोपचितसर्वाङ्गं वर्तुलानयनोल्वणम् ।
चित्रं तन्नागरं ज्ञेयं स्वल्पमाल्यविभूषणम् ।।४।।

मिश्रं मिश्रं समाख्यातं समासान्मनुजोत्तम ।
तिस्रश्च वर्तनाः प्रोक्ताः पत्राच्छैदिकबिन्दुजाः ।।५।।

1a. दैशिकं *conj.* N वैशिकं ABV वैणिकं CF वेणिकं D वोणकं 1b B विश्रमेव 1c D < चित्रं चतुर्विधं >1d D प्रवक्ष्यामि 2a DN श्लोकसादृश्यं 2b D तत्यमुच्यते

2c. A दीर्घाङ्ग V दीर्घाङ्गे V सप्रमाणं 2d CF सुभूमिपम् N सुधूमिकं

3a. AB चतुरश्रं 3b दुर्घटोल्वणाकृतिम् *conj.* BCFVNS1S2 दीर्घं D दीथं BCFVNS1S2 नोल्वणाकृतिं A दीर्घ ने < < ल्व > > ल्वणाकृतिम् D -लोल्वणाकृतिः

3c. ABCFV प्रमाणं- CFV- स्थानलम्भाढ्यं AB -लंबाढे N -लम्भाघं

3d दैशिकं *conj.* NV वैणिकं CF वेणिकं D वोणकं AB वै < < ल्वा > > णाकं निगद्यते

4a. N दृटोपचित D दृढोषरिर-

4b. वर्तुलानयनोल्वणम् *conj.* D वर्तुल- ABCFNV वर्तुलं ABCF नघनोल्वणम् N वर्तुलंनघनोतनं BV - नद्यनोल्वणम् D -नुद्यालोल्वनं

4c. V तं नागरं 4d N नामाल्य- A -भूषिणम्

5a N मिश्रमिश्रं Cf चित्रंमिश्रं ABV चित्रमिश्रं 5b N समासान्मपजोत्तम

5c CF वर्तना प्रोक्ता N वर्तनां प्रोक्तां D वर्तन D प्रोक्ता

5d -च्छैदिक- *conj.* BV पत्राहैविक- CF पत्राहैविर्क- A पत्राहैरिक- D यत्राहैविक- N कथिताबिन्दुयत्तना

ADHYĀYA 41

Mārkaṇḍeya spoke :

1. Painting is said to be of four types : *Satya* ("Naturalistic"), *Daiśika* (Provincial/local), *Nāgara* (Urban/Professional) and *Miśra* (Mixed). I shall speak about its (their) characteristics (s).

2ab. Whichever painting that bears a similarity with the world [that painting] is called *Satya* ("Naturalistic").

2cd-3. That [painting] which has elongated figures, is large in size *(supramāṇam)* effortless, [ly painted] *(sukumāram),* profusely decorated *(subhūṣaṇam),* symmetrical [in composition] *(caturasram)* fully complete *(susampūrṇam),* in which the figures are neither difficult to accomplish nor strong in shape *(na durghaṭolvaṇākṛtīm)* and in which the plumb line is used for making symmetrical [i.e. frontal] postures *(samānasthāna)* is called *Daiśika* (Provincial/local).

4. [That painting] in which all the figures are firmly developed, *(dṛḍhopacitasarvāṅgam)* [so as to appear three dimensional], in which calculation [for foreshortening] is derived from a circle (*vārtulānayanolvaṇam*) and very little decoration in form of garlands *(svalpamālyāṅbhūṣaṇam)* is used, such a painting is called *Nāgara.*

5. O Best of Men, a *Miśra* [painting], in short, is known to be mixed [i.e.a combination of the three types as listed above]. The three types of line-rendering *(vartanā)* are said to be: *Patrajā* (leaf/paper born), *Acchaidikā* (unbroken) and *Bindujā* (dot-born).

कृताकृताभी रेखाभिः कथिता पत्रवर्तना ।
अतीव कथिता सूक्ष्मा तथाच्छैदिकवर्तना ।। ६ ।।

उक्षावष्टम्भनायुक्ता कथिता बिन्दुवर्तना ।
दौर्बल्यं स्थूलरेखत्वमविभक्तत्वमेव च ।।७ ।।

बृहद्गण्डौष्ठनेत्रत्वं संविरुद्धत्वमेव च ।
मानविकारता चेति चित्रदोषाः प्रकीर्तिताः ।।८ ।।

स्थानप्रमाणभूलम्बा मधुरत्वं विभक्तता ।
सादृश्यं क्षयवृद्धी च गुणाश्चित्रस्य कीर्तिताः ।। ९ ।।

रेखा च वर्तना चैव भूषणं वर्णमेव च ।
विज्ञेया मनुजश्रेष्ठ चित्रकर्मविभूषणाः ।। १० ।।

N lacks verse 6

6a. कृताकृताभी *conj.* CF कृत्राकृतिभि V पत्राकृतिभि AB पत्राकृतिभी D यत्राकृतिभि

6b. Dयत्र वर्तना V कथितात्र च

6d. तथाच्छैदिकवर्तना *conj.* D तथाहैलिकवर्तना ABCFV तथाहैरिकवर्तना

N lacks 7a 7ab उक्षावष्टम्भनायुक्ता *conj.* D उखावस्तम्भनायुक्ता तथा व बिन्दुवर्तन ABCFV तथा च स्तम्भनायुक्ता

7cd. AB दौर्बल्य- ABCFV -बिन्दुरेखत्वम- N -लेखत्वंप्रविभक्तत्वमेव

N lacks verse 8

8a DV बृहदण्डौ- 8b CDFV -मविरुद्धत्वमेव D -मविरुद्धस्तथैव

8c . मानविकारता *conj.* F मानवाकारिता ABCV मानवाकारता D मानवाकारतोले

N lacks verse 9

9a. CF स्थानप्रमाणं D स्थानप्रदानभूलम्भा ACFV -भूलम्बो

9c. क्षयवृद्धी *conj.* ADF पक्षवद्धि च BC पक्षवृद्धीश्च V पक्षवद्धिश्च 9d A गुणाचित्रस्य

10d DN चित्रकर्म्मविभुषणा ABCF चित्रकमैर्व भूषणा V चित्रकर्मसु भूषणम्

6ab. The *patra* [type] of line-rendering is drawn by lines which are partly done [drawn] and partly undone [not drawn] *(kṛtākṛtābhi rekhābhiḥ).*

6cd. *Acchaidika* (unbroken/continuous) type is said to be extremely fine *(atīva sūkṣmā).*

7ab. A *Bindu* (dot) type employs dotting [lit. sprinkling] *(ukṣāvaṣṭambhanā).*

7c-8. The demerits of a painting are as follows: Lines that are either [too] weak [thin] or [too] thick *(darbalyamsthūlarekhatvam)*, lack of variety *(avibhaktatvam)*, oversized eyes, lips and cheeks *(bṛhadgaṇḍoṣṭhanetratvam)*, inconsistency *(samviruddhatvam)* and deviation from [the rules of] proportion *(mānavikāratā).*

9. Merits in a painting are said to be :

[The use of] perpendiculars for postures and proportion *(sthānapramānabhūlamba)*, loveliness *(madhuratvam)*, variety *(vibhaktatā)*, verisimilitude *(sādṛśya)*, and foreshortening *(kṣayavṛdhi).*

10. The ornaments of painting are, O Best of Men, to be understood as the lines, line-rendering, decoration and colour.

रेखां प्रशंसन्त्याचार्या वर्तनां च विचक्षणा: ।
स्त्रियो भूषणमिच्छन्ति वर्णाढ्यामित्तरे जना: ।।११ ।।

इति मत्वा यथायत्नं कर्तव्यश्चित्रकर्मणि ।
सर्वस्य चित्तग्रहणं यथा स्यान्मनुजोत्तम ।।१२ ।।

दुरासनं दुरालीनं पिपासा चान्यचित्तता ।
एते चित्रविनाशस्य हेतव: परिकीर्तिता: ।।१३ ।।

शुभ्रलिप्तावकाशा च निर्दंशमशका शुभा ।
+सुप्रसन्नाभिगुप्ता+ च भूमि: स्याच्चित्रकर्मणि ।।१४ ।।

सुस्निग्धविस्पष्टमनोज्ञरेखं विद्वन् यथादेशविशेषवेशम् ।
प्रमाणशोभाभिरहीयमानं कृतं भवेच्चित्रमतीव चित्रम् ।।१५ ।।

इति श्रीविष्णुधर्मोत्तरे तृतीयखण्डे मार्कण्डेयवज्रसंवादे चित्रसूत्रे रङ्गवर्तना नामैकचत्वारिंशत्तमोऽध्याय: ।।४१ ।।

N lacks 11a.-12b.

11b A विलक्षणा: 11c D भूणमिच्छन्ति 11d F जना

12a C सत्वा DV तथा यत्न: 12b A कर्त्तव्य: F कर्त्तव्यं D श्चित्रकर्मलि 12c D -वित्तग्रहणं

12d C यस्यान्मनुजोत्तम F यस्यास्यान्मनुजोत्तम

N lacks 13-14

13a ABCDFV दुरानीतं 13b D -पिसाचान्यचित्तया 13c A पते F चित्रं 13d CF हेहव:

14a D सुभ्रलिप्त- C स्वनुलिप्त- F स्वन्नलिप्त 14b CF निर्दशंमधुका BV निदेशं मधुका

14c S1S2 सप्रसभामि- 14d D सुप्रसक्षा- F भूमि D -च्चि?कर्मणि

15a ABCF { ..... } सुस्निग्धविस्पष्टरेखं V -सुवर्णरेखं- ABCDFNV विद्वान्

15b D विशेषवे < . > N -यथादेवविशेषवेषं 15d Cf भवे चित्र- N ends this adhy. with इति श्रीविष्णुधर्म्मोतरे वर्त्तनोऽध्याय: ।।

11. The master *(ācaryā)* praises the lines, critics *(vicakṣaṇa)*, the shading, women, the ornamentation and common people, the richness of colour.

12. O Best of Men, keeping this in mind, effort should be made in such a way that there comes about captivation of the minds of everyone.

13. The (following) are the reasons for an unsuccessful painting: A bad manner of sitting, of crouching, being thirsty, and state of being distracted [lit. thinking about something other than painting] *(anyacittatā)*.

14. The site of painting should be spotlessly plastered *(śubhraliptam)*, spacious, free of insects, bright, very pleasant and secluded (?).

15. A painting, O learned One, made with lines that are smooth, clear, having beautiful colour [representing] dress appropriate to that particular country, without lacking in the beauties of proportion is indeed an extraordinary one *(atīva citram)*,

NOTES TO ADHYĀYA 41

41.1a. *satyam.* See infra 3.41.2. for various interpretations by AKC, SK, SM, GS and PS. See Raghavan's "Some Sanskrit Texts on Painting" **The Indian Historical Quarterly 1933 vol.9** for his criticism of AKC's translation as "sacred" or "pure".

41.1a. *daiśika.* Note that this is a conjecture based primarily on sense and paleography. The former requires a type of painting which could be set against the *Nāgara* type. If *Nāgara* here is understood as relating with a city or an urban context, its counterpart would be *Daiśika* as in *Deśī* or provincial or local context. The reconstruction of the possible mode of corruption is best illustrated in the *Newārī* script. Assuming that the archetype was in *Newārī,* this reconstruction is as follows:

DAIŚIKA ... >	VAIŚIKA ...>	VAIṆIKA ....>	VEṆIKA
	N	ABV	CF

Moreover, in *Newārī* script, -da- and -va- do not resemble one another as much as they follow the same direction graphically. By repeated copying from one MS to another, if the gap in -da- is not maintained, it would turn into -va-. Cf the same corruption in BCFDV's *patrāhaivika* of *patrācchaidika* in 5d.

This emendation throws light on the rest of the attributes of this variety of painting. As opposed to the *Nāgara* type of painting which demands a certain degree of academic training in shading so as to create a three dimensional effect and in foreshortening in the representation of figures, the *Daiśika* type relates with local taste of the people. While the former eschews ornamentation which is regarded as vulgar as it forces attention to the surface, the *Daiśika* painting revels in bright colours, profuse ornamentation and arrangement of figures which respects symmetry.

The usage of *deśī* is quite well established in the context of drama and music and is commonly contrasted with the classical or the *mārgī* style of representation. Note its usage in Mataṅga's ***Bṛhaddeśī*** (14) which it refers to a particular taste and a kind of songs which are very popular amongst women children, cowherds and even the kings, sung spontaneously and passionately without any formal training in one's own land/province.

अबलाबालगोपालैः क्षितिपालैर्निजेच्छया ।
गीयते सानुरागेण स्वदेशे देशिरुच्यते ।। १४ ।।

Bharatakoṣa offers following references:

तदेव रुचिवैचित्र्यच्चित्तरञ्जनकृतज्जनैः ।
प्रयुक्तं स्वस्वदेशे यत्ततो देशीति कीतिर्तम् ।। कुम्भः (p. 282)

And:

देशेषु देशेषु नरेश्वराणां
रुच्या जनानामपि वर्तते या ।
गीतं च वाद्यं च तथा च नृत्तं
देशीति नाम्ना परिकीर्तिता सा ।। जग (ibid)

vaiṇikam yields no appropriate sense. Neither of the attempts of previous interpreters to make sense of it (< *veṇā* > *vīṇā*) is convincing.

SK: Painting is said to be of four kinds. (1) "true" (to life) (Satyam) (2) *"of the lute player" (Vaiṇikam)* ..... (p.45)

PS is of the view that *vaiṇika* is derived from *veṇā* a name of a river in Southern India. Hence, the association of *Vaiṇika* type of painting with the Dravidian style of architecture.

> Vaiṇika is a little more difficult to explain. it can be grammatically explained as follows: -
>
> *Veṇāyam bhavaḥ vaiṇikaḥ bhāvārthe ṭhak ṭhasyekaḥ* It would mean born in or coming from *Venā.*
>
> Now what is Venā ? Following the geographical line of inquiry we find that veṇā is a name of a river in Daksiṇāpatha and Veṇātata is the name of a city in Ābhira Deśa, which is also in Dakṣiṇāpatha. On the strength of this indentification we can explain *Vaiṇika* as a style of painting current in the regions round about *Veṇā* or in the city of *Veṇātaṭa* and consequently equate it with the Dravidian style. (p. 123)

SM takes it as *Vaiṇika* and reasons it out as follows:

> The reason for the *Vīṇā* being brought in here is not quite clear. May be it is to suggest that this is the best variety like the *viṇā* which is rare gem though not from the milky ocean, *Vīṇā hi nāmāsa-mudrotthitam ratnam, Mṛcchakaṭika,* 3. (p. 67)

Motichandra prefers to derive *vaiṇika* from *venī,* a form of coiffure and regards *vaiṇika* type of painting as purely decorative.

> In the Visṇudharmottara, III, 41, this motif seems to have been mentioned under the name of vaiṇika, which is derived from *veṇī* coiffure. The entwined meanders are of the same shape as the coiffure twisted in basket-work pattern.

The technique of Mughal Painting The U.P. Historical Society, 1949 p.68

AKC takes it as "lyrical" (pp.13). This interpretation is justified as follows:

> The name lyrical is given to this kind of painting because these various poses and movements reflect the motives and emotions of the actors; in other words, because we recognise in this kind of painting just such *bhāvas* and *rasas* as belong to the drama and music. (p.15)

Visṇudharmottara, III, 41, Journal of the American "Oriental Society 1932 vol. 52.

The generally accepted sense of *Vaiṇika* (eg. ***Amarakoṣa Kaṭhāsaritsāgara*** 161a, 162) texts, it is recorded in the sense "lyrical'. *Viṇā* and *vaiṇika* do not stand with each other as "lyre" and "lyrical" but as an instrument and its player. In short, *vaiṇika* is likely to be a corruption.

AKC is totally mistaken in his interpretation. The only reason why he takes *vaiṇika* in this sense is the special English sense of lyric (from lyre) in which it means not merely "pertaining to the lyre", "associated with lyre" but by metaphorical extension of the term, "having the aesthetic quality of a kind of poetry" (that was originally associated with the lyre, lyric poetry etc.).

41.2. All scholars take verse 2cd as part of *satyam* except D. N. Shukla. See ***Vāstuśastra: Hindu Canons of Iconometry and Painting*** p. 385, ch. III, vol.II, 1958. The definition of *satyam* is confined to verse 2a,

Notice in all other definitions, the description precedes the term mentioned. SK, AKC, PS, SM, and Motichandra have symmetrically alloted a verse per term. Following this division, *dīrghaṅgam* would be ascribed to the Satyam type of painting which contradicts the definition given in the text. This error has led some scholars to justify their claim that naturalism in ancient Indian art is no different than idealisation of form.

SK : Whatever painting (bears) a resemblance to this earth, with proper proportion tall in height, with a nice body , round and beautiful, is called "true to (life)". (p. 45)

AKC : Painting that represents any of the worlds *(kincillokasādṛśya)*, that is elongated, and has ideal proportion (*sukumāra*), and has godly background (*subhūmika*), is called Pure or Sacred. (p. 13)

Note how AKC reiterates this in the commentary:

> (Verses.2-4) Painting done on an upright canvas, in harmonious colours, and having an ample background (or perhaps, provided with an honourable setting), with subject matter derived from the world of gods or any other sphere, is called Sacred; here, as also in Lyrical painting, where heroes such as Rāma are represented, the rules of ideal proportion are to be carefully followed, but this is not so essential in Secular painting. (ibid. pp. 11)
>
> PS : Whatever (yatkiñcid) painting depicts semblance of the world (lokasādṛśyam citram) is called Satya. It is elongated,(*dīrghāṅgam*), well proportioned (*pramāṇa*), delicate (*sukumāra*), and has a proper background (*subhūmika*). (p. 120)
>
> SM : What is known as Satya faithfully portrays any object of the world that it intends to represent. It has the limbs somewhat elongated though following proportion in all other respects, is delicate in treatment and with the right background. (p. 183)

41.2c. *dīrghāṅgam.* This term is ambiguous and can refer to both the figures in a painting or the picture frame. According to me, it refers to the figures in a painting and not to the frame or the size of the painting. SK, AKC and PS take it in the latter sense.

SK : ...... *tall in height,* ..... (p. 45)

AKC : .....*that is elongated,* ..... (p.13)

PS : *It is elongated* ..... (p.120)

This has led Raghavan to think that the differentiation amongst the types of painting was based merely on the shape of the frame.

> My impression on reading the Viṣṇudharmottara is that even to its author the exact import of these names was not clear. The text seems to have been written after a cut in the flow of tradition of the artists who were using these words as paribhāṣās. Otherwise one would not, in differentiating types of pictures on the basis of prominent and noteworthy features, mix with these such trifling features as the oblong or square nature of the frame, as the author of the Vi. Dha. does. (p.905)

Some Sanskrit Texts on Painting, V. Raghavan, The Indian Historical Quarterly, 9, ed. Narendra Nath Law, 1933.

41.1c. *supramāṇam. Sapramāṇam* is emended to *supramāṇam* based on MSS N, F, A and B. It alliterates well with *sukumāram, subhūmipa* and *susampūrṇam.* Its meaning as "largesized" (referring to the size of figures) sheds light on this type of painting as a whole.

Note how *supramāṇam* is taken by the scholars :

SK : ... *with proper proportion*......... (p. 45)

AKC : ......*ideal proportion*........ (p. 13)

PS : .... *well proportioned*...... (p. 120)

SM : ... though following proportions in all other respects, ... (p. 183)

41.2d. *sukumāram.* Here, this term is understood in a technical sense. Its common meaning "delicate" or "tender" does not seem to be intended. ***Bharatakośa*** again offers a more nuanced and technical meaning:

अम्लानप्रतिमोद्भिन्ननवशब्दार्थबन्धुरः ।
अयत्नविहितस्वल्पमनोहारि विभूषणः ।।
भावस्वभावप्राधान्यन्यक्कृताहार्यकौशलः ।
रसादिपरमार्थज्ञमनस्संवादसुन्दरः ।।
अविभावितसंस्थानरामणीयकरञ्जकः ।
विधिवैदग्ध्यनिष्पन्ननिर्माणातिशयोपमः ।।
यत्किञ्चनापि वैचित्र्यं तत्सर्वं प्रतिभोद्भवम् ।
सौकुमार्यपरिस्पन्दस्यन्दि यत्र विराजते ।।
सुकुमाराभिधस्सोयं येन सत्कवयो गताः ।
मार्गेणोत्फुल्लकुसुमकाननेनेव षट्पदाः ।।

This meaning of *sukumāra* fits in well with *Daiśika. ayatna-* above becomes significant in this context. It refers to a type of painting which can be executed even without a formal acadamic training by anyone who possesses the talent *(pratibhodhavam)*. Hence the technical meaning would be "effortless" or "spontaneous".

41.2d. *subhūṣaṇam.* MSS CF show *subhūmipam* which yields a poor sense in the context and in Monier Williams dictionary, it is recorded as a varia lectio for *subhūṣaṇam* which fits in with the context.

41.3a. *caturasram susampūrṇam.* Cf. adhy. 39.31ab and adhy. 38.4 cd. In this adhy. also *susampūrṇam* means "fully complete", as in unforeshortenend figures where no limbs or parts of the body are hidden from view. *Caturasram* does not mean literally as "four-sided". It also means "regular" or "symmetrical". It is semantically associated with *susampūrṇam,* i.e. that which is symmetrical is also fully complete.

Note the various translations:

SK : .... *placed in an exactly square field,.......* (p. 45)

PS : ...... *which is four sided.....* (p. 120)

AKC : .....*Painting that fully fills a square field,....* (p. 13)

41.3b. *durghaṭolvaṇākṛtim.*. The emendation of *dīrgham-* to *durghaṭ-* is compelled by sense and context. The negative *na* preceding this compound indicates that this attribute is not likely to be present in the *Daiśika* type of painting. And the context suggests that while the *Nāgara* painting demanded a high level of skill based on training, the *Daisika* type with its preference for frontal postures(*samānasthāna*) was more accessible, i.e. not difficult to accomplish(*nadurghaṭo*). Likewise, whereas all the figures in the *Nāgara* type were strongly developed, simulating three-dimensionality, they were not so on the *Daiśika* painting (*na......olvaṇākṛti*). This interpretation is further corroborated by the presence of *caturasram* and *susampūrṇam* in 3a.

41.3c. *samānasthāna-*. Here, *samāna* is supplied by D and it is preferred over *pramāṇa-* of the rest of the MSS. It is taken to mean similar or common postures as in frontal or profile ones.

41.4b. *vartulāyanolvaṇam-*. This emendation is mainly suggested by the context.

Regarding the phrase immediately following *na ghanolvaṇam,* the poor sense that it yields indicates its corrupt state. It closely echoes *na dīrgha-m-**nolvaṇa**-* of 3b. I suggest the following emendation, keeping in mind the technical sense of '*vartula*' as a method for deriving foreshortening discussed in adhyāya 39.

vartulam na **ghanolvaṇam** -> vartulānayanolvaṇam

The sense that this emendation conveys is that in *Nāgara* painting the figures are derived by applying the rules of foreshortening. The latter method assumes that the human figure or model is rotated around its vertical axis.

SK : ...... which is *round,*.... (p. 20)

PS : ...... *circular* ... (p.120)

AKC: Painting that *closely covers every part of a circular field (dṛḍhopacita-sarvāngam vartulam)*,..... (p. 13)

SM : *well rounded* .... (p. 183)

41.4c. *nāgara.* This term has lent itself to various interpretations. AKC (p. 13) associating it with *nāgaraka* of ***Kāmasūtra*** translates it as

"Urban"or "Seculat" it is further explained in his commentary:

> Secular painting is quite different; it is usually done on a circular field, for it consists chiefly in portraiture, and it is in a circular mirror that sees one's own face. Here the faces or figures of the persons represented are relatively large, filling the whole area, and leaving scarcely any background. The multiplicity of garlands and attributes proper to the representation of the deities will not be required. This kind of painting is called Secular or urban, because it is practised by princes and other amateurs and men about town such as we call Nāgarika, and has much to do with gallantry. (p.15-16)

Note how his associating the *Nāgara* type with portraiture hinges on *vartulam* which is now regarded a corrupt reading.

SK (p. 45) takes "*nāgaracitram*" as painting "of the city " or "of common man". PS is of the opinion that this style of painting was the pictorial counterpart of the *nāgara* style in architecture thereby establishing its epicentre in the Nortern India.

AKC connects the sixty four *kalās* or arts mentioned in the ***Kāmasūtra*** as an auxillary branch with the *nāgara* type of painting. He cites the following verse from ***Kāmasūtra*** *(adhikaraṇa* 1, chapter 4) to substantiate such a view. Connecting the *nāgaraka* of the ***Kāmasūtra,*** AKC puts forward his following deductions:

> the term nāgara applies primarily to secular painting executed by amateurs on panels and that its main themes included portraits and more specifically crotic subjects.
>
> "Nāgara Painting", Rūpam , 37, p. 24.

However, in the light of the emended reading *Daiśika,* AKC's identification of the *Nāgara* type of painting can no longer be considered valid.

> I have also suggested that whenever painting is mentioned amongst the sixty-four kalas, the reference is solely to this "Urban" painting on panels by skilled aristocratic amateurs and never to wall paintings by professional artists.

The term *"nāgara"* appears in Pāṇīni's ***Aṣṭādhyāyī*** (4.2.128) as follows:

नगरात् कुत्सनप्राविण्ययोः

From the *nāgara,* for abuse and proficiency derives *nāgara.*

Kāśikā:

नागरकश्चौरः । नागरः चित्रलेखकः

A Nāgaraka is a thief. A Nāgara is a painter.

Now let us turn to the style of painting prescribed for the *Nāgara* type. The figures that it contains are firmly developed so as to appear three-dimensional as opposed to the brightly coloured and profusely decorated figures of *Daiśika* paintings and possess very little ornamentation. And it endorses the use the circular method (*vartulānayana*) in which the figures are viewed from different angles and undergo foreshortening (*kśayavriddhi*) . From this it is clear that much stress was laid on the representation of the figures in the *Nāgara* type as opposed to the ornamentation in the *vaiśika* type. Note that in the adhy. 43, a *citravit* or an expert in painting is considered to be able to draw neck, hands, feet and ears unadorned. This seems to fit in well with the meaning of *Nāgara* as skillful or proficient. In fact, the reference above shows that *Nāgara* also refers to a *citrakāra* or painter. Now the question arises as how does a *Nāgara* painting differ from the *Daiśika.* The difference may exist in terms of degrees and the kinds of skill required for both these types of painting. While the former is more academic in the sense of being more bound by the rules of foreshortening and line-rendering, the latter is more easy to learn and practice and is more popular in both its skill level and appeal.

The fourth type of painting being *Miśra* further underlines a lack of water tight compartmentalisation of the *Satya, Daiśika* and *Nāgara* painting.

41.5a. *miśrammiśram.* This is adopted in place of *citramiśram.* This reading comes from N and D. All the scholars settle for *citramiśram.* Also note that *samāsān-* has not been correctly translated. All it means is "in short" whereas all the scholars translate it as "combination / mixture".

SK : (Oh) best of men the miśram derived its name from being composed (of the three categories). (p. 45)

AKC : Painting is called Mixed (*miśra*) when there is a combination (of the three kinds), O best of men (p. 13)

PS (p. 120) and SM(p.183) closely follow SK and AKC.

41.5c. *vartanā.* It is variously translated by all scholars. SK and SM translate it as "light and shade" AKC as "shading", GS as "modelling" (le modele) and PS as "smearing or applying of paint (See p. 126-127 ViDhUp *khaṇḍa* III, vol. II for her interpretation of in *vartanā* which she identifies it with *lepaviśeṣah / paṭalepa* and ignores a more commonplace meaning of *vartanā*).

See ***Tantrāloka***, vol. 12, adhy. 31, v. 35, p. 42 in which *vartanā* is employed in connection with the drawing of the *maṇḍalas*. It refers to a drawing involving different rotation or movement of the brush/ pencil.

Thus *candra* has 12 types of vartanās due to different rotations.

चन्द्रस्येत्थं द्वादशधा वर्तना भ्रमभेदिनी

Śṛṅgavartanā and *daṇḍavartanā* are listed as another type of *vartanās*. *Vartanā* has yet another sense when found in the texts on the dramaturgy as for instance Śārṅgadeva's ***Saṅgītaratnākara*** and Aśoka's Saṅgīta work name of which is not known.

बाहूनां करणानां च समस्तव्यस्तयोजनात् ।
क्रमात् द्रूतादिवैचित्र्याज्जायन्तेऽत्र सहस्त्रशः ।
वर्तनाश्चतुरैरुह्या ताश्शोभाभरसंभृताः ।। शार्ङ्गदेवः

That which unites a multitude of beauty arising from the variety of tempo etc. in a thousand fold ways of manifold, succesive, organisation of arms and dance postures, taken together or separately is understood by the wise as vartanā.

कराभिनयशोभां यां विचित्रां रचयन्ति हि ।
ततो मयेह लिख्यन्ते वर्तनास्ता मनोहराः ।। अशोकः

> Which create that manifold beauty of the hand movements, those enchanting vartanās are depicted or written by me.

Bharatakoṣa compiled by M. Ramakrishna Kavi.

These references point to another level of meaning of *vartanā* specific to dance which can be translated as "choreography". In the CitSūt. however, *vartanā* refers to the varied handling of the lines. From the plural in *rekhābhi,* it is clear that it means several lines in a particular order. Therefore, it would be more accurate to translate *vartanā* in this context as certain types of lines or line-rendering .

41.6b. *patravartanā. Patra* has led to some speculation amongst scholars. SK, AKC and SM take *patra* to mean a leaf.

SK : Crossing lines (lit. lines in form of leaves *patrajā*), (p. 45)

AKC : The leaf shading *(patra-vartanā)* is done with lines (*rekhā*) like those on a leaf; (p. 13)

SM : *Patravartanā* is so called as it is composed of lines crosshatched in leaf pattern. (p. 183)

PS and GS offer an alternative interpretation.

PS suggests that we take *patra* to refer to a leaf of a *tamāla* tree and concludes that:

> When the paint is applied in wavy lines, it was called Patra vartanā. (p. 127)

PS notes the ambiguity about whether *patrākṛtibhiḥ rekhābhiḥ* meant criss cross lines found on the surface of a leaf or leaf shaped strokes painted in.

GS (p. 69-70 ***Le technique de la Peinture Indienne***) completely reinterprets the term. The translation is as follows:

> Beyond its general meaning as leaf of vegetation, patra would mean lead of paper or that which is a metal leaf. Thus wide like metal leaves. In painting, such brush strokes evidently make layers of colour. Because here, it is about not simply application of colour but modelling. Layers of colour means repeated layer of the same col-

our. It is clear that only one layer of the same colour could not give impression of shadow.

41.6a. *kṛtākṛtābhī.* MSS CF's *kṛtrākṛtibi* throws light on this problem of interpreting the *patravartanā.* All the scholars follow ABV's *patrākṛtibhi* which is metrically not permissible (- - 0 - 0 - 1 - - - -). CF's reading clearly appears to be a corruption of *kṛtākṛtābhi* which refers to lines that are "partly drawn and partly undrawn" as in a row of dashes. ABV's *patrākṛti-* can now be explained as a banalisation facilitated by the term *partavartanā.* It seems pointless that a definition of a term is carried out using the term itself. Besides, in the Ajanta painting, such lines have been employed.

41.6d. *acchaidikavartanā.* MSS BCF read *āhaivikā* and V, *āhairikā.* Although this reading has been recognised by all the scholars as corrupt, the emendation that they have put forward are as diverse as they are unconvincing.

> AKC: The āhairika vartanā, which is called 'delicate' (sūkṣma) can be no other than that modelling in a deeper shade of the self-same colour which has been described above. The word āhairika, hitherto unexplained, is probably to be connected with aharya, 'gotten', 'acquired', 'costume' as part of the apparatus of the stage (and including 'make-up'), and ahara as 'pabulum' or 'nourishment' (eg. kabālinkāhara-bhakkha, 'using concrete nourishment', Aṅguttara Nikāya, III 17, 6, and dharmāhāra in Mahāyāna texts as the food of the Buddhas and Bodhisattvas, etc.') In as much as the modelling is produced by repeated application of the self-colour, which is thus 'fattened' (sthūla), this kind of modelling may well have been called 'nourishing' (āhairka), although in effect 'subtle' (sthūla).

(See A Reprint from ***Technical Studies in the Field of Fine Arts. The Technique of Indian Painting vol. III, Oct. 1934***)

Note how GS's interpretation of *patrā vartanā* coincides with AKC's interpretation of *āhairika vartanā.* The explanation put forward by AKC does not stand to the definition given in the text in which emphasis is laid on *atīva sūkṣmā* or excessively fine -a fattening process which is very fine in effect is contradictory.

SK emends it to *airikā* which makes the meter less by a syllable and translates it as "stumping" (p. 45). Since the reading itself is doubtful, we cannot consider the translation.

PS emends to *hairikā* deriving it from "hira" meaning "a band , a strip or a fillet, a vein or an artery". Thus *hairikā vartanā* is translated as 'applying paint with thin bands" (p. 127-128).

> 1) If we, however, take Hirā or Hīrā = gmeline Arborea, the meaning would be lines in the shape of leaves of gmelina Arborea. (p. 127-128)

She also offers an alternative interpretation as follows:

PS elaborates :

> The word patra ordinarily means a leaf. But leaf of which tree ? This is not clear. When the word patra alone is used, it means a Tamāla tree. So we may take here the word patra to mean a leaf of a Tamāla tree. Still there remains a difficulty whether the lines of a paint are to be taken leafy in shape or whether they are like lines on the leaf as Dr. A. K. Coomaraswamy takes it. Whichever the meaning we take the purport seems to be that when the paint is applied in wavy lines, it was called patravartanā.

SM emends to *raikhikā*:

> F.N. 4-5) It should be read as here shown. हैविक makes no sense. But we know that रैखिक is an accepted mode like बिन्दुज. हैरिक has an obscure meaning 'thief'. If the shading is so subtle as be elusive हैरिक may be accepted with a pinch of doubt. (p. 153)

Note SM's emendation yields a redundant sense given that *rekhābhi* has already been mentioned in 6a and that all the *vartanās* are composed of lines.

Ahaivika, as suggested by GS, might be a corruption of *āharyaka,* the latter deriving from the root हृ and also containing the idea of accidental or reported. In noting a link between *āharyaka* and *āharya,* he follows Coomaraswamy but differs in interpretation. Rejecting Coomaraswamy's formulation of it being a repeated application of the same colour and maintaining that *āhairika* is corruption of *āharyaka,* Gunasinghe interprets it as that which is introduced further (ce qui est introduit en plus).

He further infers that *āharyaka* is about the introduction of a different colour, different from that laid down earlier.For example, for an object painted yellow, one would introduce red or blue (Ajanta). For an object painted white, one would use blue (Central Asia and Seistan). This is for marking the shadows. He holds that this kind of explanation, on one hand, allows one to incorporate the rules laid down in the ŚilpRat. and the MānaUll. and the ViDhUp. on the other. It equally takes account of "susūkṣma" used in the CitSūt.; atleast in the parts of painting, where the two colours must merge into one another when they are juxtaposed. If they had not been this delicate (mixing) of colours, it would not have been modelling but a simple juxtaposition of different colours. (see p. 66-67). This is clearly a case of over interpretation and reading in of sense not substantiated by the text.

Motichandra emends to harika (printing error)

> Hairika is derived from hiraka "diamond" which was rhomboidal and is that same as jalida pardaz.

MSS B,C, and F read *patrahaivikabindujāḥ* and V and D have -*hairika.*-None of these makes any sense. My emendation *ācchaidika* derived partly from context and partly from the similarity between -h- and -ch- in the *Śāradā* script. Note that in the adhy. 38, *chātodarī,* a corruption of *śātodarī* was further corrupted to *hātodarī* owing to the confusion between -ch- and -h-. Note that it also accounts for the long vowel -ā- in *patrāhaivika-.* Besides, *ācchaidika* yields a sense consistent with the two *vartanās* i.e. it offers a contrast to the *Patra* and *Bindu vartanās.* It means "not deserving to be cut", "that which needs no cutting", i.e. unbroken, continuous and so forth. ***Kāśikāvṛtti*** (vi. 2. 155) define this term as:

> छेदमर्हति छैदिकः। न छैदिकोऽच्छैदिकः।

Note in the light of the radically different definition of the *patrā vartanā* meaning- "lines partly drawn and partly undrawn", *Acchaidika vartanā* seems to mean its opposite. In contrast to the *Patra* type, *Acchaidika* refers to unbroken, continuous line which is drawn extremely fine.

SM draws our attention to an interesting reference from a *Kannaḍa* text of the ***Kallināthapurāṇa*** which in fact mentions the three types of *vartanā* - the two of which, the *patraka* and *binduka* parallel the *patrajā* and *bindujā* of the CitSūt. The third type is called *anilaka (analaka ?)*.

> This Kannada terminology is given by B.V.K. Sastri in his book on Karnataka chitra kala. The word in the kannada text has probably a stress on not only fine linework but indicates a somewhat shaky sketch of lines after the movement of the flames of fire. (p. 58)

It could be possible that fine continuous lines i.e. *ācchaidika vartanā* was used to create various atmospheric effects i.e. to represent fire or smoke.

41.7a. *ukṣāvaṣṭambhanā* This emendation derives from D's *ukhāva-stambhanā*-while the rest of the MSS have *tathā ca* which are clearly banalisation of *Ukṣāva* due to the similarity of -u- and -ta- in the Sāradā script. *ukṣā-* is taken to mean sprinkling so as to create dotting. Note that *stambhanā* is emended to *-avaṣṭambhanā* and taken to mean "taking recourse to" or "depending upon".

41.7b. *binduvartanā* has been translated differently. In this case again scholars who follow the literal meaning of the term are more correct than those who strive to reinterpret it. As for instance, SK and AKC translate the term *bindu* as a "dot". SM while defining this mode of *vartanā* employs "stippling". The word *stambhanā* being associated with this mode has led some scholars to interpret *bindu* in a different light. Note PS's theory:

> The word Bindu would mean a dot. But that meaning cannot be taken here because in verse 7 (ad. 41) Bindurekhatva i.e. dotty lines are regarded as defects in painting. Therefore, the word Bindu could be taken in accordance with the other two words as the name of a tree. Hemachandra in his Nighaṇtuśeṣa gives the word bindu in the synonym of Iṅgudī. Its leaves have the shape of an egg. Its oil is famous for stickiness. (Compare Sakuntala etc. and Sanskṛta Sāhityaman Vanaspati by Bāpālal Vaidya). So Binduja vartanā would mean applying paint with lines in the form of the leaves of Ingudi.

> This identification of Bindu with Iṅgudī has an additional justification because its oil is well known for its stickiness and therefore would serve as an astringent (stambhanāyukta).

PS bases this supposition on a wrong reading in verse 7b. Note the emendation of bindu to *sthūla* based on N's reading. The basic premise of her interpretation is overthrown by this because it establishes that *bindu* as in *bindurekhatva* was not a demerit of a painting. Besides, it is not necessary for all the types of *vartanās* to derive from leaves. If this was the case, the distinction of the *vartanās* in terms of different categories would be meaningless.

The only way to derive the meaning of stippling is by the emendation mentioned above. A line that is neither broken as in *patra* nor continuous as in *ācchaidika* but formed of dots is what is referred by *bindu vartanā*.

SK :

> Vindujā method was called so from the restrained (i.e. not flowing) handling of the brush. (p. 46)

AKC :

> While that done with an upright (stambhanāyukta) (brush) is dot-shading (bindu-vartanā). (p. 13)

PS takes *stambhanā* to mean an astringent or styptic which forms the basis of her interpretation of the term *bindu*. SM derives the meaning "stippling" from *stambhanā*.

Gunasinghe translates it as

> le vehicule; le detrempe; le lait de chaux que l'on ajoute aux colours pour les << degrader >>.

From this, he drives the following definition:

> Le technique du modele qui utilise le juxtaposition dcs tons clairs et sombres d'une meme couleur. (p. 188)

The technique of modelling which employs the juxtaposition of light and dark tones of the same colour. (My translation)

41.7c. *daurbalyam.* It is to be taken as a separate word and in meaning being opposite of *-sthūla,* as a qualifier of *rekhatvam.* A line too weak or too thick is regarded as a defect in a painting.

41.7c. *sthūlarekhatvam.* This is adopted from N and D against *sthūlarekhatvam* found in all the other MSS. The mention of *bindu* is verse 5d and 7b accounts for this scribal error. Besides it makes better sense given that it is part of the demerits of a painting. All the scholars follow the corrupt reading- *bindurekha-*.

SK : Indistinct, *uneven and inarticulate* delineation,...... (p. 46)

AKC : Weakness of *dots* or lines ,..... (p. 13)

PS : (1) Daurbalya - feebleness, (2) Bindurekhatva - dotty lines, ... (p. 128)

SM : Weakness and vague drawing, *coarse dotty lines in sketches,*..... (p. 183)

41.8a. *bṛhadgaṇḍoṣṭha-*. Both SK (p. 46) and AKC (p. 14) accept V's *bṛhadaṇḍo-* and hence their translation of it as "big testicles".

SK : ... representation of the human figure with lips, (too) large, eyes and *testicles* (too) big ,... (p. 46)

AKC : the representation of human figures, with lips or eyes too large, ... (p. 14)

41.8c. *mānavikāratā* is emendation of *mānavākaratā.* The latter reading seems unlikely considering the detailed iconometry laid down in adhyāya 36 of CitSūt based upon human proportions. SK connects *mānavākāratā* with *bṛhadaṇḍoṣṭhanetratvam :*

> representation of the human figures with lips (too) thick eyes and testicles (too) big, (p. 46)

AKC on *mānavākaratā* :

> the representation of human figures (mānavākārata),...... are said to be the faults (dośa) of painting.

PS (p. 128) takes *mānavakaratā* in the following sense drawing connection with other art treatises - ŚilpRat. and MānaUll. :

> If we, however, take the clue from vakrarekhatva, the meaning might be that merely drawing a curve line in the form of a human figure is no art. This is supported by the words ākāramātrakamsattve in the description of aviddha variety of painting in Mānasollāsa Ad.1, Vimśatiḥ 3, verse 902 (G.O.S.) and nālamākāramātrakam in Śilparatna Ad.

> 46, verse 164. The point emphasised in both the works is that merely drawing a form is no art. Our text adds the word mānava which would mean that merely drawing a human figure with a zigzag line is really a defect. (p. 128)

Note the text does not mention any *vakrarekhatva* which PS uses in her argument. The emendation *mānavikāratā* makes PS's explanation redundant and connection with the two texts forced.

Note how this corrupt reading further misleads PS making her see an affinity between this defect in a painting and the aviddha type of painting stated in the MānaUll. :

> Mānasollāsa gives two kinds of painting-one called viddha and the other aviddha. The viddha is one where the sādṛśya or semblance is like a reflection in a mirror. This is the approved type. When a painter without any purpose just draws something without any clear notion as to what he wants to do and just draws a mere form of being is called aviddha which is not the approved type. This idea is more clearly stated in Śilparatna, where it is said that that is a citra or painting in which semblance is like a reflection in a mirror, *mere form is not enough.* (ibid)

SM takes it as "*celestial figures looking commonplace human figures.*" (p. 184)

41.9a. *sthānapramāṇabhulambo.* There is a problem in interpreting this compound. *Bhūlamba* by itself does not yield a good sense as a merit of painting. It only makes sense in connection with *sthāna* and *pramāṇa.* But in this case, the number of the merits becomes reduced in number whereas in the adhy. 43, they are supposed to be eight merits (*guṇāṣṭakam,* 43.19c). *Bhūlamba* which means a plumb line cannot be one of the merits and is to be taken as an instrument employed to determine the proportions and postures. Moreover, if *kṣaya* and *vṛiddhi* are taken as two *guṇas,* then the total number would add up to six. Cf. the six means of accomplishment or the *ṣaḍaṅgas* mentioned by Yaśodhara in his commentary on the *Kāmasūtra* (on *ālekhyam*). SK (p. 46), AKC (p. 14) and SM (p. 184) translate *bhūlamba* as "background".

41.10d. *citrakarmavibhūṣaṇāḥ.* SK, PS and SM follow V's corrupt reading *citrakarmasubhūṣaṇam. Citrakarmaiva bhūṣaṇa* found in MSS AF, have given rise to interesting speculations amongst all scholars. Only AKC gets the sense correct.

SK : (oh) best of men, in works of chitra delineation, shading, ornamentation and colouring should be known as decorative (i.e. as the elements of visualisation).

PS expresses doubts about the reading :

> How bhūṣaṇa should be interpreted is not clear, literally it means decoration. line 2 of verse 10 (Ad. 41), according to the reading adopted in the text means one should know what is bhūṣaṇa in citrakarma i.e. acts of painting. If we, however, adopt the reading of Mss. A and F. citrakarmaiva bhūṣaṇa, it would mean that the act of painting is itself a decoration. This, however gives no definite meaning because we cannot say what is implied by decoration. Does it mean ornaments worn by male and female figures in a picture or it refers to the decorative parts of a picture such as beautiful borders found in old paintings ? These two meanings would be inappropriate here because ordinarily we would have the reading bhūṣaṇāni and not bhūṣaṇam and secondly because in this analysis of general elements, reference to particular items in painting such as ornaments worn by human figures or decorative borders would be very clumsy. I, therefore, prefer to take the word bhūṣaṇa in the sense of śobhā or saundarya i.e. beauty in general. With this meaning citrakarmaiva bhūṣaṇas mean that the act of painting itself is the act of creating beauty. (p. 130)

SM : Line, shading, decorative design and colour are the decorative element in pictures. (p. 184)

AKC's translation agrees with the emendation made on the basis of N's reading.

> Outline (rekhā) shading (vartanā), adornment (bhūṣaṇa) and colour (varṇa) are regarded, O best of man, as the ornaments of painting. (p. 14-13)

41.13a. *durālīnam.* Note that this reading is a slight emendation of D's reading *durālītam. Ālīnam* means "having come close to", "crouched", "stooped" and with the prefix "dur" it would be "badly stooped" (in case of miniature painting or panel painting) and "having come badly (i.e. too) close (to the painting) in case of a mural painting.

Note this emendation conforms to the metre in contrast to *durānatim* as emended by AKC. Both PS and SM follow the reading of C and F.

SK seems to have interpreted V's reading *durānītan as duranītim :*

> Bad seat, thirst, inattentiveness, and *bad conduct* ....(p. 46)

AKC questions SK's interpretation but leaves it as a problem. PS and SM do not translate it.

41.14c. *abhiguptā.* Note that this reading which yields an inappropriate sense is regarded as corrupt.

41.15a. *-suvarṇa-.* N shows an interesting variant - *manojña* in place of *suvarṇa.* This is possibly a gloss on *suvarṇa* to cut down the ambiguity of meaning. It is not to be taken as "golden" but "beautiful colour".

41.15b. *vidvan.* All the MSS show *vidvān* which is a corruption of *vidvan* as the context and grammar require a vocative.

द्विचत्वारिंशोऽध्यायः

मार्कण्डेय उवाच

यथा देवास्तथा चित्रे कर्तव्याः पृथिवीश्वराः ।
एकैकं कूपके लोमं कर्तव्यं पृथिवीक्षिताम् ।। १ ।।

ऋषयश्चैव गन्धर्वा दैत्याश्च सह दानवैः ।
मन्त्रिणश्च महाराज सांवत्सरपुरोहितौ ।। २ ।।

कार्या भद्रप्रमाणेन ब्राह्मणाश्च नरेश्वर ।
ऋषयस्तत्र कर्तव्या जटाजूटोपशोभिताः ।। ३ ।।

कृष्णाजिनोत्तरासङ्गा दुर्बलास्तेजसा युताः ।
देवतुल्याश्च गन्धर्वा मुकुटेन विवर्जिताः ।। ४ ।।

कर्तव्यास्ते महाराज शेखरैरुपशोभिताः ।
दैत्याश्च दानवाश्चैव कर्तव्या भ्रुकुटीमुखाः ।। ५ ।।

1a. CF यथ V देवस्तथा CF देवस्तथां AB देव N चित्रैः 1b V कर्तव्यः पृथिवीश्वर
1c. N कुपकै D कूयके ABCVF रूपके ABCDFV लोम N लास
2a. ABCDV ऋषयश्च 2b ABCDV सगन्धर्वा D यहदानवैः ABV दानवाः
2d. ACF संवत्सर-
3c. N ऋषयश्चैव D ऋषयश्च A ऋषस्तत्र N कर्त्तव्या D प्रकर्तव्या
4a. N कृष्णां- 4b N दुर्वारा- A तेजसान्विताः CF तैजसा N युता
4c. CF देवतुश्चाश्च AB देवताश्च V देवताश्चापि AB सगंधर्वा 4d D विवर्जिताः
5b. CFV शिखरै- 5c N दैत्याच्च

ADHYĀYA : 42

Mārkaṇḍeya spoke:

1. In a painting, kings should be made just like gods. One and only one hair should be made in the pore(s) of the kings.

2-3ab. Sages, *gandharvas, daityas, dānavas,* ministers, astrologer, priest and the *brāhmins* should be drawn, O Lord, according to the *Bhadra* mode of proportion.

3cd. O Lord of men, the sages are to be made possessing matted locks.

4ab. [They] should be clad in an upper garment made of black antelope skin, emaciated and full of radiance.

4c-5b. The *gandharvas* should be made just like the gods, [except that they should be made] without a crown. They, O Lord, should be adorned with a *śekhara.*[1]

1. The *Śekhara* is a kind of coiffure in which a garland is tied around the top of the head.

वर्तुलाक्षास्तथा कार्या भीमवक्त्रास्तथैव च ।
तेषामत्युद्धतो वेषः कर्तव्याः पृथिवीपते ।।६।।

मन्त्रिणश्च महाराज सांवत्सरपुरोहितौ ।
सर्वालङ्कारसंयुक्ता नैवोल्वणविभूषणाः ।।७।।

ब्रह्मवर्चस्विनो विप्राः शुक्लाम्बरधरास्तथा ।
मुकुटेन विहीनास्तु सोष्णीषान्कारयेच्च तान् ।।८।।

भद्रप्रमाणाः कर्तव्यास्तथा विद्याधरा नृप ।
सपत्नीकाश्च ते कार्या माल्यालङ्कारधारिणः ।।९।।

खड्गहस्ताश्च ते कार्या गगने वाऽथवा भुवि ।
मालव्यपरिमाणेन किन्नरोरगराक्षसाः ।।१०।।

6a. N वर्तुलोक्षा-
6b. V म्युद्धतो ABCNF -प्युद्धतो 6d ABCFNV कर्तव्यः
7a. CF मन्त्रिणस्तु AB मन्त्रिणंतु 7d V -नेवोल्वण- D -नैवोल्वत- V -विभूषणान् N सर्वलक्षणलक्षितः
8a. N ब्रह्मक- -F वर्चसिनो N विप्र 8b N -म्बरविभूषणा
8c. D मुङ्गटेन ABF विहीनास्तु N विहीनानां 8d N मोष्लीषांकारयेच्चतां D कारयेहतान् C तान्
9a. ABCFV रुद्र- 9b N -धराचये 9c ये -9d N धारिणा 10b F गमने N तुवि
10c. D गालन्यपरिणामेन 10d N किन्नरोरगराक्षसः F -राक्षसा

5c-6. The faces of the *daityas* and *dānavas* should be shown frowning; their eyes, globular and mouths, terrifying. O Lord of earth, they should be dressed in gaudy clothes.

7. O Lord, the ministers, astrologer and the priest are [drawn] wearing all the [appropriate] ornaments [but] none more than that [i.e. superfluous].

8. The wise who have prominence in holiness *(brahmavarcasvi)* [should be shown] likewise wearing white clothes. They should be made devoid of crowns and [their hair] should have a top-knot.

9. The *vidyādharas* should [also] be made according to the *Bhadra* mode of proportion. They should be made accompanied by their wives and wearing garlands and ornaments.

10. They should have swords in their hands and shown either [flying] in the sky or standing on earth. The *Kiṇnaras,* the snakes and the *Rākṣasas* [are to be made] according to the *Mālavya* mode of proportion.

रुचकस्य प्रमाणेन यक्षाः कार्या नराधिप ।
शशकस्य प्रमाणेनाप्रधानं मानवं लिखेत् ।। ११ ।।

पिशाचा वामनाः कुब्जाः प्रमथाश्च महाभुज ।
मानानियमतः कार्या रूपानियमतस्तथा ।। १२ ।।

स्वानुरूपप्रमाणाश्च सर्वेषां योषितः स्मृताः ।
किन्नरा द्विविधाः प्रोक्ता नृवक्त्रा हयविग्रहाः ।। १३ ।।

नृदेहा अश्ववक्त्राश्च तथान्ये परिकीर्तिताः ।
+अश्ववक्तास्तु+ कर्तव्याः सर्वालङ्कारधारिणः ।। १४ ।।

गीतवाद्यसमासक्ता द्युतिमन्तस्तथैव च ।
उत्कचा राक्षसाः कार्या विवृताक्षा विभीषणाः ।। १५ ।।

11d. ABCDFNV प्रधानं
12a. D वानराः 12b D -प्रथमाश्च D महाभुजाः F महीभुज AV महीभुजः C महीभुजाः
12c. V मानन्नियमतः CF मानानियमनः 12d F रूपां V रूपन्नियमतस्तथा
13a. CF स्वानुरूपं N स्वानरूप-
13b. ABCN योषिताः CF योषित N स्मृतः
13c. DN द्विविधा 13d N नृवक्त N हयविग्रहा
14a. D नृदेहाःश्ववक्तश्च ABCF - नृदोहाश्चाश्वक्ताश्च
14c. D अश्ववक्ताश्च AB अश्वक्तातु AN कर्त्तव्या
15a. N lacks 15ab. C -वाद्यसमायु < > F -वाद्यसमायु < < क्त > > AV -समायुक्ता
15c. D उत्करा N उत्कटा 15d V विकलाक्षा N विवृताख्यातिभीषणा ABCF विकृताक्षा बिभीषणाः D विकृताख्या

11. O King of men, the *yakṣas* are to be made according to the *Rucaka* mode of proportion. A subordinate man *(apradhānam mānavam)* is to be drawn according to the *Śaśaka* mode.

12. O Long-armed one, the *piśācas,* the dwarfs, the hunch backed the tormenters *(pramatha)* should be made disregarding the laws of proportion and in the same way, irrespective of rules of colour.

13-14. The wives of all are said to have proportion appropriate to themselves. The *Kinnaras* are said to be of two types - one with human heads and equine bodies and the other type is said to have human bodies and equine faces. The equine faced ones should be made endowed with all the decorations.

15) They should be engaged in singing and playing musical instruments, and possessing brilliance. The *Rākṣasas* should be made with their hair rising upwards, dilated eyes and terrifying to look at.

प्रांशवस्तनुमध्याश्च क्रुद्धरूपा भयावहाः ।
यक्षाः कार्या महाराज न सौम्या न विभीषणाः ।। १६ ।।

देवाकाराश्च कर्तव्या नागाः फणविराजिताः ।
सालङ्काराः स्मृताः सर्वे यत्र तेऽभिहिता मया ।। १७ ।।

सुराणां प्रमथाः कार्याः प्रमाणेन विवर्जिताः ।
पिशाचाश्च तथा कार्याः प्रमाणेनैव वर्जिताः ।। १८ ।।

नानासत्त्वमुखाः कार्या देवतानां तथा गणाः ।
नानावेषा महाराज नानायुधधरास्तथा ।। १९ ।।

नानाक्रीडाप्रसक्ताश्च नानाकर्मकरास्तथा ।
एकरूपास्तु कर्तव्या वैष्णवास्तु तथा गणाः ।। २० ।।

16. ABCFS1S2V lack 16.
16b. N भयावहा D भयङ्कराः 16d D न च विभीषणाः
17a. V देवकाराश्च 17b N नागा फणविभूषणाः
N lacks 17cd and 18 ab.
17c. F सालङ्कारा 17d CF य एते AB य पते V यक्षास्ते CF ऽभिहता
18a. CDF प्रथमाः
D lacks 18cd.
18cd. N कार्य्या प्रमाणेन विवर्जिता
19a. N -मुखा 19b CF गुणाः 19c N -वेश
N lacks 20.
20a. D -शुसक्ताश्च
20d. V वैष्णवानान्तथा N वैष्णवानां गणास्तथा

16. They should be made towering, slender-waisted, having wrathful expression and awe inspiring.

The *Yakṣas* are to be made, O Lord, neither tranquil nor terrifying.[2]

17. The *Nāgas* should be depicted like the gods [but] except that they should be endowed with snake hoods. They all are said to have ornaments wherever specified by me.

18. The goblins [attendants] *(pramatha)* of the gods are to be made devoid of [fixed] proportion and the *piśācas,* in the same manner, are made proportionless.

19. The attendants of the gods *(gaṇa)* are made having faces of various animals. O Lord, they should be clad in various types of dress and hold various kinds of weapons.

20. The attendants[3] of Vaisnava deities (of gods) should be engaged in various sports and should be made similar in form.

2. see Notes.

3. नानाकर्मकरास्तथा : कर्मकरा must be a synonym for a गणा

तत्रापि तेषां कर्तव्या भेदाश्चत्वार एव तु ।
वासुदेवसमाः कार्या वासुदेवगणाः शुभाः ।। २१ ।।

सङ्कर्षणेन सदृशास्तद्गणाश्च तथा स्मृताः ।
प्रद्युम्नेनानिरुद्धेन तद्गणाः सदृशास्तथा ।। २२ ।।

तत्प्रभासदृशाः सर्वे तदायुधधरास्तथा ।
नीलोत्पलदलश्यामाश्चन्द्रशुभ्रास्तथैव च ।। २३ ।।

तथा मरकताकाराः सिन्दूरसदृशप्रभाः ।
रुचकस्य तु मानेन वेश्याः कार्यास्तथा स्त्रियः ।। २४ ।।

वेश्यानामुद्धतं वेषं कार्यं शृङ्गारसम्मितम् ।
मालव्यमानतः कार्या लज्जावत्यः कुलस्त्रियः ।। २५ ।।

21b. N भेदाचत्वार CFN तु ABDV च

21c. N -समा

22b. N स्मृता

23a. ACDFNV तत्प्रभावास्स्मृताः 23 bN -धराः स्मृताः

24a. FN -कारा 24b N -प्रभा
N lacks 24cd-25.

25a. CFS1S2 वेशानाम- S1S2 -मद्धुतं 25a A वेश्यं कार्यं

25b. CDFV -सम्मतम् A -सस्मृतम्

25c. D आलव्य- V मालव्यमानतः 25d A लजावत्यः

21. But even amongst them, four distinctions ought to be maintained. The auspicious attendants of *Vāsudeva* should be made similar to *Vāsudeva*.

22. Similarly, the attendants of *Saṃkarṣaṇa* are said to resemble *Saṃkarṣaṇa*. In the same manner, the attendants of *Pradyumna* and *Aniruddha* should resemble them [their respective gods].

23. All of them (i.e. the attendants) should have colours similar to them (i.e. their respective gods) and hold the (corresponding) weapons. (The attendants of *Vāsudeva*) should be dark green like that of the colour of the leaves of a blue lotus and (the attendants of *Saṃkarṣaṇa*) should be moon-white in colour.

24. [The attendants of *Pradyumna*] should have an appearance of an emerald and [the attendants of *Aniruddha*] have a colour resembling red lead. The courtesans are made according to the *Rucaka* mode of proportion.

25. The attire of the courtesans should be made flamboyant and full of the erotic [sentiment]. The modest women of noble families should be made based on the *Mālavya* mode of proportion.

नात्युद्धतेन वेषेण सालङ्कारास्तथैव च ।
दैत्यदानवयक्षाणां राक्षसानां तथैव च ।। २६ ।।

रूपवत्यस्त्रियः कार्याः पत्न्यो मनुजसत्तम ।
मातरस्तेन रूपेण तेषां कार्या नराधिप ।। २७ ।।

पिशाचानां तु पत्न्योऽपि कार्यास्तद्रूपसंयुताः ।
विभर्तृकास्तु कर्तव्याः स्त्रियः पलितसंयुताः ।। २८ ।।

शुक्लवस्त्रपरीधानाः सर्वालङ्कारवर्जिताः ।
कुब्जा वामनिका वृद्धा तथारूपवती भवेत् ।। २९ ।।

राजस्त्रीणां परिवारे वृद्धः स्यात्कञ्चुकी पुनः ।
रुचकस्य तु मानेन वैश्यमानं विधीयते ।। ३० ।।

N lacks 26 ab.
26a. A नात्युन्नतेन CFV नात्यनुन्नतेन
26c. A दैत्यादानव- N देवदानव
27a. ABV रुपवत्यस्तथा N -स्त्रियः कार्य्या CF -स्त्रियस्कार्यः F कार्यः
27c. ABCDVF -स्वेन- 27d ABV तथा कार्या
N lacks 27cd.
28a. V च 28ab N कर्तव्या कार्य्या तद्रूपशोभिताः 28c V कर्तव्या 28d A पुलित-
N lacks 28cd-34ab.
29. A परीधाना 29b A नाना- 29cd CF वृद्धास्तथा
30b. D कञ्चुको

26-27ab. They should possess the ornaments but not very excessively showy garments. O Best amongst men, the wives of the daityas, danavas *Yakṣas* and *Rākṣasas* should be made, in the same manner as beautiful women.

27cd. O King of men, their mothers should be made based on that [type of] proportion (i.e. *Mālavya*).

28-29b. Even the wives of the *Piśācas* should be made incorporating their (i.e. the *Piśācas*) appearance. The widows should be made full of grey hair, clothed in white dress and bereft of all ornaments.

29c-30) In the retinue of the noble ladies, there should be a hunch-backed woman, a female dwarf and such an ugly woman. The chamberlain should be old.

The proportion of those belonging to the trading class, is made according to the *Rucaka* type.[4]

4. Note that the type of proportion prescribed for the courtesans or *veśyā* is also *Rucaka.* (see verse 25a).

शशकस्य तु मानेन शूद्रमानं तथैव च ।
यथाजात्यनुरूपेण रूपेण मनुजेश्वर ।। ३१ ।।

दैत्यादियोजिता कार्या परिचारस्त्रियस्सदा ।
महाशिरा महोरस्का महानासो महाहनुः ।। ३२ ।।

पीनस्कन्धभुजग्रीवो परिमाणेन चोच्छ्रितः ।
त्रितरङ्गललाटश्च श्येतदृष्टिर्महाकटिः ।। ३३ ।।

दृप्तश्चित्रविदा कार्यः सेनायाः पतिरूर्जितः ।
योधाः कार्या महाराज प्रायशो भ्रुकुटीमुखाः ।। ३४ ।।

किञ्चिदुद्धतवेषाश्च कार्याश्चोद्धतदर्शनाः ।
अभ्युङ्गताश्च कर्तव्या आयुधीयाः पदातयः ।। ३५ ।।

N lacks 31 and D and N lack 32-34 ab.

31b. C श्छुद्रमानं

31d. V वेषेण CF < .... > AV कार्याः

32a. ABV दैत्यादियोषितां 32b. CF परिचास्त्रियस्सदा

32c. AB महारस्का CF महोस्को महानासो

33a. AB पीनस्कंद- CFV -भुजग्रीवः AB -भुजग्रीवाः 33b AB चोच्छ्रिताः

33c. AB ललाटाश्च 33d. ABCFV -श्येनदृष्टि- V व्योमदृष्टि-

34a. CF -दृप्ता- B कार्या 34b. A सेनाया A. पतिऊर्जितः C पतिरुर्जितम् 34c N योधा

34d. N प्रांशवो N -मुखा

35b. D -दसनाः

35 N lacks 35.

35a. ABCF दुद्धत

35c A अत्युद्धताश्च 35d CF पदातया

31. Similarly, the proportion for the *Śudras* is made according to the *Śaśaka* mode. O Lord of men, their proportion should be in accordance with the caste.

32. The female attendants should always be accompanied by the Daityas etc. (such as) the *Mahāśira* (the big headed one) (being) big chested, the *Mahāhanu* (the big jawed) (having) muscular shoulders, arms and neck, (being) huge in proportion, and the *Mahākaṭi* with three lines on the forehead and being red eyed *(śyetadṛṣṭi)*.

34. The commander of an army should be depicted by the expert painting as arrogant and mighty. The warriors should be done, O Lord, as towering and with a frown on their face.

35. The foot-soldiers should be done with their dress somewhat lifted up, possessing a haughty appearance, marching forth and armed with weapons.

खड्गवर्मधराः कार्याः कर्णाटकवपुर्धराः ।
वरबाणधराः कार्या नग्नजङ्घाश्च धन्विनः ।। ३६ ।।

नात्युद्धतेन वेषेण सोपानत्कास्तथैव ते ।
यथोक्तलक्षणाः कार्याः कुञ्जरास्तुरगास्तथा ।। ३७ ।।

हस्त्यारोहास्तु कर्तव्या मुद्गश्यामास्तु वर्णतः ।
केशैश्च जूटसटालैः सालङ्कारास्तथैव ते ।। ३८ ।।

उदग्वेषाः प्रकर्तव्याः तुरगाणां तु सादिनः ।
उद्धतेन तु वेषेण कर्तव्या बन्दिनस्तथा ।। ३९ ।।

सिरादर्शितकण्ठाश्च तथैवोन्मुखदृष्टयः ।
आह्वरकास्तु कर्तव्याः कपिलाः केकरेक्षणाः ।। ४० ।।

36b. N कर्णाटकवपुद्धरा
36c. N -बाणधरा D < वरबाणधरा- >
37. N lacks 37 ab
37b. Cf सोमानर्कास्तथैव B च
37cd. N लक्षणा कार्या DN तुरगाः कुञ्जरास्तथा V तुरगादयः
38a. F हस्त्यारोहाश्च C हस्त्यरिहाश्च कर्तव्या
38ab. N मुद्गश्यामस्तु कर्तव्या हर्म्यावाहाश्च संयुता
38ab. VB मुहुः श्यामस्तु D -श्यामस्तुकर्त्तव्याहर्म्या वाहास्तु संयुता CF कर्णतः
38c. A जूटेटसरैः BCDFV जूटटमरैः N जूटठमरैः 38d CFN च
39a. ABCDFV उदीच्य- ACF -वेश्याः N उदीवशाः N प्रकर्त्तव्या ABCDFV कर्त्तव्या
39b. D पापि > नः
39c. CF उद्धतुनतु 39d. CF कर्तव्याः V वणिजस्तथा
40a. N lacks 40 ab.
40c. N आव्हारकास्तु ABDFV आव्हानकास्तु N कर्त्तव्या 40d A कापेलाः

36. [The warriors] bearing the sword and shield should be made based upon the *Karṇāṭaka* variety of physique. Excellent bowmen and archers are to be made with naked shanks.

37. Their dress should not be too flamboyant and moreover they should be wearing foot-wear. The elephants and horses ought to be made according to the characteristics already defined.

38. As for the complexion of the riders of the elephant, it should be made as dark as a bean. They should be accompanied with decorations and likewise with twisted and matted hair.

39. On the other hand, the riders of the horses should be made dressed in Northern style and likewise the bards are made accompanied with ostentatious apparel.

40. Moreover, they [i.e. the bards] should have the sinews of the throat visible and their faces looking upwards. Low caste people (*Āhvarakas*) ought to be made of ruddy complexion and cross-eyed.

किञ्चिद्दानवसंकाशाः प्रांशवो दण्डपाणयः ।
न केकरान् न कपिलान्द्वन्द्वस्थाने समालिखेत् ।। ४१ ।।

नात्युद्धतेन वेशेन दशान्तरेण शस्यते ।
पार्श्वबद्धेन खड्गेन प्रतीहारस्तु दण्डवान् ।। ४२ ।।

संवेष्टितशिरस्काश्च कर्तव्या वणिजस्तथा ।
गायका नर्तका ये च वाद्यवादविदश्च ये ।। ४३ ।।

उद्धतेन तु वेषेण कार्यास्ते मनुजोत्तम ।
आसन्नपलिताः कार्याः सुभूषणविभूषिताः ।। ४४ ।।

पौरजानपदाः श्रेष्ठाः शुभ्रवस्त्रविभूषणाः ।
प्रश्रिताः प्रवणाः पह्वाः स्वभावप्रियदर्शनाः ।। ४५ ।।

41a. A किंचिदानव- 41b V प्रायशो
41cd. N lacks 41cd. CF न केकरा न कपिला D न्नकपिलास्तु द्वन्द्वास्थान ABCFV द्वंद्वान् ABCF युद्धे
42a. N lacks 42ab. ACF तत्युन्नतेन 42b AV न च शान्तेन
42d. N कारयेत् F दण्डवत्
43. N lacks 43-45.
43a. D सचेष्टितालेरक्षाश्च
43c. ABCDFV गायना- ACF नन्तकाये B न तु काये V ये वा
43d. C -वादविस्तद्धये ABFV -वादविशुद्धये
44c. D आसन्नः 44d CV स्वभूषण-
45a. V -जानपदाः F -जानपदः C -जनपदः
45c. D प्रश्रितः ABCFV प्रसृत- ABCDF -प्रवणः AB प्रव्हः CF प्राहुः D प्रदः
45d. B -दर्शिर्नः

41. The staff-holders should be made tall and somewhat resembling a *Dānava.* In a battlefield, no squint-eyed or tawny coloured [low-caste] people should ever be portrayed.

42. The doorkeeper should be [clad] in a dress which is not too ostentatious, is lacking in loose ends and with a sword tied by the side.

43ab. Merchants should be made with turbaned heads.

43c-44ab. O Best amongst men, those singers and dancers who are proficient in playing musical instruments are to be made dressed in flamboyant clothes.

44cd. Those approaching old age are to be adorned in beautiful ornaments.

45. The prominent amongst the citizens should be dressed in white clothes. They should be endowed with courteousness, be humble and pleasant looking by nature.

स्वकर्मोपस्करव्यग्रः कार्यः कर्मकरो जनः ।
प्रांशवः पीनगात्राश्च पीनग्रीवशिरोधराः ।। ४६ ।।

उदग्रा नीचकेशाश्च मल्लाः कार्यास्तथोद्धताः ।
वृषाः केसरिणश्चैव पश्चाद्यास्सत्त्वजातयः ।। ४७ ।।

यथाभूमि निवेश्यास्ते लोकं दृष्ट्वा नराधिप ।
एतद्रूपसमुद्देशं संदृष्टानां तवेरितम् ।। ४८ ।।

दृष्टानां सादृशं कार्यं सर्वेषामविशेषतः ।
चित्रे सादृश्यकरणं प्रधानं परिकीतिर्तम् ।। ४९ ।।

बुद्ध्वा रूपं यथावेषं वर्णं च मनुजोत्तम ।
देशे देशे नराः कार्या यथावत् तत्समुद्भवाः ।। ५० ।।

N lacks 46-50
46a. AS1S2 सुकर्मो- 46b A कार्य
47a. V उग्राश्च D नीवकेशाश्च मन्दाः
47d. ABV याश्चान्याः D पाश्चद्याः CF यथान्यास्-
48a. CF यथा भूमिं D यथाभूमीः V -निवेशास्ते
48d. CDFV मदृष्टानां AB -मदृष्टानं
49a. ABCFV दृष्टं D सदृशं ABCF ससदृशं V सुसदृशं
49c. A प्रयाणं
50a. D तथावेयं
50d. D यथावर्त्तसुभवा ACFV यथावत्तत्समुद्भवा

46ab. The labourers should be made preoccupied with the instruments of their trade.

46c-47b. The wrestlers should be made towering, short haired *(nīcakeśa)* with muscular limbs, and possessing thick neck and head.

47c-48b. O Lord of men, bulls, lions and other animals [like] cattle etc. should be [depicted] after looking at the world, [and] how they are located in the respective regions of it.

48cd. This exposition of that which is completely visible has been instructed to you.

49. Regarding the visible things, a very close resemblance ought to be made without any exception [because] in a painting, the accomplishing of verisimilitude is said to be vital.

50. O Lord of men, men in every land should be painted just as they are, after understanding [their] appearance, the way they dress and [their] colour.

देशं नियोगस्थानं च कर्म बुद्ध्वा च यत्नतः ।
आसनं शयनं यानं वेषं कार्यं नराधिप ।।५१ ।।

सरितां सशरीराणां वाहनानि प्रदर्शयेत् ।
पूर्णकुम्भकराः कार्यास्तथा नमितजानवः ।।५२ ।।

शैलानां शिखरं मूर्ध्नि दर्शयेन्मनुजोत्तम ।
द्वीपानां च करे कार्यं तथा भूमण्डलं शुभम् ।।५३ ।।

राजन् तथा शिखरिनः कार्याः शिखरपाणयः ।
रत्नपात्रकराः कार्याः सागरा मनुजोत्तम ।।५४ ।।

समुद्राणां प्रभास्थाने सलिलं तु प्रदर्शयेत् ।
आयूधानां च तच्चिह्नं किञ्चिन्मूर्धनि दर्शयेत् ।।५५ ।।

N lacks 51.

51a. D देशे ABCFV वियोगं स्थानं 51c. D पानं 51d C वेमं 52b N वाहानानि

52c. N –करा 52d AC नमित– N नमततजानवः F निमितजानवः

53a. N शिखलं 53b A दर्शयन्मनु N –जोत्तमः

53c. ABV करैः N कार्य्या 53d N मण्डलं तु तथा

54ab. CFV < .... > राजंस्तथा A < < पर्वताश्च तथा > > राजंस्तथा N कर्त्तव्या वर्ष्णाणि राज तथा 54b D कार्यश्च ABCFNV शिखरपाणयः

54C. N रत्नपात्रधराः 54d N सागरो A मुनुजोत्तम N –जोत्तमः

55c. N आयुधानांश्च D आयुधानंश्च C तच्चिह्नः FV2 तद्वद्धिः V1 तद्वद्धिः

55d N –मूर्ध्नि प्रदर्शयेत्

51. O Lord of men, the posture of sitting,[or a stool], sleeping [or a couch or bed], going or riding [or a chariot] and [the way of] of dressing should be made after understanding carefully the country, rank of authority and activity.

52. Of the Rivers which are personified, [their] vehicles should be shown. Moreover, their hands should be made to hold pitchers full [of water] and their knees bent downwards.

53. O Best of men, of the [embodied] mountains, a peak should be made on the top of the head. And in the same manner, an auspicious circle of earth [a globe] should be made in the hands of the [personified] islands.

54. O King, the [personified] mountains ought to be made with peaks in their hands. O Best amongst men, the [personified] oceans should be made with jars of jewels in their hands.

55. On the top of the halo of the oceans, water is to be shown. And in case of the [personification] of the weapons, their symbol should be shown on the top of the head.

निधीनां दर्शयेत्कुम्भं शङ्खं शङ्खस्य दर्शयेत् ।
पद्मं पद्मस्य राजेन्द्र शेषाणामनुरूपतः ।।५६ ।।

कालस्यावयवाः कार्याः स्वदेहसदृशाः पृथक् ।
विद्यानां दर्शयेच्चिह्नमक्षमालां च पुस्तकम् ।।५७ ।।

अतः परं प्रवक्ष्यामि रूपं सर्वस्य दृश्यते ।
आकाशं दर्शयेद्विद्वान् स्ववर्णं खगमाकुलम् ।।५८ ।।

तथैव दर्शयेद्रात्रिं तारकामण्डितं दिवम् ।
भूमिं च जाङ्गलानूपमिश्रांश्च स्वैस्तथा गुणैः ।।५९ ।।

पर्वतं तु शिलाजालैः शिखरैर्धातुभिर्द्रुमैः ।
निर्झरैर्भुजगैश्चैव दर्शयेन्नृपसत्तम ।।६० ।।

56c. D पद्म
57a. N कालस्यावयवाकार्या ABCFV कार्यस्यावयवाः A कार्या
57b A सदेहास्- NV स्वदेहसदृशा CF स्वदेहसदृशः
57c. ABCFVB दिव्यानां -57d N मालाञ्च D मालांश्च < ..... > कम्
58b. AB यदस्य CFNV यद्यस्य D मद्यस्य 58c CF -द्विद्वात्
58d. N -स्ववर्ण V विवर्णं A वर्वणं
59a. ABCFNV दर्शयेद्राजन् D दर्शयेद्राचन् 59b C -स्तारका- D ताकरा-
N lacks 59cd.
59c. D भूमीश्चजङ्गला 59d ABCV -मिश्रां स्वैः स्वैस्- F -मिश्रांस्वस्स्वैस्तथा गुलैः
60a. DN पर्वतन्तु
N lacks 60cd.

56. Of the *Nidhis,* a pitcher should be shown. *Śamkha* is to be shown by conchshell. O King, a lotus [is to be shown] in case of *Padma* and the rest according to what is appropriate.

57. The limbs of *Kāla* should be made separately resembling its own body. And the *vidyās* [or *vedās*] are to be shown by a rosary and a book as their symbols.

58. Now, I shall instruct about forms which are visible to all. One proficient (in painting) ought to show the sky with its own colour and full of birds.

59. O King, in the same way, night is to be shown with the sky studded with stars. And the earth (is to be shown) as arid, watery and mixed with their respective features.

60. O best of men, the mountain is to be shown by a multitude of rocks, peaks, minerals, trees, waterfalls, and snakes.

वनं नानाविधैर्वृक्षैर्विहगैः श्वापदैस्तथा ।
तोयं च दर्शयेद्विद्वानाकुलैर्मस्त्यकच्छपैः ।।६१ ।।

पद्माद्यैश्च महाराज तथान्यैर्जलजैर्ग्रहैः ।
देवतावेश्मभिश्चित्रैः प्रासादापणवेश्मभिः ।।६२ ।।

नगरं दर्शयेद्विद्वान्राजमार्गैश्च शोभनैः ।
वसत्या दर्शयेद्ग्रामं किञ्चिदुद्यानभूषितम् ।।६३ ।।

सर्वेषामथ दुर्गाणां कर्तव्यं दर्शनं तथा ।
स्वभूमिविनिवेशेन वप्राट्टालकपर्वतैः ।।६४ ।।

पण्ययुक्तास्तु कर्तव्यास्तथैवापणभूमयः ।
आपानभूमिः कर्तव्या पानयुक्ता नराकुला ।।६५ ।।

61a. V -विहङ्गैः
61b. N स्वापवैस्तथा
61d. N -विद्वान्रावतै- CF विद्वान्नारन्तैर्मस्त्य- AV -नन्तैर्मत्स्य-
62a. N पद्माख्यैश्च CF पद्माख्यै < . > ABV पद्माक्षैश्च N महाराजस्तथा
62b. N -जलजैग्ग्रहैः D -जनजेर्गुणैः ABCFV -जलजैर्गुणैः
N lacks 62cd.
63c. V वमत्या
64c. A सुभूमि- B साभूमि- 64d F प्राट्टालकपर्वतैः D प्राट्टालकदर्शनैः N प्राट्टालकनिदर्शनैः
N lacks 65.
65. A आदान- CFV आधान- 65d D मानयुक्ता F पात्रयुक्ता D नरांगला

61-62b. The well-versed [in painting] shows the forest by different types of trees, birds and beasts of prey and shows water, O Lord by flurrying fishes and tortoises, lotuses etc. and other water-born creatures [crocodiles etc].

62c-63b. The learned [in painting] shows a city by means of various kinds of palaces of gods [temples], palaces, shops, houses and magnificent highways.

63cd. The villages are shown by settlements and somewhat beautified by the gardens.

64. Moreover, the depiction of all the fortresses should be made as located on appropriate ground and [furnished] with mounds, watch-towers and hillocks.

65. The market place should be made full of articles of trade. The Drinking places should have [alcoholic] liquors and be crowded with people.

उत्तरीयविहीनांश्च द्यूतसक्तान्प्रदर्शयेत् ।
जिताञ्छोकसमायुक्तान्हृष्टान् लब्धजयांस्तथा ।। ६६ ।।

चतुरङ्गबलोपेतां प्रहरद्भिर्नरैर्युताम् ।
मृतावयवरक्ताढ्यां रणभूमिं प्रदर्शयेत् ।। ६७ ।।

चिताकुणपसंयुक्तं श्मशानं च तथा नृप ।
युक्तं सभारुष्ट्रैराद्यैर्मार्गं सार्थं प्रदर्शयेत् ।। ६८ ।।

सचन्द्रग्रहनक्षत्रां तथा दर्शितलौकिकाम् ।
आसन्नतस्करां रात्रिं दर्शयेत्सुप्तमानवाम् ।। ६९ ।।

प्राग्रात्रे दर्शयेत्तत्र तथा चैवाभिसारिकाम् ।
सारुणो म्लानदीपश्च प्रत्युषो रुतकुक्कुटः ।। ७० ।।

N lacks 66-70.
66a. D -विहीनां B द्यूतमुक्ता- CDF द्यूतसक्तान्
66d. CF -हृष्टा- A -लघुजलांस्तथा
67c. CF -रक्ताढ्या 67d CF राजभूमिं
68d. D -र्मार्गै
69d. CF -मानवान्
70b. ABCF चैवाभिचारिकम्
70d. AB प्रदोषो CF प्रदोषा ACF हृतकुक्कुटः

66. Those seated for gambling [gamblers] should be shown without their upper garments.Those who are won over [loosers] should be overwhelmed with grief and the winners should be shown joyful.

67. The battlefield should be shown [smeared] with blood, with [mutilated] limbs of the dead, accompanied with attacking men and approached by the four limbed army [i.e. elephants, chariots, cavalry and infantry].

68. The funeral ground, O King, should be full of dead bodies and funeral pyres. The caravan road is to be shown by the camels etc. carrying burdens.

69. The night is to be shown by people sleeping, a thief in the proximity and by the ordinary happenings [associated with the night] made visible and by moon, planets and the stars.

70. In the first half of the night, an *Abhisārikā* [a woman secretly meeting her lover] is to be shown. The Dawn is shown accompanied by a [rising] sun, dimmed lamp and cock shown crying.

कर्मव्यग्रजनप्रायः कर्तव्यो वासरस्तथा ।
द्विजैर्नियमिभिर्युक्तां रक्तां संध्यां प्रदर्शयेत् ।।७१।।

तमसो दर्शनं कार्यं हस्तसंसर्पकैर्नरैः ।
कुमुदानां विकासेन ज्योत्स्नां चन्द्रेण दर्शयेत् ।।७२।।

दर्शयेत्सरजस्कां च वात्यां पर्णोत्करावृताम् ।
सछत्रमानवप्रायां वृष्टिं वृष्ट्यां प्रदर्शयेत् ।।७३।।

वृक्षैर्वसन्तजैः फुल्लैः कोकिलैर्मधुपोत्कटै ।
प्रहृष्टनरनारीकं वसन्तं तु प्रदर्शयेत् ।।७४।।

प्राणीनां क्लमतप्तानामादित्येन च दर्शयेत् ।
क्लान्तैः कार्यं नरैर्ग्रीष्मं मृगश्छायागतैस्तथा ।।७५।।

71a. A -विग्रजनप्राय: 71b ABCFV वानरस्तथा 71c D -द्विजैभूमिभि-

72b. F -संसर्पकेन्नरै: V वासैसंसर्प- 72cd N विकाशेन द्योस्त्लां

72d ACFV विकासे च ज्योत्स्नां चन्द्रे प्रदर्शयेत्

73a. D सरमस्कांश्च 73a ACFV -सरजस्यं N सरजस्का V शय्यां 73b N वात्यां D वात्य ACF वाप्यां V कणोर्त्करावृताम् N कणोर्त्करावृता D मणोर्त्करावृताम्

N repeats 73ab N कणोर्त्करावृतं

73c. N सछन्त- D सहत्र- AFV सद्वृत्त- C सद्वृत्ति N -प्रायो

73d. ABDN वृष्टया AFV -मदर्शयेत् AB स दर्शयेत् DN च दर्शयेत् V निदर्शनम्

N lacks 74.

74a. A फुलै: 74b ACDFV कोकिलामधुपोत्कुटै: 74d N सचतन्तु

75ab. ABCDFV प्राणिनां N प्राणिन्तं N क्रमतप्त- V क्लेशतप्त- D < .? > मतप्त- CF निदर्शयेत् V निदर्शनम्

N has 73 after 73ab.

75b. V तु 75c N क्लान्तं कार्यैन्नरैग्रीष्मं- 75d ABCFN मृगैच्छाया-

71. Day is usually painted by men toiling away at work. The dusk should be shown reddish [in hue] with the twice-borns engaged in their rituals.

72. The darkness is made visible by [showing] people reaching out with their hands. The moonlight is shown by the blooming of the lotuses and the moon.

73. A gale *(vātyā)* is to be shown by [depicting] dust and scattered leaves. The rain [that accompanies it] is shown by a downpour and people going out with their umbrellas.

74. Spring *(Vasanta)* is shown by overjoyed men and women, swarms of bees, cuckoo birds, flowers and trees which blossom in this season.

75-76. The summer *(Grīṣma)* is made [i.e. represented] by fatigued people and likewise deer lying under the shade, by the creatures languid and

महिषैः पङ्कसंलीनैस्तथा शुष्कजलाशयम् ।
विहङ्गैर्द्रुमसंलीनैः सिंहव्याघ्रैर्गुहागतैः ।।७६ ।।

तोयनम्रघनैर्युक्तां सेन्द्रचापविभूषणैः ।
विद्युद्विद्योतसंयुक्ता प्रावृषं दर्शयेत्तथा ।।७७ ।।

सफलद्रुमसंयुक्तां पक्वसस्यवसुन्धराम् ।
सहंसपद्मसलिलां शरदं तु तथा लिखेत् ।।७८ ।।

सबाष्पसलिलस्थानं तथा लूनवसुन्धरम् ।
सनीहारदिगन्तं च हेमन्तं दर्शयेद् बुधः ।।७९ ।।

हृष्टवायसमातङ्गं शीतार्तजनसङ्कुलम् ।
शिशिरं तु लिखेद्विद्वान् हिमच्छन्नदिगन्तरम् ।।८० ।।

76a. D महिषै N -सलीनै- BCV पङ्कमलीनस्तथा 76b N शुष्का- A जलाश्रयम्
N lacks 76cd.
76c. ABVDF विहगै- 76d V -व्याघ्रैर्गु- CF -व्याघ्रैस्दहागतैः
77a. N तोयेनसघनैर्य्युक्तां D तोयनघद्यनै- ABCF -युक्तं
77c. V विद्युद्विद्योतनै- D विद्युद्वद्योत F विद्युदुद्योतयन्युक्तो ABC विद्युदुद्योतयत्युक्तां N विद्युदुद्योनसंयुक्तां 77d D प्रावृषा
78a. N संयुक्ता 78b CFV पक्वसस्यां-N -वसुन्धराः A सस्यवसुन्दराम्
78d. A तदा A खिखेत् 79a CF -सलिलं 79b N ह्लनवसुन्धरम्
79c. N -विगन्तं 80a D हृष्टपाय- 80a CF मीतान्त-
80d. CF हिमच्चन्नं

suffering due to the sun and by buffaloes sporting in mud, dried up ponds, birds clinging to the trees [for shade] and lions and tigers resorting to caves.

77. The rainy season *(Prāvṛṣam)* is likewise shown with water laden clouds, ornaments in form of rainbows and flashes of thunderbolt.

78. The autumn season *(Śarada)* is painted with lakes full of swans and lotuses, with fields full of ripened corns and trees laden with fruits.

79. The learned [in painting] shows the winter *(Hemanta)* season with horizons full of fog, with fields harvested and water vapour [mist] hanging over the water areas.

80. The cool, *(Śiśira)* season is to be painted with snow obscured horizons, people huddling together afflicted with cold, and with delighted elephant and crows.

वृक्षाणां पुष्पफलतः प्राणिनां मदतस्तथा ।
ऋतूनां दर्शनं कार्यं लोकं दृष्ट्वा नराधिप ॥ ८१ ॥

रसभावाश्च कर्तव्या यथापूर्वमुदाहृताः ।
यथायोगं तु युञ्जीत नृत्ताभिहितमत्र च ॥ ८२ ॥

शुष्कं वर्तनया यस्तु चित्रं तन्मध्यमं स्मृतम् ।
शुष्कार्द्रमधमं प्रोक्तं सार्द्रमेव तथोत्तमम् ॥ ८३ ॥

यथादेशं यथाकालं यथादेहं यथावयः ।
क्रियमाणं भवेद्धन्यं विपरीतमतोऽन्यथा ॥ ८४ ॥

इति विचक्षणबुद्धिविकल्पितैः
करणकान्तिविलासरसादिभिः ।
लिखितमीक्षणलोभनमादरा-
द्भवति चित्रमभीप्सितकामदम् ।। ८५ ।।

इति श्रीविष्णुधर्मोत्तरे तृतीयखण्डे मार्कण्डेयवज्रसंवादे चित्रसूत्रे रूपनिर्माणं नाम द्विचत्वारिंशत्तमोऽध्यायः ॥

81a. D पुष्पकलतः 81b A प्राणिनां D प्रालिनाम-N मुदतस्तथा
81c. N कार्य्यं 81cd ABCFV लोकान् 81d D लोक
N ends after 81
83a. D शुष्क AV वस्तु
83cd. A शुकांद्रम- CF प्रोक्तमार्द्रमेव 83d V चार्दू- A चांद्रमेव
84a. V यथादेयं 84b CF यथादेमं यथायवः ABV यथादेशं
84d. CF -मथो ऽन्यथा 85a AV -विकिल्पतैः-
85b. CF करणकीर्ति- D विशाल- D लिखितवीक्षिण- AV -लोचनमाद-

81. The representation of the seasons should be done, O King of men, after observing the world and in accordance with the flowers and fruits of the trees and also the ruttishness of the animals.

82. The sentiments, *rasas* and emotions, *bhāvas* are to be depicted as explained already. All that which has been said [in the chapter on] dance [in connection with the *rasas* and *bhāvas*] should be employed in a painting accordingly.

83. That painting is said to be mediocre *(madhyama)* which employs only the dry line-rendering. The inferior *(Adhama)* is said to be that which is dry and wet. And the best *(Uttama)* is that which has wet line-rendering.

84. [A painting] which is being made according to the instructions *(yathādeśam)*, time *(yathākālam)*, age *(yathāvayaḥ)* and the body type *(yathādeham)* becomes auspicious. Otherwise, it becomes its opposite. [i.e. unfavourable.]

85. Thus that painting which is [imbibed] with the [dance] postures, beauty, playfulness and sentiments etc. visualised by discerning mind, which is a form of a painted visual enticement fulfills desires.

NOTES TO ADHYĀYA 42

42.1b. *pṛthivīśurāḥ* . PS's text reads *pṛthivīśvarā,* possibly a printing error. The correct reading, *pṛthivīśvarāḥ* is found in MSS ABDCN and followed by SM.

42.1c. *kūpake.* Only MSS N preserve this reading. Both SK (p. 46) and PS (p. 130) adopt ACV's *rūpake.* Note how it affects their translations:

SK : In the case of kings (however) the hair on the body should be drawn *one by one.*

PS : The bodily hair of the kings should be *drawn one by one.*

SM (p. 185) takes it to mean "features"

> Kings in general are to be depicted in pictures like the celestial, while individually each one of them should be portrayed in consonance with his features.

kūpake meaning "in the pore" is to be understood in the light of the following citation from BṛSaṃ.

> रोमैकैकं कूपके पार्थिवानां (B.S. 67.5)
>
> Kings have only one hair in the pore.

Bhaṭṭa Utpala explains it : एकरोमा भवेद्राजा "Kings should be single haired."

This helps us to appreciate the stress laid on "one" in *ekaikam* and how this characteristic operated within a physiognomic hierarchy and its association with prognostication.

42.1c. *lomam.* SM (p. 155) emends to *lokaḥ* on the following grounds:

> F.N. 1) The reading लोमं is wrong. It should be लोक: . The painting of hair one by one appears very queer. It is probably लोक: as पृथिवीक्षितां लोक: meaning the whole class of kings.

SM's emendation reflects his failure to view *lomam* in the appropriate context supplied by the *BṛSaṃ.*

42.2. Verse 2 is a list of personages to be portrayed in groups. For eg. the sages are to be painted next to the *gandharvas, daityas* alongside the *dānavas* and so on. The next verse tells us that they are all to be painted following the *Bhadra* mode. According to 4b, the *gandharvas* are like the gods [in appearance] except that they lack crowns and are smaller in proportion (in the *Bhadra* mode).

Note N at this point has a different word order.

MS N	OTHER MSS
ऋषयश्चैव गन्धर्वा दैत्याश्च सह दानवैः ।	ऋषयश्चैव गन्धर्वा दैत्याश्च सह दानवैः ।
मन्त्रिणश्च महाराज सांवत्सरपुरोहितौ ।।	मन्त्रिणश्च महाराज सांवत्सरपुरोहितौ ।। २ ।।
सर्वालंकारसंयुक्तो सर्वलक्षणलक्षिताः ।	कार्या भद्रप्रमाणेन ब्राह्माणाश्च नरेश्वर ।
कार्या भद्रप्रमाणेन ब्राह्माणाश्च नरेश्वर ।।	ऋषयस्तत्रकर्तव्याजटाजूटोपशोभिताः ।।३ ।।
ऋषयश्चैव कर्तव्या जटाजूटोपसोभिताः ।	कृष्णजिनात्तरासंगा दुर्बलास्तेजसान्विताः ।
कृष्णाजिनोत्तरासंगा दूर्वारास्तेजसायुताः ॥	देवताश्चापि गन्धर्वा मुकुटेन विवर्जिताः ॥ ४ ॥
देवतुल्याश्च गर्न्धवा मुकुटेन विवर्जिताः ।	कर्तव्यास्ते महाराज शिखरैरुपशोभिताः ।
कर्तव्यास्ते महाराज शेखरैरुपशोभिताः ॥	ब्रह्मवर्चस्विनो विप्राः शुक्लाम्बरधरास्तथा ॥ ५॥
ब्रहांवर्चस्विनो विप्रः शुक्लाम्बरविभूषणाः ।	मन्त्रिणश्च महाराज सांवत्सरपुरोहितौ ।
मुकुटेन विहीनानां मोष्णीषां कारयेत् ॥	सर्वालङ्कारसंयुक्ता नैवोल्वणविभूषणाः ॥ ६ ॥
	मुकुटेन विहीनांस्तु सोष्णीषान्कारयेत् ।

In all the other MSS, *mantriṇaśca .... purohitau* is repeated twice. On a close scrutiny, it will be evident that it is not a case of dittography but is deliberate. At first, sages etc. are listed and grouped and then they are again mentioned in a greater elaboration.

The list consists of (1) sages, (2) *gandharvas,* (3) *daityas /dānavas,* (4) ministers, (5) astrologer / priest and (6) Brahmins. Note that regarding the sequence in which the sages and *gandharvas* are mentioned, all the MSS agree. It is after verse 2 that an arbitrary order sets in where the ministers, astrologer and priest are mentioned before the *daityas* and *dānavas.* This inconsistency has been rectified by reshuffling the word order whereby 7b, 8 and 6 of the other MSS are inserted in that sequence between 5 and 6 of N's order.

In one instance the *Newari* wordorder seems more appropriate. Compare verse 6 from N and verse 6 and 7a from other MSS. The description given in 6b of N -*"mukuṭena vihīnānstu .... kāryeśca tān"* connects better with *"brahmavarcasvinaḥ"* or the brahmins than the ministers. The sense that other MSS convey, is that the ministers are to be painted without crowns and with a topknot. Topknots are more the distinguishing features of the priests and the brahmins than of the ministers.

42.3d. *yutāḥ*. This reading is preferrable to *-tejasānvitāḥ* on the grounds that it is found in MSS CDN.

42.4a. *devatulyāśca*. The *deva-* in this reading (> MSS DN) goes better with *devaḥ* of 1a than *devatā* found in ABV followed by all. What it implies is that the *gandharvas* resemble the gods in all respects except in one feature - while gods are portrayed with crowns, *gandharvas* possess *"śekhara* i.e. garland of flowers tied around the heads. SK translates., (p. 47), "Gods and gandharvas should be represented *without crowns*". PS follows SK in her translation (p. 131). SM tr., (p. 185), "Devas (celestials) and gandharvas *do not wear a crown.*"

42.4d. *śekhara-*. It comes from MSS D and N. SK, PS, and SM follow ABCFV *śikhara-* SK and SM translate it as "crest". SM (p. 185) appears to have followed one of the lexical meanings of *"śikhara"* as "erection of the hair of the body. (see Monier Williams) and translates as follows:

> Devas (celestials) and Gandharvas with groomed and well-dressed hair shooting up.

42.6c. *teṣāmatyuddhato.* It is adopted from MSS CFD according to which the dress of the *daityas* and *danavas* should be excessively showy. SK and PS follow V's *-abhyuddhato.* Cf. verse 26a.

42.9a. *bhadrapramāṇāḥ*. MSS D and N preserve this reading *rudrapramāṇāḥ* in ABCFV is a corruption based on the similarity between -ru- and -bh- in the *Śāradā* script. DN's reading confirms the conjecture made by all the scholars. It refers to a well known mode of proportion listed and explained in adh. 35, verse 11.

प्रमाणं नृप हंसस्य भद्रस्य तु षडुत्तरम् ।
चतुर्भिरधिकं ज्ञेयं मालव्यस्य तथा नृप ।। 35. 11

42.11d. *aparadhānam.* The emendation of *pradhānam mānavam* found in all MSS to *apradhānam mānavam* is prompted by sense and context. The former referring to the *śudras* could not possibly mean "the chief among men". Nor can *pradhānam* be taken as "usually, generally" because *Śaśaka* mode addresses not all men but specifically the subordinate or inferior men belonging to the *Śura* caste given its smaller proportions (92 *aṅg*) as opposed to *Rucaka* (100 *aṅg*) and *Bhadra* (106 *aṅg*) for the *vaiśyas* and the *brāhmaṇas.*

42.12b. *mahābhuja.* This reading comes from MS N. It is a vocative meaning "the great armed one". All scholars take it as *mahibhuja* but translate it differently. SM, (p. 47). "Piśāchas, dwarfs, hunch-backed men, pramathas and (those) who enjoy the earth,...". PS (p. 137) translates:

> "In the representation of the piśācas, dwarfs, hump-backed and pramathas enjoying the earth, ... ".

SM (p. 156) emends it correctly but his translation of *mahābhuja* as "valorious" in place of "O Long armed one" is not correct.

42.12cd. *mānāniyamataḥ - rūpāniyamastathā,* This reading found in MSS ADNF is adopted.

SK (p. 47) follows the corrupt reading from V-मानन्नियमतः कार्यं रुपन्नियमतस्तथा and translates:

Piśāchas, ...should be represented consistent with the rules of (proportionate) measurment and in accordance with the rules of *rūpa* (creative form).

PS follows V's corrupt reading in the text but corrects the translation by following F (p. 131).

42.14c. *aśvavaktrāsca...* That this particular type of hybrid form should alone be ornamented seems odd and makes the last two *pādas* of this verse doubtful.

42.15cd. *vivṛttākṣā.* It is derived from N's *vivṛtakhyā- tibhīṣaṇa.* Note that ACF and a slightly different variant of D read *vivṛtakṣā* which means blind. (for eg. Pāṇ. vi. 3.3) (vārtt. 2. Pat). Whereas *vivṛttākṣa* means "(glaringly) wide eyes" and fits in better with the context.

SK (p. 48) follows *vikalākṣa* from V and translates it as "bewildered eyes". PS (p. 131) translates *vikṛtākṣa* as "eyes deformed". SM (p. 186) translates it as "ugly eyes". Cf. verse 1. *adhyāya* 57 of ViDhUp.:

मार्कण्डेय ॐ विरुपाक्षो विवृत्ताक्षः प्रांशुदण्डोज्ज्वलाननः ।
ऊर्ध्वकेशो हरिच्छमश्रुद्विर्बाहुर्भीषणाननः ।।

42.16. प्रांसवस्तनुमध्याश्च कुद्धरुपा भयावहा ।
यक्षाः कार्या महाराज न सौम्या न विभीषणाः ।।

This verse found only in D and N appears to be dropped from all the MSS of the 'C' group. This strengthens the argument that these two MSS are the independant witnesses to the archetype. Besides this verse also is an important source of information about the representation of *yakṣas.*

42.17d. *yatra.* Only D preserves this reading. It makes a much better sense than *yaksaḥ* which is found only in V. MSS ABCF read *ya ete* which yields a poor sense. What it means is that the figures are said to be represented with ornaments in all the cases where the author has specified. Note this reading alters the meaning of this half verse.

SK (p. 48) accepts V's reading and translates:

> All *Yakṣas* are said to be decorated with ornaments and they have been dealt by me (already).

PS's text and translation (p. 131) follows SK.

SM (p. 131) includes *nāgās* and *rākṣasās* with *yakṣās:*

> All of them including the *Yakṣas* already described have to be decorated with ornaments.

42.18d. I agree with SM in adopting the reading in MSS ABC- *pramāṇenaiva varjitāḥ.* The monotoneity of repetition can thus be avoided.

42.21b. *tu.* MSS CN's reading *tu* is preferred to *ca* of ABDV.

42.23a. *tatprabhāsadṛśāḥ sarve.* The reading *-prabhāvāḥ smṛtāḥ* is corrupt because the context requires *"prabhā"* as found in verse 24a. *Smṛtāḥ* appears to be corrupt, echoing its mention in 22b. The scribe seems to have confused *-sadṛśāḥ* for *-vāḥ smṛtāḥ.* Moreover, -mṛ- and -dṛ- look fairly similar in the *Śāradā* script.

42.24b. Note SK's (p. 48) serious mistranslation of this verse in which she connects 24a and 24b :

> Prostitute women should have the size of a "Ruchaka". (They should be painted) with vermillion or emerald colour,

moonwhite (in complexion) or dark like the petals of the blue lotus.

Verse 24a is connected with 23 and is a continuation of the description of the colours of *Vāsudeva* etc. and their attendants.

42.25a. *veṣyānā-*. This reading is preserved in MSS ABDV. PS and SM adopt corrupt reading *veṣānām* from C and F.

42.25b. *śṛṅgārasammitam.* Note that *-sammatam* found in all the MSS is clearly a corruption of *-sammitam* meaning "furnished with". The compound means "having a dress (suitable) for amorous purposes".

42.27a. *rūpavatyasstriyāḥ.* This reading is more reliable and is adopted from C and N.

42.27b. *mātarastena.* The emendation of *-svena* to *-stena* is crucial to derive an appropriate sense. *Tena* which parses with *rūpeṇa* refers to the *Mālavya* mode of proportion which is prescibed for the wives as well as the mothers of *daityas* etc.

Note verse 11a throws more light on this:

> SK: The wives and mothers of daityas, dānavas, yakṣas and rākṣasas ought to be according to the rules (laid down for their men). The same holds good for the wives of pisachas. (p.48)

PS: Their mothers should be shown in their own forms. (p. 131)

> SM : While the wives of Daityas, Dānavas, Yakshas and Rākshasas are to be portrayed as beautiful, their mothers are to be delineated *in their own fierce forms.* (p. 187)

42.28b. *kāryāstadrūpasaṃyutāḥ.* Note the "*tadrūpa-*" is ambiguous for it could refer to either the *Mālavya* mode or the form of the *piśācas* which is to be followed for portraying the wives of the *piśācas.* For SK's translation. see above. PS and SM follow the latter sense. PS, (p. 131), "The wives of Piśācas should have the forms of Piśācas." SM translates. (p. 187), "The wives of Piśāchas, however, are to be shown fearful after their male forms."(p.181)

42.29a. *sarvālaṅkāravarjitāḥ* . This reading from MS C makes more sense than *nānālaṅkāravarjitāḥ.* Note SM also prefers this reading but for a different reason.

> F.N. 1. If visarga is to be retained for परीधाना:, सर्वालंकार is required. This reading is preferable to नानालङ्कार (p. 157)

42. 29b. *tathārūpavatī.* This compound which can split either as *tathā* + *rūpavatī* or + *arūpavatī* leads to contradictory meanings. However, judging by the context in which lists a hunch-backed, dwarfish and old woman, this problem can be resolved by taking it as *-arupavatī.* The subsequent verse makes the sense clearer. In a retinue of the noble ladies, these mis-shapen characters i.e. a hunch-back etc should be portrayed along with a similarly ugly woman *(tathārūpavatī).*

SK : A hunch-backed,a dwarfish and an old woman also should be (represented) in (their) *natural condition.* (p. 48)

PS : Kubja- Hunch-backed Vāmanikā dwarfish, and old woman should *not be shown beautiful.* (p. 131)

SM : The retinue of princesses should be composed of hunchbacks, dwarfs, aged woman and *beautiful damsels* with an old chamberlain. (p. 187)

42.31d. *rūpeṇa.* This reading of MSS AD is preferred to V's *veṣeṇa.* Note that by this, the various formula of proportion such as the *Bhadra, Mālavya* etc. are implied.

42. 32ab. *daityādiyojitāh kāryāh paricāra striyaḥ sadā.*

PS rejects CF's perfectly sound reading in favour of AV's *daityādi yoṣitam.* Note that D lacks 32-34a and N lacks 31-34a. CF's reading yields a completely different sense. According to this reading, the attendant women should be drawn accompanied *(-yojitā)* by the *daityas* etc.

SK (p. 49), PS (p. 132) and SM (p. 187) take it to mean that the wives of daityas etc. should always have attendant women.

42.32cd. *mahāśirā mahorasko mahānāso mahāhanuḥ.*

The adoption of CF's reading above has a notable bearing on the interpretation of the verses 32cd-33. All the scholars have been led to regard the attributes mentioned as belonging to an army commander *(senāyāḥ patiḥ)* mentioned in verses 32cd - 33. These epithets are far too diabolical for an army commander and apply better to the *daityas.* However, it is important to bear in mind that they are either attributes or epithets of the *daityas.*

These *daityas* etc. , as the text maintained, form a part of the retinue with the assigned function of accompanying the women attendants.

Note the use of *suhanuḥ* and *mahāśirāḥ* in ***Mahābhārata:***

पताकिनो मण्डलिनः फणवन्तश्च सर्व्वशः । एते चान्ये च बहवः सर्पास्तस्यां युधिष्ठिर ।
उपासते महात्मानं वरुणं विगतकल्माः । बलिवैरोचनो राजा नरकः पृथिवीजयः ।
संह्रादो विप्रचितिश्च कालखंजाश्च दानवाः । सुहनुर्दुर्मुखः शङ्खः सुमनाः सुमतिस्ततः ।
घटोदरो महापार्श्वः क्रथनः पिठरस्तथा । विश्वरुपः स्वरुपश्च विरुपोऽथ महाशिराः ।
दशग्रीवाश्च बाली च मेघवासा दशावरः । टिटिभो विटभूतश्च संह्रादश्चेन्द्रतापनः ।
दैत्यदानवसंघाश्च सर्व्वे रुचिरकुण्डलाः । स्रग्विणो मौलिनश्चैव तथा दिव्यपरिच्छदा ।

these and many other Snakes wait on the great-spirited Varuṇa in that hall unwearied, Yudhisthira, King Bali Vairocana and world conquerer Naraka, Samhrāda and Vipracitti, all the Kālakhanjās, Suhanu, Durmukha, Saṅkha, Sumanās, Sumati, Ghatodara, Mahāpārśva, Krathana, Piṭhara, Visvarūpa, Svarūpa Virūpa, Mahāśiras, Daśagrīva, Vālin, Meghavāsās, Daśāvara, Ṭiṭibha, Viṭabhūta, Samhrāda, Indratāpana, all the hosts of Daityas and Dānavas with their bright earrings, all garlanded and diademed and divinely garbed,

Note that *mahāśirā* and *suhanu* are amongst the names of the demons. *mahāhanu* is an epithet belonging to *piśācas* or *dānavas.* For eg. see ***Harivamśa:***

तेषामनु महाघोरौ पिशाचौ विकृतानौ । प्रांशु पिङ्गलरोमाणौ दीर्घजिह्वौ महाहनू ।
(***Bhaviṣyapurāṇa*** adh. 269 / 270)

मांसपो मासभक्षश्च वेगवान्केतुमानशिविः । पङ्कदिग्धशरिरश्च वृहत्कीर्तिर्म्महाहनुः ।

(Ibid. adh. 239/ 12938)

42.33a. *pīnaskandhabhujagrīvo.* Note that it is likely that *Mahāhanuḥ* is a name of a *daitya* who has a similar attribute and *pīnaskandhabhujagrīvo* being another of its attributes.

42.33b. *tritaraṅgalalāṭaśca mahākaṇiḥ.* It seems to be a name of a *daitya* and *tritaraṅga* being its attribute. The three wavy lines on the forehead has often been used to create a diabolical expression on the faces of demons. (see example I, 'Gods paying Homage to Durga' from

Bundelkhand, circa. 1875, ***The Classical Tradition in Rajput Painting Pratapaditya Pal, 1978, New York*** plate 53, p. 152/example II, a scupture of Rahu from the Navagraha panel, Sun Temple, Konarak, Orissa, 1238-58 A.D. ***The Art of Ancient India, Susan L. Huntington, 1985, New York)***

42.33d. *śyetadṛṣṭir.* This emendation of *śyena* to *śyeta* is based on a reference to *śyetākṣa* found in, for eg. texts such as ***Vājasaneyasaṃhitā*** and ***Śatapathabrāhmaṇa*** where it means "reddish eyes" शुद्धवाल: सर्वशुद्धवालो मणिवालस्तऽअश्विना: श्येत: श्येताक्षोऽरुणस्ते रुद्राय पशुपतये कर्णा यामा अवलिप्ता रौद्रा नमोरुपा: पार्जन्या:, (Vājasaneya Saṃhitā, 24.3.ed. Weber). See also Mahidhara's commentary: श्येत: श्वेतवर्ण: श्येताक्ष: अरुण: रक्त:. Besides, in the *Śāradā* script, "ta" and "na" are easy to confuse.

SK (p. 49) follows V's *vyomadṛṣṭir* and translates., "*...with eyes raised up towards the sky ...* "PS (p. 132) and SM (p. 188) accept *śyanākṣa* from ABCFV and take it to mean "hawk like eyes".

42.34a. Note the translation by other scholars who connect verses 32 and 33b with the description of *"senāyāḥ patiḥ"* in 34a.

SK's translation which sets a precedence for PS (p. 132) and SM (p. 188) is worth citing in full:

> By one who knows painting, the commander of an army should be represented (as) strong, proud, tall, with fleshy shoulders, hand and neck, with big head, powerful chest, powerful nose and broad chin, with eyes raised up towards the sky, and with firm hips. (p. 49)

See ***Mahābhārata,*** for an interesting description of a king named Bṛhadratha who was also alleged to be a commander of army:

> अक्षौहिणीनां तिसृणामासीत्समरदर्पित: । राजा बृहद्रथो नाम मगधाधिपति: पति: ।।
> रुपवान्वीर्यसंपन्न: श्रीमानतुलविक्रम: । नित्यं दीक्षाकृशतनु: शतक्रतुरिवापर: ।।
> तेजसा सूर्यसदृश: क्षमया पृथिवीसम: । यमान्तकसम: कोपे श्रिया वैश्रवणोपम: ।।

(***Mahābhārata***, 2.16.12-14 ed. Edgerton, Poona, 1944)

> There was a king, Bṛhadratha by name, the overlord of Magadha, the commander of three armies, and proud warrior. He was a handsome man of personal bravery, illustrious

> and incomparably powerful; his body was always lean from fasts at sacrificial consecrations, and he had the appearance of a second Indra. In splendour he resembled the Sun, in patience the earth, in ḥis anger Yama the Finisher, in wealth Kubera.

Note that this seems a more convincing description of an army commander than what is given in verses 32cd-33.

42.36a. *khaṅgacarmadharāḥ.* This reading is adopted from A,C,F,D and V, *carma* here means "shield" and fits in with *khaṅga* or "sword". PS and SM follow *khaṅgavarmadharāḥ.*

PS (p. 132) suggests the correct emendation only in the footnote:

> The soldiers carrying swords and *armours*[1] ....
>
> F.N. 1. If we amend the reading "varma" into "carma", then the meaning would be shield.

42.37b. *kuñjarāsturagāstathā.* This is adopted from MSS A, C and F in place of *kuñjarāsturagādayaḥ* found only in V and is accepted by all the scholars. It seems to be a correct reading because *tathā* employed forms a correlative to *yathā* in *yathoktalakṣaṇāḥ* in the same line. Note that MSS N and D have same in a reverse word order.

42.38a. *kartavyā.* PS's text has "*kartavyaḥ*" and is not supported by any of the MSS. It is probably a printing error.

42.40c. *āhvarakāstu.* This is a slight emendation of D's reading *-āhvārākāstu.* There is a wide variance in interpretation put forward by the scholars. SK, PS and SM accept *āhvanakāstu.* SK (p.49) translates it as "heralds", PS. (p. 132) as "the town criers" and SM (p.188) as "announcers". The Sanskrit term for "messenger" is *āhvāyaka.* The description given in the text does not agree with any of the translation given above. Besides, the messengers or *bandinaḥ* in verse 39b have already been discussed.

See the ***Aṣṭādhyāyī*** for eg. in which it refers to "low castes" or "untouchables".

अन्नमपहर्तार आह्वरका भवन्ति श्राद्धेसिद्धे पा० ३.२.१३५

Note that the description given in the text fits in with this reading. The readings found in other MSS clearly seem to be a corruption of *āhvaraka* which means "a low or expelled man (who after having offered a sacrifice to the manes takes the sacrificial food for himself) (Apte).

42.41a. *kimciddānava ....pāṇayaḥ*. SK in the translation treats verse 41a as a description of *āhvānaka.*

> *heralds* should be drawn tawny and squint eyed, slightly resembling the danavas and as a rule carrying staffs in their hands. (p. 49)

SM: translates *"kekarekṣaṇāḥ"* as "sidelong looks"

> *Announcers* are to be shown reddish and *with sidelong looks.* (p. 188)

42.41cd. *dvandvasthāne.* Note that only D seems to preserve a reading which with a slight emendation of *dvandvāsthane* to *-sthāne* and an elimination of the superfluous syallable *tu* gives out a good sense. Both the MSS C and F show corrupt reading in which *yuddha* seems to be gloss on *"dvandva"*, the former being a lectio facilior. The meaning seems to be that in a battle field, never should a squint eyed or a tawny coloured person be depicted. Note the double negative is for emphasis and not in the sense of "neither / nor". See (supra) 40cd and the association of these features with the *āhvarakas* or the low-caste people.

Note the various translations:

SK : In a fight (one) should not represent the squint-eyed and the tawny *(heralds)*. (p.49)

PS : In the battle, one should not represent the fighting pairs as tawny or squint-eyed. (p. 132)

SM : Pairs in combat engaged like wrestlers are to be shown somewhat like the Dānavas tall and stately , club in hand neither swarthy nor with oblique eyes. (p. 188)

These are clearly incorrect translations. Verse 41a describes the staff bearers in terms of different nominative plurals *kimciddānavasaṃkāśāḥ prānśavā).* 41b, on the other hand, is about the squint-eyed etc. in accusative plurals.

42.42b. *daśāntareṇa.* This reading comes from MSS CF. All the scholars follow the corrupt reading, *na ca śāntena* from AV. What it means is that the door-keeper should be drawn clad in a dress which has no loose ends or hem. *daśā* refers to a fringe of a garment, loose ends of any piece of cloth and *antareṇa* here means "without". SK (p. 49) takes it as an attribute of the dress and translates it as, "... does not look very mild....."; PS (p. 132) translates, "Their dress should be neither very showy nor very mild"; SM (p. 188)," ..... nor too subdued in his apparel".

42.43b. *vaṇijastathā.* Note that this reading comes from D, A and V.

42.43c. *gāyaka.* I accept SM's emendation of *gāyanatogāyaka.* SK and PS follow *gāyana* which is obviously a corruption.

42.43d. *vādyavādavidaśca ye.* Only MSS preserves this reading. It yields a good sense meaning "those proficient in playing the musical instruments. All the other MSS show corrupt readings, for eg. AFV's *vādyavādaviśuddhaye* followed by all.

> SK : ... those who can correctly regulate the sound of musical instruments... (p. 49)

PS emendas to *vādyavādanaśuddhaye* (see her Critical Notes p. 398, vol. I):

> The singers and dancers should be shown in showy dress and engaged in tuning the musical instrments (p. 132)

42.45c. *praśritāḥ pravaṇāḥ* . Following D, I have separated the compound. The former is derived from D's *praśritaḥ* meaning "courteous". *prasṛta-* found in the other MSS is listed in the Monier Williams' dictionary as a wrong reading for *praśrita.*

42.47a. *nīcakeśāca.* PS mistranslates it as "with hair hanging downwards". (p.132)

42.47b. *paśvādyaḥ.* This reading is a slight emendation of D's reading *pāśvādyaḥ.* It yields a better meaning than *yāścānyāḥ* followed by all. It goes with *vṛṣāh kesariṇaścaiva* and can be translated as "The bulls and the lions, animals like cattle etc.-"

42.48a. *yathābhūmi niveśyāste.* Note that *yathābhūmi* is indeclinable and to be found in BV. It means "into the respective country of each". To derive sense, these two words are not to be taken separately and but as a compound as taken by all the scholars.

42.48d. *saṃdṛṣṭānām.* Note that this emendation which reverses the meaning is crucial to get the sense demanded by the context. The verse preceding evidently deal with the description of the visible things. It also derives support from the similarity between -m- and -s- in the *Śāradā* script. *saṃdṛṣṭānām* means "of the (things) completely visible". Note the following translations which yield a contradictory sense.

SK: I have given hitherto the full description of the appearance of *objects not (usually) seen.* (p. 50)

PS : *The forms of invisible entities* have been described on the analogy of things found in the world. (p. 132)

SM realising the contradiction of meaning settles for the following translation supplying "not to be seen so easily":

> *Though what may not be seen so easily* has been explained at some length, what can be easily observed and studied should be so sketched and painted as to lay stress on their proper semblance to the original. (p. 189)

Compare verse 48b with 57a:

अतः परं प्रवक्ष्यामि रुपं सर्वस्य दृश्यते ।

Note that verses that are roughly between them i.e. 52-57 in contrast are concerned with the objects not commonly seen in the natural world such as the various allegorical representation of rivers, seas, mountains etc. The description after verse 57 reverts to the natural objects perceptible to human eye.

42.49a. *dṛṣṭānām.* This comes from D and is preferred to ACF's *dṛṣṭam sasadṛśam* and V's *dṛṣṭam susadṛśam*; the latter is adopted by all. Note how well it goes with *saṃdṛṣṭānām* of 48d.

42.51a. *niyogasthānam.* This comes from D. The compound makes a better sense than taken as separate words. It means "rank of authority" or "job status".

42.54a. *rājanstathāśikhariṇaḥ kāryaḥ śikharapāṇayaḥ*. Note that only MS D preserves the correct reading except for the corruption of *śikhariṇaḥ* to *śikhariśaḥ*. MSS C and F show a lacunae standing for 6 missing syllables. MS A has this gap filled in a *parvatāśca tathā* which is clearly an interpolation. Both PS and SM follow A's unreliable reading. It refers to the personification of mountain in which a human figure is depicted with peaks in the hands.

43.55c. *Ca*. It is preferred to *tu* of MSS CNDV.

42.57a. *kālasyāvayavāḥ* . All the scholars follow *kāryasyāvayāḥ* from MSS ABCFV which yields no sense. MSS D and N (to some extent) preserve the correct reading. *kāla* refers to Time personified. *avayavaḥ* stands for the limbs of time. The ViDhUp. mentions *kālam* and *kālasyāvayavaḥ* as follows:

> अहमावाहयिष्यामि मुहूर्तान् सूक्ष्मरूपिणः ।
> मुहूर्ताः शीघ्रमायान्तु कालस्यावयवाः शुभाः ।। 49, adh. 103.
>
> I will invoke the moments possessing subtle form. May the moments which are auspicious limbs of Time come soon.

SK forces sense out of the corrupt reading:

> and of all things representations (should be drawn) resembling (what is seen in nature). *Every part of the object to be represented should agree with the general treatment of the whole object.* (p. 50)

PS expresses her doubts the soundness of reading in the footnote 1 but in the commentary takes it as follows:

> F.N. 1) Verse 56 is obscure. I have connected the first line with the second line of verse 55 and taken the following order of words-śesānām (nidhinām) kāryasya nidheḥ avayavaḥ anurūpataḥ sadṛśāḥ sadehāḥ pṛthak kāryā.

PS translates it as follows:

> and *of the remaining nidhis each one i.e. to be executed should be distinct and with proper body.* (p. 133)

SM (p. 190) seems to follow PS in replacing *nidhīnām* with *śeṣāṇām* in the translation:

The pot is a symbol in general for all treasures and should be shown in the hands of personified Saṅkhanidhi, the lotus similarly for Padmanidhi, and similarly for other *nidhis* like Makara, Kacchapa, etc. *All the nidhis are to be personified, all of them almost alike, but each differing in his attribute.*

42.57b. *svadehasadṛśāḥ.* This reading is adopted from MS D. It should be taken as compound or there results a semantic break between *svadeha* and *sadṛśaḥ.* Note all the scholars accept *sadehāssadṛśāḥ.* Note that if *sadeha* is accepted, then *sadṛśāḥ* makes little sense. On the other hand, *svadehasadṛśāḥ* would mean that the form of the limbs of *kāla* should be modelled after the personified Time itself.

42.57c. *vidyānām.* This reading is adopted from MSS D and N and it makes much more sense than *divyānām* which has been interpreted variously. It is possible that by *vidyānām,* what was in fact implied was *vedānām.* This supposition is based on the verse order in *adhyāya* 103 of the ViDhUp. which echoes the one given in adhy. 42.

कालमावाहयिष्यामि देवं सावयवं शुभम् ।
आगच्छ भगवन् काल देवदेव जनार्दन ।।५४।।
वेदानावाहयिष्यामि यज्ञमूर्तिधरानहम् ।
देवा वेदास्समायान्तु वरदा बहुरूपिण: ।।५५।।

All the scholars adopt *divyānām.* SK (p. 50) translates, "Of divine beings"; PS (p. 133), "of celestial things"; and SM (p. 190) tr., "In case of celestial of a high order".

42.58.a. *sarvasya.* The reading *yadyasya* of CDFNV is corruopt for it yields a poor sense. It is emended to *sarvasya* according to the sense demanded by the context. It is possible to explain the corruption in the *Śāradā* script thus:

सर्वस्य → < स > र्वस्य → र्वस्य → र्वस्यस्य → यद्यस्य

Note that in this script, -rva- and -y- look similar. In contrast to objects not seen by ordinary mortals as described in verses 52-59, the author now resumes the description of things perceptible to everyone *(sarvasya).*

It is difficult to see how SK (p. 51) and SK (p. 190) derive the following sense from *yadyasya:*

Now I am going to speak about the *appearance of things actually seen.*

SM : And now I shall narrate the form that suits appropriately *any particular object intended.*

42.58d. *svavarṇa.* All MSS preserve the correct reading - *svavarṇa* except V which shows *vivarṇa.* All the scholars follow V's corrupt reading against a perfectly reasonable reading. SK bases much of her speculations on the symbolic nature of Indian art on this corrupt reading.

> The colour thus has partly descriptive and partly suggestive significance. The dṛṣṭam and adṛṣṭam hold their sway; symbol and illustration are amalgamated into an expressive language, keenly alive to all those visual impressions that are on a small scale, obstrusively finite and seem to carry their meaning within their outlines, as local colour. But this ambiguity of the colour in its suggestive and descriptive faculty was clearly kept apart. While in a naturalistic and descriptive sense the sky, the atmosphere has to be painted as almost without any "special colour (part III ch.42) ... " (p. 16-17)

SK : A learned (artist) should show the sky *without any special colour* and full of birds (oh) king... (p. 51)

Note how closely PS (p. 133) and SM (p. 190) follow SK in their translations:

PS : The sky should be shown *colourless but* full of birds.

SM : The well-versed artist should represent the sky as *having no colour in particular but* full of birds.

The adoption of *svavarṇa* in place of *vivarṇa* not only disqualifies their translations but nullifies the grounds on which SK proposed her theory about the symbolic nature of Indian art in the first place.

42.59a. *darśayedrātrim.* Note *rājan* in place of *rātrim* is an obvious corruption resulting from banalisation. It is easy to arrive at the conjecture from the context. What is under question is not any sky but specifically the night sky studded with stars *(tārakāmaṇḍitam divam).*

42.59cd. *jaṅgalānūpāmiśrāṃśca svaistathā.* Note that the correct reading comes from MS D. The -śc- in *miśrāṃśca* which in the *Śāradā* script looks like -sv- appears to have led to a dittographical error in ACV (F) 's *miśram svaiḥ svair.* This also explains why this line is hypermetrical with 2 superfluous syllables. What it means is that the ground should be depicted as combination of arid, watery and mixed regions.

42.61d. *-ākulair matsyakacchapaiḥ. -ākulair* is derived from D's reading *āku + air.* Note X stands for a faded letter in D's reading which I have filled in by *la.* It qualifies *matsyakacchapaiḥ* and yields this meaning- "flurrying fishes and crocodiles". All the scholars follow *"anantai"* from V which is corruption. SK (p. 51), PS (p. 133) and SM (p. 190) take it to mean "innumerable fishes and tortoises".

42.62a. *padmādyair.* Note this reading is taken from D. MSS C and N show *padmākhair* followed by all. In *Śārada* script, -dy- and -khy- look very similar. D's reading meaning "with lotuses etc." fits in well with the context.

PS (p. 133) translates *padmākṣair* as *"with lotus-eyed* aquatic animals"; SM (p. 190) takes it as *"swans and ducks"* following more PS's translation than the text itself.

42.62b. *grahaiḥ.* This reading is adopted from MSS N and D *guṇaiḥ* accepted by translation is clearly a corruption. It perhaps echoes *guṇair* of 59b. *grahaiḥ* means "a crocodile" (Apte). *grāhair* may have been implied meaning "any large fish or marine animal (crocodile, shark, serpent, Gangetic alligator, water elephant or hippopotamus" (Monier Williams). For metrical consideration, *grahaiḥ* might have been favoured.

SK (p. 51), PS (p. 133) and SM (p. 190) take it to mean "other or similar aquatic life".

42.64c. *svabhūmi* This is from MSS CDFNV. Note that in the *Śāradā* script, it is easy to confuse -sv- with -su-. Apart from meaning "one's own place", it could also mean "proper place" as it does in BṛSam.

जवजातिबलस्थानहर्षसत्त्वस्वरान्विताः ।
स्वभूमावनुलोमाश्च तदूनाः स्युर्विवर्जिताः ।। १९.८६

SK follows V's correct reading but translates literally (p.51) as "in their enclosures"; PS adopts A's *subhūmi* and translates it "on good ground".

SM emends to *sabhūminiveśanam* (translates well-planned) without any explanation.

F.N. 1) सभूमिनिवेशेन is better than सुभूमिविनिवेशेन (p. 160)

42.71b. *vāsarastathā.* This reading comes from MS D. *vāsara* means a "day". This goes with the context and fits in with the temporal sequence falling in between *pratyuṣa* or Dawn and *sandhyā* or Dusk. The corruption has led to interesting speculation amongst the scholars.

SK separates V's reading - *vānarastathā* into *vā narastathā* in the translation. Hence the translation - "or a man".

Note SK takes this line as a continuation of the description of the dawn:

> ... or *a man* should be drawn as if ready for work. (p. 52)

PS :People should be shown ready for work *so also a monkey.* (p. 134)

SM disapproves of this translation by PS as follows:

> F.N.1) The reading वानर has misled and has resulted in a mention of a monkey to suggest morning. The reading removes the error.(pp. 161)

SM considered *"vā narastathā"* as the correct reading: (p. 161)

> Another way of representing daybreak is by showing men sallying forth and engaged in their pursuits ..... (p. 191)

Given that *jana* is already mentioned in the compound *karmavyagra-janaḥ,* separating *vānarastathā* into *vā narastathā* leads to a reduntant meaning.

42.72b. *hastasamsarpakair*. Note V's reading *vāse* in place of *hasta* leads SK to translate thus:

> The (setting in) of darkness has to be shown by men *approaching their abodes.* (p. 52)

42.72cd. *vikāsena jyotsṇām candreṇa darśayet.* MSS D and N preserve the best reading except for a minor emendation required of *jyotsnā as dyotslām* in N. Note that the verb *darśayet* has *jyotsnām* as its object i.e. this verse refers to the representation of moonlight.

SK: *That the moon in shining* should be shown by the Kumuda flower in full bloom, (p. 52)

Note SK takes *kumuda* flower in singular perhaps to stress the suggestive nature of Indian art.

42.73a. *darśayet saraskām ca vātyām parṇotkarāvṛtām.* In these two *pādas,* where all the manuscripts show corrupt readings, MSS N and D preserve the correct one to a large extent. The emendation of *vāpyām* to *vātyām* puts the rest of the words into perspective because the latter is the key to a feasible interpretation. The subject of representation is the gale which is to be represented full of dust and scattered leaves. However, *karṃotkarāvṛtām* in N is clearly a corruption of *parṇotkarāvṛtām.*

SK follows V's reading:

दर्शयेत्सरजस्यं च शय्यां कर्णोत्करावृताम्

SK connects this verse with 72b and takes it as a continuation of the representation of moonlight.

> That the moon is shining should be shown by the Kumuda flower in full bloom while the *many petals of the lotus flower should be closed.* (p. 52)

PS acknowledges the corrupt state of this verse and puts down her conjecture *vāpim* which seriously misleads her reading of this verse.

> दर्शयेत्सरजस्कां च वाप्यां (पीं) पर्णोत्करावृताम्
>
> *A step-well* should be shown with *full of flower-dust and covered with heaps* of leaves. (p. 134)

SM's text reads:

दर्शयेत्सरजस्यां च शय्यां पर्णोत्करावृताम्

Note SM basically adopts V's reading except for the emendation in form of *parṇotkarāvṛtām.* Like SK, SM connects this verse with previous one i.e. 72b. His translation reads:

SM : Also it [refering to the moonlight in 72b] is indicated by a *cool leaf-spread bed (śayyām) with lotus pollen strewn to indicate the mitigating of the heat experienced from the moonlight by the love-lorn damsel (virahiṇī) in separation.* (p. 191)

SM's intepretation turns out to be most fanciful.

Note in this context, "*utkara*" means "scattered" and not "heap".

42.73c. *sachatramānavaprāyām*. Even-though N's reading *sachantamānavaprāyo* calls for emendation, it sufficiently preserves the clue as to the correct reading. It is clear that the reading should be *sachatra-* meaning "along with umbrella". In *Newārī* script, -nt- and -tr- look alike. Also note that MS D show *sahatramānava-*. The confusion between -ch- and -ha- is noticed to be common in both *Bengālī* (D) and *Newārī* (N) scripts.

SK follows V :

> सद्वृत्तमानवप्रायां वृष्टि वृष्ट्याम्प्रदर्शयेत्
>
> When depicting a shower of rain, (that it is) raining should be shown *by a man well covered.* (p. 52)

PS. (p. 134) expresses her misgivings about this verse offers tentative emendations:

> सद्वृ (? संवृ)त्त(?त) मानवप्रायां
>
> Rain should be shown pouring and *a man well covered.*

SM emends to *sampṛktamānava-* and translates:

> संपृक्तमानवप्रायां वृष्टिं बृष्ट्या प्रदर्शयेत्
>
> Rain is indicated by a downpour *to avoid which men and women would cover themselves.* (p. 191)

The reading derived from MSS DN makes good sense and puts an end to these confusions.

42.75a. *klamataptānām*. Note *klama-* is an adoption of the reading from MSS ACDF. *klama* means "fatigue, exhaustion, langour, weariness" and fits in well with the description of summer. Note that this line which is obviously about summer is part of the description of this season in the following verse.

42.76d. *guhāgataiḥ.* MSS ADV preserve the correct reading and confirm PS's conjecture.

42.77c. *vidyudvidyotasamyuktām.* This reading from N is preferred to *vidyudvidyotanair.*

42.80d. *himachannadigantaram.* I have dropped *ca* in this compound following N.

43.81b. *madatastathā.* Note that *mada-* in the given context clearly means "sexual intoxication" or "ruttishness" but both SK and SM seem to emend to *mudatastathā* in their translations. They take it in the sense of "delighted" and "joy or happiness" respectively.

> SK: (Oh) lord of men seasons should be represented by trees in flowers and fruits and creatures *delighted (or otherwise)* and by looking at nature. (p. 52)

SM (p. 192) closely follows SK.

42.81d. *lokam.* Note this reading from N makes more sense than its accusative plural *lokān.* All the scholars appear to accept *lokam* in their translations but leave the text unchanged.

42.83d. *sārdrameva.* Note that this is the correct reading adopted from MSS CDF. All scholars accept AV's *cārdrameva.*

42.84a. *yathādeham.* This comes from D and it makes good sense meaning 'the body type'.

SK follows V's *yathādeyam* and translates

> ... everything is drawn in *an acceptable (form)* ... (p. 53)

PS puts forward the conjecture *yathādeham* but does not translate it.

SM takes it in the sense mentioned above:

The picture painted *in conformity with the region,* ... (p. 193)
Note that *deha* here refers to the body types such as the *Haṃsa, Mālavya* etc.

ADHYĀYA 43

त्रिचत्वारिंशोऽध्यायः

मार्कण्डेय उवाच

शृङ्गारहास्यकरुणवीररौद्रभयानकाः ।
वीभत्साद्भुतशान्ताश्च नव चित्ररसाः स्मृताः ।। १ ।।

+तत्र यत्कान्तिलावण्यं+ लेखामाधुर्यसुन्दरम् ।
विदग्धवेशाभरणं शृङ्गारे तु रसे भवेत् ।। २ ।।

यत्कुब्जवामनप्रायमीषद्विकटदर्शनम् ।
वृथा हि हस्तसंकोचं तत्स्याद्धास्यकरं रसे ।। ३ ।।

याञ्चाविरहसंत्यागविक्रियाव्यसनादिषु ।
+अनुकम्पितकं+ यत्स्याल्लिखेत्तत्करुणे रसे ।। ४ ।।

पारुष्यविकृतिक्रोधद्विषत्त्वार्थान्नदूषणम् ।
दीप्तशस्त्रावरणवत्कृतं रौद्ररसे भवेत् ।। ५ ।।

1a. AV -हास- 1b N -भयानका 1c CF -शान्ताश्चैव 1d NF चित्ररसा A स्मृता
2a. N यत्रयत्कार- - 2ab ACDFNV लावण्य-
2b. CF -लेखामाधुर्य- 2c F विदग्धे N -लेखाभरणं
3a. A -कुब्जा- 3b N -म्रायइषवि- F -म्रायमी- N विकटदर्शनः D -विकटदलनं
3c. BD वृषा V च ABCDN विहस्तं CFV हस्तं CF ABCDFNV संकोच्य
3d. AB -द्धास्यकरे CDNF -रसं
4a. D या < . > विरह- V -विरहा- N -विहग- 4b ABCDFNV -विक्रय- B -व्यमनादिषु
4c. CD अनुकल्पितकं N अनुकल्पितकं 4d N करुणो
5a. N पारुष्यं- CFN -विकृत- N विकृता- D क्रोधे-
5b. A -विषस्वर्था- FV -विषस्त्यर्था C विषस्त्यता N -विप्रस्तार्था- D विष्त्यक्षा- V न दूषणम् N -नुदूषणम् D -दिदूषणम्
5c. ACFV दीप्र- D दीष- CFV -शस्त्रा AD -शस्ता- N -मम्तास- 5d CDF रौद्रे N -रसो

ADHYĀYA 43

Mārkaṇḍeya spoke :

1. There are said to be nine kinds of sentiments of painting *(citrarasāḥ)* - Erotic *(Śṛṇgāra)*, Comic *(Hāsya)*, Tragic *(Karuṇa)*, Heroic (*Vīra*), Wrathful *(Raudra)*, Terrible *(Bhayānaka)*, Disgusting *(Bībhatsa)*, Marvellous *(Adbhuta)* and Tranquil *(Śānta)*.

2. In the Erotic sentiment, the figures should be depicted clad in sophisticated dress and ornaments *(vidagdhaveṣābhūṣaṇam)* and in which their amorous beauty *(kāntilāvaṇyam)* is expressed by the exquisite beauty of the lines.

3. In the [representation of the] Comic sentiment, the portrayal of the hunch-backed, dwarfs, that which looks somewhat distorted and [gestures such as] the unnecessary clenching of the fists is said to bring about laughter.

4. In case of the Tragic sentiment, one should paint situations that evoke sympathy such as begging, separation from the beloved, renunciation, ailment, calamity etc.

5. To express the Wrathful sentiment in a painting, one should depict harshness, agitation, anger, hostility, and the destruction of property and foodgrains. It should be furnished with glinting weapons and armours *(dīptaśastrāvaraṇavat-)*.

प्रतिज्ञागर्वशौर्यादिष्वथेर्ष्वौदार्यदर्शनम् ।
सस्मयं सभ्रुकुटिवद्वीरं वीररसोद्धतम् ।। ६ ।।

दुष्टदुर्दशनोच्छुष्कहिंस्त्रव्यापादकादि यत् ।
तत्स्याद्भयानकरसे प्रयोगे चित्रकर्मणः ।। ७ ।।

श्मशानगर्हिताघातकरणं स्थानदारुणम् ।
यच्चित्रं चित्तविक्षेप्तृ तद्बीभत्सरसोद्भवम् ।। ८ ।।

यदाविर्भूतरोमाञ्चं विस्तृताक्ष्युन्मुखाननम् ।
प्रदर्शयति स्वेदेन तदद्भुतरसाश्रयम् ।। ९ ।।

यद्यत्सौम्याकृतिध्यानधारणासनबन्धनम् ।
तपस्विजनभूयिष्ठं तत्तु शान्तरसे भवेत् ।। १० ।।

6a. C -गर्ब- DN -गर्थ- ABVC -गर्भ- F -गभ- 6b A -र्थेष्टौदार्य- N -थेष्वेनार्य्य-
6c. N सम्मयं CDF -यद्वीरं 6d CDFV -रसे N -रसद्धतं A -रसे ACDFV ऽद्धुतम्
7a. V1 दुष्टकेदर्श- DN -नाच्छुष्क- ABF -नोच्छुष्म- V1 नोच्छष्म- C नोच्छुष्द- V2 -नालुत्य- V -नोन्मत्त-
7b. D -हिंश्र N -हिम्र- D -व्यायोदिकादि 7c N तस्माद्भयानक 7d F चित्रकर्मण
8a D श्मशाविलर्हिता- V -गर्हितं घात- 8b CFN -करण- D करणा- B -दर्शनम् A -दर्शितम्
8c. AB सूत्रितं B चित्रविच्छेष्ट- A चित्रविछ्रेष्ट- D चित्रि < ? ? छे < ? > CFNV चित्रवच्छ्रेष्टं
8d. V -त्सरसे भवेत्
9a. C -विनीभु- FDNV -विनीत- A -विनीते- AFDNV -रोमाञ्च- N रोमाच- A -रामाञ्च-
9b. N -विस्तान्तं- D -चिन्तास्र्ता- A -चिन्तार्ता- CF -चिन्तान्ता- V -चिन्तार्ता- S1S2 -चिन्तार्ता- V -क्ष्र्यमुखानतम् CFDN -क्षुन्मुखानतम् S1S2 -क्षुणमुखानतम् A -क्षुत्मुखनतम्
9c. N चान्येन ABCDFV चान्योऽन्यं
10a. N यद्यन- - D यदा- A -सौम्याहति- N -मौन्याकृति- D -स्यैसाकृति
10b. N -धाराना- A सत्रबन्धनम् 10d CFN तन्तु N सान्तरसं ACFV शान्ते रसे

6. In [a painting expressing] Heroic sentiment, there should be [a display of] nobleness in form of oath [taking], pride, in the matters of heroism etc; the hero should [be depicted] with a frown and an arrogant expression.

7. In a painting which expresses the Terrible sentiment, the subject of portrayal should be vile, frightful [lit. difficult] to look at, fading away in decay [lit. shrivelled up ?] and that which [looks] contemptible and murderous.

8. That painting which disturbs the mind *(cittavikṣeptṛ)* due to its terrifying [subject matter such as the] funeral grounds *(śmaśāna)* and [the] acts of reprehensible violence gives rise to the sentiment of Disgust.

9. The [lit. abode of] Marvellous sentiment is conveyed by depicting someone showing horripilation *(āvirbhūtaromāñcaṃ)*, having a wide eyed look *(vistṛtākṣī)* an expectant face *(unmukhānanam)*, and [beads of perspiration *(svedena)*.

10. The representation of the Tranquil sentiment consists mainly of ascetics in meditative postures with a band [clasping their legs] and of any [other] subject that expresses calmness.

शृङ्गारहास्यशान्ताख्या लेखनीया गृहेषु ते ।
परिशेषा न कर्तव्या कदाचिदपि कस्यचित् ॥ ११ ॥

देववेश्मनि कर्तव्या रसाः सर्वे नृपालये ।
राजवेश्मनि नो कार्या राज्ञां वासगृहेषु ते ॥ १२ ॥

सभावेश्मसु कर्तव्या राज्ञां सर्वरसा गृहे ।
वर्जयित्वा सभां राज्ञो देववेश्म तथैव च ॥ १३ ॥

युद्धश्मशानकरुणमृतदुःखार्तकुत्सितान् ।
अमङ्गल्याश्चं न लिखेत्कदाचिदपि वेश्मसु ॥ १४ ॥

निःशृङ्गाश्च वृषान्राजन्निर्हस्तांश्च मतङ्गजान् ।
निधिविद्याधरा राजन्नृषयो गरुडस्तथा ॥ १५ ॥

11b. ABCF लेखनीय
11c. ABFV परशेषा N परसेवा C परमेषा D परषये D कर्तव्या:
12a. AN कर्त्तव्याः
12c. N ना
13a. AB सभयेषु न 13b A राज्ञं
13d. N -वेश्मन्तथैव
14a. V करुणामृत F वरुणमृत 14b CF दुःर्खान्त- N दुःषार्त- C -कुत्सितात् N -कुत्सितं
14c N अमंगल्यं
15ab. ABCDFNV निधिशृंगान्- वृषान्रजन्निधिहस्तान् CF वृषराज- ABDFNV -न्निधिहस्तान्- C -विधिहस्तान्- CF मतेङ्गजान् B -न्रताङ्गजान्
15c. BV निधिविर्द्याधरा A निधिन्विद्या- CFDN निधीन्विद्याधरान् V राजनृषयो
15cd. ABCFD -नृषीन्- N ऋषीन् ABCDN गरुडमेव च F -वरुडमेव च

11. Only the paintings that represent the Erotic, Comic and Tranquil sentiments are allowed in houses. None of the remaining sentiments should ever be painted in anyone's house.

12. [On the other hand] in temples and palaces, all of the sentiments may be portrayed. [However], not all of them should be depicted in the palaces.

13a. In the royal assembly hall, all the sentiments may be represented in the paintings.

13b.-15b. [Scenes such as] the representation of battles, funeral grounds, the tragic, death, pain, people tormented with grief and the villainous, bulls without horns *(niḥśṛngān vṛṣān)* and elephants without trunks *(nirhastān mataṅgajān)* are regarded as inauspicious and they are not allowed to be painted in houses. They are only permitted in the royal assembly halls and the temples.

हनुमन्तश्च मङ्गल्या ये च लोके प्रकीर्तिर्ता: ।
लिखितव्या महाराज गृहेषु सततं नृणाम् ।। १६ ।।

चित्रकर्म न कर्तव्यमात्मन: स्वगृहे नृप ।
दौबल्यं स्थूलरेखत्वमविभक्तत्वमेव ।। १७ ।।

बृहद्दण्डौष्ठनेत्रत्वं वक्ररेखत्वमेव च ।
वर्णानां संकरश्चात्र चित्रदोषा: प्रकीर्तिता: ।। १८ ।।

स्थानं प्रमाणं भूलम्बो मधुरत्वं विभक्तता ।
सादृश्यं क्षयवृद्धी च गुणाष्टकमिदं स्मृतम् ।। १९ ।।

स्थानहीनं गतरसं शून्यदृष्टि मलीमसम् ।
चेतनारहितं यत्स्यात्तदशस्तं प्रकीतिर्तम् ।। २० ।।

16a. ABCF हनुमन्तं V हनुमांश्च सुमङ्गल्या N मंगलेषु 16b N च सर्वेषु हनुमन्तं DN प्रकीर्तितम्

16cd ABCDFV लिखितव्या N महाराज शूलमुद्गलपाणय

17a. N कर्तव्या- 17b N -मात्मन प्रकितं गृह ABV -मात्मना

18a. NV lack 18 ab. AC बृहद्दण्डोष्ठ- D -स्वनेत्रत्वं 18b D स्थूलरेखत्वं

18c. N शङ्करश्च 18d V -चित्रदीपा: N प्रकीर्तिता

19a. V स्थानप्रमाणं N तुलम्भो AB भूलम्ब: 19b AB सपुरत्वं

20b C -च्छुन्यदृष्टि- N सभ्यदृष्टि-

20cd. V वा स्यात्तद- N यस्यान्मदसप्तं

15c-16. O King, [only] those which are regarded as auspicious in [this] world such as the [nine] treasures *(nidhi)*, *vidyādharas*, sages, the *garuḍa*, and monkeys are to be painted in the houses.

17ab. O King, portrait of one self [i.e. self portrait] *(ātmanaḥ citrakarma)* must never be made in one's own house.

17b-18. The following are said to be the [eight] demerits of a painting:

Lines that are either [too] weak or [too] thick, lack of details *(avibhaktatvam)* oversized cheeks, lips and eyes, crooked lines and the (undue) merging of colours *(varṇānām saṃkaraḥ)*.

19. The [following] are said to be the eight merits of a painting: postures, proportions, [the use of the] plumbline, charm, details, verisimilitude and the loss and gain [i.e. foreshortening].

20. A painting that lacks postures, sentiments, has [figures with] vacant stare [or without eyes], is dirty and bereft of life [likeness] is considered to be unpraiseworthy.

लपतीव तु भूलम्बो श्लिष्यतीव तथा नृप ।
हसतीव च सादृश्यं सजीव इव दृश्यते ।। २१ ।।

सश्वासमिव यच्चित्रं तच्चित्रं शुभलक्षणम् ।
हीनाङ्गं मलिनं शून्यं बद्धं व्याधिभयाकुलम् ।। २२ ।।

वृतं प्रकीर्णकेशैश्च सोऽमङ्गल्यं विवर्जयेत् ।
प्रतीतं च लिखेद्धीमान्नाप्रतीतं कथञ्चन ।। २३ ।।

शास्त्रज्ञैः सुकृतं दक्षैश्चित्रं हि मनुजाधिप ।
श्रियमावहति क्षिप्रमलक्ष्मीं चापकर्षति ।। २४ ।।

निर्णजयति चोत्कण्ठां निरुणद्ध्यागताशुभम् ।
शुद्धिं प्रथयति प्रीतिं जनयत्यतुलामपि ।। २५ ।।

21a. N लपभीव ADV लसतीव CF लमतीव V च CDFN भूलम्भो 21b NV बिभ्यतीव N नृपं
21c. B हसंतीव A हसतीच N साधुर्य्यं ABCDFV माधुर्यं 21d D सज्जीव
22a. ABCFVD सश्वास इव N यः चित्रं
22c. C च्छुन्यं N -नं सुप्त्वं 22d ABCDFV बद्ध- ABCDFNV -व्याधिमयाकुलैः
23a. V वृत्तं A वृत्रं ABCDFV -केशैश्च
23b. D समङ्गल्येर CFNV सुमङ्गल्यैर् AB स्वमंगल्यैर् ABCDF विवर्णयेत्
23c. D प्रतीतश्च 23cd N -द्धीमाना- C द्धीमावा- F -प्रतीते CV प्रतीतेः N कथंच < . ? >
24a. N has चित्रेन हरते दुःखं चित्रं लक्ष्मी प्रवर्धयेत् in the place of 24.
24a. ABCDVF सुकृतै ABVF -र्दक्षै- C -र्चक्षै- D र्दान्तै- 24d A क्षिपरं अलक्ष्मीं F -मलक्ष्मी
25a. N lacks 25 ab.
25b. ACDFV निरुणद्ध्याहतं S1S2 निरुणागतं ACDFV शुभम्
25c. ABCDFNV शुद्धां CF प्रथ < . . > N प्रीतां

21-22b. O King, a perfect (lit. auspicious) painting is one that incorporates such a high degree of verisimilitude *(sādṛśya ?)* that it [i.e. the figures painted in it] appears to be smiling, alive and breathing; the [ingenious] use of the plumbline makes it look as if it were talking and reaching out [lit. embracing] [the onlooker].

22c-23b. [If a painting is to be executed in a house] a painter should avoid painting the inauspicious [subject matter] - figures that are disproportionate, dirty, numb, overwhelmed by fear or sickness and those with dishevelled hair.

23cd. A wise painter only depicts that which is recognisable [or trustworthy] *(pratītam)* and never should he paint that which is unconvincing *(apratītam)*.

24. O King of men, a painting is best painted by he who is well-versed with the treatises. [Such a painting] brings about prosperity and wards off misfortune.

25. [Such a painting] dispels one's anxiety and obstructs misfortune which has befallen. It spreads purity *(śuddhim)* and brings about incomparable joy.

दुःस्वप्नदर्शनं हन्ति प्रीणाति गृहदेवताम् ।
न च शून्यमिवाभाति यत्र चित्रं प्रतिष्ठितम् ॥ २६ ॥

गलं हस्तं च पादं च कर्णमप्यनलङ्कृतम् ।
शल्यविद्धं च वृद्धं च यः करोति स चित्रवित् ॥ २७ ॥

सुप्तं च चेतनायुक्तं मृतं चैतन्यवर्जितम् ।
निम्नोन्नतविभागं च यः करोति स तु चित्रवित् ॥ २८ ॥

तरङ्गाग्निशिखाधूमं वैजयन्त्यम्बरादिकम् ।
वायुगत्या लिखेद्यस्तु विज्ञेयः स चित्रवित् ॥ २९ ॥

एतेषां खलु सर्वेषामानुलोम्यं प्रशस्यते ।
सम्मुखत्वं तथा तेषां चित्रे यत्नाद्विवर्जयेत् ॥ ३० ॥

26b. F प्रणाति F गृहदैवताम् N गृहदैवता V गृहदैवतम्
N lacks 26cd.
26c. D तदशुन्य- C - - V तु
27a. D गल- N ऋजुहस्तं 27ab D -हस्तम्तथा- CF < .... > दं कर्णचाप्य- A < < मशुभ > > दं कर्णचाप्य- V < .... > द कर्ण चाप्य- D कस्तुंनाप्यलङ्कृतम्
AB lack 28.
28a. N सुसुप्तं चतयायुक्तं
CF lacks 29.
29b. V -यास्वरादिकम् ABC -यास्वारादिकम्
29d. V विज्ञेयो V मत्तचित्रवित्
30ab. N सर्वेषांमानुलाम्यं 30 c C -त्वमथेतेषां AFV -त्वमथैतेषां

26. It annhilates bad dreams and propitiates the house deity. The place where a painting is installed does not appear to be empty.

27. He who is able to paint throat, hands, feet and ears unadorned, a person wounded by an arrow and an old person.

28. He who is able to paint the distinction between the [apparent] depth and projection *(nimnonnatavibhāgam)* and between a person sleeping full of consciousness and dead person devoid of vitality is said to be an expert.

29. He who is able to paint waves, flames, smoke, flags and garments etc. with the speed of the wind *(vāyugatyā)* is considered to be an expert.

30. In all these cases, conformity with the natural order *(ānulomyam)* is recommended. The placement of figures facing one another [in strict profile] should be carefully avoided.

यथा चित्रे तथैवोक्तं खातपूर्ते नराधिप ।
सुवर्णरुप्यताम्रादि तच्च लोहेषु दर्शयेत् ॥ ३१ ॥

शिलादारुषु लोहेषु प्रतिमाकरणं भवेत् ।
अनेनैव विधानेन यथा चित्रमुदाहृतम् ॥ ३२ ॥

तथानेन विधानेन पुस्तकर्म विधीयते ।
द्विविधं तच्च कथितं घनं सुषिरमेव च ॥ ३३ ॥

घनैर्लोहैः शिलाभिश्च दारुमृद्भिः सदा भवेत् ।
चर्मणा सुषिरः कार्यो दारुलोहैस्तथैव च ॥ ३४ ॥

देयो मृत्तिकया लेपः पुस्ते चर्मकृते दृढम् ।
सूत्रेऽनेन विधानेन चित्रवस्त्रे तथा लिखेत् ॥ ३५ ॥

N lacks 31 ab.

31a. D तथा ABCDFV चित्रं D खातपृतं ABFV खातपूर्वं CF खातपूर्व

31c. A -रौप्य- 31d CF लोकेषु 32a N शैलदारुषु

N lacks 32cd.

32c. A प्रधानेन D अनेनैव 32d A यथावित्र-

33a. ND अनेनैव 33b N पुस्तकर्म्मं विधीयते 33c D तत्वितं 33d N घनंमुखिलमेव च

34a. N घनं D घन- 34c N वर्त्मना सुषिरः D सुषिरं

35ab. DN देयं D मृतुकपालेयं N लेपप्रस्ते चर्म्मकृतं भवेत् V दृढः 35c ABCDFV सूत्रे ABCF वा न

35d. D चित्रं वस्त्रे

N in place of 35b, has:

राज्ञां वासगृहे तेषां पूर्व्यसच्चरितं लिखेत्
श्रीरामदेवचरितं शिवकेशवयोः (पि वा ?)
देवता चलितं पूण्यं तेषां विजयमेव च
सर्वारिष्टं महाघोरं नाशनं शुभवृद्धिदं

31. O King, what has been said about [the rules of] painting should be followed for sculpture *(khātapūrtam lit.* digging and filling). And that [set of rules also] applies to metals such as gold, silver, copper etc.

32. Following this very method by which painting has [so far] been expounded, images in stone, wood and metals are constructed.

33. Likewise, [the rules of] modelling are devised according to the same method. It is said to be of two types - solid *(ghana)* and hollow *(suṣira)* modelling.

34. The solid modelling is always employed for [images made out of] metals, stones, wood and clay. The hollow method is used while working with leather, wood and [some] metals.

35. When leather is used in modelling a coating of clay is laid firmly. In the case of *Citravastra,* it is painted by this very method[mentioned] in [this] text.

एतदुद्देशमात्रेण यदा ते कथितं नृप ।
अशक्यो विस्तराद्वक्तुं बहुवर्षशतैरपि ॥ ३६ ॥

यदत्र नोक्तं तन्नृत्ताद्विज्ञेयं वसुधाधिप ।
नृत्तेऽपि नोक्तं तच्चित्रात्तत्र योज्यं नराधिप ॥ ३७ ॥

कलानां प्रवरं चित्रं धर्मकामार्थमोक्षदम् ।
मङ्गल्यं परमं ह्येतद् गृहे यत्र प्रतिष्ठितम् ॥ ३८ ॥

यथा सुमेरुः प्रवरो नगानां यथाण्डजानां गरुडः प्रधानः ।
यथा नराणां प्रवरः क्षितीशस्तथा कलानामिह चित्रकल्पः ॥ ३९ ॥

इति श्रीविष्णुधर्मोत्तरे तृतीयेखण्डे मार्कण्डेयवज्रसंवादे चित्रसूत्रे शृङ्गारादिभावकथनं नाम त्रिचत्वारिंशत्तमोऽध्यायः ॥ ४३ ॥ समाप्तं चित्रसूत्रम् ।

36b. D यया
36d. D वक्तुमपि वर्षशतैरपि
37c. S1S2 नृत्तेऽपि यन्नोक्तं तच्चित्रं 37cd V तच्चित्रं नात्र
38c, BV प्रथमं 38d ABV चैतद्गृहे
39b. A यथां द्रुजानां
39c. ACDFD जनानां B सतानां
39d. D कलयामिह चित्रकर्म

36. O King, what you have been told [so far] is only a summary, for it is not possible to relate [the rules] in detail even in many hundred years.

37. O King of Earth, all that has been left untold should be understood from [the section on] Dance. O King of men, that which has been left untold in Dance should be improvised from Painting.

38. Painting is the most excellent of all arts and grants *dharma artha,* and *kāma.* The house which has a painting is considered auspicious.

39. Just as *Sumeru* is the most excellent mountain, *Garuḍa* the chief amongst birds, king best of all men, painting is the best of all the arts.

43.2a. *tatrayatkāntilāvaṇyam.* This reading found in ACDF is somewhat dubious. Note that *yat-* is not followed by its correlative pronoun *tat* which is odd. Based on N's *yatrayatkāra-,* I have hazarded a conjecture *-gātrasaṃskāra-*, a commonly used compound. (For example, see ***Daśakumāracarita,*** the commentator explains it as *śarīrasya saṃskāra parikarmādir yayā sā* p. 69). The possible mode of corruption could be as follows:

Gātrasaṃskāra -> Patrasaṃskāra -> Yatrasatkāra - > Yatrayatkāra

The compound *gātrasaṃskāralāvaṇyam* yields good sense- "loveliness due to adornments of the body" which conforms with the erotic sentiment and more specific than *yatkāntilāvaṇyam.* On the other hand, if *kāntilāvaṇyam* is adhered to, then *kānti* should be taken in a sense used in rhetorics (eg. ***Sāhityadarpaṇa***) where it means much more than "beauty" - कान्तिर्मन्मथाप्यायिता द्युति "splendour enhanced b amorous desire" (see Apte).

43.3b. *vṛthā hi hastasaṃkocam.* Note that *saṃkocya* found in all the MSS leaves the sense incomplete. This can be rectified by emending it to *-saṃkocam* and making it a compound with *hasta.* It is possible that the phrase *vṛthā hi hasta saṃkocya* may have been lifted from another text which explains its incomplete meaning. Mammaṭa's ***Kāvyaprakāśa*** throws light on this problem and helps to contextualise the phrase. In ullāsa IV. 37, the author illustrates the *Hāsya Rasa* or Comic sentiment.

आकुञ्च्य पाणिमशुचिं मम मूर्ध्नि वेश्या मन्त्राम्भसा प्रतिपदं पृषतैः पवित्रे ।
तारस्वनं प्रथितभूत्कमदात्प्रहारं हाहा हतोऽहमिति रोदिति विष्णशर्मा ।।

In the CitSūt., although there is no reference to *Viṣṇuśarmā* or the prostitute, it is clear that the condensed phrase in the CitSūt. comes from a common stock of what was considered to be comic situation. Perhaps the humour lies in the incongruity of the situation in which a brahmin after ablutions is hit by the unclean hands of a prostitute. *Hastasaṃkocam* refers to the clenching of the palm of the hand into a fist (as the commenator *Vāmanācārya* explains). Notice the following translations:

SK : ... *with the unnecessary shortness of hands* should be laugh exciting in sentiment. (p. 53)

PS : ... *somewhat deformed in appearance with a hand contracted without purpose* expresses *Hāsya Rasa.* (p. 135)

SM : ... as well as *movements like the hand awkwardly drawn in a comical mode of shyness* excites it. (p. 194)

43.4b. *-vikriyāyasanādiṣu.* Note that *vikraya* found in all the MSS meaning "selling of goods" does not fit in with the definition of Tragic sentiment. It clearly seems to be a corruption of *vikriyā* which stands for "ailment, indisposition, failure, misadventure" and so on. Note other translations:

SK (p. 53), PS (p.135) and SM (p. 194) translate it as "sale".

43.4c. *anukampitakam*. This (>ABF) is regarded as a doubtful reading. Nor is CDN's *anukalpitakam* any more reliable. I offer a very tentative emendation based on the context - *anukampanajam* referring to that "gives rise to compassion / trembling / sympathy".

43.5b. *dviṣattvārthānnadūṣaṇam.* MSS ACFV retain correct reading as far as *-annaduṣanam* is concerned. However, the wrong reading *viṣa-* found in all the MSS has misled all the scholars. *Dviṣatva* is suggested tenatively and draws some support from the ***Kāvyaprakāśa*** of Mammaṭa which mentions *dviṣad-* in its definition of *Raudra Rasa.*

क्रोधस्थायिभावको द्विषदालम्बनकस्त्वपकाराद्युद्दीपितो
विकत्थनाद्यनुभवितो गर्वादिसंचारितो रौद्रः । ४ उल्लासः

The reading *viṣastyarthānnadūṣaṇam* is perhaps a corruption of *dviṣattvārthādidūṣaṇam.* Note that in the *Śāradā* and *Newārī* scripts, *-ty-* and *-tv-* are easy to mistake. *arthadūṣaṇam* is a well known compound meaning "prodigality, destruction of property, etc.". Note its use in the ***Manusaṃhitā***, 7.48:

पैशुन्यं साहसं द्रोहं ईर्ष्यासूयार्थदूषणम् ।
वाग्दण्डजं च पारुष्यं क्रोधजोऽपिगणोऽष्टकः ।।७.४८

Note other translation:

SK : Harshness anger, *slaughter* - these things befit the *"roudra"* ... (p. 53)

PS : The depiction of harshness, passion, anger, *poisoning food for killing* ... (p. 135)

SM (p. 194) emends to *visasyarthoktaduṣaṇam:*

> In *raudra* flavour should be depicted harsh, unnatural, angry, *unworthy language and impost used in abuse and action* ...

43.5c. *dīptaśastrāhananavat-*. Note that the emendation of *ābharaṇam* to *āhananam* derives support from a common confusion in the *Śāradā* script between -bha- and -ha- and also between -ra- and -na-. *āhananam* is taken to mean "acts of killing" with sharp weapons should accompany a painting depicting *Raudra Rasa*. SK and PS follow *ābharaṇam* and translate it as "ornaments".

43.6a. *-garvaśauryā-*. Note this emendation of *garbha* found in the C Group of MSS *-garva* is demanded by the context. MS N has *-gartha-* which also lends support to the emendation. In the *Newārī* script, *-rv-* (in which the -v- becomes double barrelled) resembles *-th-*. Moreover, the *Vīra rasa* or the heroic sentiment is described in the ***Nāṭyaśāstra*** (68.6) in the following way:

स्थितिधैर्यवीर्यगर्वैरुत्साहपराक्रमप्रभावैश्च ।
वाक्यैश्चाक्षेपकृतैर्वीररसः सम्यगभिनेयः ।।

Note that all translations omit *gartha (bha)*.

43.6c. *vīrarasoddhatam*. The reading *-rase'dbhutam* is found in most of the MSS. It seems unlikely that *adbhuta* which is associated with the *Adbhuta rasa* should be employed in *Vīra rasa*. It seems to be a corruption of *rasoddhatam* meaning "full of *Vīra rasa*". Note how this confounds SM :

SM: In *Vīra* or heroic mood there is a certain *wonder* suggested in the portraying a smile ... (p. 194)

43.7a. *-darśanocchuṣka-*. Note that there is a wide variance of reading in the MSS. Only MS D preserves a reading *-nocchuṣka-* which makes some sense. *Ucchuṣka* means "withered, dried up, etc.". Could it perhaps refer to an aged person with dried up, withered and wrinkled skin? This sense does not fit in well with the context and it should be regarded with caution. Note that all scholars follow V's reading- -*nonmatta-* :

SK : Wicked, hardlooking, and *almost mad* vindictiveness... (p. 53)

PS : The depiction of that which is wicked, unpleasing to look at *furious*.. (p. 135)

SM : ... there is to be depicted the wicked, the abhorrent, *the mad*,... (p. 195)

43.8b. *sthānadāruṇam.* This reading is found in MSS C, F, N and V. Yet PS favours MS A's reading *sthānadarśitam.* It refers to that painting *(yaccitram)* which is "terrible because of (depiction of) cremation ground ... "

43.8c. *Cittavikṣeptṛ.* Note that this emendation is strongly demanded by the context. All the MSS readings are corrupt. C anf F show *citravacchreṣṭam* which gives out a poor sense "best decorated with painting". Note that MSS A, B and D preserve the *-i-* vowel in the *-vi-* (In D's reading the script loses clarity but the vowel -i- is legible). The mode of corruption in the *Śāradā* script seems to follow this pattern.

1.	2.	3.
Cittavikṣeptṛ ->	*Cittavicchiptam* - >	*Citravacchreṣṭam*

The corruption of *-kṣ-* to *-cch-* is a common occurrence. There is a similarity between *-ptṛ-* and *-ṣṭam-* in the *Śāradā* script. The corruption of *citta* is understandable given the presence of *yaccitram* just preceding it. This emendation yields a sense which is consistent with the context- "mind-tormentor". Cf *vikṣiptacitta,* a common compound meaning "distraught in mind".

SK: The painting (which depicts) a terrible position (i.e. a scene of execution) and (is) loathsome on account of the (representation of the) crematorium ground, should be *the best of all paintings*.....(p. 53-54)

PS omits its translation.

SM : That which is born of *bībhatsa* mood *in a picture chosen by an artist, adept in his art,* ..... (p. 195)

43.9ab. *yad āvirbhūtaromāñcam vistāryakṣyunmukhānanam.* This half verse, particularly the second *pāda* has been seriously misunderstood by all the scholars. Note that *yadāvinīta-* gives out a poor sense and must be emended to *yad avirbhuta-*. Regarding the second compound, N's reading *-vistāntam-* is a clue to its correct interpretation. It is clearly a corruption of *(vistāri + aksi + unmukhānanam - >) vistāryakṣyun-mukhānanam.* What its means is a "face with a wide eyed and expectant look". Cf. ***Nāṭyaśāstra*** (ed. Ramakrishna Kavi, p. 329, adhy. vi, vol. I. GOS 36, Baroda, 1956) where *nayanavistāra* is used in the definition of the *Adbhuta rasa.*

तस्यनयनविस्तारानिमेषप्रेक्षणरोमाञ्चाश्रुस्वेदहर्षसाधुवाददानप्रबन्धहाहाकारबाहुवदन- चेलाङ्गुलिभ्रमणादिभिरनुभवैरभिनयः प्रयोक्तव्यः ।

Note how the corrupt readings have confused all the scholars. SK followed V's reading deriving a sense which is unrelated to the context.

> Whenever (a painting) depicts (lit. shows) *thought* and a slight horripilation (and) *the submissive face of Tārksaya and other (similar figures),* it is indicative of *adbhuta* sentiment.

Note that PS omits reference to the second compound.

PS : The depiction of people showing one another, something with subdued horripilation expresses[1] *Adbhuta Rasa.* (p. 135)

F.N.1) The meaning of the first line of verse 9 is not at all clear.

Atleast, PS expresses doubt about an obviously corrupt reading.

SM (p. 195) adopts S1S2's *cintārtākṣuṇāmukhānatam* and translates:

> That partakes of *adbhuta* or the mood of wonder where one gazes at another, *revealing on his face, rather pulled down, a certain humility,* horripilation, *thoughtful mood apparent.*

43,9c. *svedena.* Note that is an emendation partly derived from N's reading *cānyena* and mainly from the context. The *adhyāya* 30 of the ViDhUp. Khaṇḍa III which, in its definition of the *Adbhuta rasa,* refers to *svedena.*

आश्चर्येण समुत्पत्तिरद्भुतं तत्प्रकीतिर्तम् ।। २७ ।।
प्रस्फुरिताक्षिरौमाञ्चैरङ्गुलीभ्रमणादिभिः ।
स्वेदेन चाभिनेयस्स्याद्भुतस्तु तथा रसः ।। २८ ।।

The last line above mentions perspiration as being one of the expressions of the *Adbhuta rasa.* Note that N's *anyena* seems to preserve the instrumental case i.e. implying that the word in question is that by means of which this *rasa* is visually expressed (*pradarśayati*). From the reference cited above, *cānyonyam* which conveys a poor sense, appears to be a corruption of *svedena*.

SK (p. 54) seems to follow V's *anyena* and takes it as 'and other (similar figures)". PS (p. 135) translates it as "The depiction of showing one another.... ". SM (p. 195) follows PS and translates its as "where one gazes at another, revealing on his face".

43.10d. *sāntarase.* Note that this reading comes from MS D and it is preferred to all other readings since it makes better sense.

43.11a. *pariśeṣā.* MS D preserves the correct reading. All the scholars follow the corrupt reading *paraśeṣā.*

43.15ab. *niḥśṛngāṅśca urṣānrājannirhastāṇśca mataṅgajān.* Note that none of the MSS preserves the correct reading. The emendation above is made entirely from the context i.e. how verse 15ab relates to the preceding verse 14. The verse 14 is about certain inauspicious themes which an artist should not paint in houses. The verse 15a is a continuation of verse 14 adding to the list of prohibited subjects of depiction such as bulls without horns and elephants without trunks. *Nidhiśṛngān* and *nidhihastān* make no sense. The corruption may have also been brought about by *nidhi* in the next verse and also the context. SK connects 15ab with the preceding verse:

> Except in assembly (halls) of kings and in temples, the inauspicious, (as for instance) *bulls with horns (immersed) in the sea, and (men) with their horns (sticking out of) the sea (whilst their) body (is) bent (under water)* .... (p. 54)

PS : All those which are regarded as auspicious by people such as *bulls with nidhi horns, elephants with nidhi trunks*........ (p. 136)

SM : *Bulls with horns holding treasure and elephants holding treasure pots in their trunks* .... (p. 195)

18.43.15cd. *nidhividyādhara rājann ṛṣayo garuḍastathā.* It is quite clear from the next verse that the auspicious themes of painting are being discussed. *Likhitavya* in verse 16c has determined my emendation of *nidhin* to *nidhi* and the adoptation of variant *vidyādhara* from MSS A, B and V and *-ṛṣayo garuḍastathā* from V.

43.16ab. *hanumantaśca maṅgalyā ye ca loke prakīrtitāḥ*. This emendation derives from ABCF and D reading. Note that all the scholars take *hanumantam* as referring to *"Hanumān"* when it seems to have a general sense of "monkey".

43.17b. *-ātmanaḥ*. Note that *-ātmanaḥ* is preserved in MSS BCDF. Yet PS followed V's corrupt reading *ātmanā*, also accepted by SM. The adoption of this reading here has a dramatic bearing on the meaning. *Ātmanaḥ* is to be connected with *citrakarma* of the preceding *pada* and means the same as *ātmapratikṛti* or *ātmaprakṛti* meaning a "self-portrait". Note that N's *-ātmanā prakṛtim gṛhe* is clearly an attempt at interpolation. Notice the use of both *ātmapratikṛti* and *ātmanaḥ prakṛti* in the ***Bhaviṣya Purāṇa***. Note that the adhy. 85, (v. 1and 3). is called *Ātmapratikṛtidānavidhivarṇanam.*

आत्मप्रतिकृतिर्नाम यथोक्तं कस्यचित्पुरा ।
तत्तेऽहं संप्रवक्ष्यामि दानं मानविवर्धनम् ।। १ ।।
लोहजां प्रकृतिं भव्यां कारयित्वात्मनो नृप ।
अभीष्टवाहनगतामिष्टालंकारसंयुताम् ।। ३ ।।
इममुच्चारयेन्मत्रं विप्रस्य पुरतो बुधः ।
आत्मनः प्रतिमा चेयं सर्वोपकरणैर्युता ।। ९ ।।

In the ***Mahābhārata*** (5,2222), this term is used as follows:

ध्वजे हि तस्मिन् रूपाणि चक्रस्ते देवमायया ।
महाधनानि दिव्यानि महान्तिच लघूनि च ।
भीमसेनानुरोधाय हनुमान् मारुतात्मजः ।
आत्मप्रतिकृतिं तस्मिन् ध्वज आरोपयिष्यति ।

In the present context, verse 17ab means that self-portraits should never be painted in one's own house perhaps due to certain magical associations attached to them.

All the scholars follow the corrupt reading and hence the following translations.

SK : (Oh) king in one's own house *the work of painting* should not be done *by oneself.* (p. 54)

PS : In one's own house *the work of painting* should not be done *by oneself.* This seems to be an advice given to the artist. (p. 136)

SM : *Painting* should never be done *by anyone with his own hand for decorating his own house.* (p. 195)

43.21ab. *lapatīva ....sajīvamiva dṛśyate.* This verse lacks any coherent grammatical structure. What is obvious is that the merits of a painting such as the *bhūlamba* and *sādṛśya/mādhurya* are being discussed. Note *lapatīva* comes from, MS D. N has *lapabhīva* retaining the -p-. All scholars accept the reading *lasatīva* from A and V. From the context, it is possible to understand the sense. It appears to exalt the naturalistic aspect of painting. A painting should be so lifelike that it should appear as if alive *(sajīva iva).* In this given context, the reading from D *-lapatīva* (as if talking) seems to be most probable. It is also consistent with the other verbs mentioned *-śliśyatīva* (as if embracing) and *hasatīva* (as if smiling).

43.21c. *sādṛśyam.* The context strongly demands this emendation which is based on N's *sādhuryyam.*N's reading retains the -s- of the correct reading. *Mādhuryam* found in all the MSS yields a poor sense. This emendation draws further support from the mention of *sādṛśyam* as one of the eight merits in 19c.

43.22c. *baddham vyādhibhayākulam.* The instrumental ending found in all MSS *(-kulair)* is corrupt.

43.23b. *prakīrṇakeśaiśca so 'mangalyam vivarjayet.* MS D's reading *samaṅgalyair* is emended to so *'maṅgalyam'* to get the sense compatible with the context. "So" refers to the artist who is instructed not to paint inauspicious themes such as the disproportionate bodies, dishevelled haired figures and so on. Here, such a restriction seems to refer only to paintings made in the houses. Note the other translations:

SK : *No* (painting depicting a) figure with a defective limb *covered all over* with hair, overwhelmed with fear due to internal disease, *or smeared with a yellow pigment (ought to be executed).* (p. 55)

PS : *Those who desire auspiciousness should avoid pictures depicting a figure with defective limbs, stained, dispirited and incidence (vṛtam) by persons overcome with fear and disease and with dishevelled hair.* (p. 137)

SM : *The artist should ever avoid painting what is devoid of auspiciousness,* defective in form, tainted, vacant, agitated from being overpowered, disease-stricken or fear struck, wild with dishevelled hair. (p. 196)

43.23d. *-dhīmānnapratītam.* Note the correct reading is preserved in D which does not alter the meaning so much as to improve the grammar. *Pratītam,* a part from its commonly understood meaning of "probable, recognisable etc" also means "cheerful, glad or gladdening" Perhaps it is an instruction to the artist to paint only what is cheerful and never to depict any depressing theme [when painting in a house]. The other translations are not precise.

43.25b. *-āgatāśubham.* I follow SM's emendation since it entails a minor alteration and yields a feasible meaning. All MSS show *-āgatam śubham* which gives a contradictory sense. Note how SK and PS take it.

SK : A painting ..... *augments future good,* ..... (p. 55).

PS : A painting ..... *brings forth prosperity.* (p. 134)

43.27a. *galam hastam ca pādam ca.* Note that this emendation is derived from MSS ND. *Gala* is adopted from D and the rest from N. All the remaining MSS lack this *pāda.* PS's text followed by SM show *dharmārthakāmaśubhadam* which is clearly an interpolation for it has no semantic connection with the rest of the verse. However, the emended *pāda* means that he who is able to paint a human figure with its throat, hands, feet and ears unadorned (i.e. parts of the body which are normally hidden by ornaments), is an expert in painting. Note that SK and PS omit its translation. SM (p. 196) translates it as," it *assures the auspicious fruit of their puruṣārthas, dharma, artha and kāma.*

43.29b. *-ambarādikam.* Note that the correct reading which means "garments etc." is only preserved in MSS ND. This confirms SM's conjecture. SK (p. 55) is misled by V's corrupt *svarādikam* and translates it as "streamers *fluttering in the air ...* "

43.28c. *vāyugatyā.* Note that all the scholars are seriously mistaken in their translations of *vāyugatyā.* It means "with the speed of wind" and refers to the speed with which an artist paints. He should be able to paint waves, flames, banners, clothes etc. with the speed of the wind.

Note the following mistranslation by SK (p. 55) which is followed by PS (p. 137) and SM (p. 196).

> He who paints waves, flame, smoke and streamers fluttering in the air *according to the movement of the wind* should be considered a great painter.

43.29ab.SM (p. 197) appears to supply "pig" in translation this verse, " ..... depict the difference between a sleeping *pig* and that is alive and breathing and a dead one bereft of life,... ". Perhaps SM interpreted it in such a way in order to draw a connection between this verse and a Kangra painting of the 18th century (in the Government Museum, Art Gallery, Chandigarh) in which pigs are sketched in various reclining postures. (see SM's ***Chitrasūtra of the Viṣṇudharmottara***, fig. 13).

43.29c. *nimnonnatavibhāgam*. SK's (p. 55) translation is misleading.

> SK: He knows *chitra* who *makes one portion of the body lower than the other, ...*"
>
> Note that *nimnonnata* refers to technique in painting by which illusory depth and projection are created. It literally means "sunken/raised".

43.30b. *-ānulomyam*. None of the translations of this term is precise. Literally it means "in the direction of the hair". It also means "produced in natural or direct order" or "conformity". However, SK (p. 55) settles down for "regular series or succession" which is lexicographical meaning.

SK : In every case (their) *regular succession* is praiseworthy.

PS (p. 137) takes it as "harmony in different parts of a painting" and SM (p. 197) "proper arrangement of figures in the composition of a picture".

43.30c. *sammukhatvam*. Note that the mistranslation of this term has had a serious bearing on the theorisation of Indian art. It should be taken as "confrontation, the state of being face" as demanded by the context. In this case,it connot mean "in front of". In fact, verse 28 of adhy. 39 strictly prohibits a quarter based symmetry or *ardhārdhasārūpyam* which is a result of placing for example, two profiles facing one another.

SK: In painting (one) should carefully avoid in the case of all these, *placing one (figure) in front of another.* (p. 55)

PS (p. 137) completely follows SM's line of interpretation.

SM (p. 197) reiterates it by elaborating it further.

> By special effort the crowding of figures, one directly in front of another, should be avoided.

43.31b. *khātapūrtam.* This emendation derives from D's reading *khataprtam. khāta* which literally means "digging" and *pūrta* "filling" but when they form a compound, they yield a technical sense. Note its mention in the *Amarakośa:*

त्रिष्वथ क्रतुकर्मेष्टपूर्तखातादि कर्म यत् ।

The commentator, Maheśvara, explains:

खातं वापिकूपादि आदिना देवालयादि यत् कर्म तत् पूर्तं स्यात् ।

However, in the CitSūt., it appears to refer to sculpture or modelling. SK (p. 56) translates it as "*carving in* iron, gold, silver ..." and SM (p. 197) "dug up metals". PS (p. 136) offers a different interpretation in from of *"that in which digging is done first"*.

43.31c. *loheṣu.* The reading from MSS ABDNV is preferred to *lokeṣu* and its meaning fits in well with the context.

43.34c. *suśiram.* Note that MSS CD preserve the retroflex -ṣ- in place of the palatal one.

* * *

SELECT BIBLIOGRAPHY

Bachhofer, L. *Early Indian Sculpture.* London: Pegasus Press, 1939; Reprinted, New Delhi: Munshiram Manoharlal, 1973.

Banerjee, J.N. *The Development of Hindu Iconography.* Calcutta: Calcutta University, 1941; Revised and enlarged, 1956; Reprinted, New Delhi: Munshiram Manoharlal, 1974.

——— "Pratimālakṣaṇam", *Journal of Department of Letters* 23 (1933): pp.1-85.

Baumer, B.(ed.) *Kalātattvakośa: A Lexicon of Fundamental Concepts of the Indian Arts.* Vol. II, New Delhi: Indira Gandhi National Centre for the Arts, 1988.

Benjamin, W. *Illuminations.* "The Task of the Translator". London: Fontana Press, 1992.

Bhat, G.K. *Bharatanāṭyamañjarī: Bharata on the Theory and Practice of Drama.* Poona: Bhandarkar Oriental Research Institute, 1975.

Bhattacharya, D.C. *Pratimālakṣaṇa of the Viṣṇudharmottara.* New Delhi: Harman Publishing House, 1991.

Bhattacharya, T. *The Canons of Indian Art: A Study of Vastuvidya.* Calcutta: KLM, 1963.

Birdwood, G. *Industrial Arts of India.* London, 1880.

——— *Journal of the Royal Asiatic Society of Arts,* (1910): pp. 286-287.

Boner, A. *Principles of Composition in Hindu Sculpture : Cave Temple Period.* Leiden: E.J. Brill, 1962.

Bose, M. *Classical Indian Dancing: A Glossary.* Calcutta, 1970.

Bühler, G. *Detailed Report of a Tour in Search of Sanskrit MSS made in Kashmir, Rajputana and Central India.* Bombay, 1977.

——— Rev. of Alberuni's India by Edward C Sachau", *Indian Antiquary* 19 (1890): pp. 380-410.

Chaitanya, K. *Sanskrit Poetics: A Critical and Comparative Study.* Bombay : Asia Publishing House, 1965.

Coomaraswamy, A.K. *Medieval Sinhalese Art.* Broad Campden: Essex House, A.K. Press, 1908.

——— *Art and Swadeshi.* Madras: Ganesh, 1911.

——— "A Connection between Indian Aesthetics and Philosophy", *Rupam* 27-28 (1926): pp.21.

——— "Nagara Painting." Rupam 37 (1929).

——— *The Dance of Shiva : Indian Images with Many Arms.* Bombay: Asia Publishing House, 1948.

——— "Viṣṇudharmottara Chapter XLI", *Journal of American Oriental Society,* 52 (1932) b: pp.31-21.

——— "Introduction to the Art of Eastern Asia", Boston: *The Open Court* XLVI (1932): pp.185-215.

——— "Reactions to Art in India", *Journal of American Oriental Society* 52 (1932): pp.213-220.

——— "The Painter's Art in Ancient India : Ajanta", *Journal of Indian Society of Oriental Art,* 1 (1933): pp 26-29.

——— "The Technique and Theory of Indian Painting", *Journal of American Oriental Society* 32 (1934): p.79.

——— *The Transformation of Nature in Art.* Cambridge, Mass: Harvard University Press, 1934.

——— "Figures of Speech and the Figures of Thought", *Selected Papers.* I Roger Lipsey. Bollingen Series, Princeton: Princeton University Press, 1977.

Dasgupta, S.N. *History of Indian Philosophy.* Cambridge: Cambridge University Press, 1922.

Dehejia, V. *Representing the Body: Gender Issues in Indian Art.* New Delhi: Kali for Women, 1997.

Dvorak, M. *Idealism and Naturalism in Gothic Art,* Trans. R.J.Klawiter. Notre Dame, Ind.: 1967.

Fleet, J.F. "The Standard Height of an Indian Man", *Journal of Royal Asiatic Society* MDCCCCXI (1911): pp.208-9.

Ghosh, A. (ed.) *Ajanta Murals.* "The Murals, their Composition and Technique", New Delhi: B.B.Lal, 1967.

Ghosh, M. "The Nāṭyaśāstra and the Abhinavabhāratī", *Indian Historical Quarterly* 10 (1934): pp.161-163.

Gnoli, R. *The Aesthetic Experience according to Abhinavagupta.* Rome: Instituto Italiano Per il Medio ed Estremo Oriente, 1956.

Goswami, B.N. trans. *An Early Document of Indian Art*: The & Picolla Dahmen, *Citralakṣaṇa of Nagnajit.* New Delhi : Manohar, A.L. 1976.

Gunasinghe, S. *Le Technique de la Peinture Indienne d'apres les Textes du Silpa.* Paris: *Annales Musse Guimet,* 1957.

Grunwedel, A. *Buddhist Art in India.* Trans. A.C.Gibson. London: Bernard Quaritch, 1901.

Gupta, K. *A Socio-Religious Study of Viṣṇudharmottara Purāṇa.* New Delhi: Harman Publishing House, 1994.

Hadaway, W.S. "Some Hindu 'Śilpa' Śāstras – In Their Relation to South Indian Sculpture", *Östasiatische Zeitschrift* 3 (1914-15): pp.34-50.

Havell, E.B. *Indian Sculpture and Painting.* London: John Murray, 1908.

Hazra, R.C. *Studies in Upapurāṇas.* Calcutta: Sanskrit College, 1958.

Huntington, S.L. *The Art of Ancient India: Buddhist, Hindu, Jain.* New York: Weatherhill, 1985.

Jayaswal, K.P. "A Hindu Text on Painting", *Journal of Bihar and Orissa Research Society* 9 (1923): pp. 30-39.

——— "Nagara and Vesara", *Journal of Society of Oriental Art* 1 (1933): pp.57-58.

Kane, P.V. *History of Sanskrit Poetics.* New Delhi: Motilal Banarsidass, 1961.

Kleinbauer, W.E. *Modern Perspectives in Western Art History.* Los Angeles: University of California, 1971.

Kramrisch, S. "The Representation of Nature in Early Buddhist Art", *Rupam* 8 (1921): pp.7-9.

——— "Review of A Handbook of Indian Art by E.B.Havell", *Journal of Royal Asiatic Society of Great Britain and Ireland* (1922): pp.454-455.

——— "The Expressiveness of Indian Art", *Calcutta Review* 1-2 (1922): pp.19-25.

——— "The Religious and Grotesque in Indian Art", *Modern Review* 33-34 (1923): pp.567-69.

——— "Influence of Race on Early Indian Art", *Rupam* 18 (1924): pp.73-76.

——— "A Treatise on Indian Painting", *Journal of Department of Letters*, 2 (1924) pp.1-56.

——— *Indian Sculpture*, Calcutta: Heritage for India Series, 1933.

Krishna, A. "Certain Citrasūtra Traditions and Their Application in Rajasthani and Mughal Painting", *Veroffentlichungen des Museums für Indische Kunst Berlin* (1977):pp.267-278.

Lipsey, R. *Coomaraswamy 1: Traditional Art and Symbolism*. Princeton: Princeton University Press, Bollingen Series, 1977.

——— *Coomaraswamy 2: Metaphysics*. Bollingen Series, Princeton: Princeton University Press, 1977.

Coomaraswamy 3: His Life and Work. Bollingen Series, Princeton: Princeton University Press, 1977

Maillous, S. "Interpretation", *Critical Terms for Literary Studies*. ed. Frank Lentricchia & Thomas MacLaughlin. Chicago: University of Chicago Press, 1990.

Maxwell, T. "Śilpa versus Śāstra", *Shastric Traditions in Indian Arts*, ed. A. L. Dallapiccola, Stuttgart: Steiner Verlag , 1989: pp.5-15.

Sontag, S. "Against Interpretation", *Twentieth Century Criticism*, ed. David Lodge. Hongkong: Longman, 1988.

Masson J.L. *Aesthetic Rapture: the rasādhyāya of the Nāṭyaśāstra*. & M.V. Poona: Deccan College, 1970.

Patwardhan "The Dhvanyāloka and the Dhvanyālokalocana: A Translation of 4th *Uddyota*, pt. I", *Journal of American Oriental Society* 97.3(1977): pp. 285-304.

Miller, B.S. "Stella Kramrisch: A Biographical Essay", *Exploring India's Sacred Art*. ed. Philadelphia: University of Pennsylvania Press, 1983.

Misra, R.N. *Yaksha Cult and Iconography*. New Delhi: Munshiram Manoharlal, 1981.

Misra, S.S. *Fine Arts and Technical Sciences in Ancient India: with special reference to Someśvara's Mānasollāsa*. Varanasi: Krishnadas Academy, 1982.

Mitter, P. *Much Maligned Monsters : History of European Reactions to Indian Art*. Oxford : Clarendon Press, 1977.

Monier-Williams, M. *A Sanskrit –English Dictionary*. Oxford: Oxford University Press, 1974.

Mosteller, J.F. *The Measure of Form : A New Approach for the Study of Indian Sculpture.* New Delhi: Abhinav Publications, 1991.

Moti Chandra. *The Technique of Mughal Painting.* Lucknow: The U.P. Historical Society, 1949.

Nadkarni, K.M. *Indian Materia Medica.* Vol. I. Bombay: Popular Book Depot, 1954.

Ojha, G.H. *The Paleography of India.* New Delhi: Munshiram Manoharlal, 1975.

Oursel, P.M. "Une Connexion dan l'Esthetique et la Philosophie de l'Inde", *Review des Arts Asiatique* (1925).

Page, T.E. & *Vitruvius* Book III, Ch.1 "Vitruvius on Architecture."

Capps E. ed. trans. Frank Granger & W.H.D. Rouse, London: William Heinemann, 1933.

Pal, Pratapaditya. "A Brahmanical Triad from Kashmir and Some Related Icons", *Archives of Asian Art* 27 (1973-74) pp. 33-45.

——— *The Classical Indian Tradition. Traditions in Rajput Painting.* New York: The Gallery Association of New York State, 1978.

Pandey, K.C. *Comparative Aesthetics: Indian Aesthetics.* Vol. I. Varanasi: Chowkhamba Sanskrit Series Office, 1950.

Panofsky, E. *The Codex Huygens.* London: Warburg Institute, 1940.

Pillai, C. D. *Samudrikā or a Treatise on the Hindu Sciences of Palmistry and Physiognomy*: A Translation From Tamil Puruṣa Samudrikā Lakṣaṇa, Bangalore, 1886.

Pingree, D. *Jyotiṛśāstra : History of Indian Literature,* 6 (2). Weisbaden: Otto Harrassowitz, 1981.

——— "The Paitamahāsiddhānta of the Viṣṇudharmottarapurāṇa", *Adayar Library Bulletin* 31-32 (1967-68): pp.472-473.

——— (ed.) *The Yavanajātaka.* Vol.2, Cambridge, Massachusetts: Harvard University Press, 1978.

Raz, Ram. *Essay on The Architecture of the Hindus.* London, 1834.(repr. Varanasi: Indological Book House, 1972.)

Raghavan, V. "Some Sanskrit Texts on Painting", *Indian Historical Quarterly* 9 (1933): pp.904-5.

Rao, Gopinath. *Elements of Hindu Iconography*. Madras: Law Printing House, 1914-16.(repr. Delhi, 1968).

"Painting in Ancient India", *Modern Review* 23-24 (1918).

——— "Tālamāna or Iconometry", *Memoirs of the Archeological Survey of India* 3 (1920): pp. 32-115.

——— "Pratimālakṣaṇam", *Journal of the Department of Letters*, University of Calcutta 23 (1933).

Ruelius, Hans (ed.) *Sāriputra und Ālekhyalakṣaṇa Zwei Texte zur Proportionslehre in der indischen und ceylonesischen Kunst*. Gottingen, 1974.

Sachau, E.C. *Alberuni's India*. 2 vols. London: Kegan Paul, Trench, Trubner & Co., 1910.

Sarma Sastri, V.V. "Method of Plastering Walls for Painting", *Indian Historical Quarterly* 3 (1927): pp.53-59.

Schwab, R. *The Oriental Renaissance: Europe's Rediscovery of India and the East, 1680-1880*. Trans. Gene Patterson-Black and Victor Reinking. New York: Columbia University Press, 1984.

Shah, P. *Shri Viṣṇudharmottara: A Text of Ancient Indian Arts*. Ahmedabad: Krishna Printery, 1990.

Sontag, S. "Against Interpretation", *20th Century Criticism*. (ed. David Lodge. Hongkong: Longman, 1988).

Stein, M.A. *Catalogue of Sanskrit Manuscripts in the Raghunath Temple Library at Jammu & Kashmir*. Bombay: Nirnaya Sagar Press, 1894.

Swamikannu. *An Indian Ephemeris*. 5 vols. Delhi: Agam Prakashan, L.D. 1922.

Timm, J.R. ed. *Texts in Context: Traditional Hermeneutics in South Asia*. Albany: State University of New York Press, 1992.

Vatsyayana, Kapila. *Classical Indian Dance in Literature and the Arts*. New Delhi: Sangeet Natak Akademi, 1968.

——— *The Square and the Circle of the Indian Arts*. New Jersey: Humanities Press, 1983.

Williams, J. *The Art of Gupta India: Empire and Province*. Princeton: Princeton University Press, 1982.

Williams, R. *Keywords*. London: Fontana Press, 1988.

Wollheim, R. *Painting as an Art*. Princeton: Princeton University Press, 1984.

Sanskrit Texts

Agni Purāṇa, ed. Rajendralal Mitra, vol.I. Calcutta: Asiatic Society of Bengal, 1873.

Aparājitapṛcchā of Bhuvanadeva, ed. B. Bhattacharya. *GOS* 115, Baroda: Oriental Institute, 1950.

Aṣṭādhyāyī of Pāṇini, ed. S.C. Vasu. Delhi: Motilal Banarsidass, 1962.

Bhaviṣya Purāṇa, ed. By several authors. Bombay: Venkateswara Press, 1959.

Bṛhatsaṃhitā of Varāhamihira, ed. Ramakrishna Bhatt, 2 vols. Delhi: Motilal Banarsidass, 1982.

Citralakṣaṇa of Nagnajit, ed. B. Laufer; trans. to English by B.N.Goswamy and A.L.Dahmen Piccola: *An Early Document of Indian Art*. New Delhi: Manohar, 1976.

Kāmasūtra of *Vātsyāyana*: with Comm. by Yaśodhara, ed. D.Shastri. Varanasi: Vidya Vilas Press, 1929.

Kāvyālaṃkāra of Rudraṭa: with Comm. by Namisadhu, ed. Durgaprasad and Wasudeva Laxmana Sastri Pansikar. Bombay: Nirnaya Sagar Press, 1928.

Kāvyaprakāśa of Mammaṭa: with Comm. by Vidyācakravartin and Bhaṭṭagopala, ed. R. Harihara Sastri, 1-5 Ullasa. Trivandrum Sanskrit series 88, 100, Trivandrum, 1926.

Kāvyaprakāśa of Mammaṭa: ed. N.D. Banhati. Bombay: Nirnaya Sagar Press, 1917.

Kriyāsamuccaya; reproduced by Lokeshchandra. Śata Piṭaka series. vol. 237. New Delhi, 1977.

Kumārasambhava of Kālidasa : with Comm. by Mallinātha, ed. Kanakalal Sarma. Kasi Sanskrit series 14. Varanasi, 1923.

Lalitavistara, ed. R.L.Mitra. Calcutta: Asiatic Society of Bengal, 1877.

Mānasollāsa of Someśvara, ed. G.K.Shrigondekar, 2 vols. Gaekward Oriental Series 84, Baroda, 1939.

Mṛcchakaṭika of Śudraka: with Comm by Pṛthvīdhara and Lalla Dīkṣit, ed. N.B. Godabole, Bombay: Bombay Sanskrit Series 52, 1896.

Mahābhārata, ed. V. S. Sukthanker and S. K. Belvalkar. Poona: Bhandarkar Oriental Research Institute, 1927- 59.

Matsyapurāṇa, ed. Hari Narayana Apte. Anandasrama Sanskrit series 54. Poona, 1907.

Nāṭyaśāstra : with Abhinavabhāratī, ed. Manavalli Ramakrishna Kavi, Vol. I. Gaekward Oriental series 36. Baroda, 1926.

——— ed. Manomohan Ghosh. Calcutta: Royal Asiatic Society of Bengal, 1950.

Yogasūtra of Patañjali, with Comm. Yogavārtika by Vijñānabhikṣu. ed. Ramakrishna Sastri and Kesava Sastri. 2 vols. Varanasi: Medical Hall Press, 1883-84.

Samarāṅgaṇa-Sūtradhāra of Bhojadeva, ed. T. Ganapati Sastri. 2 vols. Gaekward Oriental series 25, 32. Baroda, 1924-25. Rev. edn. by V. S. Agrawala. Baroda: GOS 25, 1966.

Samudralakṣaṇam, ed. T.N.Subramanyam. Madras, 1959.

Saṅgītaratnākara of Sārṅgadeva: with Comms. by Kallinātha and Siṁhabhūpāla, ed. S. Subramanya Sastri. 4 vols. Adayar Library series 86. Madras, 1953.

Sārāvalī of Kalyāṇavarman, ed. Murlidhara Chaturvedi. Delhi: Motilal Banarsidass, 1977.

Śatapatha Brāhmaṇa with Comms. by Sāyana and Hariswāmi, ed. several persons. Bombay: Venkateshvara Steam Press, 1940.

Śilparatna of Śrīkumāra, ed. T. Ganapati Sastri. 2 vols. Trivandrum Sanskrit series 75, 98, Trivandrum, 1922-25.

Tantrāloka of Abhinavagupta, with Comms. by Rajanaka Jayaratha and Mukund Ram Sastri. Srinagar, 1918-38.

Vaikhānasāgama of Marīci, ed. K. Sambasiva Sastri. Trivandrum Sanskrit series 121. Trivandrum, 1935.

Vākyapadīya of Bhatṛhari: with Comm. by Helarāja, III. 1-77, ed. K. Sambasiva Sastri. Trivandrum Sanskrit series CXVI. Trivandrum, 1935.

Vājasaneya Saṃhitā, ed. A. Weber. Berlin: Royal Academy of Sciences, 1849.

Viṣṇudharmottara Purāṇa Khanda III, ed. Pandit Madhusudana and Madhavaprasada Sarma. Bombay: Venkatesvara Press, 1912.

——— ed. Priyabala Shah. Gaekwad Oriental series 130, 137, Baroda, 1958.

——— 1961. ed. and Trans. (Hindi) Asoke Chatterjee Sastri. Gaṅgānātha Jhā Granthamālā, 4. Varanasi, 1971.

GLOSSARY

Acchaidikā	one of the three types of line rendering (vartanā); extremely fine, unbroken lines. Others: Patrajā, Bindujā (adhy.41).
Adhyardhā locana	one of the 9 types of rotated postures (sthāna); a three quarter posture with one eye fully visible and the other, half-visible. Others: Ṛjvāgata, Sācīkṛta, etc. (adhy. 39).
Adhvaidha	one of the three types of postures (sthāna) ; a type which yields only one variation= Ṛjvāgata and Pṛṣṭhāgata. Others: Citra, Vicitra (adhy. 39).
Āhvaraka	a low-caste person (adhy. 42).
Ālīḍha	one of the three types of dynamic (maṇḍala) stances (sthānaka) associated with archers. Others: Vaiśākha, Pratyālīḍha (adhy. 39).
Aṅga	major parts of the body—torso, head, arms and legs (adhy. 36).
Aṅgula	the lowest unit of measurement of any whole divided into 108 parts (adhy. 35).
Ānulomya	literally, along the direction of the growth of the hair; conformity with the natural order = pratīta (adhy. 43).
Anyacittatā	one of the four causes of spoiling a painting; a state of being distracted while painting (literally, thinking about something other than painting) Others: pipāsā durālīnam, durāsana (adhy. 41).
Adhyardha locana	one of the thirteen postures (sthāna); the fourth of the nine rotated postures = Adhyardhākṣa. Others: Ṛjvāgata, Sācīkṛta, etc. (adhy. 39).
Ardharju	one of the thirteen postures (sthāna); the second of the nine rotated postures; afrontal; = Anṛju. Others: Ṛjvāgata, Sācīkṛta, etc. (adhy. 39).

Asamapada	one of the two stances; a stance which is symmetrical and wherein the legs are unbent = Maṇḍala (adhy. 39) .
Avibhaktatvam	one of the eight demerits of art (citradoṣa); lack of details. Others: Daurbalya, Sthūlarekhatva, etc. (adhy.43).
Āyāma	(context-dependant) 1. width; measurement along the horizontal axis. 2. height (when juxtaposed with pariṇāha) (adhy.35).
Balbaja	coarse grass; constituent of wall plaster (adhy.40).
Barbara	one of the seven types of hair (keśajāti); curly hair. Others: Kuntala, Dakṣiṇāvarta, etc. (adhy.37).
Bhadra	one of the five stereotypes for male body (puruṣa) measuring 106 aṅgulas in height. Others: Haṃsa, Mālavya, Rucaka, Śaśaka (adhy.35).
Bhāga	1. a unit of measurement comprising 4 aṅgulas. 2. quadrant of a circle (adhy. 39).
Bindu	one of the three types of line rendering (vartanā); dots. Others: Acchaidikā, Patra (adhy.41).
Bhittika	one of the nine rotated postures (sthāna); fully profile = Pārśvāgata. Others: Ṛjvāgata, Sācīkṛta, etc. (adhy. 39).
Bhudara-puccha	hog's tail; the means of applying astringent on painted surface (adhy. 40).
Bhūlamba	a particular use of the plumb line to derive proportions of foreshortened figures and postures (sthāna) viewed from different angles (adhy.41).
Bṛhadgaṇḍ-oṣṭhanetratva	the three out of eight demerits of art (citradoṣa); oversized cheeks, lips and eyes. Others: Sthūlarekhatva, avibhaktatva, etc. (adhy.43).
Calita	one of the thirteen postures (sthāna); walking. Others: Calita, 'Ullepa', etc. (adhy. 39).
Cāpākāra	one of the five types of eyes (netra); bow-shaped eye. Others: Matsyodara, Padmapatra, Utpalapatra, Vaṭākṛti (adhy.37)

Carmakvātha	decoction of leather (adhy. 40).
Caturasram	1. symmetrical 2. unforeshortened (adhy. 38, 39).
Chavi	the colour tone (adhy. 40).
Chāyāgata	one of the nine rotated postures (sthāna); a frontalthree-quarter = Adhyardhākṣa. Others: Ṛjvāgata, Sācīkṛta etc. (adhy. 39).
Citra	1. By and large refers specifically to painting. 2. Can also refer, in different contexts, to 'works of art' in other mediums. The Citrasūtra, for example, mentions that all that is said of "citra" also applies to stone and metal sculptures. 3. one of the three types of posture (sthāna) which yields two variations = Pārśvāgata. Others: Adhvaidha, Vicitra (adhy. 39).
Citradoṣa	a serious fault or demerit in art; eight in number (adhy. 41, 43).
Citraguṇa	a positive attribute or merit in art; eight in number (adhy. 41).
Citrakarma-	four ornaments of painting. See Rekhā, Vartanā, Bhūṣaṇa and Varṇa (adhy. 41).
Citrarasa	sentiment/emotion as expressed in art (adhy. 43).
Citravastra	painting on cloth (adhy. 43)
Citravid	a fully trained and proficient artist, having skills in drawing difficult parts of the body (for example, unadorned ears), wounded soldiers, aged people, waves, flames, flags and garments; one who can create a distinction between a sleeping and a dead person; one who can draw with the speed of wind (vayugatyā) (adhy. 43).
Dakṣiṇāvarta	one of the seven types of hair (keśajāti); hair associated with South India. Others: Barbara, Kuntala, etc. (adhy. 37).

Daiśika	one of three types of painting/sculpture (citravidha) that is locally prevalent and is more accessible in terms of skill acquisition than the Satya type. Others: Satya, Nāgara, Miśra (adhy. 41).
Daurbalya	one of the eight demerits of art (citradoṣa); weakness (due to use of weak lines). Others: Sthūlarekhatva, Avibhaktatva, etc. (adhy.43).
Drāvaka	liquifier such as mica to melt impervious metals (adhy. 40).
Durālīna	one of the four causes of spoiling a painting; crouching. Others: Pipāsā, Anyacittatā, Durāsana (adhy. 41).
Durāsana	one of the four causes of spoiling a painting; an uncomfortable posture while painting. Others: Pipāsā, Anyacittatā, Durālīnam (adhy. 41).
Gaṇḍa-parāvṛtta	= Parāvṛtta
Gaurichavi	a colour tint obtained by mixing white to any colour (adhy.40).
Gomutrika	one of the two types of dynamic (maṇḍala) stances (sthānaka); a stance in which both the legs are bent; associated with sword, shield, lance, javelin, stone and arrow bearers. Other maṇḍala type in which only one leg is bent and the other straight—Vaiśākha, Ālīḍha, Pratyālīḍha (adhy.39).
Guḍa	jaggary; constituent of wall plaster (adhy. 40).
Guggulu	a fragrant gum resin or the exudation of *Amyris agallochum*; constituent of wall plaster (adhy. 40).
Haṃsa	one of the five stereotypes for male body (puruṣa) measuring 108 aṅgulas in height. Others: Bhadra, Mālavya, Rucaka, Śaśaka; also regarded as the standard type (adhy. 35).
Juṭaka	one of the seven types of hair (keśajāti); hair twisted like that of ascetics. Others: Kuntala, Dakṣiṇāvarta, etc. (adhy. 37).
Kala	a unit of measurement comprising of 2 aṅgulas (adhy. 39).
Kāla	Personification of Time (adhy. 42).

Karaṇa	co-ordination of the movement of the hands and feet (adhy. 37).
Khātapūrtam	literally means digging and filling. Perhaps it implies large scale sculptures (adhy. 43).
Kṣayavṛddhī	literally means increase and decrease; one of the eight merits of art (citraguṇa); a type of 'foreshortening' which occurs when the body/model is rotated around its vertical axis, stage by stage. Others: Sthāna, Pramāṇa, etc. (adhy.39,43).
Kundura	an extract of Deodar or *Avaria longifolia*; constituent of wall plaster (adhy. 40).
Kuntala	one of the seven types of hair (keśajāti); hair in form of locks. Others: Dakṣiṇāvarta, Taraṅga, etc. (adhy. 37).
Kusumbha-taila	safflower oil; ingredient of wall plaster (adhy. 40).
Loma	body-hair; an index of hierarchical status. One single hair per pore denotes highest status. One hair per pore—kings; two hair per pore—ministers, etc. (See Bṛhatsaṃhitā 67.5) (adhy. 38, 42).
Māna-bhūmayaḥ	area of various dimensions (for painting) (adhy. 40).
Madhya	intermediary angles of vision or location within the circle for the postures to avoid strict profiles or fully frontal or backviews. Madhya makes possible the three-quarter view (adhy.39).
Madhūcchiṣṭam	beeswax; constituent of wall plaster (adhy.40).
Madhuka	an extract of a flower, *Bassia latifolia*; constituent of wall plaster (adhy. 40).
Madhuratva	one of the eight merits of painting/art (citraguṇa); a certain kind of charm or attractiveness (adhy. 43).
Mālavya	one of the five stereotypes for male body (puruṣa) measuring 104 aṅgulas in height. Others: Haṃsa, Bhadra, Rucaka, Śaśaka (adhy.35).

Mānavikāratā — one of the eight demerits of art (citradoṣa); deviation from [the rules of proportion]. Others: Bṛhadgaṇḍoṣṭhanetratva, Daurbalya, etc. (adhy. 41).

Maṇḍala — one of the two type of stances (sthānaka); a stance which is asymmetrical (asamapada) wherein one leg bears the weight and is straight and the other is bent. Other: Samapada (adhy. 39).

Mataṅga — a kind of wild grass, *Eleusine aegyptica*, used as an astringent to give durability to colours (adhy. 40).

Matsyodara — one of the five types of eyes (netra); eyes resembling "fish's belly". Others: Cāpākāra, Padmapatra, Utpalapātra, Vaṭākṛti (adhy.37)

Miśracitra — one of the three types of painting; a type which is a combination of the other three. See others: Satya, Vaiśika, Nāgara (adhy. 41).

Mūlaraṅga — five basic colours—white, black, red, yellow and black (adhy.40).

Nāgara — one of the three types of painting; a type requiring high levels of skill and proficiency in "foreshortening." Others: Satya, Vaiśika, Miśra (adhy. 41).

Nata — = Samānata

Nimnonnata — apparent "ups" and "downs" specifically in painting which result from a skillful use of foreshortening and colour tones (adhy.43).

Pada — a unit of measurement comprising of three aṅgulas (adhy. 35).

Pada — space between the eyebrows (adhy. 39).

Padmapatra — one of the five types of eyes (netra); eyes resembling "petal of a red lotus." Others: Cāpākāra, Matsyodara, Utpalapatra, Vaṭākṛti (adhy.37).

Parāvṛtta — one of the thirteen postures (sthāna); the sixth of the nine rotated postures; Turned Away = Gaṇḍaparāvṛtta. Others: Ṛjvāgata, Sācīkṛta, etc. (adhy. 39).

Pariṇāha	(context-dependant) 1. circumference. 2. breadth; when juxtaposed against Āyāma (adhy. 35).
Pārśvāgata	one of the thirteen postures (sthāna); the fifth of the nine rotated postures; profile. Others: Rjvāgata, Sācīkṛta, etc. (adhy. 39).
Patrajā	one of the three types of line rendering (vartanā); partly drawn, partly suggested, discontinuous lines. Others: Acchaidikā, Bindu (adhy.41).
Patravinyāsa	application of metallic colours in form of foils (adhy.40) .
Pipāsā	one of the four causes of spoiling a painting; a state of being thirsty. Others: Anyacittatā, Durālīna, Durāsana (adhy. 41).
Pramāṇa	1. one of the eight merits of art (citraguṇa); a sense correct proportion and right measure. Others: Sthāna, Bhūlamba, etc. (adhy. 41).
	2. breadth, when juxtaposed against vedha (adhy. 36).
Prāṅnata	oriented or bending towards the east (adhy.38).
Pratītam	1. manner of representing the plausible; 2. also objects of such representation (adhy. 43).
Pratyālīḍha	one of the three types of assymmetrical (maṇḍala) stances (sthānaka) for archers; a stance in which the left foot is brought forward and the right one drawn back. Others: Ālīḍha, Vaiśākha (adhy. 39).
Pratyaṅga	minor parts of the body—the forehead, nose, chin, fingers, etc (adhy. 36).
Pṛṣṭhāgata	one of the thirteen postures (sthāna); the seventh of the nine rotated postures; backview. Others: Ṛjvāgata, Sācīkṛta, etc. (adhy. 39).
Purovṛtta	one of the nine rotated types of postures (sthāna); three-quarters rear-view. Others: Ṛjvāgata, Sācīkṛta, etc. (adhy. 39).
Pustakarma	method of modeling by which solid (ghana) and hollow (suśira) figures or objects can be made (adhy. 43).
Rājavarta	lapis lazuli (adhy.40).

Ṛjvāgata — one of the thirteen postures (sthāna); the first of the nine rotated postures; fully frontal; undergoing least foreshortening. Others: Sācīkṛta, Adhyardhākṣa, etc. (adhy. 39).

Rucaka — one of the five stereotypes for male body (puruṣa) measuring 100 aṅgulas in height. Others: Bhadra, Haṃsa, Mālavya, Śaśaka (adhy.35).

Sācīkṛta — one of the thirteen postures (sthāna); the third of the nine rotated postures; averted. Others: Ṛjvāgata, Adhyardhākṣa, etc. (adhy. 39).

Sādṛśya — problematic term. One of the eight merits of art (citraguṇa); often taken to mean 'resemblance'. Others: Pramāṇa, Bhūlamba, etc; one must be careful to distinguish its usage in the context of western art history (verisimilitude and its consequent association with Realism/ Naturalism) from its use in the context of ancient Indian art practice. Refers to conformity between what is seen and what is depicted. At the same time, it is important to recognise certain semantic overlap between 'sādṛśya' and resemblance (adhy. 41, 42, 43).

Samānata — one of the thirteen postures (sthāna); the last of the nine rotated postures; Completely Bent = Nata; the body bends along its horizontal axis. Others: Ṛjvāgata, Sācīkṛta, etc. (adhy. 39).

Samapada — one of the two types of stances (sthānaka); a stance with erect posture (Ṛjvāgata) and unbent legs = Ṛjvāpada. Other: Asamapada, eg. the Maṇḍala stances – Ālīḍha, etc. (adhy. 39).

Sammukhatva — literally means figures facing each other; figures rendered in perfect symmetry and strict profile (adhy. 43).

Saṇa — a type of hemp-fibre; constituent of wall plaster (adhy. 40); one of the eight demerits of art (citradoṣa); uncontrolled, (varṇa).

Saṅkara — untidy merging of colours (adhy. 43).

Sarja-taila — oil of *Vartica robusta*; rubbed on dried wall plaster for smoothness (adhy. 40).

Śarkaratoyena	sugar solution; constituent of wall plaster, used for smoothening (adhy. 40).
Śaśaka	one of the five stereotypes for male body (puruṣa) measuring 92 aṅgulas in height. Others: Bhadra, Haṃsa, Mālavya, Rucaka (adhy.35, 42).
Satya	one of the four types of painting/sculpture (citravidha); a type which is similar to the world/people depicted (lokasādṛśyam). Others: Daiśika, Nāgara, Miśra (adhy. 41).
Siṃhakeśara	one of the seven types of hair (keśajāti); hair resembling a lion's mane. Others: Juṭaka, Kuntala, etc. (adhy.37).
Sthambana	1. astringent 2. method of mixing colours in which one colour is treated as constant (adhy. 40).
Sthāna	one of the eight merits of art (citraguṇa); posture of a body viewed from a fixed vantage point and rotated around its vertical axis; 9 rotated types (Ṛjvāgata etc.)+ 4 bent around its horizontal axis (Ullepa etc.) = 13 sthānas all together (adhy. 39).
Sthānaka	stance; two types- Symmetrical (Samapada) and Asymmetrical (Asamapada) (adhy.39).
Sthūla-	one of the eight demerits of art (citradoṣa); use of thick rekhatva lines. Others: Daurbalya, Avibhaktatvam, etc. (adhy.43).
Sumeru	the best mountain in the world, Mount Meru (adhy. 43).
Susampūrṇa	fully [visible]complete [undergoing least degree of foreshortening] (kṣayavṛddhī) (adhy. 38, 39).
Svenaivā-aṅgulamāna	measurement derived from its own smallest unit = aṅgula, (adhy.35).
Śyāmā chavi	the shade of a colour derived by adding black to it (adhy. 40).
Tāla	a large unit of measurement comprising of twelve aṅgulas in length (adhy. 35).
Taraṅga	one of the seven types of hair (keśajāti); wavy hair. Others: Juṭaka, Kuntala, etc. (adhy.37).

'Ullepa' — one of the thirteen postures (sthāna); posture in motion ? Others: Calita, Valita, etc. (adhy. 39).

Utpalapatra — one of the five types of eyes (netra); eyes resembling "petal of a blue lotus." Others: Cāpākāra, Matsyodara, Padmapatra, Vaṭākṛti (adhy.37).

Uttāna — one of the thirteen postures (sthāna); reclining. Others: Calita, Ullepa, etc. (adhy.39).

Vaiśākha — one of the three types of assymetrical (maṇḍala) stances (sthānaka) for archers; a stance in which the right foot is brought forward and the left one drawn back. Others: Ālīḍha, Pratyālīḍha (adhy. 39).

Vakra-rekhatva — one of the eight demerits of art (citradoṣa); use of crooked line. Others: Sthūlarekhatva, avibhaktatvam, etc. (adhy.43).

Valita — one of the thirteen postures (sthāna); turning around (both the horizontal and vertical axes). Others: Calita, Ullepa, etc. (adhy. 39).

Vartana — three types of line rendering. See Acchaidika, Binduja, Patraja(adhy. 41).

Vaṭākṛti — one of the five types of eyes (netra); eyes resembling "Cowrie shell". Others: Cāpākara, Matsyodara, Padmapatra, Utpalapatra (adhy.37).

Vāyugati — literally means the speed of wind; draughtsmanship entailing drawing at very high speed (adhy. 43) .

Vedha — depth (adhy. 36).

Vicakṣaṇa — expert or connoisseur of art who is conversant with its norms(adhy. 41).

Vicitra — one of the three types of posture (sthāna); a type which yields maximum (i.e. three) variations of the three-quarters view = Sācīkṛta, Anṛjvagata and Adhyardhākṣa. Others: Advaidha, Citra (adhy. 39).

Vibhaktatā	one of the eight merits of art (citraguṇa); rendering of details through which differences between objects are established.
	Others: Sthāna, Bhūlamba, etc.(adhy. 41).
Vidyā	allegorical representation of Vedas (adhy. 42).
Virāga	shades of grey when black is mixed with white (adhy. 40).
Yava	a small measure of length = 1/12 of an aṅgula (adhy. 37).

LIST OF DIAGRAMS

***

DIAGRAM I

Two dimensional projection of Foreshortening (Kṣayavṛddhī)

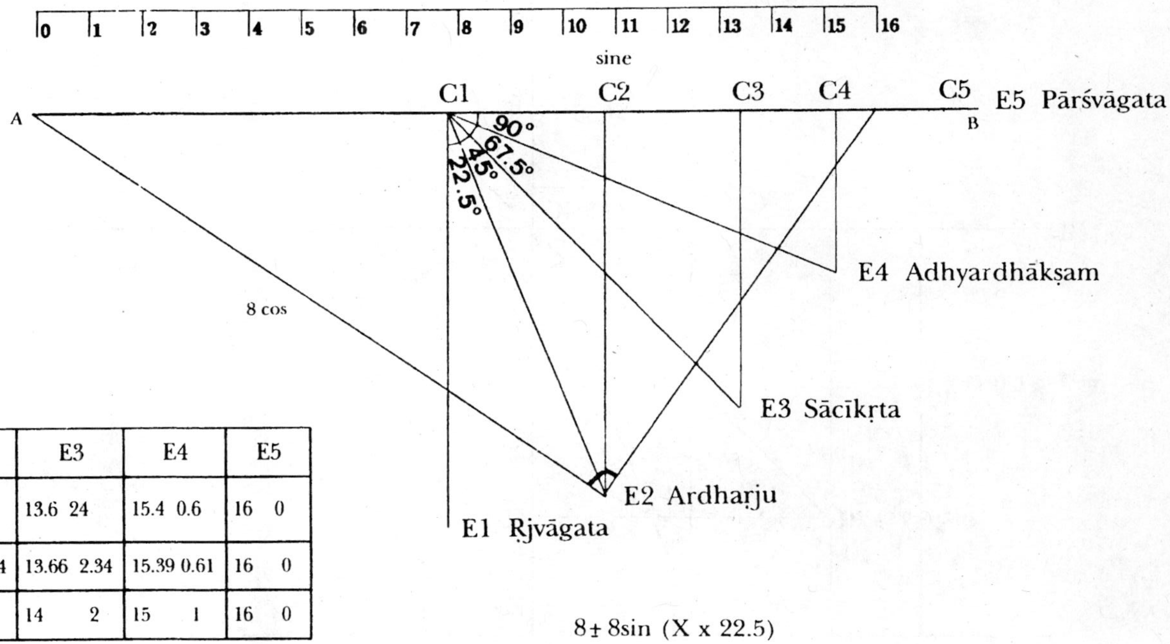

	E1	E2	E3	E4	E5
Measure-ment	8 8	11 5	13.6 24	15.4 0.6	16 0
Calculation	8 8	11.06 4.94	13.66 2.34	15.39 0.61	16 0
Given value	8 8	11 5	14 2	15 1	16 0

E : Viewing point
AB : Distance between the nipples
C : Centre
AB : Stationary ; E Shifts

DIAGRAM II

Two dimensional projection of Foreshortening (Kṣayavṛddhī)

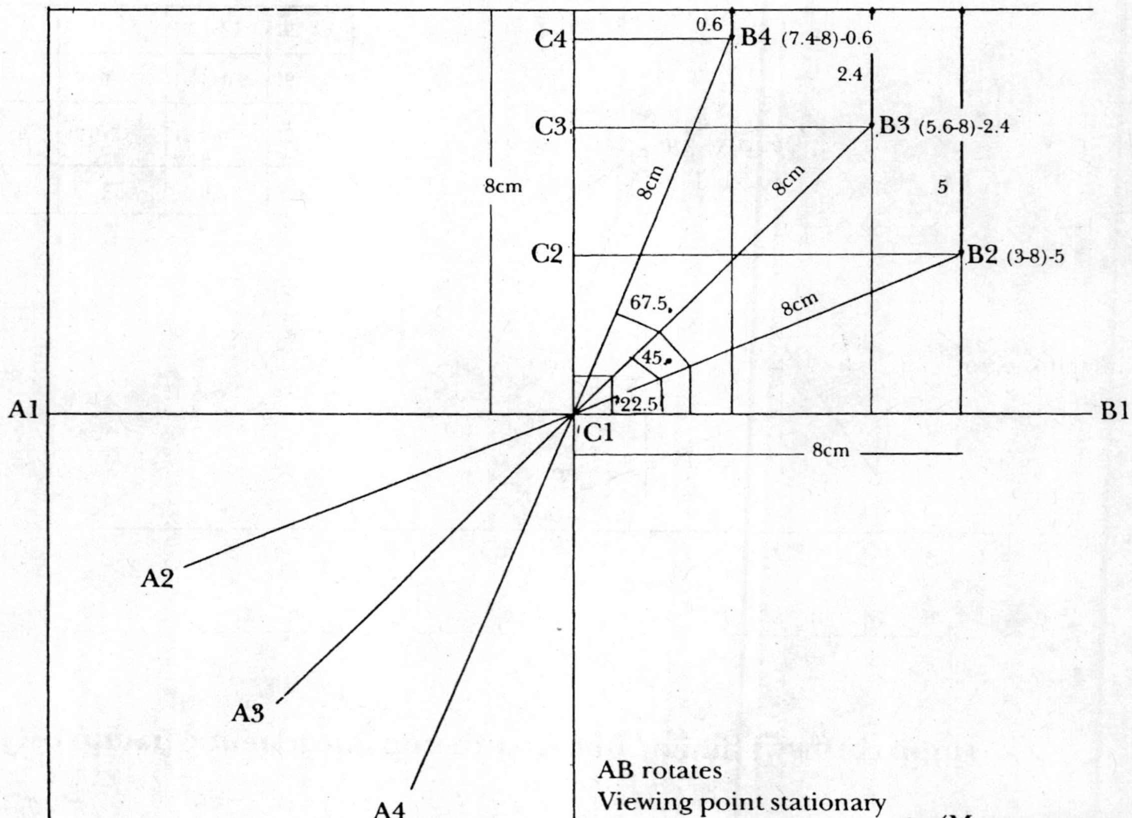

(Measurements : cms)

DIAGRAM III

THE HAṂSA MODE
[NAVATĀLA]

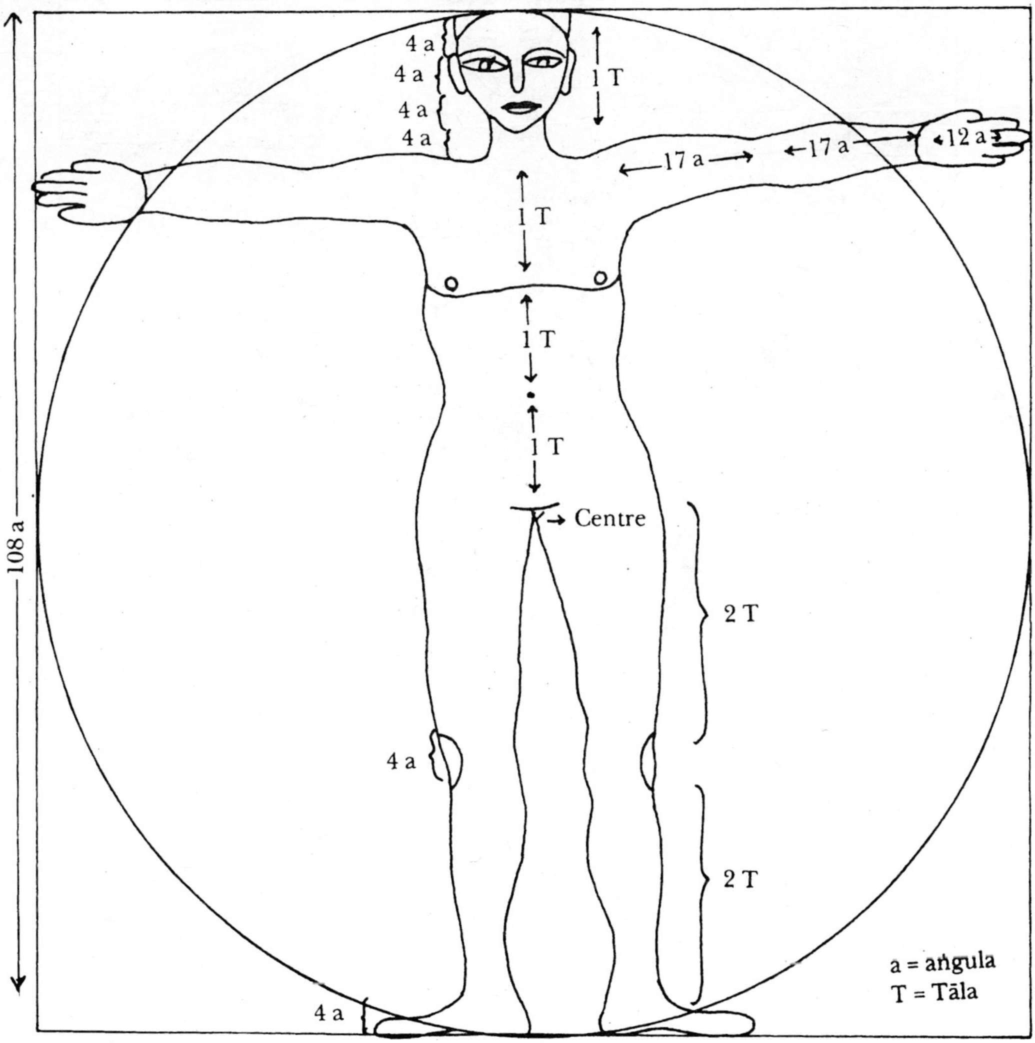

HORIZONTAL MEASUREMENT : 8+17+17+12 =5 4x2 =108 a
VERTICAL MEASUREMENT : 12+4+12+12+12+24+4+24+4 =108 a
(FROM HAIRLINE BELOW)

DIAGRAM IV

THE BHADRA MODE

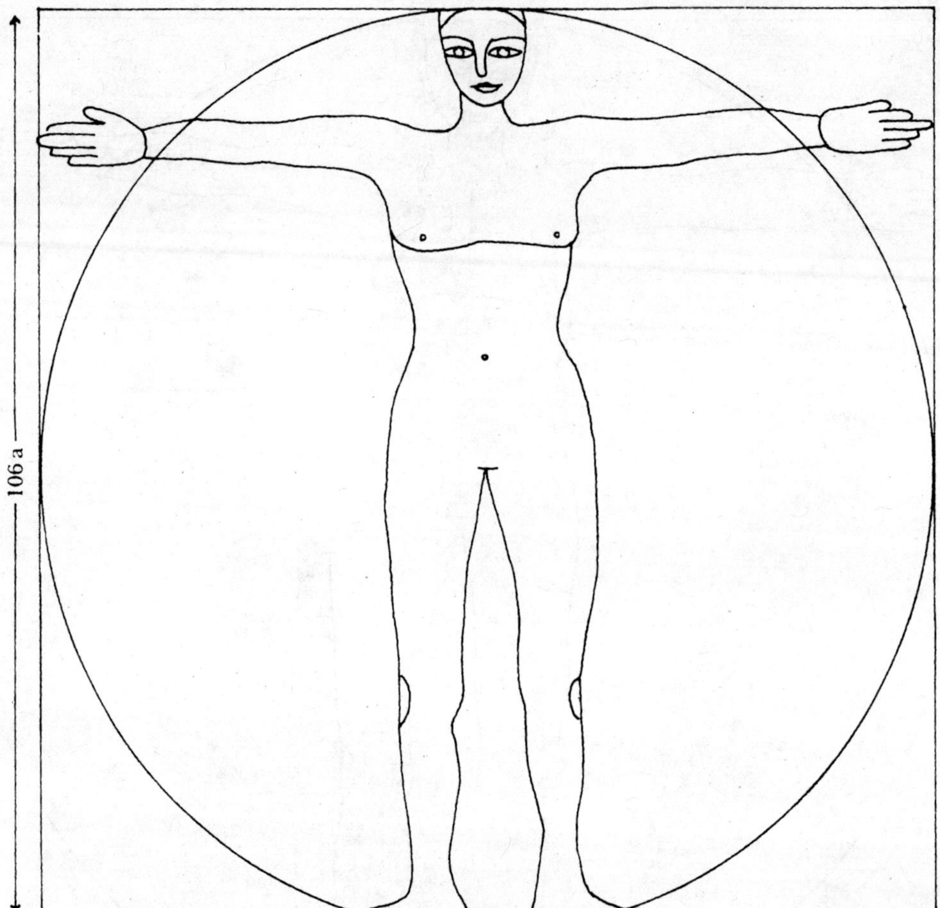

DIAGRAM V

THE MĀLAVYA MODE

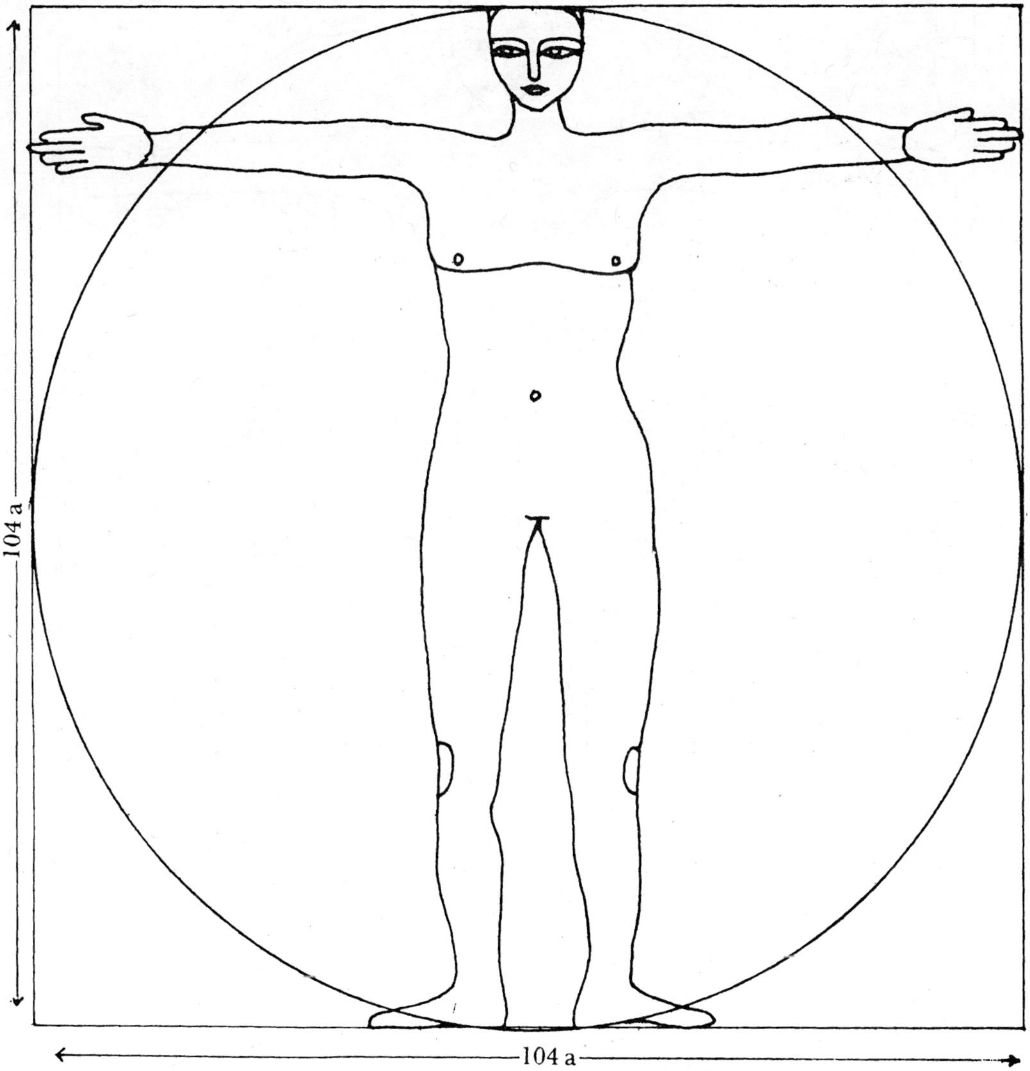

DIAGRAM VI

THE RUCAKA MODE

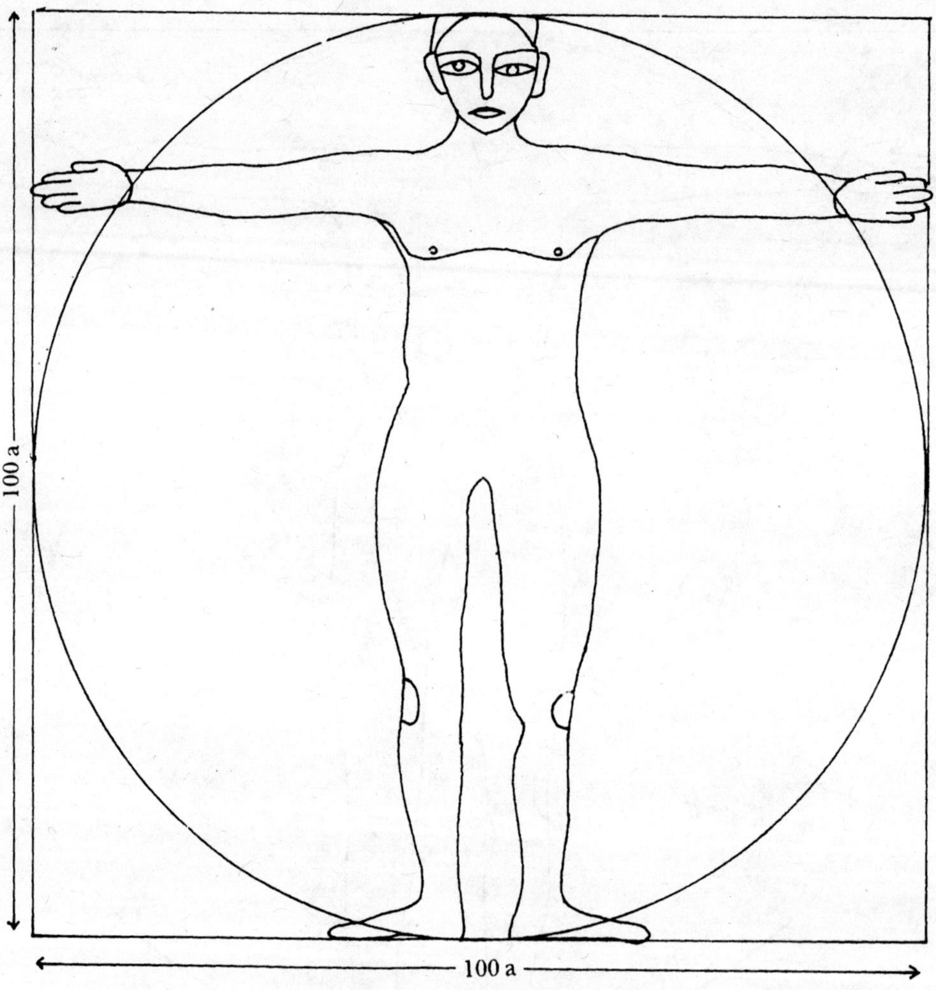

DIAGRAM VII

THE ŚAŚAKA MODE

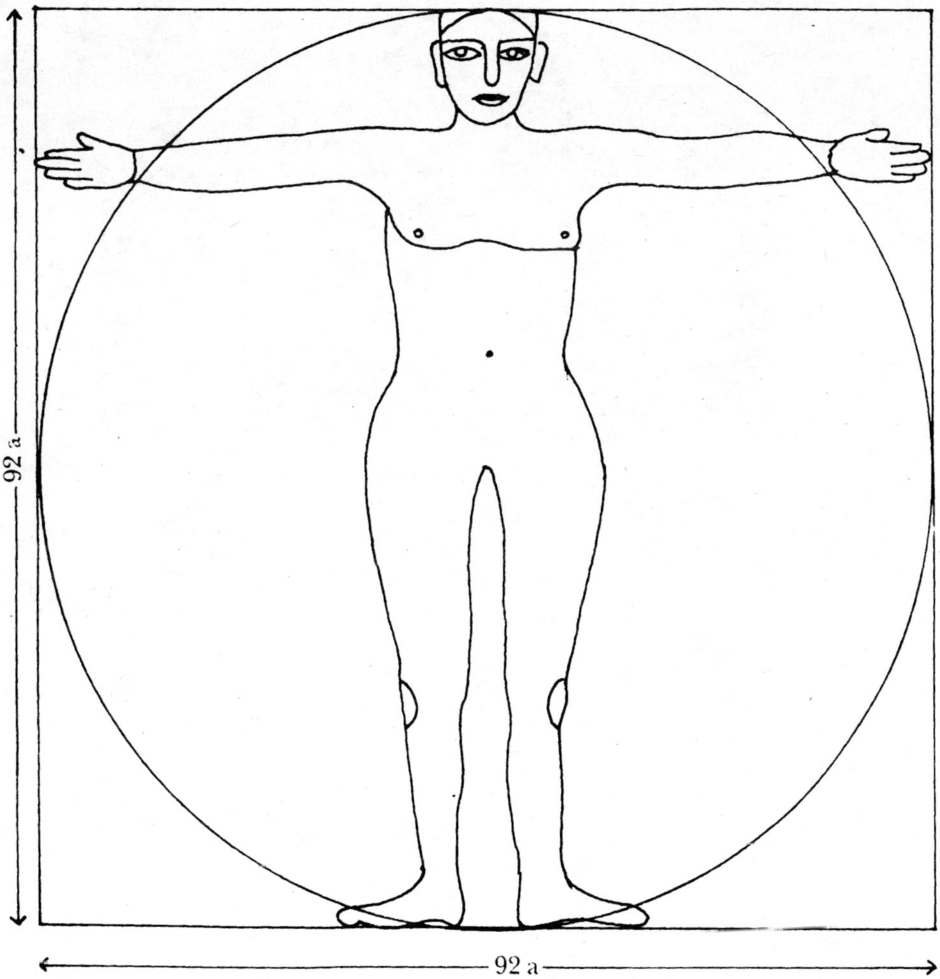

INDEX

* * *